THE LANGUAGE OF THE MUSIC BUSINESS

THE LANGUAGE
OF THE
MUSIC BUSINESS

by

Leston Huntley

A HANDBOOK OF ITS CUSTOMS
PRACTICES AND PROCEDURES

del capo publications inc.
800 horner avenue • nashville, tennessee 37204

ⓒ *Copyright by Leston Huntley 1965*
International Copyright Secured
All Rights Reserved

Music Illustrations by Music Type Service,
2535 Franklin Road, Nashville, Tennessee 37204

Library of Congress Catalog Card No. 65-28722

Manufactured in the United States of America

REFERENCE

ML
3790
H95ℓ

1093401

To
my wife, Natalie,
wise and understanding,
who made it possible

REFERENCE

foreword

As a music publisher, it is my privilege to know the most interesting and probably the most diversified group of people ever engaged in one overall activity.

There is the songwriter who writes the song, the arranger who arranges the song, the musician who plays the song, the singer who sings the song, the A and R man who records the song, the disk jockey who spins the record, the retailer who sells the song, and these are only a few.

Between the time a song is written and sold, in sheet music or record form, there are dozens of others who play important roles in manufacturing, printing, advertising, merchandising, promoting and keeping tab on the songs that are continuously being written, published and recorded day in and day out.

And each of these has a language of his own, unique to his particular activity. The disk jockey doesn't play the *recto* or *verso* side of a record, the printer doesn't measure the size of sheet music in *decibels*, to a songwriter the word *mother* means someone to whom songs like MY MOM are written, to a record manufacturer a *mother* is a die used in making records, yet each of these terms is a part of the overall language of the music business.

In his book, The Language of the Music Business, Leston Huntley has made an important contribution to the music industry in gathering these many and varied tongues and combining them in one source, by including an amazing amount of varied information that otherwise could require endless search.

For those like myself, here is a book that provides the excitement of learning. For those who know all these things, here is a book to be handed to the newcomer in the music business as a valuable requisite to communication, to fulsome understanding.

To paraphrase the great Scottish poet Bobby Burns, The Language of the Music Business gives those in the music business the opportunity *to hear ourselves as others hear us.* The music business being the audible industry that it is, hearing is always important.

Wesley H. Rose
President
Acuff-Rose Publications, Inc.

intro.

Entries

The entries in this book are listed in alphabetical order and are grouped into twenty-six sections. Each section is designated by a letter of the English alphabet.

Pronounciations

Pronunciations are given only for entries for which it is felt this might be desired. Where given, pronunciations appear (in parentheses) immediately following the entry and are in the simplest possible form of phonetic spelling.

Accents

The prime accent (′) is used in pronunciations to designate the syllable which is the heaviest stressed. The secondary accent (″) is used to designate the syllable of lesser stress.

Field Labels

The language of the music business comes from many sources, both within the industry and without. The sources from which entries originated are designated by one or more field labels, as SW (songwriting), MP (motion pictures), TE (theater), etc. A list of these field labels, together with their designations, follows this introduction.

Parts of Speech

Where an entry is listed more than once as, for instance, first as an adjective or verb and then as a noun, its grammatical category is designated by a small letter, immediately following the field label. These letters and their meanings are:

a., adjective.　　v., verb.　　n., noun.　　p., prefix.

ix

Definitions

A word or phrase might mean one thing to one person and something else to another, both of whom are in the same field of activity. For this reason, several definitions are given for some entries, even though in some instances the shadings in difference are but slight. These definitions are designated by Arabic numerals, as 1, 2, 3, etc. The order in which definitions are given, the numeral by which each is identified, does not necessarily imply preference of use or importance of meaning.

Foreign Words and Phrases

The language of music, itself, is universal. Even so, herein is given the language of the *English-speaking* music business. Foreign words and phrases listed in the main sections of this book are those which have long been permanently established in music idiom and for which there are no commonly used English synonymns. Foreign words and phrases which appear in the Coda are those for which English synonymns are becoming more frequently used.

Selection of Entries

There is a saying among songwriters that "Today's topical song is tomorrow's historical song." Like the topical song, there always will be expressions that are but short lived. The entries in this book were chosen for their seemingly reasonable permanency. Words and phrases that are obviously transitory have been omitted.

♩ ♩ ♩ ♩

field labels

♩ ♩ ♩ ♩

AI	Additional information	NM	Newspapers and Journalism
AP	Advertising and Publicity		
AS	Acoustics	PB	Publishing
AT	Art	PG	Printing
		PF	Performers
BD	Broadcasting	PH	Photography
BH	Barbershop harmony	PM	Prosody and Music
BR	Broadcasting and Recording	PN	Music publishing
BS	Business and Economics	PP	Printing and Publishing
BY	Barbershop singing	PS	Psychology
		PY	Prosody
CH	Church music		
CM	Country music	RB	Record business
		RC	Rhetoric
DG	Dancing	RD	Record manufacturing
		RG	Recording
EI	Entertainment business	RM	Rhythm and blues
ET	Electronics	RN	Religion
		RO	Radio
FK	Folklore and Song	RT	Radio and Television
FM	Folk music		
		SA	SPEBSQSA
GI	General information	SB	Show business
GM	Gospel music	SE	Science
		SG	Singers
HM	Hill music	SI	Speech input
		SN	Sound reproduction
JB	Juke box industry	SS	Song sharks
JM	Journalism	SW	Songwriters
JZ	Jazz		
		TE	Theater
LC	Lyrics	TH	Theatrical production
LW	Law	TV	Television
		TR	Theater relations
MB	Music business		
MD	Merchandising	VL	Vocal
MN	Musicians	VN	Versification
MP	Motion picture business		
MR	Film recording	WE	Writing and Editing
MS	Musicians and Singers	WG	Wording
MT	Music typography	WR	Writers and Writing
MU	Music		
MY	Mythology		

contents

♪ ♪ ♪ ♪

Music is the fourth great, material want of our nature—first food, then raiment, then shelter, then music.

Bovee

a

A

MU. 1. The first letter of the musical alphabet, representing a standard pitch of 440 vibrations per second. 2. The letter applied to any octave above or below this pitch. 3. The tone (usually played by the oboe) from which orchestras are tuned. 4. The sixth tone, note or degree in the ascending major scale of C. 5. The major key that has three sharps in its key signature. 6. The caption for an A major triad. 7. The key or string of a musical instrument that produces the tone of A. 8. The fifth string on the Spanish guitar. 9. The fourth string on the ukulele (tuned A-D-F♯-B). 10. The capital letter used to designate the first phrase in song structure, as in AABA, AABC, etc. 11. The small letter used to designate the first rhyme in a rhyme scheme, as in abab, abba, etc. MB. 12. The capital letter used to designate the preferred side of a phonograph record, as the *A side*. 13. The capital letter used to designate *alto* in multiple-voice arrangements, as in SATB. MP. 14. The capital letter used to designate a feature motion picture, as an *A picture*.

A♭

MU. See A FLAT.

A♯

MU. See A SHARP.

A and R (ae and ahr)

RB. Abbreviation, *artist and repertoire*.

1

A and R department

RB. The department in a phonograph record company that has to do with recording songs.

A and R director

RB. Usually called *A and R man.* See A AND R MAN.

A and R man

RB. An employee of a phonograph record company whose duties include: (1) selecting and/or approving songs to be recorded by the artists to whom he is assigned and (2) supervising and directing the recording of these songs. AI. Same as *A and R director.*

abandon

LW. To forsake, to give up, as the right to a song.

abbreviation

MU. 1. A method of indicating the repetition of a note or chord. 2. A shortened form of notation. RC. 3. A shortened form of a word or phrase, as *aug* for augmented, *dim* for diminished, *maj* for major, etc.

ABC (ae-bee-see)

BD. Abbreviation, *American Broadcasting Company.*

above

MU. 1. Higher than, as in pitch. 2. To the right of, as on the piano keyboard.

absolute music

MU. 1. Music that does not try to tell a story, describe a scene, etc., as distinguished from program music. 2. Music that is born with no purpose other than the delight of combining musical tones.

absolute pitch

MU. 1. The ability to identify a musical sound (tone) accurately upon hearing it, or to reproduce a given tone without having it sounded beforehand. 2. The ability to sing (or whistle) any tone at

2

will. Compare with *tin ear*. AI. Actually the term absolute pitch, as it is generally used, should be called *absolute judgment of pitch*. See RELATIVE PITCH.

A CAPP

MU. Abbreviation, *a cappella*.

a cappella (ah kah-pel'lah)

MU. In a chapel style, without instrumental accompaniment, said of choral singing.

accent

MU. v. To emphasize or stress, as a syllable, word, phrase, note or chord.

accent

PY. n. 1. Emphasis or stress given a particular syllable or word in speaking it. PY. 2. A mark used to show the placement of this emphasis or stress, as the primary accent (') and secondary accent ("). MU. 3. Emphasis or stress given a particular note or chord. 4. A mark indicating this emphasis or stress. AI. Normally, a main accent falls on the first note of each measure, with secondary (weaker) accents falling elsewhere. For instance, in Four-Four meter normally the heaviest accent is on the first beat, the weaker accent is on the third beat. Syncopation is produced by a variance in this procedure. See ACCENT MARKS. See SYNCOPATION.

accented syllable

PY. 1. A syllable that is emphasized or stressed, as distinguished from a syllable that is unaccented or not stressed. 2. A *long* syllable. AI. The opposite of unaccented syllable. See UNACCENTED SYLLABLE.

accent marks

MU, PY, WG. Any sign, symbol or other designation used to show the placement of emphasis, as *the v*, the *v-on-its-side*, the *inverted-v*, the *dot*, the *tenuto mark*, the *dash*, the abbreviations *sf* and *sfz*, the *primary accent* and the *secondary accent*.

3

access (ak′ses)

LW. The occasion to become acquainted with, as with a song. AI. For instance, willful infringement of a copyrighted song cannot be proven unless it is first proved that the alleged infringer had *access* to the song.

accidental chord

MU. Any chord that contains a note or notes that are foreign to its harmony.

accidentals

MU. All sharps, flats and naturals that are placed before notes in a song as distinguished from those used in a key signature. AI. Accidentals are so called because they seem to turn up *accidentally*. It is good songwriting practice to place an accidental (usually in parentheses) before any note whose meaning may otherwise seem doubtful. Sharps and flats used in a key signature are not called accidentals.

ACCOMP.

MU. Abbreviation, *accompaniment*.

accompaniment

MU. A secondary musical part or parts played or sung with the principal solo or melody.

accompanist (a-kum′pa-nihst)

MU. 1. One who plays or sings an accompaniment. 2. A sideman.

accordion

MU. 1. A musical instrument with keys, metal reeds and a bellows, which is alternately pulled out and pressed together between the player's hands to force air through the reeds and thus produce tones. 2. A musical arrangement, as that of a song, which can be lengthened or shortened at will to fit varying time requirements as those of radio and/or television shows. AI. For instance, a coda might be added to a song, as an *accordion*, for use if necessary, to fill out an allotted period of time. Or a song might be so arranged that part of it (the accordion) might be omitted if time is running short. See VIDE.

4

accounting

MB. 1. A statement showing debits and credits. 2. A settlement, as a balancing of an account. AI. Usually the agreements songwriters have with music publishers and artists have with record companies provide that an accounting will be made each six months. However, this can vary.

acetate

RB. 1. A phonograph record made of cellulose acetate. AI. An acetate is used as an economical and quick means of making a temporary phonograph recording, as a *demo*.

achromatic (ak″ro-mat′ek)

MU. 1. Unmodulated, without accidentals. 2. An *achromatic scale* is a scale without sharps or flats. 3. *Achromatic music* usually means very simple music in which modulations seldom occur and very few sharps and flats are used.

acoustic (a-koos′tik)

SE. 1. Having to do with hearing. 2. Heard sound. 3. The science of heard sound.

acoustics (a-koos′tiks)

SE. 1. The qualities of a room, studio, auditorium, theater, etc. that have to do with how clearly sounds can be heard or transmitted in it. 2. That branch of physics which has to do with the laws of sound.

act

TE. v. 1. To perform on the stage. 2. To play a role or a part. 3. To be an actor.

act

TE. n. 1. A section or division of a play, as the *first act, second act*, etc. 2. A prepared performance, a routine, as that of a singer, a comedian, etc. as a *night-club act*, etc.

action

MB. 1. Exposure. AI. A song is said to be getting *action* when it is being played on radio, television and/or juke boxes, etc. See CHART

5

ACTION. MU. 2. The mechanial connections between a keyboard, as that of a piano, organ, etc. and the strings or pipes. LW. 3. A legal process or court action, as a lawsuit in connection with a copyright infringement.

active tones
MU. The 2nd, 4th, and 7th tones of any major or minor scale. AI. In the key of C major, the active tones are D, F, A, and B.

act music
MU. 1. Music played between the acts of a play, a drama, etc. 2. Music written for this purpose.

Actors Equity Association
TE. The actors union, often called *equity*. Address: 226 West 47th Street, New York, N. Y. 10036.

acute (a-kute')
MU. 1. Shrill. 2. High in pitch.

acute accent
RC. A mark (') used to show: (1) the quality or length of a vowel, as in the French word idée, (2) primary stress, as in the word sweet'heart", (3) any stress on a spoken sound or syllable, as in scanning poetry. See DOUBLE ACUTE ACCENT.

adage (ad'ej)
WG. 1. A well-known saying. 2. A proverb or maxim. AI. Typical adages are: *Silence gives consent. A word to the wise is sufficient. Love will find a way.*

adaption (a-dap'shun)
MU. 1. An arrangement. 2. A version different from the original, usually made to meet certain specific requirements. AI. For instance, an adaption of a song might be made so that it will fit the plot of a musical show, a motion picture, etc. An adaption of a work in public domain is copyrightable, whereas the work itself is not.

added line
MU. Leger line. See LEGER LINE.

added-sixth chord

MU. See SIXTH CHORD.

added space

MU. Leger space. See LEGER SPACE.

additional endings: ⌐1 2 3 ¬ ⌐4 ¬

MU. All endings of a song other than the first and the concluding ending. AI. While most songs require only two endings, there are others where the requirement varies. One example of such songs is THE LOVE OF MY LIFE, from the musical *Brigadoon*, which has four sets of lyrics. Additional endings for a song with four sets of lyrics are shown above. Actually, this only means that the first ending is used three times, designated as ending number one, ending number two and ending number three, and that the concluding ending (originally ending number two) is then designated as ending number four. There are no set rules for song endings. A composer is free to use as many endings as his composition requires.

Adeline (ad′e-line)

BY. A member of the Sweet Adelines.

ad lib (ad-lihb′)

MU. Abbreviation, *ad libitum.*

ad libitum (ad lihb′e-t′m)

MU. 1. At pleasure, at will. 2. To be played or sung as the performer wishes. AI. Where music is marked *ad lib*, the time values may be changed by the performer and any part may be omitted if the performer so chooses.

advance royalties

MB. Money advanced, as to a songwriter by a music publisher, and which is charged against possible royalties to be earned and repaid at a later time. See ROYALTIES.

advice songs

MB. A classification in songwriting as to treatment. Typical advice songs are DON'T LET THE STARS GET IN YOUR EYES,

7

HEY THERE, CATCH A FALLING STAR, YOU'VE GOT TO
HAVE HEART and BUTTON UP YOUR OVERCOAT.

affidavit

LW. A written statement made under oath, usually before a notary
public or other authorized person, as an affidavit stating the date of
existence of a song.

A flat: A♭

MU. 1. The symbol shown above. 2. The tone on the piano that is
one half step below the tone of A. 3. The same tone on the piano as
G sharp. 4. The major key that has four flats in its signature. 5. The
caption for an A FLAT major triad.

A flat major scale

MU. The scale consisting of these eight notes or tones: A♭, B♭,
C, D♭, E♭, F, G, A♭. Also called *the key of A♭*. See KEY SIGNA-
TURE.

AFM (ae-eff-ehm)

MB. Abbreviation, *American Federation of Musicians*. Also called
AF of M.

after beat

MU. 1. A delayed beat. 2. The beat *after* the regular beat. AI.
When you count *one-and*, *two-and*, etc., in counting time, the word
and designates the after beat.

AFTRA (af'tra)

RT. Abbreviation, *American Federation of Television and Radio
Artists*.

AGAC (ae-jee-ae-see)

SW. Abbreviation, *American Guild of Authors and Composers*.

agent

SB. 1. Booking agent. 2. Canadian agent. See BOOKING AGENT.
See CANADIAN AGENT.

8

air

RT. v. To broadcast by radio or television, as a song.

air

MU. n. 1. A tune. 2. The melody of a song with or without words. RT. 3. The medium through which broadcasts reach their audience: a figurative use.

air check

RT. A recording made, for reference purposes, from a radio or television broadcast, as that of a song. AI. It is illegal to make an *off-the-air* recording without proper permission to do so.

airplay

MB. The radio or television broadcast of a phonograph record or one side of a phonograph record.

air plug

MB. Promotion (as the favorable mention and/or playing of a song) on radio or television.

Alberti bass

MU. A bass written or played in broken chords.

album (al'bum)

MB. 1. A collection of songs in book form. RB. 2. A book-like holder for phonograph records. 3. A set of phonograph records in such a holder. 4. A long playing record containing a number of songs or other musical compositions. 5. A long playing record containing non-musical material, as the spoken word, etc.

al fine (al fee'ne)

MU. 1. To the end. 2. Play or sing *to the end*.

alla breve (ahl'lah bre've)

MU. 1. Four-Two Time. 2. Doubled time. AI. Incorrectly but generally used and accepted to mean Cut Time. See CUT TIME.

all fields

MB. All song audiences and/or all song categories, as pop, country, western, rhythm and blues, Latin, etc.

alliteration (a-lit″er-ae′shun)

RC. 1. The repetition of an initial sound, usually a consonant, in two or more words, as *beautiful baby, lovely to look at, bewitched, bothered and bewildered, love me or leave me,* etc.

all-night sing

GM. 1. Originally, a community gathering for the purpose of singing gospel songs until dawn. 2. More recently, a commercialized version in which several groups of professional gospel singers appear at a theater to entertain from about eight o'clock in the evening until about two A.M. AI. This type of *all-night* sing is a well-established, well-patronized form of entertainment in the southeastern part of the United States.

all′ ottavo (ahl′lah ot-tah′vo) : 8va-------

MU. The sign above meaning, *to be played an octave higher than written.*

alma mater

GI. 1. The college, university or school one has attended. MU. 2. Its anthem or hymn (sometimes called *alma mater song*), as CARMEN OHIO, FAR ABOVE CAYUGA'S WATERS, DEAR OLD DUKE, etc.

al segno (al sae′nyo)

MU. 1. To the sign. 2. Return *to the sign* and play or sing (it over again) to the end.

alt

MU. Abbreviation, *alto.*

alteration

PG. 1. A change, a modification. 2. Any instructions to make differently, as those given a music typographer or printer for printing a song. See AUTHOR'S ALTERATION.

10

alternate note

MU. An optional note, written above or below another note, which a singer may take in preference, if he so chooses. AI. An alternate note is sometimes written in parentheses or as a smaller note. Also called *choice note* or *optional note*.

alternate tone

MU. The tone designated by an alternate note.

alto

MU. 1. Designating the octave beginning with the tone of G written in the fourth space of the bass staff and extending upward. 2. Designating any note (or tone) in this octave, as *alt A, alt B, alt C,* etc. 3. Designating any instrument or voice in the alto range.

AM (ae em)

RO. Abbreviation, *amplitude modulation.*

A major scale

MU. The scale consisting of these eight notes or tones: A, B, D♭, D, E, G♭, A♭, A. Also called *the key of A.* See KEY SIGNATURE.

amateur

MB. 1. An amateur songwriter. 2. One who has not learned his trade and/or his way around in the world of music. 3. One who is not a professional.

America

GI. 1. As used in this book, the word America means the United States of America.

American

GI. 1. As used in this book, the word American means of or in the United States of America, as an American songwriter. 2. Characteristic of the United States, as the American language. 3. A citizen, native or inhabitant of the United States of America.

American Broadcasting Company, The

RT. A radio and television broadcasting network, usually called *ABC.* Address: 7 West 66th Street, New York, N.Y. 10023.

11

American English

GI. 1. The English language as spoken in the United States of America, as distinguished from the English language as it is spoken elsewhere, as usually in Great Britain. 2. The language in which American songs are written.

American Federation of Musicians

MB. The musicians' union. Also called *AFM* and *AF of M*. Address: 220 Mount Pleasant Avenue, Newark, N.J. 07104.

American Federation of Television and Radio Artists

RT. The television and radio actors' and singers' union. Also called AFTRA. Address: 724 Fifth Avenue, New York, N.Y. 10019.

American Guild of Authors and Composers

SW. A voluntary association for songwriters, whose purpose it is to establish and enforce uniform songwriting contracts and promote other benefits for its members. Usually called *the guild* or *AGAC*. Requirements for membership may be had on request. Address: 158 West 55th Street, New York, N.Y. 10019.

American language

GI. 1. The language of the United States of America. 2. The language in which songs of the United States are written. 3. American English.

American Record Merchants and Distributors Association

RB. An organization of wholesale phonograph record distributors, which record manufacturers are eligible to join as associate members. AI. Also called ARMADA (pronounced as a three-syllable word). Address: 663 Fifth Avenue, New York, N.Y. 10022.

American Society of Composers, Authors and Publishers

MB. A nonprofit society founded in 1914, for the purpose of collecting payment for the performance rights of its members' compositions and distributing this revenue to its membership. AI. Usually called ASCAP (pronounced as a two-syllable word). Requirements for membership may be had on request. Address: 575 Madison Avenue, New York, N.Y. 10022.

American States, Fourth International Convention of

LW. See BUENOS AIRES CONVENTION.

amp

MN. 1. Abbreviation, amplifier, as a *guitar amp meaning a guitar amplifier*. 2. Abbreviation, ampere.

ampere (am'pihr)

SE. 1. The standard unit for measuring the strength of electrical current, as that used by amplifying equipment.

amphibrach (am'fe-brak")

PY. A metrical foot of three syllables in this order: an unaccented syllable, an accented syllable, an unaccented syllable, or ⌣ — ⌣. Example, *en-dear'ing*. The opposite of amphimacer. Musical counterpart: Three-Four Time.

amphimacer (am-fihm'a-ser)

PY. A metrical foot of three syllables in this order: an accented syllable, an unaccènted syllable, an accented syllable, or: — ⌣ —. Example, *go, man, go*. The opposite of amphibrach. Musical counterpart: Three-Four Time.

Amphy (am'fi)

MN. A nickname for any musician. AI. A shortening of the name Amphion, the son of Zeus and Antiope, in Greek mythology, who was a lute player.

amplification

ET. Increased volume, usually by means of electronics. Also called *gain*.

amplifier

ET. An electrical device for increasing the volume of sound.

amplify

ET. To increase the volume of sound, usually by means of electronics.

amplitude modulation (am'pleh-tude" mod"u-lae'shun)

RO. A method of broadcasting, often called *AM*, that is older and in more general use than *frequency modulation* or *FM*. GI. A more detailed explanation would be highly technical.

Amusement Business

SB. A show-business trade publication featuring out-door show activities. Published weekly. Issued every Monday. Dated the Saturday following date of issuance. Address: 188 West Randolph Street, Chicago, Illinois 60601.

anacrusis (an'e-kru'ses)

PY. One or more unaccented syllables added to the beginning of a line of verse which would ordinarily commence with an accented syllable. AI. The counterpart, in versification, of pick-up notes in music.

anapest (an'a-pest")

PY. A metrical foot of three syllables in this order: an unaccented syllable, an unaccented syllable, an accented syllable, or: ⌣ ⌣ —. Example, *it is spring*. The opposite of dactyl. Musical counterpart: Three-Four Time. See ENGLISH METER.

angel

SB. 1. One who provides money for producing a show, as a musical. 2. One who provides money for any enterprise, usually of a theatrical nature. 3. A financial backer. AI. Also called *backer*.

angle (an'gl)

SW. n. To give a specific point of view to a song.

angle (an'gl)

SW. n. 1. The way something appears from a particular point of view. 2. The point from which something is seen, imagined, or constructed, as a song. See YOU ANGLE.

angle song

MB. A song which has a particular reason for its being published and/or recorded, other than its merits as a song. The *angle* might be to catch a certain trend, to round out a music publisher's catalog, to please an important person, etc. AI. By no means does this necessarily imply that an angle song is not a good song. Many, in fact, are excellent songs and could qualify on their own merits regardless.

Annie

SB. Short for *Annie Oakley*, a complimentary ticket.

Annie Oakley

SB. 1. A complimentary ticket. 2. A pass. AI. So called because *comps* (complimentary tickets) are usually punched with holes, like the targets shot by Annie Oakley, the famous rifle woman (immortalized by Irving Berlin in his musical *Annie Get Your Gun*). Also called *Annie*.

anonymous

GI. 1. With no name known, as a song of unknown authorship. 2. With no name acknowledged. 3. Written by a person whose name is withheld, as a song. 4. A work of which no natural person is identified as the author.

answer

MU. 1. A musical answer phrase. 2. The consequent. See CONSEQUENT. See ANSWER SONG.

answer song

SW. A song written in reply to another song. Typical answer songs are I'M THE GIRL FROM WOLVERTON MOUNTAIN (in answer to WOLVERTON MOUNTAIN), HE'LL HAVE TO STAY (in answer to HE'LL HAVE TO GO) and I'M FALLING TOO (in answer to PLEASE HELP ME I'M FALLING).

antecedent (an"te-see'dent)

MU. 1. A musical question. 2. A musical phrase that *asks a question*. 3. A musical phrase that needs to be answered. See CONSEQUENT.

anthem

MU. 1. A type of sacred composition for voices, with or without instrumental accompaniment, intended to be sung by a choir or congregation, the words of which are usually taken from the Bible. AI. Also called *religious anthem*. 2. The official national song of a country, as THE STAR-SPANGLED BANNER, GOD SAVE THE KING and THE MARSEILLAISE. 3. Any song of praise or joy.

anticlimactic (an"teh-kli-mak'tek)

SW. Of, having, or like an anticlimax.

anticlimax (an"te-kli'max)

SW. 1. A sudden drop from the important thought or idea before the climax is reached, as in a song lyric. 2. A descent, as in a series of thoughts, that spoils the otherwise actual climax. AI. For instance, the lyric of the song THE NAUGHTY LADY OF SHADY LANE builds to a climax which tells that the subject of the song is a baby. Anything that would give this away, in advance of the climax, would be an *anticlimax* or *anticlimatic*.

antonym

RC. A word whose meaning is the opposite of another word in the same language, as *good* is the antonym of *bad, happy* is the antonym of *sad, love* is the antonym of *hate*, and vice versa. AI. The use of antonyms in songwriting is illustrated in the songs I'VE GOT IT BAD AND THAT AIN'T GOOD, FULL MOON AND EMPTY ARMS, LOVE ME OR LEAVE ME, DAY IN-DAY OUT and SUNRISE, SUNSET.

Apollo (a-pahl'o)

GI. 1. In Greek and Roman mythology, the god of songwriting. 2. The god of music and poetry.

appearance

SB. Short for *personal appearance*.

application for copyright

LW. The act of applying for the registration of a claim to copyright an original property, as a song. AI. In the United States this application is made in Form E for either a published or unpublished musical composition. In Canada this application is made in Form I for a published musical composition and in Form K for an unpublished musical composition. See INTERNATIONAL COPYRIGHT.

16

Arabic numerals

MU. The figures: 1, 2, 3, 4, 5, 6, 7, 8, 9, and 0 (zero). See NUMERALS.

archive of folk song

LW. The Library of Congress Archive of Folk Song, founded in 1928, has more than 70,000 songs on phonorecords and tapes. A catalog listing recordings available may be obtained from the Recording Laboratory, Library of Congress, Washington, D.C. 20540.

ARMADA (ahr-mah'da)

RB. Abbreviation, *American Record Merchants and Distributors Association*.

arpeggio (ahr-pej'eo):

MU. 1. The playing of the notes of a chord, one after the other, in harp style. 2. A chord so played. 3. The notation for this style of playing, as shown above.

arrange

MU. To make an arrangement, as that of a song.

arrangement

MU. 1. The adaption of a song (or other musical composition) for performance by instruments or voices other than those for which it was written, as an arranger might make a piano-and-vocal arrangement of a songwriter's lead sheet (vocal). 2. The adaption of a song (or other musical composition) for performance in a style other than that for which it was written, as a country song might be arranged for pop style performance, a pop song might be arranged for Latin style performance, etc. See SCORE. See ADAPTION.

arranger

MU. One who makes music arrangements. AI. Although arrangements of songs are copyrightable as new versions, the arrangers who make these new versions usually are employed by music publishers on an *employee-for-hire* basis and in this category have no status as copyright claimants. See WORK MADE FOR HIRE.

arsis (ar'sis)

PY. 1. The accented syllable. 2. The accent or stress itself. MU. 3. The *unaccented* part of a measure. 4. The upbeat. AI. The word *arsis* means one thing in prosody and the direct opposite in music. This is due to a misunderstanding in translating the original Greek.

artist

MB. 1. Contrary to its true meaning, the word *artist* is loosely used in the music business to designate anyone who attempts to sing or play professionally, no matter how poorly. 2. Anyone who has a recording contract, regardless of talent or skill. 3. Any performer, no talent or skill implied.

art song

MU. 1. A serious song written by a trained songwriter, as distinguished from a folk song. 2. A well-known poem that has been set to music by a skillful composer. AI. Typical art songs are TREES, ON THE ROAD TO MANDALAY and BOOTS.

ASCAP (az'kap)

MB. Abbreviation, *The American Society of Composers, Authors and Publishers.*

A sharp: A#

MU. 1. The symbol shown above. 2. The tone on the piano that is one half step above the tone of A. 3. The same tone on the piano as the tone of B FLAT.

A side (ae side)

MB. 1. The side of a phonograph record chosen (by the record company) as most likely to become a success. 2. The side of a phonograph record chosen by the record company to be promoted. 3. The side of a phonograph record opposite the B side. 4. The song on the *A side.* See B SIDE. See FLIP.

assign

LW. To make over to another, to transfer to another, as a song or any of its rights, etc.

18

assignee (a″-si-nee′)

LW. 1. A person to whom something is transferred or assigned. AI. For instance, when a songwriter assigns a song to a music publisher, the music publisher is the *assignee*. 2. A person appointed to act for another, as a lawyer.

assignment of copyright

LW. See TRANSFER OF COPYRIGHT.

assignor (a-sine′or)

LW. A person who assigns or transfers something. AI. For instance, when a songwriter assigns a song to a music publisher, the songwriter is the *assignor*. Also spelled *assigner*.

assonance (as′o-nans)

PY. 1. An imperfect rhyme. 2. A rough similarity in sound. 3. A partial rhyme in which the stressed vowels are alike, as in the words *late* and *make* or in the words *mane* and *came*. See CONSONANCE.

at liberty

SB. 1. Unemployed, as a singer, musician or other performer. 2. Open for employment.

attack

MU. The way voices or instruments start a phrase of music.

aubade (o-bad′)

MU. A morning song. AI. The counterpart of serenade.

audibility

SN. The capacity or condition of being heard.

audible

SN. Loud enough to be heard.

audience

SB. 1. Those assembled to hear and see a performance, as a play, musical show, etc. 2. Those who listen to radio or view television.

3. The song audience, as those who listen to songs, those who are interested in songs and those who buy sheet music and/or phonograph records. AI. Song audiences are also classified as to fields of interest as: *pop* audience, *country-music* audience, *rhythm-and-blues* audience, etc. The *potential* audience in any classification or field means the audience it is possible to attract or reach.

audience left

TE. 1. The left hand side of the stage, as seen from the audience in a theater. 2. The opposite of *audience right*. 3. The same as *stage right*. 4. The opposite of *stage left*.

audience reaction

SB. See REACTION.

audience right

TE. 1. The right hand side of the stage, as seen from the audience in a theater. 2. The opposite of *audience left*. 3. The same as *stage left*. 4. The opposite of *stage right*.

audio

ET. 1. Pertaining to sound. 2. Pertaining to the reproduction of sound, as *audio equipment* meaning the equipment used in recording or broadcasting sound, *audio engineer* meaning the technician who operates audio equipment, etc. 3. Designating the sound portion of television and motion pictures, as distinguished from the *video* or picture portion. 4. Short for *auditory*.

audio impression

PS. 1. The memory of sound. 2. The memory of music. AI. Also called *auditory impression*. See AUDITORY IMAGERY.

auditory imagery (au'de-tor"e im'ej-re)

ET. An instrument for measuring the intensity of sound, as used in recording and broadcasting.

audition

MB. v. To give an audition, as that of a song, a singer, etc.

audition

MB. n. A trial or test hearing, as that to evaluate a song, a singer, a musician, etc.

auditory imagery (au'de-tor"e im'ej-re)

PS. 1. The process that takes place in the mind when one *mentally* hears a song or other forms of music. 2. A *mental picture* of a song, music or sound. AI. Also called *audio imagery, auditory impression,* and *audio impression.*

aug

MU. The symbol meaning *augmented,* as used to designate augmented chords, as *Caug, Daug, Eaug,* etc. AI. The word *augmented* is also designated by a plus sign (+), as C+, D+, E+, etc.

augment

MU. 1. To add to. 2. To increase. 3. To raise. 4. To make larger by half a step (a half tone or a semitone). AI. The opposite of *diminish.*

augmented

MU. 1. Increased. 2. Made larger. 3. Raised, as an *augmented chord* or an *augmented interval.* See AUG.

augmented chord

MU. A chord composed of a root, its third and its augmented fifth. AI. For instance, the C augmented chord (designated *Caug* or C+) is composed of the tones C-E-A♭. The D augmented chord (designated *Daug* or D+) is composed of the tones D-G♭-B♭. The E augmented chord (designated *Eaug* or E+) is composed of the tones E-A♭-C, etc.

augmented interval

MU. An interval that is a half step greater than the corresponding major or perfect interval. AI. For instance, C-G is a perfect fifth, C-A♭ is an *augmented* fifth, etc.

author

SW. 1. One who writes the lyrics of songs, as distinguished (by ASCAP) from *composer.* See SONGWRITER. L.W. 2. For the

21

purpose of registration of a claim to copyright a musical composition, the United States copyright law defines the word *authors* to include *composers of music, authors of words, arrangers, compilers*, etc. The U.S. copyright law further states, "Where a work is made for hire, the employer is the author."

authorize

LW. 1. To give approval to or permission for. 2. To give power or authority to. AI. For instance, a songwriter might authorize a music publisher to act in his behalf in placing his songs with recording companies, etc.

authorless

LW. 1. With the author or authors unknown, as a song. 2. Of unknown authorship. 3. Anonymous.

author's alteration

PG. Any change made in a song by its composer or lyricist, usually after type has been set or plates have been engraved for printing. AI. Music typographers, engravers and printers make an additional charge for such alterations.

author's correction

PG. Any correction by a composer or lyricist of a tyopgraphical error in a song. AI. There is no extra charge for such corrections.

Autoharp

MU. A trade name for a stringed instrument of the zither family. Simple chords are produced by pressing keys with one hand and strumming the strings with the other. AI. The Autoharp is used by folk singers.

auxiliary notes

MU. Notes not essential to the harmony.

auxiliary tones

MU. Tones designated by auxiliary notes.

axe

MN. 1. Any musical instrument. AI. For instance, if a violinist were asked if he brought his *axe*, this would mean did he bring his *violin*.

22

If a musician is asked what kind of *axe* he blows, this means what kind of *instrument* does he play. SW. 2. Songwriters sometimes refer to a typewriter, pencil or pen, as their *axe*. MB. 3. Generally, any working tool or instrument by which one makes a living. AI. The word comes from the expression *to hack* (chop) it out. See HACK.

axiom

RC. A statement generally accepted as being true. Typical axioms are: *You can't have your cake and eat it too. Hell hath no fury like a woman scorned. A rolling stone gathers no moss,* etc.

b

B

MU. 1. The second letter of the musical alphabet, representing a pitch a whole tone higher than A. 2. The letter applied to any octave above or below this pitch. 3. The seventh tone, note or degree in the ascending major scale of C. 4. The major key that has five sharps in its key signature. 5. The caption for a B major triad. 6. The key or string of a musical instrument that produces the tone of B. 7. The second string on the Spanish guitar. 8. The first string on the ukulele (tuned B-F♯-D-A). SW. 9. The capital letter used to designate the second phrase in song structure, as in AABA, AABC, etc. 10. The small letter used to designate the second rhyme in a rhyme scheme, as in abab, abba, etc. MB. 11. The capital letter used to designate the secondary side of a phonograph record, as the *B side*. 12. The capital letter used to designate either *baritone* or *bass* in multiple-voice arrangements, as in SATB. See B MAJOR SCALE. MP. 13. The capital letter used to designate a motion picture second in importance to an *A picture* as a *B picture*.

B♭

MU. See B FLAT.

B♯

MU. See B SHARP.

BAC (bee-ae-see)

LW. Abbreviation, The *Buenos Aires Convention*.

25

baby grand

MU. 1. A baby grand piano. 2. A small grand piano, as distinguished from a *grand* or *concert grand*.

back

MU. 1. To provide a musical and/or vocal background, as for a solo. SB. 2. To supply with backing. 3. To finance.

back beat

MU. After beat.

back cover

PG. 1. The outside cover immediately following the last page, as that of sheet music or a song book. RB. 2. The cover of a record album opposite the front.

backdrop

TE. A painted or unpainted curtain hung at the back of a stage or scene. AI. Backdrops are often painted to resemble a locale, as a city street, a rural scene, the interior of a room, etc.

backed up

MU. 1. Accompanied, as a soloist might be *backed up* by a vocal or instrumental group. RB. 2. Having a backing, as a song on the A side of a phonograph record is said to be *backed up* with the song on the B side, and vice versa.

backed with: b/w

RB. 1. On the same record with. 2. On the opposite side of the record from. 3. The abbreviation shown above. AI. For instance, it might be said that OH, SUSANNA is *backed with* SWEET GENE-VIEVE or OH, SUSANNA b/w SWEET GENEVIEVE. The same as *coupled with*. See FLIP.

backer

SB. A person who gives financial assistance to another person, a business, a project, etc. See ANGEL.

26

background

MU. 1. An added musical accompaniment, as to a solo, dialog or action (as in a motion picture, a stage play, etc.) GI. 3. The whole of a person's study, training and experience, as a songwriter's background, etc.

background music

MB. 1. Mood, atmosphere or thematic music performed as a background to some non-musical subject matter being presented on radio or television. AI. This is one of the categories used by performing-rights societies in establishing credit values. 2. Music furnished by direct wire to supermarkets, stores, factories, offices, etc., sometimes is also called *background music*.

backing

RB. 1. The other side of a phonograph record. 2. The flip side. MU. 3. A musical and/or vocal background, as for a solo. SB. 4. Financial support.

backstage

TE. 1. That part of a stage which is the furthest removed from the audience. 2. The area at or to the sides and rear of a stage that is unseen by the audience. 3. The area in a theater, night club, auditorium, etc. where the dressing rooms are located.

back-to-back

RB. Songs on opposite sides of the same phonograph record are said to be *back-to-back*.

baffle board

BR. A movable partition, similar to a screen, used in broadcasting and recording studios to absorb or reflect sound (depending on the material from which it is made). See ISOLATION BOARD.

balance

SA. The effect achieved through proper voice level or volume on each tone of a chord, as used in the SPEBSQSA. A style of barbershop singing.

ballad

MU. A simple song that tells a story, usually of a sentimental nature. Typical ballads are TO EACH HIS OWN, SO IN LOVE, AMONG MY SOUVENIRS, MORE THAN YOU KNOW and MUSIC, MAESTRO, PLEASE.

ballad with a beat

MB. A beat-ballad. See BEAT BALLAD.

ballroom dancing

DG. A kind of dancing in which two people dance as partners, as distinguished from stage dancing, en mass dancing, etc. AI. Typical ballroom dances are the waltz, the foxtrot, the polka, etc.

banal (bae′n′l)

RC. Trite, hackneyed, commonplace, trivial, as a banal song.

band

MU. 1. A company of persons organized to play musical instruments. 2. An orchestra.

band card

MB. 1. A card on which music is printed or written, for use by marching bands. AI. Band cards vary in size from about 6¾″x5¼″ to 7″x5½″. Also called *march-size cards* and *quickstep* (size) *cards*.

band stand

MU. A raised floor or stage, indoors or outdoors, on which bands or orchestras perform.

banjo

MU. A stringed musical instrument with a long fretted neck and a circular body covered on top with parchment. The strings are plucked with the fingers or a plectrum. The number of strings varies. AI. This is the only musical instrument to have its origin in America. See FIVE STRING.

bar:

MU. A perpendicular line drawn across the music staff, as shown above. AI. A bar is used to divide the staff into measures. Frequently and erroneously used to mean *measure*. Also erroneously used to mean *beam*. See MEASURE. See BEAM.

barbershop

MU. Designating a particular style of four-part vocal harmony which is performed without accompaniment. AI. Typical of songs that are favorites with barbershop singers are GOODBYE MY CONEY ISLAND BABY, HEART OF MY HEART and DEAR OLD GIRL.

barbershop arrangement

MU. A four-part, close-harmony arrangement, without accompaniment, for the following voices: lead, tenor, baritone and bass, and giving preference to dominant seventh (barbershop) chords. AI. A female barbershop quartet uses these same four parts, called by these names. Women barbershoppers, however, usually do not sing as low in pitch as do men. See TWO-STAFF ARRANGEMENT.

barbershop chord

MU. A dominant seventh chord. AI. The chord immortalized by the ragtime-music man Lewis F. Muir in his song hit of 1910, PLAY THAT BARBERSHOP CHORD.

barbershopper

MU. Any devotee of barbershop harmony, male or female. Usually used to mean a member of the *SPEBSQSA* or the *Sweet Adelines*. AI. The SPEBSQSA prefers that this term be applied only to male singers and that members of Sweet Adelines, Inc. be called *Adelines*.

bard

MN. 1. A singer, usually one who also composes songs. 2. A minstrel.

bare-footed

MN. 1. Unaccompanied and often unrehearsed. 2. An impromptu performance, as that of a song.

bari (bahr′ee)

MU. Short for *baritone*. AI. Sometimes spelled *barit*.

baritone

MU. a. Having a baritone or similar range.

baritone

MU. n. 1. The range from second A below middle C to the first F above. 2. A voice having this range. 3. A singer who sings baritone. 4. An instrument that has this range. 5. A musical part written for a baritone voice or instrument. AI. Female baritones are used in barbershop harmony.

bar line

MU. An incorrect term for bar. See BAR.

barre′ (ba-rae′) :

MU. In stringed instrument playing, the stopping of two or more strings with the forefinger. AI. The above guitar diagram indicates a barré, performed by stopping the first four strings of a guitar with the forefinger. See BARRER.

barred c: ¢

MU. 1. The character shown above. 2. The time signature for *Cut Time*. Also called *C barré*.

barrel-house

JZ. a. 1. Of or in the unrestrained style of playing associated with the old barrel houses, particularly those in early New Orleans. 2. A free and easy, relaxed style of performance. 3. Honky tonk.

barrel house

GI. n. 1. An early New Orleans type of saloon which had a row of racked barrels along the wall. 2. A honky tonk. AI. Each of these old barrel houses had its featured (jazz) band, (jazz) combo or (jazz) pianist. It was these musicians who contributed to the birth of jazz.

barrer

MU. Same as the French word *barré*. See BARRÉ.

30

barrer, great

MU. The act of stopping *all* the strings on the guitar, or similar stringed instrument, at the same time, with the forefinger.

barrer, small

MU. The act of stopping *two or three* strings on the guitar, or similar stringed instrument, at the same time, with the forefinger.

bass

MU. a. Having a bass range, as a basso, a bassoon, the bass staff, etc.

bass

MU. n. 1. The range composed of all tones below middle C. 2. Low in tone. 3. Low in compass. 4. The lowest male voice. 5. A bass instrument, as the bass viol, bass saxophone, bassoon, etc. AI. Although the word *bass* is often used to mean a male singer, the lowest voice in a female barbershop quartet is also called *bass* and the woman who sings this part is known as the *bass* or *bass singer*.

bass clef

MU. 1. The clef that designates the fourth line of the staff as F below middle C. 2. The *F clef*. See F CLEF.

bassist

MU. One who plays a bass instrument, as a bass viol, tuba, bass guitar, etc.

basso (bas′so)

MU. 1. A bass voice. 2. A person who sings bass. 3. The bass part. AI. Women bass singers are seldom, if ever, called *bassos*.

bassoon (ba-sune′)

MU. 1. A double-reed instrument, the lowest in pitch in the wood wind family. 2. The wood wind bass.

basso profundo (bas′so pro-fun′do)

MU. 1. The deepest or lowest voice in the bass range. 2. The male singer who sings this voice.

31

bass strings

MU. 1. The strings of any stringed instrument whose open (un-stopped) tones are below middle C. 2. A stringed instrument whose range is below middle C, as the bass viol, bass guitar, bass banjo, etc.

baton (ba-tahn´)

MU. 1. A slender, light stick or wand used by the conductor of an orchestra, choir, etc. for directing, as in beating time. 2. A hollow rod, with a knob at one end, twirled in a showy manner by a drum major or drum majorette.

BBB (bee-bee-bee)

BS. Abbreviation, *Better Business Bureau.*

beam: ▬

MU. A heavy line used to replace flags and connect two or more beamed notes. AI. Often erroneously called a *bar*. See BAR. See DOUBLE BEAM.

beamed notes: ♫ or ♬ etc.

MU. Notes connected by a beam or beams, as connected eighth notes, connected sixteenth notes, etc.

beat

MU. 1. Mental pulsation (a throbbing sensation of the mind) that occurs when listening to music, thinking of music or performing music. AI. For instance, Two-Four Time has 2 beats to each measure. Four-Four Time has 4 beats to each measure, etc. A conductor indicates these beats by the rise (up-beat) and fall (down-beat) of his hands or baton. See BEATING TIME.

beat-ballad

MU. A ballad with a pronounced beat, marking a danceable tempo. Also called *ballad with a beat.* Typical beat-ballads are SLEEPY TIME GAL, AIN'T MISBEHAVING and SLOW BOAT TO CHINA.

32

beating time

MU. The movement, usually of a leader's (conductor's) hands or baton, to indicate the beats and tempo of a musical composition, to bring about the coordination of all musicians and/or singers. AI. The following diagrams show the most commonly used movements used in beating time for popular music:

Two-Four Time   Three-Four Time   Four-Four Time
and Cut Time.

beginner

MB. 1. A beginning songwriter. 2. A songwriter who is just getting started as distinguished from a *would-be* or an *amateur*.

bell

MU. 1. A metallic percussion instrument set in vibration by a hammer or clapper. 2. The widest part of a horn.

bell chord

MS. A chord, each tone of which is sounded individually, one after the other, to simulate the chiming of bells. AI. Also called *chime chord*.

belt

MU. To sing with vigor, volume and authority, as to *belt* out a song.

belter

MU. 1. A singer who has the ability to belt out a song. 2. A singer who sings in this manner.

bend

MU. 1. To alter the tone indicated by a note, either higher or lower, by less than a half step. 2. To change pitch slightly. AI. A singer or musician who does this is said to *bend a note*. A violin, a steel guitar, a trombone permits this variance. A piano, an organ, an accordion does not.

Berne Convention

LW. Same as *Berne Union*.

Berne Country

LW. 1. Any country subscribing to the original Berne Union or to the original Berne Union and any of its four revisions. 2. A member of the Berne Union.

Berne Union

LW. An international union for the protection of literary and artistic works, commonly called the *Berne Convention*. The Berne Union, currently consisting of some 50 members, was formed in 1886 by a group of countries who wanted to simplify the international protection of creative works by getting automatic copyright protection in other countries for their citizens. The original convention has been revised four times: at Paris in 1896, at Berlin in 1908, at Rome in 1928 and at Brussels in 1948. Not all of these revisions have been adopted by all members, as yet. A fundamental condition of membership in the Berne Convention is that every original work by a native author is automatically copyright and that no formality shall be imposed upon an author. Because the copyright laws of the United States of America require compulsory registration and compulsory notice of copyright (in order to effect copyright protection) this does not conform with the requirements for membership in the Berne Union. However, citizens of non-member countries, as the United States, may secure (international) copyright through the Berne Convention by making publication in one of the member-countries of the Convention. The original Convention requires this be *first* or *simultaneous* publication. To this, however, has been added a revision, at Brussels in 1948, which allows a citizen of a non-Berne country, as the United States, to establish *first publication* in a Berne country any time within 30 days after a work has been published in the citizen's home country. *First* in this respect means *first publication in a Berne country*. Although Canada has not as yet adopted the Brussels revision, and the 30 day leeway does not apply, because of its nearness and the lack of language difficulties, many American publishers send their songs to Canada for *same-day* publication rather than, for instance, to England or France, countries that have adopted the Brussels revision. The correct name and address of the Berne Convention is Bureau de l'union internationale pour la protection des oeuvres litteraires et artistques, 32, chemin des Colombettes, Geneva, Switzerland. A current list of countries belonging to the Berne Union may be had free of charge, by requesting "annex C to Circular 37" from the United States Copyright Office. See INTERNATIONAL COPYRIGHT.

better business bureau

BS. An organization to promote truth in advertising and to help the public obtain maximum satisfaction in its dealings with business. Any unscrupulous dealings of song sharks or others whose questionable actions are a detriment to the legitimate music business should be reported to the nearest Better Business Bureau. Better business bureaus located in principal music centers are:

National Better Business Bureau, Inc.
230 Park Avenue, New York, N. Y. 10017

Better Business Bureau of Metropolitan New York, Inc.
220 Church Street, New York, N. Y. 10013

Better Business Bureau of Greater Nashville, Inc.
Nashville Trust Building, Nashville, Tennessee 37201

Better Business Bureau of Los Angeles, Ltd.
307 West 8th Street, Los Angeles, California 90014

Better Business Bureau of Meropolitan Boston, Inc.
52 Chauncy Street, Boston, Massachusetts 02111

Chicago Better Business Bureau, Inc.
14 East Jackson Boulevard, Chicago, Illinois 60604

b.f.

PG. 1. A proof reader's mark meaning *bold face*, a heavy face type. 2. Instructions, to a printer, to set in *bold face* type. AI. Also written *bf* or *BF*.

B flat: B♭

MU. 1. The symbol shown above. 2. The tone on the piano that is one half step below the tone of B. 3. The same tone on the piano as

A SHARP. 4. The major key that has two flats in its signature. 5. The caption for a B FLAT major triad.

B flat major scale

MU. The scale consisting of these eight notes or tones: B♭, C, D, E♭, F, G, A, B♭. Also called *the key of B♭*. See KEY SIGNATURE.

B. H.

MU. Abbreviation, *both hands*. AI. Where this abbreviation is written on music, it means that both hands are used in playing the part indicated.

big downpour

CM. 1. A big performance of country music. 2. A big square dance. 3. The Grand Ole Opry, in Nashville, Tennessee, is often called *the big downpour*.

big potato

SB. 1. A big-name performer. 2. A star. MB. 3. A high-ranking or important executive, as that of a music publishing company, record company, etc.

big song

MB. 1. A big hit. 2. An important song, as the featured song in a musical. 3. The current featured song of a music publisher. 4. An important song in a music publisher's catalog.

big sound

MB. 1. A large band or orchestra. 2. A highly featured band or orchestra. 3. A big-name band or orchestra, as that of Benny Goodman, Woody Herman, Duke Ellington, Bert Kaempfert, Billy Vaughn, Henri Mancini, etc. 4. A recorded sound giving the impression of many instruments over and above the usual number.

big time

SB. 1. Major, first-rate, the best, as opposed to *small time*. AI. Originally used to designate *big-time vaudeville*, which played only two performances a day in the best theaters in major cities. 2. Often used to designate *Broadway* and/or *Hollywood*, as distinguished from elsewhere. 3. A national radio or television network, as distinguished from a local station.

bilateral copyright arrangements

LW. Agreement by a country to provide copyright protection for the residents of another country and to receive copyright protection for its own residents in return. AI. A current list of the thirty-odd countries with whom the United States has bilateral copyright arrangements may be had by requesting *circular 37 annex D* from the United States Copyright Office.

bilingual song

MB. A song with two or more sets of lyrics, each in a different language, as English-and-Italian, English-and-French, English-and-Spanish, etc.

Billboard

MB. A music-business trade publication. Published weekly. Issued every Monday. Dated the Saturday following date of issuance. Address: 165 West 46th Street, New York, N. Y. 10036.

billing

SW. 1. The listing of performers' names on a playbill, theater sign, advertisement, etc. 2. The order and size in which these names appear. MB. 3. The listing of song titles in an advertisement, etc. 4. The order and size in which these titles appear. AI. For instance, in an advertisement, a music publisher might give the song on one side of a phonograph record *top billing* over the song on the flip side, or the two songs might be given *equal billing*, etc.

binaural (bi-nau'r'l)

RD. The method of picking up and/or reproducing sound from two different sources to give a stereophonic effect. See STEREO-PHONIC.

bind

MU. A tie. See TIE.

bio (bi'o)

MB. Biography. AI. Sometimes called *biog*.

biography

MB. 1. The history of an individual's life, as used to publicize performers, musicians, songwriters and others. 2. An account of a person's life, described by another, as distinguished from *auto-biography*.

bird's eye

MU. A fermata. See FERMATA.

bistro (bis'tro)

SB. 1. A somewhat facetious name for a night club or cocktail lounge. 2. A French saloon.

bit

TE. 1. A small role, as that in a musical. 2. A very short routine. 3. A part of a routine. SW. 4. A part of a song.

black and white

MB. 1. A professional-size printed song sheet. PG. 2. A printer's proof, as that of a song.

black bottom

MU. 1. A type of dance combining intricate steps to slow fox trot time. 2. The music for this dance, as the song BLACK BOTTOM.

black out

TE. 1. The extinguishing of all stage lights to end a play or a scene. 2. A brief scene, usually in a musical show, that ends in this manner.

blank

RG. 1. A phonograph disk, usually made of hardened wax or plastic, that has not been recorded. 2. An acetate without sound. AI. Blanks are recorded by being cut (by a stylus) as distinguished from those that are *pressed*. Also called *recording blank*.

blank verse

PY. 1. Originally, unrhymed verse having five iambic feet to the line. 2. More often used to mean any unrhymed verse. AI. The lyric of the song hit MOONLIGHT IN VERMONT is written in blank verse.

blast

MU. 1. To play a horn loudly. 2. The sudden blowing of a horn, as a trumpet.

blend

MU. 1. To harmonize, as the *blend* of voices and/or instruments. 2. To go well together, as the *blend* of a song's lyric with its melody.

block in

SW. Same as *block out*.

block license

MB. Any license, domestic or foreign, whereby rights are granted with respect to two or more musical compositions. AI. Also called *bulk license*.

block out

SW. 1. To sketch or design roughly, as a song or other musical composition. 2. To plan in outline form. 3. Same as *block in*.

blow

MU. 1. To sound by blowing, as a horn. 2. To play, as a wind instrument played by mouth. MN. 3. To play, regardless of type of instrument. AI. For instance, one musician might ask another, "What do you blow?" meaning *what instrument do you play?* and the answer might be "piano" or even "drums." MS. 4. To make a mistake in playing or singing. AI. For instance, a musician or singer is said to *blow a note, blow a line, blow a measure,* etc. when he fails to play or sing at the proper time, plays or sings at the wrong time, plays or sings the wrong note or notes, etc. SB. 5. To fail. AI. For instance, to *blow* an appointment. To *blow* a date means to fail to appear for a scheduled performance, etc.

blue-grass music

MU. 1. Music typical of that played in the southern Appalachian Mountains, usually featuring three-finger (Earl Scruggs type) banjo accompanied by other stringed instruments. 2. Music similar to southern Appalachian mountain music. AI. In true blue-grass music electrically amplified instruments are definitely not used. Bill Monroe, Lester Flatt and Earl Scruggs were among the first to popularize this particular type of music by this particular name.

blue material

SB. 1. Off-color, indecent material. 2. A risqué song. AI. Blue material is not to be confused with the *blues*, which can be perfectly proper and decent. See BLUES. See OFF COLOR.

blue note

MU. 1. A sour note or tone. 2. A discordant tone. 3. A flatted third or flatted seventh.

blues

MU. 1. A type of folk song originated by the American Negro, characterized by minor harmony using flatted thirds and flatted sevenths (blue notes), slow jazz rhythm, and melancholy words. 2. Any good imitation of this kind of song. AI. The word *blues* is short for *blue devils*, a depressed, unhappy feeling. Hence the mood of the melody and the lyrics that deal with gloomy, sad and dejected subject matter. The classic of all blues is the immortal W. C. Handy's ST. LOUIS BLUES. Other typical blues are WABASH BLUES and BLUES IN THE NIGHT.

Blum's Cafe, Paul

MN. An establishment located at 116-118 Exchange Place, New Orleans, La., which was the *official* meeting place for musicians in the early days of jazz. AI. Paul Blum's Cafe is said to be the place where jazz was actually born, as it was here that the Original Dixieland (Jazz) Band came into being.

B major scale

MU. The scale consisting of these eight notes or tones: B, D♭, E♭, E, G♭, A♭, B♭, B. AI. Also called *the key of B*. See KEY SIGNATURE.

BMI (bee-em-i)

MB. Abbreviation, *Broadcast Music, Inc.*

40

bo (bee-oh)

SB. Abbreviation, *box office*. AI. Also, *B.O.*

body

MU. 1. The fullness, deepness and richness of tone. 2. That quality of tone that is full and sonorous. 3. The main structure of any musical instrument. AI. The *body* of a hollow-bodied, stringed instrument serves as a *resonance box*, as that of a guitar, violin, etc.

boffo (bahf'o)

SB. 1. Short for *box office*. 2. A good box-office attraction. AI. For instance, it might be said that a singer, a dance band, a musical show, etc., is definitely *boffo*.

boiler-room arrangement

MN. 1. A musical arrangement featuring drums and/or other percussion instruments. 2. A musical arrangement in which drumming predominates. 3. An overly loud musical arrangement. AI. Also called *boiler-shop arrangement*.

bold c (bold see) : **C**

MU. 1. The character shown above. 2. The character used as the time signature for Four-Four Time. AI. Originally the time signature for Four-Four Time was a broken circle. However, in recent years this broken circle has been replaced by the bold-faced C shown above. Contrary to a widespread but entirely erroneous belief, this character does not mean *common time*. It represents only one of several common times. See COMMON TIME.

bold face

PG. A printing type with a heavy face. AI. For instance, **these eight words are set in bold face.** Abbreviated, *b.f.*, *bf* and/or *B.F.*

bomb

SB. 1. A failure. 2. A success. AI. Paradoxically, this term is used to mean two different things, each the direct opposite of the other. See LAY A BOMB.

bona fide (bo'na fi'de")

LW. 1. In good faith. 2. Without fraud, dishonesty or deceit, as a *bona fide* contract, a *bona fide* music publisher, etc.

bongos

MU. Two small drums of different tones that are connected by a rigid brace. AI. Bongos are placed on a floor cymbal stand or held between the knees of a sitting performer and played with the fingers of both hands.

booby trap

MB. Any device, as a fine hair, a small seed, talcum powder, trick sealing of an envelope, etc., included in a song submission, by which misguided songwriters think they can tell whether or not a submission has been opened and read, as by a music publisher.

boogie (bou′ge)

MU. Short for *boogie woogie.*

boogie beat

MU. 1. Eight beats to the measure. 2. Eight-Eight Time. 3. In the tempo and character of boogie woogie.

boogie woogie

MU. A style of jazz piano playing in which repeated bass figures in Eight-Eight Time furnish the accompaniment for a blues melody played in the treble. AI. This particular style was popular with many Negro pianists in and around New Orleans even before the twentieth century began. However, it was not until the roaring twenties that boogie woogie became known nationally as a supposed new style of piano playing, said to have originated on Chicago's South Side. Because of this, it was known for a while as State Street piano. Among those prominent in popularizing boogie woogie are Meade Lux Lewis, Albert Ammons, Jimmy Yancey, Pinetop Smith and Pete Johnson. Typical boogie-woogie songs are BEAT ME DADDY EIGHT TO THE BAR, BIG FOOT PETE, SCRUB ME MAMA (With a Boogie Beat) and RHUMBOOGIE. See WALKING BASS. See NEGRO MUSIC.

book

SB. v. 1. To contract a performance or the appearance of a performer or performers. 2. To engage, as an artist, for a performance or performances. AI. For instance, a singer might be *booked* to appear at a certain night club on a certain date, a dance band might be *booked* to play at a certain ballroom, etc.

book

PN. n. 1. A number of sheets of paper with writing or printing, fastened together along one edge, usually between protective covers, as a song book. MU. 2. The words of a musical play, as distinguished from the score. 3. Libretto. 4. The book or books containing the music used by a band or orchestra. 5. Figuratively, *repertoire*. AI. For instance, if a band or orchestra does not know or play a certain song, it could be said that it is not in their *book*, etc.

booking

SB. 1. An engagement, as for a singer, a band, etc. 2. A contract or agreement to perform at a certain place on a certain date. 3. A performance. 4. An engagement. 5. A working date.

booking agent

SB. 1. A person who arranges bookings for performers, as for singers and musicians in theaters, night clubs, etc. 2. An organization for this purpose, usually called a *booking agency*. AI. A booking agent or agency works on a commission (which in some states is regulated and controlled by law). Because this commission is usually ten per cent, a booking agent is often referred to as a *ten percenter*.

book man

MS. 1. A good reader of music. 2. A musician who is able to read music. AI. Also called *paper man*.

book-title songs

MB. Songs with titles the same as those of books, usually novels. Typical book-title songs are GONE WITH THE WIND, I COVER THE WATERFRONT, MY SISTER AND I and STARS FELL ON ALABAMA.

boom-chick

MN. A Two-Four rhythm, often used as a background, as BOOM-chick, BOOM-chick, BOOM-chick, etc., with the accent on the capitalized syllable.

borsch belt

SB. The locale of the borsch circuit.

borsch circuit

SB. A number of associated resort hotels in the Catskill and White Mountains, where entertainment, as that of singers and musicians, is provided for the guests. AI. Humorously so called because of the characteristic cuisine, borsch being a Russian (kosher) beet soup. Many big-name entertainers got their start in show business by playing the borsch circuit. Also spelled *borsht.*

bounce

MU. A lively, quick-beat style of syncopation. Also called *jump.*

box office

SB. 1. A place where admission tickets are sold, as in a theater, auditorium, etc. 2. The money received from the sale of tickets of admission. AI. For instance, to count the *box office* means to count the money paid in for admission to a performance. 3. Audience appeal, popularity. AI. For instance, a song, a scene, a musical play, etc. might be said to have *good box office,* meaning that it has public appeal—good possibilities of becoming a financial success.

box-office attraction

SB. 1. A performer, act, show, etc. that normally attracts a large (ticket buying) audience. 2. A draw. 3. A drawing card.

boy-and-girl song

MU. A song written to be sung as a duet by girl and boy singers. Typical boy-and-girl songs are ANYTHING YOU CAN DO, YOU'RE JUST IN LOVE and BABY, IT'S COLD OUTSIDE.

boy lyric

MU. A lyric written to be sung by a male singer. See BOY SONG.

boy-name song

SW. A classification in songwriting as to title. AI. Typical boy-name songs are: BILL, CHARLIE BROWN, JUST A GUY NAMED JOE and JOEY.

44

boy-or-girl song

MU. A song that has both a boy lyric and a girl lyric. AI. For instance, the boy lyric of BLUES IN THE NIGHT becomes a girl lyric with such skillful changes as *son* to *hon, kneepants* to *pigtails, woman* to *man,* etc.

boy song

MU. A song with a boy lyric only. Typical boy songs are FIVE FOOT TWO EYES OF BLUE, MY MOONLIGHT MADONNA and YOU MUST HAVE BEEN A BEAUTIFUL BABY.

brace: { or [or |

MU. 1. Any of the characters shown above. 2. A character, curved or straight, used to connect two or more staves of music. 3. The group of staves connected in this manner. AI. When two or more staves are connected by a brace, this means that the notation on these staves is to be played and/or sung at the same time.

bracket

MU. A term often used to mean *brace.*

brain child

SW. 1. Any idea, plan, or thought regarded as produced by a person's mental labor. 2. A song, an idea for a song, etc.

brass

MU. A brass wind instrument (singular), as a horn, trumpet, trombone, tuba, etc. AI. BRASSES, plural.

brass band

MU. 1. A band consisting chiefly of brass wind instruments, to which are usually added some wood winds and percussion instruments. 2. A band in which the instruments are mainly brasses.

brasses

MU. Brass wind instruments (plural). AI. Brass, singular.

brass section

MU. 1. The brass instruments of an orchestra. 2. Brass group. 3. Brass choir.

brass wind

MU. The term applied to the horns, trumpets, trombones, tubas, etc. of an orchestra, as distinguished from wood winds.

break

MB. v. 1. To happen in a certain way, as a song is said to *break* when it begins to become popular and its sheet music and/or phonograph records start selling. MU. 2. To change from one quality of tone to another in singing or playing.

break

MU. n. 1. A pause in syncopated music. 2. A period of silence. 3. Tacet. 4. Erroneously but frequently used to mean *lick*. See LICK. 5. The point where the chest-tone changes to the head-tone, as those of a singer. 6. Hence, the point where one register or quality of voice changes to another, as alto to soprano, etc. 7. A similar point in the tones of a musical instrument. MB. 8. A rest period, as that taken by members of a dance band, recording musicians, etc., as a *five-minute break*, *coffee break*, etc.

breakdown

MU. 1. A shuffling, stamping dance, usually done to music played in a fast tempo. 2. A vigorously performed square dance. 3. The music for such a dance.

break out

MB. Same as *breakthrough*.

breakthrough

MB. v. To become popular, usually suddenly, as a song.

breakthrough

MB. n. A song that suddenly becomes popular. AI. Also called a *break out*.

break up

SB. 1. To put a stop to. 2. To upset. AI. For instance, a singer or musician might be said to *break up* when he is unable to continue singing or playing because of an emotional upset, laughter, tears, etc.

46

breath mark: ,

MU. 1. The mark shown above. 2. A mark placed over the staff to indicate the end of a phrase and the desired place for a singer to take a breath.

breathy

MB. Characterized by an excessive and audible emission of breath, as might be said of some singers.

breve: 1. ⌣ 2. ‖o‖

PY. 1. The curved mark shown above, which is put over or under a vowel or syllable to show that it is short. AI. A breve is the opposite of *macron*. MU. 2. The second sign shown above, meaning a note equal to two whole notes. AI. This note value was never used in songwriting and is now rarely used elsewhere.

brickyard

MN. Very solid and flawless, as said of a musician, a musical composition or performance. AI. A highly complimentary term.

bridge

SW. 1. The secondary passage of a song or other musical composition. 2. A contrasting melody. 3. The so-called *middle part* of a song chorus, also called the *release*. AI. In a song written to the AABA form, the B section is the bridge. Sometimes called *the half*. MU. 4. The arched piece of wood, or other material, that supports the strings of a stringed instrument.

bridge music

MB. Music used on a radio or television program as a connective link between segments or portions thereof. AI. This is one of the categories used by performing-rights societies in establishing credit values.

Brill building

MB. The eleven-story structure located at 1619 Broadway, New York, N.Y. The Brill Building long has been associated with the music business. At one time more than 300 music publishers were listed on its directories as tenants.

broadcast

RT. To transmit widely by radio or television, as a song.

broadcasting station

RT. 1. An organization for broadcasting radio and/or television programs. 2. The studios, offices, equipment, etc. of such an organization.

Broadcast Music, Inc.

MB. An organization whose purpose it is to collect payment for the performance rights of its members' songs and distribute these payments to its membership. More often called *BMI*. A songwriter becomes eligible to apply for BMI membership when he places a song with a music publisher who is a BMI member. Address: 589 Fifth Avenue, New York, N.Y. 10017.

Broadway

TE. 1. A street that runs in a general northward-southward direction through New York City, known for its brightly lighted theater section, night clubs, etc. 2. The New York City commercial theater or entertainment industry, or its life, world, etc.

Broadway music

SB. 1. Music and songs connected with the musical shows of New York City's Broadway theater section. 2. Music and songs typical of the music and songs written especially for Broadway musical shows.

Broadway, off

TE. See OFF BROADWAY.

broken chord

MU. A chord whose notes (tones) are played or sung successively, one following the other, in a harp-like manner, instead of all being played or sung together. Also known, in barbershop harmony, as a *stinger* or a *ringer*. See CHIME. See SOLID CHORD.

broken octave

MU. An octave whose notes (tones) are played or sung separately, one following the other, instead of being played or sung together.

48

brown sound

RB. 1. The sound of Negro voices, as distinguished from the sound of voices of other races, particularly those of the white race. 2. A good imitation of the sound of Negro voices by those other than Negroes. AI. A term used to distinguish this sound from the white sound.

Brussels Amendment (brus'lz a-mend'ment)

LW. At a meeting of the Berne Union at Brussels in 1948, the following amendment was added to the original copyright agreement: *any country that has adopted the Brussels Amendment can accept for first publication a work published in that Berne country within 30 days after its publication in the United States of America.* AI. At the time this is written, Canada had not adopted the Brussels Amendment. Both France and England had done so. This means, to meet the requirements of an international copyright, if Canada is to be the country of first publication, copies of a song must be put on sale in Canada the *same day* they are put on sale in the United States. There can be no deviation. However, if either France or England is selected to be the country of first publication, copies may be put on sale in either country at any time within 30 days of the date of first publication in the United States. Most Canadian agents, upon authorization to do so, will arrange for publication of a client's song in England or France. Usually, French or English publication is an emergency step occasioned by the failure of copies to arrive in Canada in time for same-day publication. See SAME-DAY PUBLICATION. See COUNTRY OF ORIGIN. See FIRST PUBLICATION.

B side

MB. 1. The side of a phonograph record opposite the A side. 2. The *flip* of the A side. 3. The side of a phonograph record usually considered to be of secondary importance. 4. The song on the B side. AI. There have been instances where the B side became a hit and little was heard of the A side. TENNESSEE WALTZ, recorded by Patti Page, is an example of this. See A SIDE. See FLIP.

buckwheat: ♩ ♩ ♩ ♩

MU. The original four shape notes shown above. AI. Reading from left to right, these designate the syllables fa, sol, la, mi. Also called *the four-shape notes* or simply *shape* or *shaped notes*.

Buenos Aires Convention, the

LW. The convention on Literary and Artistic Copyright, a group of some seventeen countries adhering to a copyright agreement signed at Buenos Aires, August 11, 1910. AI. The United States is a member of this group. A current list of countries contracting to the Buenos Aires Convention may be had free of charge by requesting "annex B to Circular 37" from the United States Copyright Office. Also called *BAC*.

buff

GI. 1. A devotee, as a *jazz buff*, a *country-music buff*, etc. 2. A fan.

build

WG. 1. To construct (write) a series of thoughts or ideas in such a manner that each adds something more than the one preceding it. 2. To construct (write) a series of interest-building thoughts. AI. For instance, a songwriter might speak of *building* or *building up* to a climax. A good example of such building is the lyric for the song hit, GEE, BUT YOU'RE SWELL. See CLIMAX.

build up

SB. 1. A sales talk. 2. A series (usually at some length) of favorable comments. AI. For instance, a music publisher might be said to give a song a *build up* to a record company. A booking agent might be said to give a singer a *build up* to a night club operator, etc.

built-in finish

MS. 1. A special-arranged ending for a song. 2. A stirring, audience-arousing song ending. 3. A big ending to a song.

bullet

MB. A colored star, dot or other emblem, used in song and/or record popularity charts to designate a song or the side of a record that has taken a sharp rise in popularity, sales, etc. AI. Also called a *star* (if so shaped), red star, etc.

business

TE. 1. An action in a play or musical, especially for a particular effect. 2. Any action by a performer for a particular effect. AI. For

50

instance, a singer might pause to light a cigarette, put on a hat, slowly tear up a letter, wipe away a tear, etc. GI. 3. One's work, occupation, profession, etc., as the *song business, music business, show business,* etc.

business manager

SB. See MANAGER.

by-line

MB. 1. A written or printed line, as on a manuscript, a song sheet or record, that tells who wrote the song and/or who published the song, etc. 2. The line beginning with *words by, lyric by, words and music by, music by,* etc. 3. The *credit line.* See CREDITS.

b/w (bee-dub'l-yu)

RB. Abbreviation, *backed with.* Same as *c/w.* See BACKED WITH.

C

C

MU. 1. The third letter of the musical alphabet, representing a pitch one half tone higher than that of B. 2. The letter applied to middle C. 3. The letter applied to any octave above or below middle C. 4. The first tone, note or degree, the keytone, the keynote in the ascending major scale of C. 5. The only major key that has no sharps, no flats, no key signature. 6. The caption for a C major triad. 7. The key or string of a musical instrument that produces the tone of C. 8. The capital letter used, in a certain bold-faced style, as the time signature for Four-Four Time. 9. The capital letter used, in a certain bold-faced style, with a bar through it, as the time signature for Cut Time. 10. The capital letter used to designate (choir) boy's voice in multiple-voice arrangements, as in SSCB. SW. 11. The capital letter used to designate the third phrase in song structure, as in AABC, ABAC, etc. 12. The small letter used to designate the third rhyme in a rhyme scheme as in ababbcc, aabbcc, etc. LW. 13. The letter used, in a circle, to mean *copyright*. See BOLD C.

C

MU. See BOLD C.

¢

MU. See BARRED C.

C ♯

MU. See C SHARP.

53

©

LW. See C IN A CIRCLE.

cabaret (kab"a-rae')

SB. A restaurant or cafe where entertainment, as singing, dancing, etc., is given during meals, as on the dining room floor.

cacophony (ka-kof'o-nee)

GI. A harsh or disagreeable sound, as bad enunciation of a singer.

cadence (kae'd'ns)

PY. 1. Rhythmical or measured flow of movement as in poetry. 2. Fall of the voice. 3. Modulation of the voice. MU. 4. Measured movement, as in marching or dancing, or the beat of such movement. 5. Two or more chords which bring a line of melody to a point of rest. 6. A chord progression written at the close of a song, a section or a phrase. AI. A cadence creates the effect of a temporary or final conclusion. A close.

cafe society

SB. 1. A set of frequenters of cafes or night clubs in New York City. 2. Any similar set elsewhere. 3. Regular attendants of night clubs.

call

SB. 1. A notice to appear. 2. A summons. AI. For instance, a record company might issue a *call* for certain musicians to play a recording session on a certain date. A producer might issue a *call* for entertainers to appear for audition or rehearsal for a musical, etc.

call letters

RT. 1. The letters used to identify radio and television stations. 2. The name of a radio or television station, as KDKA, WINS-TV, WMAQ, KGO-TV, etc.

calypso (ka-lip'-so)

MB. a. 1. Designating or of songs improvised and sung by natives of Trinidad. 2. Similar to or in the style of such songs.

54

calypso

MB. n. 1. A song in the calypso style. 2. Music in the calypso style. AI. Calypso songs are lively folk ballads, often on topical themes done in a light or humorous manner, characterized by wrenched syllabic stress, loose rhyme and journalistic language set to a characteristic (island) beat. Typical of songs written in the calypso style are LITTLE GIRL IN KINGSTON TOWN, SING ME A TROPICAL SONG, SOMEBODY BAD STOLE THE WEDDING BELL and STONE COLD DEAD IN THE MARKET.

camera-ready

PG. 1. A form in which modern music typography is furnished, as a *camera-ready master, camera-ready copy* or *camera-ready proof*, etc. 2. Ready to be photographed. AI. This means that the copy is furnished in a form that is ready to be photographed by the (printing) plate maker's camera.

can

MB. Any container in which master recordings are stored. See IN THE CAN.

Canadian agent

MB. A person or firm, in Canada, who acts in behalf of clients elsewhere, as music publishers in the United States, usually in securing publication in Canada, for which these agents issue a certificate of publication.

Canadian copyright

LW. By virtue of a copyright treaty between the United States and Canada, both American citizens and Canadian citizens enjoy equal rights of copyright protection in both countries. This means that an original work, as a song, for which copyright has been secured in the United States, is automatically protected by copyright in Canada, and vice versa. No additional copyright notice is required. No additional copyright registration is necessary, except under one condition. As Canadian judges are forbidden by law to hear a case involving an unregistered copyright, it is therefore necessary that a copyright be registered in Canada before action in its behalf can be instituted in a Canadian court. This registration can be obtained at any time during the life of the United States copyright applying to the same work. The life of a Canadian copyright is for the life of the author, plus fifty years after his death. A Canadian copyright is not to be confused with an International copyright. A Canadian copyright does not apply to any country other than Canada. See FORM I. See FORM K.

canary

SB. A female singer. Also called *thrush* and *lark*.

C and W (see and dub'l-yu)

MB. Abbreviation, *Country and Western*.

canned music

MB. Music that is recorded (in any form), as distinguished from *live* music.

cantata (kan-tah'tah)

MU. A musical composition consisting of a vocal solo or solos and/or vocal choruses which tell a story. AI. Cantatas are sung but not acted.

cap, caps

PG. 1. Abbreviation, capital letter, capital letters. 2. A printer's mark meaning *set in a capital letter* or *set in capital letters*.

capital

PG. A capital letter, as distinguished from *lower case*. AI. For instance, THESE SEVEN WORDS ARE SET IN CAPITALS. these eight words are set in lower case. These Ten Words Are Set In Capitals And Lower Case. AI. Abbreviation *cap* (singular), *caps* (plural).

capitalize

PG. To set in a capital letter or capital letters.

capo (kah'po)

MU. 1. Head. 2. Top. 3. The beginning of a song or other musical composition. See TOP. 4. A mechanical device that clamps on the neck of a stringed instrument, as a guitar, a ukulele, etc., in a manner to stop all strings at the same fret. Changes in keys are made by moving the capo up or down the neck, thus changing the pitch of each string in correct relationship to that of all other strings.

card-carrying musician

MB. 1. A union musician. 2. A member of the American Federation of Musicians. AI. The word *card* means *union card.*

caret: ∧

WG. 1. The mark shown above. 2. A mark used in writing and editing to show where something is to be added, as to include an omission. AI. For instance, here is the way a caret is used to add the word *broken* to the following song title:

BROKEN
THE BOULEVARD OF ∧ DREAMS.

carillon (ker′e-lon″)

MU. 1. A set of stationary bells, each producing a tone of the chromatic scale, sounded by means of a keyboard. 2. A melody played on such bells.

carioca

MU. 1. A variety of South American dance. 2. The music for this dance. GI. 3. A native of Rio de Janeiro, Brazil, where the dance and its music originated.

carol

MU. v. 1. To sing joyously. 2. To praise or celebrate in song. 3. To sing a song of Christmas.

carol

MU. n. 1. A joyous song of praise and devotion. 2. A joyous song in praise of Christmas. 3. A joyous song in praise of Easter. AI. Typical Christmas carols are: O LITTLE TOWN OF BETHLE-HEM, JOY TO THE WORLD and, the greatest of all, SILENT NIGHT.

caroler

MU. A singer, particularly one who sings Christmas carols.

Cash Box

MB. A music-business trade publication. Published weekly. Issued every Monday. Dated the Saturday following date of issuance. Address: 1780 Broadway, New York, N. Y. 10019.

castanets (kas″ta-nets′)

MU. Small, hollowed pieces of hard wood, ivory, or other material, used in pairs to beat time to music by clapping one against the other to produce a hollow clicking or rattling sound, especially for Spanish rhythms.

cat

JZ. 1. A jazz musician. 2. A jazz devotee. AI. A *cat* may be either cool or hot, male or female. The name originated from musicians being night workers. Thus, their waking and sleeping habits are similar to those of the night-prowling feline. The name is complimentary and implies a degree of proficiency and/or knowledge. The opposite of *long hair*.

catalectic (kat″a-lek′tik)

PY. 1. Lacking part of the last foot. 2. Lacking one or two syllables. AI. For instance, in the following, the second line is catalectic:

> Lives of | great men | all re- | mind us
>
> We can | make our | lives sub- | lime

catalog

MB. 1. The list of songs and/or other publications published by a publisher. 2. The properties of a publisher. 3. The list of songs written by a songwriter. 4. The songs included in such a list. 5. The list of records offered for sale by a phonograph record company.

catalog of copyright entries

LW. An official publication of the United States Copyright Office, published semiannually, in which all copyright entries are recorded and indexed for the respective six-month period, as January-June and July-December. AI. The *catalog* is published in sections, each pertaining to a particular form of work, as Part 1—Books and Pamphlets. Part 2—Periodicals. Parts 3 and 4—Drama and Works Prepared for Oral Delivery. Part 5—Music, etc. Sections may be purchased sep-

58

arately. For further information and prices write: Superintendent of Documents, U. S. Government Printing Office, Washington, D. C. 20402.

catch
SB. 1. To see and/or hear, as a member of an audience, as *to catch* a performance, a performer, an act, a show, a recording, etc. 2. To witness.

catch line
WG. 1. A sentence or phrase that catches attention, as in a song. 2. A thought that catches or is meant to capture popular attention. 3. A gag line.

catchy
MB. 1. Catching attention. 2. Arousing interest. 3. Easily caught up and remembered, as a catchy tune. 4. Likely to catch on (become popular).

C barré (see bah-rae′) : ¢
MU. 1. The character shown above. 2. The time signature for Cut Time. Also called *barred* C.

CBS (see-bee-ess)
RT. Abbreviation, *Columbia Broadcasting System.*

Cecilia, Saint
SW. See SAINT CECILIA.

celesta (se-les′ ta)
MU. A small keyboard instrument, somewhat resembling an upright piano, whose bell-like tones are produced by the striking of hammers against small metal plates. AI. A celesta has a compass of five octaves.

cell
SB. A theater or night club dressing room, especially a small one.

cello (chel′o)
MU. 1. An instrument of the violin family, between the viola and double bass in size and pitch. 2. The violoncello.

certificate of assignment

LW. A written statement testifying that the owner of a copyright, as a songwriter (called the assignor), transfers this ownership to another person or persons, as a publisher (called the assignee). See ASSIGNMENT OF COPYRIGHT.

certificate of publication

LW. A written statement testifying that a work, as a song or book, has been duly offered for sale, therefore published, in a certain country, as Canada or England, as of a certain (publication) date.

certificate of registration

LW. A written statement testifying that the statements set forth in an application for Registration of a Claim to Copyright have been made a part of the records of the Copyright Office, as that of the United States. AI. See page 3 of FORM E.

changing notes

MU. Notes that indicate changing tones.

changing tones

MU. Passing tones that occur on an accent. See PASSING TONES.

channel

ET. 1. An electrical circuit, as used to convey sound, as the *channel* from a microphone to a loud-speaker, etc. 2. A frequency band assigned to a radio or television station.

chant

MU. v. 1. To sing. 2. To sing a chant. 3. To sing a song in the manner of a chant.

chant

MU. n. 1. A song or a melody. 2. A simple song in which a number of syllables or words are sung in a monotone. 3. A monotonous tone of voice.

chanter

MU. A male singer, particularly a chorister.

chanteuse (shan-tuse')

MU. 1. A female singer, pop or otherwise. 2. A female soloist. 3. A female chorister. AI. Also, *chantress*.

chantey (shan'te)

MU. 1. A work song of sailors. 2. Folk songs of the sea. GI. Sailors sing chanteys in rhythm with their motions while working. Chanteys are divided into classifications as to the particular work they fit. For instance, there are *capstan* (pushing) chanteys, *halyard* (pulling) chanteys, etc. Typical chanteys are DON'T CRY LITTLE FISH, BLOW THE MAN DOWN, THE BOLD FISHERMAN, HAUL AWAY JOE and EIGHT BELLS.

chantress (chan'tres)

MU. Same as *chanteuse*.

character

MU. 1. A general name for any musical sign or abbreviation, as a note, a rest, a clef, etc. WG. 2. A person in a story, play, song, etc., as the unnamed woman in SHE'S FUNNY THAT WAY, the gentleman described in MR. FIVE BY FIVE, JOHNNY ONE NOTE described in the song of the same name and the man known as THE OLD LAMPLIGHTER.

characteristic music

MU. 1. Music that is typical of a people or a place, as *characteristic Latin music*, *characteristic hill music*, *characteristic Irish music*, etc. 2. Ethnic music.

character songs

SW. A classification in songwriting as to subject matter. There are two kinds of character songs: 1. Songs that describe the particular qualities, traits, etc. of a person. 2. Songs that establish a character for the singer and are intended to be sung in a *characterful* manner. AI. Typical character songs that describe the qualities, traits, etc. of a person are A LITTLE BIT INDEPENDENT, OH, MY PAPA and MACK THE KNIFE. Typical character songs that establish a character for the singer are JUST A GIGOLO, MAÑANA and THAT'S AMORE.

61

Charleston

MU. A lively dance in Four-Four Time, characterized by a twisting step, popular in the 1920's.

charleston beat

MU. The tempo for the dance by the same name.

chart

MB. A list of songs in the order of their current popularity, sales of phonograph records, sales of sheet music, etc. AI. Charts of this nature are featured in the music-trade publications and in some newspapers.

chart action

MB. The changing position, from one chart to the next, of a song, a phonograph record, etc. AI. A song is usually said to be getting chart action when its *moves* are sharply upward.

cheapie

RB. Any phonograph record that is made to sell at a cheap price, as *mirrors* often are.

Child ballads

FK. A five-volume collection of folk songs, compiled by Harvard-professor Francis J. Child, titled *The English and Scottish Popular Ballads*, published in the 1880's and generally regarded as a highly authoritative source in its field.

chime

MU. 1. To sing or play the notes (tones) of a chord or an octave successively, one following the other. 2. To sing or play a broken chord. 3. To sing or play a chord brokenly. 4. To *chime* a chord. 5. To *chime* an octave. 6. To ring or play a chime or chimes.

chimes

MU. 1. A percussion instrument consisting of a set of bells, metal bars, metal tubes, etc., tuned to a scale, or part of a scale. 2. The musical sounds or harmony produced by striking a set of bells or

62

chimes. AI. Also called *tubular bells, rhythm bells, tuned resonator bells,* and *orchestra bells.* See GLOCKENSPIEL.

Chinese blocks

MU. A percussion instrument similar to a clog box.

CHO.

MU. 1. Abbreviation, chorus. 2. The sign sometimes used to designate the *chorus* of a song.

chocolo (cho-ko'lo)

MU. A Latin American rhythm instrument consisting of a short metal tube, sealed at both ends, with seeds enclosed, which produces a swishing sound when shaken. Also called *metal tubos* (plural) or *tubo* (singular).

choice note

MU. 1. An alternate note. 2. An optional note. See ALTERNATE NOTE.

choice tone

MU. 1. An alternate tone. 2. An optional tone. See ALTERNATE TONE. See ALTERNATE NOTE.

choir

MU. 1. A group of singers, usually trained. 2. A group of singers of sacred music. 3. A group of instruments, as *brass choir*, etc.

choral

MU. a. 1. Pertaining to a choir or a chorus of singers or musicians, as a *choral* group, a *choral* composition, etc. 2. Of, for, sung by, or recited by a choir. 3. Designating a size of printed music, the same as *octavo.*

choral

MU. n. 1. A song or other musical composition for choral performance. 2. A musical arrangement for choir, vocal or instrumental.

chord

MU. 1. Three or more tones sounded together in harmony. 2. A combination of tones selected according to the laws of harmony. 3. The notation representing these tones. 4. A diagram representing these tones, as that for a guitar, ukulele, etc. AI. The five principal chords are: major triad, minor triad, augmented triad, dominant seventh and diminished seventh. The four lesser chords are: major seventh, minor seventh, sixth and ninth. Two simultaneous tones are considered an *interval*, not a chord. See INTERVAL.

chord caption

MU. The abbreviated name of a chord, as *C7, Em, Gmaj*, etc. AI. Chord captions are often placed above the melody line, on lead sheets and/or piano-and-vocal arrangements of songs, to show chord progressions. Chord captions are used both with and without chord diagrams.

chord diagram:

MU. 1. A symbol composed of vertical lines representing the strings of a stringed instrument, horizontal lines representing the frets, and small dots indicating the fingering to be used in playing a chord, like that shown above. AI. Chord diagrams for the guitar are often included in popular music. Diagrams for the ukulele are not as popular as they once were. The name of the chord, as the letter F (shown in connection with the above diagram), is called the *chord caption*. Chord captions are often used without diagrams.

chord family

MU. 1. A group of chords that are related. 2. The chords that make up a chord progression.

chord progression

MU. An orderly arrangement of chords that make up a harmony sequence. AI. Expressed in Roman numerals, the chord progression most often used in song writing is: I-VI-V7-I. Applied to the key of C, this is: C-F-G7-C.

chord tones

MU. The tones that make up a chord, as distinguished from *passing tones*. AI. For instance, the chord tones C, E, and G make up the chord of C MAJOR. The chord tones G, B, D, and F make up the chord of G7, etc. Compare with PASSING TONES.

choreographer (ko-re-og'ra-fur)

MU. One who designs or arranges the movements of a dance.

choreography (ko-re-og'ra-fee)

DG. 1. Dancing, especially ballet dancing. 2. The arrangement of the written notation of the movements of a dance. 3. The art of devising, designing and planning of a ballet.

choriamb (kor'e-amb")

PY. A metrical foot or four syllables in this order: an accented syllable, an unaccented syllable, an unaccented syllable, an accented syllable, or — ⌣ ⌣ —. Example, *Sat'ur-day night'*. Musical counterpart, Four-Four Time.

chorine (kor'een)

TE. 1. A girl member of a chorus, as that in a musical show. 2. A chorus girl.

chorister

MU. 1. A singer. 2. Usually, a singer who is a member of a group, as a chorus or choir. 3. Rarely, a choir leader.

chorus

MU. 1. The major part of a song. 2. The refrain of a song, following the verse. 3. A group of singers. 4. A group of dancers. 5. A group of singers and dancers, as those in a musical show. 6. Music written for group singing.

chorus girl, or boy

TE. 1. A girl, or boy, who dances and/or sings in a chorus, as that of a musical show. 2. A member of a chorus, as that of a musical show.

chorus line

TE. 1. A line of chorus girls (and/or boys). 2. A group of chorus girls who appear as a unit. 3. The assemblage of chorus girls in a musical show.

chromatic (kro-mat′ihk)

MU. a. 1. Using or progressing by half tones, half steps or semitones, as a *chromatic scale*. 2. Producing tones of such a scale, as a *chromatic instrument*.

chromatic

MU. n. A tone modified by an accidental, as B♭, F♯, D♭, etc.

chromatic keys

MU. 1. The black keys on a keyboard instrument, as those of a piano, accordion, etc. 2. The keys on a keyboard instrument which sound the tones D♭-C♯, E♭-D♯, G♭-F♯, A♭-G♯, B♭-A♯.

chromatic scale

MU. The musical scale made up of thirteen successive half tones (half steps or semi tones) to the octave. AI. For instance, the chromatic scale of C consists of the following thirteen tones: C, D♭, D, E♭, E, F, G♭, G, A♭, A, B♭, B, C.

church music

MB. 1. Musical compositions that are written and published to be sung and played in a church, as distinguished from religious music that is not intended for use in a church. 2. Religious musical compositions of a particular faith, denomination or sect. 3. Musical compositions published by a church-owned publishing organization.

c in a circle: ⓒ

LW. 1. The symbol or sign shown above. 2. An abbreviation meaning *copyright* or *copyrighted*. AI. The c-in-the-circle sign is required by the Universal Copyright Convention. Many music publishers use both this symbol and the word *copyright* in their copyright notices, thus: ⓒ COPYRIGHTED. See COPYRIGHT NOTICE.

circuit

SB. 1. A number of places offering entertainment, as theaters, night clubs, hotels, etc. AI. For instance, a singer might be said to be playing the *night club circuit*, the *summer-theater circuit*, etc. ET. 2. A complete or partial path over which an electrical current may flow, as the circuit between a microphone and a loud-speaker, etc.

claimant

LW. 1. One who makes a claim, as that to copyright. 2. A copyright owner or one who pretends to be. 3. One who claims ownership, as of a song.

clambake

JZ. 1. A jam session. SB. 2. A failure, as an unpopular song, an unsuccessful show, etc.

clarinet

MU. A single reed wood wind instrument, with finger holes and keys, in the form of a cylindrical tube which is played vertically. AI. The clarinet is made in a variety of sizes, the most common of which is the soprano, with a range of over three octaves.

classic

MU. Any musical work or composition that is generally accepted, over a long period of time, as a standard of excellence.

classical

MU. 1. Designating or of music that conforms to certain established standards. 2. Belonging to the first class or rank, as judged by popular acceptance. 3. Long hair.

claves

MU. Two short, round sticks, made of hardwood or other material, that produce a clear, ringing tone when struck together. AI. Claves are Latin-American rhythm instruments. Also called *rhythm sticks*.

clavichord (klav'a-kord)

MU. A stringed musical instrument with a keyboard, somewhat resembling a small piano and the harpsichord, played by depressing the keys, which cause the strings to be struck by little hammers. AI. The clavichord was the forerunner of the piano.

clearance

MB. 1. The act or process that establishes the ownership of a song, the condition under which it may be publicly performed and the permission to do so. 2. A certificate, or other agreement, granting the right to perform a song or songs.

clearance society

MB. An organization which authorizes public performance of its members' songs, and other musical works, and collects payment for these performances in behalf of its members. AI. Typical clearance societies operating in the United States are ASCAP, BMI and SESAC.

clef

MU. A character used to denote the names and pitch of the notes on the staff on which it is written. See TREBLE CLEF. See BASS CLEF.

cleffer (klef"r)

MB. 1. A songwriter. 2. A composer. 3. An author. 4. A lyricist.

cliché (kle-shae')

RC. An idea or expression which, though it was once fresh and forceful, has become hackneyed, weak and trite through frequent repetition. AI. Typical cliches are: *doomed to disappointment, tired but happy, too numerous to mention,* etc.

click

MB. A song hit. AI. Also called *large click* and *big click*.

climactic order

SW. A series, or movement, in which each detail is progressively more forceful, of more importance, of more interest. AI. For instance, a melody can be written in climactic order. A lyric can be written in climactic order.

climax

SW. 1. The highest point of interest, of excitement, etc., as that of a song. 2. The culmination.

clinker

MU. 1. An inharmonious tone. 2. A sour note. 3. A discord. MB. 4. A song that fails to attract attention.

clog

MU. 1. A dance originally done by performers wearing wooden-soled shoes, which were called *clogs*. 2. The music for this dance. 3. An imitation of clog dancing produced by striking a clog box with drumsticks.

clog box

MU. A jazz percussion instrument consisting of a slotted wooden box which is struck with drumsticks to produce the sound of clog dancing. AI. Also called *Chinese block* and *temple block*.

clogger

CM. 1. A clog dancer, male or female. 2. A square-dancer who clogs, as distinguished from one who *stomps*.

close

SB. v. 1. To end, to bring to an end, as a singer might be said to *close* his act with music up full, or he will *close* his night-club engagement Saturday night. 2. To cease or suspend operation, as a theater might *close* forever or only for the summer.

close

MU. n. A cadence.

closed syllable

PY. A sound ending in a consonant. AI. For instance, the word *lov'er* is a closed-syllable word. The syllable *er* in the word *lov'er* is a closed syllable.

close harmony

MU. Harmony in which the notes, tones or parts are kept as close together as possible.

closing A section

SW. The final or fourth section of a song written to the AABA pattern.

club

SB. 1. Night club. 2· Dinner club. 3 Supper club.

C.M.

CH. Abbreviation, *common meter.*

CMA (see-em-ae)

CM. Abbreviation, *Country Music Association.*

C major scale

MU. 1. The scale consisting of these eight notes or tones: C, D, E, F, G, A, B, C. 2. The natural major scale. AI. So called because this is the only major scale that contains no sharps and no flats. Also called the *key of C.* See KEY SIGNATURE.

C.M.D.

CH. Abbreviation, *common meter doubled.*

coast, the

MB. 1. Generally, the western coast of the United States. 2. The Pacific Coast area of the United States, usually meaning the State of California. 3. Specifically, the area in and around Los Angeles. 4. Hollywood.

co-author

WG. v. 1. To write with another person or persons, as a song. 2. To act as a co-writer. 3. To collaborate.

co-author

WG. n. 1. A member of a writing team. 2. A co-writer. 3. A collaborator.

coda (ko′da)

MU. 1. An independent short piece of music that is added to a song. 2. An additional ending. AI. The opposite of an *introduction.*

coda mark: ⊕

MU. The mark shown above. AI. The first time a song is played, this sign is disregarded. The second time (after *D. C.*), the performer skips from this sign to the coda. Sometimes the coda mark is also placed at the coda. Also called *coda sign.* See D. C.

70

coffee-house

JZ. 1. To play or perform with wild abandon. 2. The style of singing and playing done in Greek coffee houses. 3. An uninhibited performance.

coin

RC. 1. To make up, devise or invent, as a new word or saying. 2. To create. AI. Songs using *coined words* are: THE ABA DABA HONEYMOON, ZING-ZING-ZOOM ZOOM, DOODLE DOO DOO, A-TISKET A-TASKET and INKA DINKA DOO.

coin box

JB. 1. A container for money. 2. The box that holds the coins dropped into a juke box. 3. A juke box. AI. Also called *cashbox*. The juke-box industry is sometimes referred to as the *coin-box* trade, the *coin-box* business, etc.

cold

TE. 1. Without warmth or feeling. 2. Without enthusiasm. 3. Indifferent, as the performance of a song. 4. Without preparation. AI. A singer or musician is said to sing or play a song *cold* when he does so without rehearsal or other preparation. When used for this meaning, the term does not necessarily imply an unfeeling performance. A song can be performed both *cold* (unrehearsed) and warm-heartedly. Also, *cold turkey*.

cold turkey

MN. 1. Unrehearsed. 2. Extemporaneously, as to play or sing in this manner.

collaborate (ko-lab'o-rate)

SW. 1. To work together. 2. To work with another, or others, as in writing a song.

collaborator (ko-lab'o-ra-tor)

SW. 1. A person who works with another or others, as in songwriting. 2. A member of a songwriting team. 3. A co-author. 4. A co-writer.

71

collective work

LW. A work in which a number of contributions, constituting separate and independent works in themselves, are assembled into a collective whole, as a song book containing songs by various songwriters.

colloquialism (k'lo'kwe-al-iz'm)

RC. 1. A word, phrase or expression that is in general use in everyday, ordinary writing and conversation. 2. Language as it is commonly spoken and written. 3. An expression that most people understand.

colon: :

MU. 1. The sign shown above. 2. Two dots, one above the other. AI. The colon is used as a part of the bass clef and as a part of a repeat mark. AI. Sometimes called *single colon* to distinguish it from *double colon*. RT. 3. A punctuation mark used before an extended quotation, explanation, example, series, etc.

color

MU. 1. Tone color. 2. Quality. 3. Timbre. See QUALITY. See LOCAL COLOR.

coloratura (kul"er-a-tyoor'a)

MU. 1. Brilliant ornamental runs, trills, etc., used to display a singer's skill. 2. Music containing such ornaments. 3. A coloratura soprano.

coloratura soprano

MU. 1. A high soprano voice capable of singing coloratura. 2. A singer with such a voice.

color tones

BH. Tones sung with vibrato, as in barbershop harmony. AI. The opposite of *white tones*. Also called *colored tones*.

Columbia Broadcasting System, Inc., The

RT. A radio and television broadcasting network, usually called *CBS*. Address: 485 Madison Avenue, New York, N. Y. 10022.

combo

JZ. 1. Abbreviation for *combination*, meaning a *combination* (usually small) of musicians. 2. A small group of persons organized to play musical instruments. AI. A *combo* usually consists of from three to five musicians. The instrumentation varies.

combo-ork

MB. 1. An orchestration in abbreviated form, especially designed for use by a small group of musicians. 2. An abbreviated orchestration for a combo.

comedian

SB. 1. An actor who plays humorous or comic roles. 2. An entertainer who tells jokes and, sometimes, sings funny songs. 3. A monologuist who delivers funny monologs. 4. Anyone who entertains by evoking laughter.

comedy songs

MB. A classification in songwriting as to subject matter and treatment. AI. Typical comedy songs are the WOODY WOODPECKER SONG, GRANDMA'S LYE SOAP, MA, I'M AN OLD COWHAND and TIE ME KANGAROO DOWN, SPORT.

come off

MB. 1. To happen successfully. 2. To become a success. AI. The expression *come off* often is used in a negative connection. For instance, to say a song did not *come off* means a song did not become successful. A song that fails to *come off* is one that does not become popular, etc.

comic

SB. A comedian, usually of the *stand-up* type.

comic opera

TE. 1. A light opera. 2. An opera with a light, humorous plot that ends happily. 3. An operetta.

commercial

MB. a. 1. A type of song. 2. Designating a song written to the prescribed popular-song formula, as a *commercial type* song. 3.

73

Designating a song that is *singable, playable, danceable* and *easy to remember*.

commercial

MB. n. 1. A commercial-type song. 2. A song conveying an advertisement on or for radio and/or television. RT. 3. An advertising message as used on radio and/or television.

commercial sound

MB. 1. An acceptable recording of a commercial-type song. 2. A phonograph record, or side, of the kind that is usually acceptable to the record-buying public.

commissioner

LW. The Commissioner of patents, Canada.

Commissioner of patents, The

LW. The government official to whom applications for registration of Canadian copyrights are addressed. Address: The Copyright Office, Ottawa, Canada.

commitment

BS. 1. An agreement. 2. A pledge. 3. An obligation. AI. For instance, a songwriter might have a *commitment* to write a song for a music publisher, singer, etc. A singer might have a *commitment* to perform at a certain theater on a certain date, etc.

common chord

MU. 1. A chord consisting of a root, its third and its fifth. 2. A triad. See TRIAD.

common law

LW. The unwritten law of a country based on custom, usage, and the decisions of law courts, as distinguished from *statute law*.

common-law copyright

LW. See COPYRIGHT, COMMON LAW.

common-law literary property

LW. This type of protection is a matter of state law, and comes into being when a work, as a song, is created. It requires no action in the Copyright Office. It may last as long as the work is unpublished but it ends when the work is published or copyright is secured. AI. To enforce this protection, in case the need should arise, an undeniable date of existence always should be established. This is one of the two types of protection for which an unpublished song is eligible. The other is *statutory* copyright.

common meter

CH. Designating a metrical count of 8.6.8.6., as that of a hymn tune. AI. Abbreviated, *C.M.*

common property

LW. 1. Something that is regarded as being possessed by all and which is not the exclusive property of one or a few, as a song that is in public domain. 2. Something to which no one person or a few people can claim proprietorship. 3. Something, the use of which is open to all without restriction.

common time

MU. Any time that has an even number of beats to the measure. AI. The common times most often used in songwriting are Two-Four, Four-Four and Cut Time. It is erroneously believed by many that *common time* means Four-Four Time exclusively.

community sing

CM. A public gathering for the purpose of audience-participation singing.

comp

SW. 1. Short for *comprehensive*, as an outline of a song. PG. 2. Short for typographical *composition*, as that for a song. SB. 3. Short for *complimentary*, as a free admission ticket.

company

BS. 1. A group of people engaged in a particular business enterprise, as a music publishing company, phonograph record company, etc.

SB. 2. All those who put on a particular show, as the actors, singers, dancers, musicians, stagehands, business management, etc.

compass

MU. The range of tones a voice or instrument is capable of producing.

compatible

RC. Capable of getting along well together. AI. For instance, a melody is *compatible* with a lyric when it expresses the same mood and vice versa. Songs are *compatible*, one with the other, when they blend well together as to tempo, mood and/or subject matter, etc., as in a medley or interpolation. Songs that are *compatible* are: THAT OLD GANG OF MINE with HEART OF MY HEART, YOU'RE A HEAVENLY THING with I MARRIED AN ANGEL, ME AND MY SHADOW with I'M SO LONESOME I COULD CRY, etc.

compilation

LW. A work formed by the collection and assembling of pre-existing materials that are selected, coordinated, or arranged in such a way that the resulting work as a whole constitutes an original work of authorship.

compiler

LW. 1. One who gathers and puts together (literary or musical material, facts, etc.), in an orderly form, as the compiler of a song book, a book of music, etc. 2. An author. AI. United States Copyright Form E states, "Authors include composers of music, authors of words, arrangers, compilers, etc."

complimentary

SB. 1. A complimentary ticket. 2. A pass, as to a theatrical or musical performance, etc. 3. A comp. See ANNIE OAKLEY.

compose

MU. 1. To put together in proper form and/or order. 2. To create, as an original literary or musical work. PG. 3. To set type or matter to be printed, as for a song. See COMPOSER. See COMPOSITOR.

76

composer

MU. 1. A person who composes, as a song. 2. One who writes the music for a song as distinguished (by ASCAP) from *author*. 3. A songwriter. See SONGWRITER.

Composers and Lyricists Guild of America, Inc.

MB. A labor organization representing composers and lyricists in screen, radio, television, stage, recording and transcription activities. Address: 8157 Sunset Boulevard, Los Angeles, California.

composite work

LW. A work formed of distinct and separable parts, as distinguished from a joint work. AI. For instance, a new lyric or a new arrangement for an existing song might be considered to be a composite work, which avoids the complications that can arise from a jointly owned copyright.

composition

MU. 1. A musical work, as a song. 2. The manuscript of a song or musical work. PY. 3. The lyrics for a song in manuscript form. PG. 4. Typesetting, as that for printing a song. 5. Typography.

compositor

PG. 1. A person who sets type, as that from which music or songs are printed. 2. A typesetter. 3. A typographer.

compound time

MU. Any time that has six parts or more to the measure and contains two or more principal accents. AI. Examples of compound time are Six-Four Time, Six-Eight Time, etc.

comprehension, level of
See LEVEL OF COMPREHENSION.

comprehensive

SW. 1. A rough but understandable draft of a song. 2. A lead sheet.

compulsory license

LW. The license to use a copyrighted musical work, as a song, for mechanical reproduction, as a phonograph record, which is automatically obtained on demand from a copyright owner who has granted this right for the same work to anyone else or has made similar use of the work himself.

concert

MU. 1. A performance of vocal or instrumental music, usually one in which a number of performers participate. 2. Musical consonance. Compare with RECITAL.

concert grand

MU. The largest grand piano as distinguished from *grand piano.*

concertina

MU. A small musical instrument of the accordion type, with bellows and keys.

concerto (kahn-cher′to)

MU. A composition for orchestra and a solo instrument, usually a piano or violin.

concord

MU. 1. A combination of simultaneous and harmonious tones. 2. Harmonious, as opposed to *discordant.*

conductor

MU. The leader or director of an orchestra, band or chorus.

conflict

SB. 1. A conflicting engagement. 2. A conflicting date, assignment or commitment. AI. For instance, if a singer, musician or other performer cannot be available for a performance because of a *conflict,* this means that he is committed to another engagement that takes place at the same time. If two shows are scheduled to play in the same community on the same day, this could be said to *conflict* and the day to be a *conflicting date.*

conga (kon′ga)

MU. 1. A ballroom dance of Latin-American origination, in which the dancers form a winding line. 2. The music for this dance, in Four-

Four syncopated time, with a heavy accent on the fourth beat of every measure.

connecting note

MU. A note used in common by two successive chords.

connecting tone

MU. The tone designated by a connecting note.

connotation

SW. An idea or thought which is associated with or suggested by a word or phrase in addition to its explicit meaning.

consecutive

GI. 1. Following in order, without interruption. 2. Successive, as of intervals in harmony.

consequent (kahn'se-kwent")

MU. 1. A musical answer. 2. The musical answer phrase. AI. When the *antecedent*, the musical question phrase, is followed by the *consequent*, this gives a feeling of completion. See ANTECEDENT.

consonance

MU. A combination of two or more tones, harmonious and pleasing in itself, and requiring no further progression to make it satisfactory. AI. The opposite of *discord* and *dissonance*.

consonant

RC. 1. An alphabetic sound not easily uttered without a vowel. 2. A letter representing such a sound. 3. Any letter in the English alphabet that is not a vowel.

consumer

MB. Anyone who buys sheet music and/or phonograph records at retail.

contact man

MB. 1. A representative of a music publisher or record company whose duty it is to *contact* the trade (disk jockeys, performers, juke-box operators, etc.) to promote his company's songs or records. 2. A (song) promotion man. 3. A song plugger.

contemporary

RC. 1. Living or happening at the same time, as a songwriter or a song. 2. A person living in the same period of history as another. 3. A person or thing of about the same age, date of origin, publication, etc.

continuity

WG. 1. The state or quality of being continuous, unbroken, uninterrupted. 2. The story told in a song. 3. The words of a song themselves. 4. A motion-picture scenario. 5. A radio or television script.

contrabass

MU. 1. Having a pitch one octave lower than a normal bass instrument, as a *contrabass* viol or a *contrabassoon*, the lowest pitched bass horn. 2. Having a pitch one octave lower than a normal bass voice, as a *contrabasso*.

contraction

RC. 1. The shortening of a word or phrase by the omission of one or more letters or sounds, as *isn't* for *is not* in the song title ISN'T IT A LOVELY DAY, *won't* for *will not* as in the song title WON'T YOU COME HOME, BILL BAILEY and *can't* for *can not*, as in the song title CAN'T HELP LOVIN' DAT MAN. 2. A word form resulting from the omission of one or more letters or sounds, as *mem'ries* for *memories*. AI. Contractions often are helpful in fitting words to music and music to words.

contralto

MU. 1. The lowest pitched female voice. 2. A woman or a girl who sings in this range. AI. Also called *alto*.

contra octave

MU. The third octave, on the piano, below middle C. AI. Keys (tones) in this octave are designated C_1, D_1, E_1, etc.

contrast

MU. The difference between two things that are similar in some

80

respects but unlike in another or others, as the *contrast* of two musical sections of a song melody.

control room

RB. 1. The room from which recordings are directed and/or *controlled*. AI. A control room is separated from the recording studio by a large glass window. Through this window the A and R man directs those in the studio. RT. 2. The room from which broadcasts are directed and/or *controlled* in radio and television stations.

convention

LW. 1. An assembly of members or delegates. 2. An agreement reached by such an assembly. 3. Hence, an agreement between persons or nations, as the Universal Copyright Convention, the Berne Convention, etc.

cool

MU. 1. Designating a relaxed, almost dreamy style of jazz with complex harmonies and involved rhythm patterns. 2. Relaxed, assured, highly capable, as a performance of jazz, or a jazz performer. AI. A performer of this type is called a *cool cat*. Cool jazz came into popularity in 1949 with Miles Davis, trumpeter, and Leonard Joseph Tristano, pianist, as its earliest exponents.

copies of lost songs

LW. Subject to certain conditions, the facilities of the United States Copyright Office are available for furnishing photocopies of both published and unpublished songs. AI. Request must be authorized by copyright owner. A fee is charged. Information may be had, free of charge, on request to Register of Copyrights.

copr.

GI. Abbreviation, *copyright* or *copyrighted*. AI. Authorities agree that it is always better to spell out the word *Copyright* in full than to use this, or any other, abbreviation.

co-publish

MB. 1. To publish with another or others, as a song. 2. To share in publishing, as a song.

co-publisher

MB. A publisher who shares publication, as that of a song, with one or more other publishers.

copy

PG. 1. Any manuscript to be set in type, as the *copy* for a song, the *copy* for an advertisement, etc. MB. 2. Any reproduction or duplicate, as a *copy* of a (printed) song, a (copy of a) phonograph record, etc. LW. 3. Any material object in which a work is fixed or reproduced and from which the work can be perceived, reproduced or otherwise communicated, either directly or with the aid of a machine or device.

copy cat

RB. 1. Anyone who produces phonograph records that are intentional imitations of other records. 2. A singer who records for such records. 3. A musician who records for such records. See MIRROR.

copyist

MB. 1. A person who makes written copies, as those of music, songs, etc. 2. A transcriber. Also called *music copyist* or a *music transcriber*.

copyright

LW. The right of exclusive use which protects the literary, dramatic, artistic and *musical* works of authors, for a certain limited period. AI. Only an author or those deriving their rights through an author can lawfully claim copyright in a work. Basically, there are two kinds of copyrights: *common-law* copyright and *statutory* copyright. There are two kinds of statutory copyrights in which an American author need be interested. These are *domestic* copyright and *international* copyright. See NINE RIGHTS, THE.

copyrightable

LW. 1. Legally acceptable to be copyrighted. 2. Meeting with the requirements of copyright law, common-law or statutory. AI. It is possible for certain material to be copyrightable in one form and not in another. For instance, a musical revue, consisting of a melee of novel arrangements, adaptions, dramatizations and new patterns of earlier works, may be copyrightable as *new matter*, although the component parts may not be separately copyrightable. See ADAPTION.

copyright application, Canada

LW. The Canadian Copyright Rules say: An application for registration of copyright in a published work shall be in Form I. An application for registration of copyright in an unpublished work shall be in Form K. All documents submitted in connection with an application for registration must be legibly and neatly written, printed or typewritten on paper that is 8 inches wide and 13 inches long with a margin of 1 inch on the left hand side. An application for registration shall be signed (a) by the applicant or his duly authorized agent in the case of an individual, (b) by a partner in the case of a firm, or (c) by a director, secretary or other principal officer in the case of a corporation. All remittances should be made payable at par in Ottawa and to the order of the Receiver General of Canada, The Copyright Office, Ottawa, Canada. All individual checks should be certified. All communications concerning copyright shall be addressed to The Commissioner of Patents, The Copyright Office, Ottawa, Canada. See FORM I. See FORM K.

copyright application forms

LW. The forms in which application for registration of a claim to copyright are made. AI. The United States Copyright Office provides the following blank forms free of charge: Form E, for a musical composition, as a song, by an author who is a citizen of the United States. Form E Foreign, for a musical composition, as a song, by an author who is not a citizen of the United States. Form R, for renewal of copyright. The Canadian Copyright Office does not provide blank forms. For Canadian forms, see FORM I and FORM K.

copyright application, United States

LW. See COPYRIGHT APPLICATION FORMS.

copyright clearance

PB. The act of checking on songs and securing permission of use, as in compiling a song book, to make certain that copyrighted works are not infringed upon.

copyright, common-law

LW. Common-law copyright provides exclusive rights to a common-law property, as a song or other musical composition, as distinguished from statutory copyright. AI. This type of protection is a matter of state law, and automatically comes into being when a work is created. It requires no action in the Copyright Office. It may last as long as the work remains unpublished. It ends when the work is published or statutory copyright is secured. See PROOF OF EXISTENCE.

copyright deposits

LW. See DEPOSIT COPIES.

copyright, domestic

LW. 1. A domestic copyright is a copyright that provides protection solely in the author's home country, as distinguished from an *international* copyright. 2. A domestic copyright for an American author is the copyright provided by the law of the United States.

copyright entries, catalog of

LW. See CATALOG OF COPYRIGHT ENTRIES.

copyright, international

LW. An international copyright is a copyright that provides protection in a number of nations, as distinguished from a *domestic* copyright. AI. For the greatest possible international copyright protection, an American author need be concerned with four sources of copyright protection. These are (1) The United States Copyright Office, (2) The Universal Copyright Convention, (3) The Buenos Aires Convention and (4) The Berne Convention.

copyright law revision bill

LW. Congressional bill H. R. 4347, jointly introduced (in the U. S. Senate) by Senator John L. McClelland and (in the House of Representatives) by Congressman Emanuel Celler, during the first session of the 89th Congress, February 4, 1965, "for the revision of the copyright law, title 17, of the United States code."

copyright lawyer

LW. A lawyer trained in copyright law and who specializes in this particular field. AI. Lawyers who devote themselves to general practice and those who specialize in fields other than that of copyright law are not expected to know or to be able to interpret the intricacies of copyright laws.

copyright notice

LW. A written or printed statement, usually in the form of a footnote, which warns that a work, as a song or other musical composition, is protected by copyright. AI. Basically, there are two forms of copyright notices. These are *domestic* and *international*. See COPYRIGHT NOTICE REQUIREMENTS.

copyright notice, complete

LW. A complete copyright notice is a copyright notice, usually in the form of four statements, that meets the requirements of the United States Copyright Law, The Universal Copyright Convention, The Buenos Aires Convention and The Berne Convention. See COPYRIGHT REQUIREMENTS.

copyright notice, domestic

LW. A domestic copyright notice is a copyright notice that states that copyright has been secured in an author's home country. AI. There are two kinds of domestic copyright notices used in the United States. These are the *original* copyright notice and the *renewal* copyright notice (sometimes called *notice of renewal*). See COPYRIGHT NOTICE REQUIREMENTS.

copyright notice, international

LW. An international copyright notice is a copyright notice which states that international copyright has been secured, or otherwise complies with certain international copyright requirements. AI. For no particular reason, an international copyright notice is usually assumed to apply to the Berne Convention and to be the copyright notice reading INTERNATIONAL COPYRIGHT SECURED. See COPYRIGHT REQUIREMENTS.

copyright notice, renewal

LW. A copyright renewal notice, as the wording implies, is a written or printed statement that copyright renewal has been secured. See COPYRIGHT REQUIREMENTS.

copyright office, Canada

LW. All communications should be addressed to:
  The Commissioner of Patents
  Patent and Copyright Office
  Ottawa, Ontario
  Canada

AI. The Canadian Copyright Office does not have blank forms for distribution, as does the United States Copyright Office.

copyright office, United States

LW. All communications should be addressed to:
REGISTER OF COPYRIGHTS
Copyright Office
Library of Congress
Washington, D. C. 20540
AI. On mail originating outside the United States, the initials *U.S.A.* should be added to the above address as a fifth line. For information concerning the functions and proceedings of the Copyright Office, write the Register requesting *Circular No. 96—Regulations of the Copyright Office*, which is distributed free of charge.

copyright owner

LW. 1. The proprietor of a *published* or *unpublished* work, as a song, for which copyright protection has been secured. 2. The proprietor of an *unpublished* work, as a song, protected by common-law copyright. 3. Anyone to whom copyright has been legally transferred or assigned. 4. Anyone having legal title to a copyright. AI. There are two kinds of copyright owners. These are the *original* owner and the *subsequent* owner. A copyright owner can be one or more persons, a company, an organization, a corporation, etc.

copyright registration

LW. The formality of having a claim to copyright made a matter of record, as those maintained by the United States Copyright Office, the Canadian Patent and Copyright Office, etc.

copyright renewal

LW. The act of causing copyright protection to exist for an additional term, as provided by law. AI. The United States Copyright law (Title 17) provides that copyright protection for a second term, in addition to the first and original term, may be secured, under certain conditions. Information concerning renewal of United States copyright is to be found on page 4 of United States copyright Form R. See COPYRIGHT REQUIREMENTS.

copyright requirements, published work

LW. For a published musical composition, as a song, the author of which is a citizen of the United States or which was first published in the United States, these requirements apply: *United States* law requires that application be made on Form E (Form E Foreign for a non-citizen) and that a copyright notice shall appear as prescribed by this form. Line 1 below meets this requirement. Privilege of renewing this copyright may be had by application on Form R. Line 2 below meets the suggestions for copyright notice in this connection offered by the United States Copyright Office. The *Universal Copyright Convention* grants copyright protection in all of its member countries to all citizens of the United States who obtain copyright in their own country. The only requirement is that the c-in-a-circle symbol © be used in connection with the copyright notice required by the United States. Line 1 below meets this requirement. The *Berne Convention*, and its four successive revisions, grants copyright protection to citizens of the United States, but only if they publish their works first or simultaneously in a country that subscribes to this convention (the United States does not), as Canada, England, France, etc. (See SIMULTANEOUS PUBLICATION.) The first 3-word statement in line 3 below is the most often used, the most generally accepted copyright notice indicating that this has been done. The *Buenos Aires Convention* grants copyright protection to citizens of the United States, who have secured copyright in their own country, providing "the work contains *notice of reservation*," in addition to a domestic copyright notice. The second 3-word statement in line 3 below meets this requirement. The following four statements are usually called a *complete copyright notice*. The numbers 1, 2, and 3 at the left are for line identification only and do not appear in an actual notice:

1. © COPYRIGHT JOHN DOE 1930
2. © COPYRIGHT RENEWED BY MRS. MARY DOE 1958
3. INTERNATIONAL COPYRIGHT SECURED ALL RIGHTS RESERVED

copyright requirements, unpublished work

LW. An unpublished musical composition, as a song, is automatically protected by common-law copyright, as prescribed by individual state law, until such time as statutory copyright is secured. While no formality is required for this protection, proof of existence should be established. When and as an author wishes to secure statutory copyright for an unpublished work, *United States* law requires that application for registration of a claim to copyright an unpublished musical composition be made on Form E (or on Form E Foreign for a non-resident). Basically, the *Universal Copyright Convention* requires a participating country, as the United States, to give the

87

same protection to foreign works which meet the Convention requirements as it gives to its own domestic works. Thus the Universal Copyright Convention affords automatic protection to unpublished works for which United States copyright has been secured, without notice or other formalities.

copyright search

LW. The United States Copyright Office can and does make a search of its records, under certain conditions and on payment of the required fee. AI. Further information may be obtained from the Register of Copyrights by giving full details of search requested, why search is wanted and stating the purpose for which resulting information is to be used.

copyright, statutory

LW. A statutory copyright is the exclusive right to a literary, dramatic, artistic or *musical* work, as prescribed and obtained by *legal* formalities, as distinguished from a *common-law copyright*, for which no application is made.

Copyright, United States

LW. 1. A United States Copyright is a copyright prescribed and granted by the laws of the United States of America. 2. A domestic copyright, as applied to an American author.

corn

WG. 1. Ideas, wording, humor, music, etc. regarded as old-fashion, trite, banal or lacking in taste. 2. Anything that is overly sentimental. 3. Crude or rustic. AI. There are no exact standards by which anything can be judged to be corn or anyone declared to be *corny*. What is *corn* or *corny* to one person may be wholly acceptable to another.

cornet

MU. A brass-wind instrument of the trumpet class, having three valves which are worked by pistons.

counterfeit

LW. 1. Any imitation of something genuine made with intention to deceive or defraud, as unauthorized copies of a phonograph record, unauthorized copies of sheet music, etc. 2. A forgery.

counterpart

GI. 1. Anything closely resembling something else. 2. Something correspondingly reverse, as the right hand to the left. 3. The direct opposite.

counterpoint

MU. 1. A melody accompanying another melody note for note. 2. The art of adding a related but independent melody or melodies to a basic melody, in accordance with the fixed rules of harmony, to make a harmonic whole. 3. This kind of composition. AI. The study of counterpoint is intricate. It is unnecessary to know counterpoint in order to write songs.

counting time

MU. The act of numbering musical beats. See BEAT.

country and western

MB. A category of songwriting and song listing. AI. Abbreviated *C and W*.

country dance

MU. 1. An early English dance in which men and women formed in pairs and danced opposite one another. 2. A square dance, so called because of its *square* formations. 3. The music for this dance.

country music

MB. 1. A category of songwriting and song listing. 2. Simple, sincere music that reflects the everyday emotions and customs of the common people, anywhere and everywhere, the *country* over. AI. By no means does the word *country*, used in this respect, necessarily imply a rural or rustic setting or viewpoint. *Country* is not to be confused with *hillbilly*. Typical country-music songs are: GOODNIGHT IRENE, COLD COLD HEART, OH LONESOME ME and YOU ARE MY SUNSHINE.

Country Music Association

MB. A non-profit trade organization for the purpose of fostering, publicizing and promoting the growth of and interest in country music. Also called *CMA*. Address: 801 Sixteenth Avenue, South, Nashville, Tennessee 37204.

country of origin

LW. 1. The country in which first publication is made, as of a song. 2. The first of two or more countries in which copyrights are secured for the same published work, as a song. AI. When same-day publication is given a song in a country belonging to the Berne Convention, as Canada, and a country that does not belong, as the United States, *the member country is considered to be the country of origination* by the Berne Convention. See FIRST PUBLICATION.

country song

MB. A country-music type song. See COUNTRY MUSIC.

country style

CM. 1. Designating a particular kind of vocal and/or instrumental performance, characterized by deep feeling and utmost sincerity (that defies immitation), as established by such all-time great performers as Jimmie Rodgers, Hank Williams and Roy Acuff, *the king of country music*. 2. Designating a kind of music and/or song. See COUNTRY MUSIC.

coupled with

MB. 1. On the opposite side of the record from. 2. Backed with. AI. Abbreviated, *c/w*. See BACKED WITH.

couplet

PY. 1. A two-line rhymed verse. 2. Two successive lines of verse, especially two of the same length, as to number of feet, that rhyme.

coupling

MB. 1. The song on the other side of a phonograph record. 2. The flip.

cover

MB. v. To prepare and release a competitive phonograph record, using the same song as that recorded on the original record. AI. A phonograph record company is said to *cover* the recording of another phonograph record company when it releases a competitive recording of the same song.

90

cover

MB. n. 1. A phonograph record that competitively *covers* a record released by another company. PG. 2. The outside pages of a sheet of music, as the front cover and the back cover, etc. 4. The exterior of a folio or song book. 5. The exterior of a phonograph record jacket.

co-writer

SW. 1. A member of a writing team, as that of songwriters. 2. A co-author. 3. A collaborator. 4. One who writes with another or others.

creamy

MU. Smooth flowing, as used in describing the timbre or quality of a tone. AI. For instance, it might be said that the clarinet is more *creamy* in timbre than the (more nasal sounding) oboe. See QUALITY.

credit

MB. 1. Credit line, usually plural, as *credits*. 2. The unit of value used by ASCAP in their credit weighting formula. See USE CREDIT.

credit line

MB. Any written or printed line that gives *credit*, as to an author, composer, publisher, etc. See CREDITS.

credits

MB. 1. The statement or statements that give *credit* to the writer or writers and composer or composers of a song, as those on sheet music, on record labels, etc. 2. The phrase or phrases that state who wrote the words or lyrics and who wrote the music of a song. 3. The statement as to who published a musical work. 4. The list of songs a songwriter has written, and has to his *credit*. SB. 5. Any acknowledgement or acknowledgements of work done, as that on sheet music, on a phonograph record label, in a motion picture, a radio or television show, a play, a musical, etc. AI. Also called *credit line, author-credit line, publisher-credit line* and *by-line*. See BY-LINE.

credit system

MB. The method used by performance-rights societies, as ASCAP and BMI, in distributing payment to their members.

credit weighting formula

MB. See WEIGHTING FORMULA.

cres.

MU. Abbreviation, *crescendo*. AI. Also spelled *cresc*.

cresc.

MU. Abbreviation, *crescendo*. AI. Also spelled *cres*.

crescendo (kre-shen'do): ⊂

MU. 1. The sign shown above, indicating a gradual increasing in loudness or intensity. 2. A gradual increasing in loudness or intensity. 3. A musical passage played in this manner. AI. The opposite of *decrescendo*.

crooner

MU. A singer, especially a man, who sings in a crooning style.

crooning

MU. A soft, sentimental manner of singing, usually devoted to popular ballads. AI. Crooning was introduced in the 1930's by Bing Crosby and Rudy Vallee.

crossover

TE. A very brief comedy hit, used in burlesque, revues and other forms of musical shows. AI. A crossover usually follows the form of a brief interruption of a scene by a comedian. For instance, one of the favorite crossovers used by the famous Marx Brothers was to have a supposedly serious scene interrupted by a scantily-clad girl dashing across the stage pursued by Harpo.

crow

MB. 1. Anyone who does not or cannot sing. 2. Anyone who sings badly. AI. Bad singing is said to be *for the crows*.

cue

TE. 1. Any sign, signal or sound by which performers are directed when and how to perform, as a sign written on music, a signal given by hand, a certain tone or tones, etc. AI. For instance, in recording or broadcasting, singers and/or musicians might be given a *hand cue* telling them when to begin by the A and R man or director. 2. A few notes or measures played as an introduction to an instrumentalist's or a vocalist's part to tell a soloist when to begin. See HAND CUE. See CUE NOTE.

cue card

MT. Large cards or boards on which song lyrics, dialog, directions, instructions, etc., are written. AI. These are held up off-camera for performers to read. Also called *idiot card* or *idiot board*.

cue music

MB. Music used on a radio or television program to introduce, but not identify, a personality or event thereon. AI. The term *cue music* includes, but is not limited to, introductions (intros), play-ons and play-offs. This is one of the categories used by performance-rights societies to establish credit values.

cue note

MU. 1. A note (tone) used as a signal to performers. 2. A note used to tell singers and/or musicians when to begin singing or playing.

cue sheet

MU. 1. A written outline, usually giving the camera directions, action, dialog and musical notation, scene by scene, of a motion picture, by which background music is added to a motion picture. 2. Written directions used by the orchestra leader to *cue* music to the action of a musical show. AI. Also called *dope sheet*, particularly when used to cue the music of animated cartoons. As cue sheets also are used to direct the lighting effects of motion pictures, plays, etc., the terms *lighting cue sheet* and *music cue sheet* often are used to distinguish one from the other.

cut

MB. 1. To record. AI. For instance, a singer is said to *cut* a record when he makes a recording. A music publisher, or musicians, might be said to *cut* a session, etc. 2. To stop. AI. For instance, if an error is made in recording, the A and R man will call or signal *cut*, as a cue to the singer or singers and musicians to stop singing and playing.

3. To shorten. AI. For instance, a song might be *cut* to fit certain time requirements on a radio or television program. 4. To share. AI. For instance, if three songwriters equally share the royalties from a song, this means that each *cuts* a third, etc. *To share* is also called *cutting in*.

cut in

SB. A financial share, as a *cut in* on royalties, a *cut in* on profits, etc. AI. Also called a *cut*, as a *cut of the box office*, meaning a share of the money received from *ticket sales*, etc.

Cut Time: ¢

MU. The time designated by the time signature (barred C) shown above. 2. Fast Four-Four Time that is counted two beats (instead of four) to the measure. AI. Cut Time is the time most often used in songwriting and also the time most often misused. All too many misguided songwriters use the barred C thinking this indicates ordinary Four-Four Time. All too many misguided musicians play Cut Time as though it were Four-Four Time. Alla breve, the erroneous name by which Cut Time is often called, adds to this general misunderstanding. See BARRED C.

cutting contest

JZ. 1. A competitive jam session. 2. A friendly jam session. AI. In the early days of New Orleans jazz, rival bands often met on street corners to see which could *out-play* the others. These free-for-all jazz gatherings were known as *cutting contests*. A losing band was said to have been *cut down* by the winner. The term *cutting contest* is now sometimes used in a humorous sense to mean a (friendly) jam session.

c/w (see-dub'l-yew)

RB. Abbreviation, *coupled with*. Same as *b/w*. See COUPLED WITH.

cycle

RC. 1. A series that repeats itself. 2. A recurring series, as a *cycle of songs* or a *song cycle*, etc.

cycle of songs

MB. A series of songs that are, in some manner, related or similar.

94

AI. For instance, a cycle of *moon* songs might be MOON OVER MIAMI, SHINE ON HARVEST MOON, PALE MOON, THE MOON IS LOW, BY THE LIGHT OF THE SILVERY MOON and BLUE MOON.

cymbal

MU. 1. Either of a pair of circular, slightly concave plates made of brass, used as percussion instruments. When struck together, they produce a sharp ringing sound. 2. A single brass plate, struck with a drumstick. AI. Cymbals vary in size from small *finger cymbals* used by oriental dancers, to the large cymbals used by orchestras and marching bands.

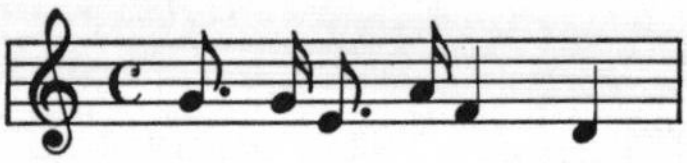

d

D

MU. 1. The fourth letter in the musical alphabet, representing a pitch a whole tone higher than C. 2. The letter applied to any octave above or below this pitch. 3. The second tone, note or degree in the ascending major scale of C. 4. The major key that has two sharps in its key signature. 5. The caption for a D major triad. 6. The key or string of a musical instrument that produces the tone of D. 7. The fourth string on the Spanish guitar. 8. The third string on the ukulele (tuned A-D-F♯-B). 9. The small letter used to designate the syllable *doh* in the English system of tonic sol-fa. CH. 10. The capital letter used as an abbreviation meaning *doubled*, as applied to the metrical count of a hymn tune.

D♭

MU. See D FLAT.

da (dah)

MU. From.

da capo (da ka'po)

MU. 1. From the beginning. 2. Play or sing it over again *from the beginning*.

da capo al fine (da ka'po ahl fee'ne)

MU. 1. From the beginning to the end. 2. Play or sing it over again *from start to finish*.

dactyl (dak´til)

PY. A metrical foot of three syllables in this order: an accented syllable, an unaccented syllable, an unaccented syllable, or — ◡ ◡. Example, *mer´ri-ly*. The opposite of anapest. Musical counterpart: Three-Four Time. Dactyl is one of the four kinds of English meter.

daisy mae

MB. A song that has good possibilities but one which needs considerable polishing.

dal (dahl)

MU. 1. From the sign. 2. Go back to the sign and play or sing it over again. See SEGNO.

dal segno (dahl sae´nyo)

MU. 1. From the sign. 2. Go back to *the sign* and play or sing it over again. See SEGNO.

damper

MU. A mechanical device, as that on a piano, which stops a string from vibrating, thus terminating its sound. AI. When a piano key is depressed the damper is lifted so that the string is free to vibrate and sound. When a piano key is released this causes the damper to muffle the string so that no further sound is produced. Without dampers, piano strings would sound longer than desired and build up a confusion of blurred tones. Dampers are also controlled by the right pedal, called the *damper pedal*, which raises all dampers, allowing all strings to vibrate (sound) at will.

dance band

MB. A band or orchestra that specializes in playing dance music, as distinguished from a *stage band*.

dance beat

MU. Any tempo suited to dancing.

dance songs

MB. A classification in songwriting as to subject matter. Typical dance songs are BALLIN' THE JACK, CHARLESTON, THE TWIST and THE BOSSA NOVA.

dash: '

MU. 7. The accent mark shown above. 2. A mark that is written above or below a note to indicate that it is to be played staccato.

date

SB. 1. The time of some event, as a performance. 2. An engagement, as that of a singer, to perform at a certain place and time. 3. A booking.

dated

MB. 1. Out of date. 2. Old fashioned, as a dated song or dated material. 3. Identified with an earlier time.

date of existence

LW. 1. The earliest time at which something is known to have reality or to have occurred, as a song. 2. The earliest time at which a song is known to have been written. AI. Songwriters often establish a date of existence by one or more of the methods described under *protection*. See PROTECTION.

date of publication

LW. The date when printed copies, as those of a song, are first placed on sale, sold or otherwise publicly distributed. AI. The date on which a publication is *printed* should not be confused with date of *publication*. See SAME DAY PUBLICATION.

day people

SB. 1. People who work by day and sleep by night, as distinguished from the majority of people in show business. 2. Those whose waking and sleeping habits are opposite to those of *night people*.

db (dee bee)

SI. Abbreviation, *decibel*.

D. C.

MU. Abbreviation, *da capo*.

dead-end rhyme

SW. 1. A rhyme scheme consisting of four lines, the first three of which rhyme, each with the others, and the fourth line does not. 2. A

99

rhyme scheme written to the following pattern: aaab. AI. For instance:

> Here is a brief sample
> Of all that is ample
> To show an example
> Of a dead-end rhyme

dead mike

ET. 1. A microphone that is not turned on. 2. A microphone that is not in working order.

deal

MB. 1. A business transaction, as that of a songwriter with a music publisher. 2. An agreement on which a business transaction is based.

dealer

MB. 1. A sheet music retailer. 2. A phonograph record retailer. 3. A rack dealer.

decibel (des′ih-b′l)

SI. 1. A scientific unit for the measurement of sound. 2. One tenth of a bel. AI. A decibel (named after Alexander Graham Bell) represents the smallest degree in loudness that normally can be distinguished by the human ear. The softest violin tone registers about 25 decibels. A full symphony orchestra registers about 100 decibels. Abbreviated *db*.

deck

MB. One side of a phonograph record.

decres. (de″kre-shen′do)

MU. Abbreviation, *decrescendo*. AI. Also spelled *decresc.*

decrescendo (de″kre-shen′do) $\diagdown$

MU. 1. The sign shown above, indicating a gradual decreasing in loudness or intensity. 2. A gradual decreasing in loudness or intensity. 3. A musical passage played in this manner. AI. The opposite of *cres endo*. Also called *diminuendo*.

100

deejay (dee-jae)

MB. Abbreviation, *disk jockey*. Also abbreviated *D.J.* or *DJ*.

degree

MU. 1. A line or space on the staff. 2. An interval between one staff line and the next staff line. 3. An interval between one staff space and the next staff space. AI. A degree is either a whole step or a half step, but it is always from one letter to the next letter. For instance, from A to B is a whole step. From B to C is a half step. Both are degrees.

degree mark: °

MU. 1. The sign shown above. 2. The small circle used to designate *diminished*, as C°7 (C diminished 7th), D°7 (D diminished 7th), E°7 (E diminished 7th), etc. See DIM.

del (de-leet')

PG. Abbreviation, *delete*. Also spelled *dele*.

del

MU. Of the.

del capo

MU. 1. Of the top. 2. The top.

delete (de-leet') : ℈

PG. The proof-readers' mark shown above, meaning erase, omit, leave out, as a letter, a word, etc.

delivery

RG. 1. The manner or style in which something is done. 2. The manner in which a song is sung, as a singer's *delivery*. 3. Style of performance.

demand

BE. 1. The desire for a commodity, as for a phonograph record or sheet music, together with the ability to pay for it. 2. The quantity of anything that people are ready to buy and pay for. AI. For in-

101

stance, the *demand* for a record of a certain song might be 100,000 copies, etc.

demo (dehm′o)

MB. Short for *demonstration record,* or *demonstration recording.* AI. Also used to mean a *demonstration tape.*

demonstration recording

MB. 1. A demonstration record. 2. A demonstration tape. 3. Any recording made to demonstrate a song, the ability of a singer or musician, etc. 4. A recording for audition. AI. A demonstration recording is also called a *demo* and is sometimes called a *dub.*

density

PG. 1. The quality or condition of being dense or crowded. 2. Quantity or number of units in a given area, as the number of music notes in a system, on a page, etc. 3. The term is used by music typographers in evaluating the quantity of notation in a song. AI. For instance, a song that has more notes than another is said to have *greater density* or *greater density of notation.* Music typographers charge according to density and the quantity of lyrics.

deposit copies

LW. 1. Copies of a work, as those of a song or book, deposited with the Register of Copyrights, as is required in securing registration of copyright. 2. Copies of a work sent to a Berne Union country to be placed on sale in order to establish date of publication.

derivative work

LW. 1. A work based upon one or more pre-existing works, such as a translation, as of a song lyric, a musical arrangement, abridgement or any other form of adaption by which a work may be recast or transformed. 2. A work that is not original.

development

MU. 1. The elaboration of a musical theme by changing its rhythm, melody and/or harmony. SW. 2. A step or stage in growth or advancement, as the step between an idea and a song.

102

devotee (dehv″o-teh′)

RC. 1. A person warmly devoted to something or someone, as a *devotee of country music, a progressive-jazz devotee,* etc. 2. A fan. 3. A buff.

D flat major scale

MU. The scale consisting of these eight notes or tones: D♭, E♭, F, G♭, A♭, B♭, C, D♭. Also called *the key of D♭.* See KEY SIGNA-TURE.

diagram

MU. See GUITAR DIAGRAM. See UKULELE DIAGRAM.

dialect

RC. 1. Any form of speech considered as deviating from a real or imaginary standard speech. 2. English speech as employed by a foreign-born or minority group, as Irish dialect, Jewish dialect, West Indian (calypso) dialect, etc.

dialect song

MB. 1. Any song that is written to be sung in a dialect. 2. A song written in a dialect. AI. Typical dialect songs are WHERE DO YOU WORK-A, JOHN? (Italian), COME ON-A MY HOUSE (Armenian), THROW MAMA FROM THE TRAIN A KISS (Pennsylvania Dutch) and JAMBALAYA (Cajun).

dialog (di′a-lawg)

RC. 1. A written work in the form of a conversation, as a song, a play, a radio show, etc. 2. The passage of talk in a play, a motion picture, a radio or television story, etc. AI. An outstanding example of songwriting using the dialog form is BABY, IT'S COLD OUT-SIDE, by Frank Loesser.

diatonic

MU. Designating the regular tones of a scale (or key), as distin-guished from chromatic tones.

diatonic major scale

MU. 1. The scale most often used in songwriting. 2. A scale con-sisting of two tetrachords, one following the other, separated by a full step. AI. For instance, the tones of the diatonic C major scale are: C, D, E, F, G, A, B, C. All major scales given in this book are *diatonic* major scales, as A major, B major, B♭ major, etc.

diction

RC. 1. The use, choice and arrangement of words, as those in a song. 2. Manner of speaking or singing. 3. Enunciation.

die

RB. See MATRIX.

dig

JZ. 1. To understand. 2. To comprehend and/or appreciate.

diletante (d'l''e-tahnt')

RC. 1. A person who follows an art, or a science, only for amusement and in a superficial way. 2. A dabbler, as one who *dabbles* in or at songwriting. 3. A trifler.

dim

MU. 1. The symbol meaning *diminished*. AI. For instance, diminished triads are designated as Cdim, Ddim, Edim, etc. Diminished seventh chords are designated as Adim7, Bdim7, Cdim7, etc. 2. The symbol meaning *diminuendo*.

dimeter (dihm'e-ter)

PY. 1. A line of two measures or two feet. 2. Sometimes, a line of four feet.

diminish

MU. 1. To make less, decrease. 2. To lessen by a half step (a half tone or semitone). The opposite of *augment*.

diminished

MU. 1. Decreased, lessened. 2. Made smaller, as a *diminished interval* or a *diminished chord*. See DIM.

diminished chord

MU. A diminished triad is composed of a root, its minor third and its diminished fifth. AI. For instance, the C diminshed chord (designated

104

Cdim, C- or *C°*) is composed of the tones C-E♭-G♭. The D diminished chord (designated *Ddim, D-* or *D°*) is composed of the tones D-F-A♭. The E diminished chord (designated *Edim, E-* or *E°*) is composed of the tones E-G-B♭, etc. See SEVENTH CHORDS.

diminuendo: >

MU. 1. The sign shown above, indicating a gradual decrease in loudness or intensity. 2. A gradual decrease in loudness or intensity. 3. Decrescendo. 4. A musical passage played in this manner. AI. The opposite of *crescendo.* Also called *decrescendo.*

diminution

MU. 1. A diminishing or being diminished, lessening, decrease. 2. The repetition of a musical theme in notes of one half or one quarter the time value of those in the original. AI. The opposite of *elongation.*

dinner club

SB. 1. Supper club. 2. Night club. See NIGHT CLUB.

dirty bird

MN. 1. A musical mistake. 2. A sour note. 3. A discord. 4. A fluff. 5. Any mistake in the playing, reading or writing of music. SG. 6. Any mistake in singing. MB. 7. Anyone whose business practices are of a questionable nature. 8. An unethical businessman.

dirty note

MN. A note that is, usually intentionally, off key. AI. For instance, in the musical phrase *without a shirt,* the word *shirt* is sung to a *dirty note.*

disc

RB. 1. Disk. See DISK.

discord

MU. 1. A lack of harmony in tones simultaneously sounded. 2. An inharmonious combination of tones. 3. Dissonance.

discothèque (dihs″ko-tehk′)

MB. An intimate, usually small and dimly lighted room which offers, usually recorded, music for a particular kind of en masse dancing. AI.

Typical *discothèque* dances are *the monkey, the mash potato* and *the frug.*

disk

RB. A phonograph record.

disk cutter

RG. A machine for recording sound into a blank phonograph record.

diskery

RB. A phonograph record company. AI. Plural, diskeries.

disk jockey

MB. A person who conducts a radio or television program of recorded music, usually interspersed with chatter, jokes, commercials, etc.

dissonance

MU. 1. A combination of tones that are lacking in harmony. 2. A chord that sounds harsh and incomplete until resolved to a harmonious chord. 3. Discord.

distortion

RG. Any variation of an original sound, as that caused by untrue pitch or any unwanted and extraneous noise or tones, etc.

distrib

MB. 1. Short for *distributor.* 2. Short for *distribute.*

distributor

MB. 1. A person or organization who distributes merchandise, as phonograph records and/or sheet music to the retail trade. 2. A wholesaler. 3. A jobber.

ditrochee (di-tro'kee)

PY. 1. Two trochees. 2. A compound metrical foot of four syllables in this order: an accented syllable, an unaccented syllable, an accented syllable, an unaccented syllable, or: — ◡ — ◡. Example, *bro'ken heart'ed.* Musical counterpart, Four-Four Time.

106

ditty

MU. A short, simple song.

Dixieland

MU. 1. In or of the style of jazz associated with early New Orleans, characterized by a fast ragtime tempo. 2. A style of music created and made famous by the Original Dixieland Band, under the leadership of Nick La Rocca. AI. Dixieland music features trumpet, clarinet and trombone in combination and in solo parts against a steady rhythm background played by a rhythm section originally consisting of piano and drums, to which bass and/or banjo was later added. Typical Dixieland numbers are PRETTY LIL, MUSCAT RAMBLE, SOUTH RAMPART STREET PARADE and CLARINET MARMALADE.

Dixie, strictly from

MN. See STRICTLY FROM DIXIE.

dj (dee-jae)

MB. Short for *disk jockey*. Also called *deejay* and *d.j.*

D major scale

MU. The scale consisting of these eight notes or tones: D, E, F♯, G, A, B, C♯, D. Also called the *Key of D*. See KEY SIGNATURE.

do: △

MU. 1. The syllable used in singing the first tone and the last (eighth) tone of a scale in the sol-fa system. 2. The shape notehead shown above representing this syllable.

domiciliary

LW. Of or in connection with one's legal dwelling place, home or residence. AI. For instance, the domiciliary of a songwriter may be of importance in obtaining an international copyright and is a term used in such proceedings.

dominant

MU. 1. The fifth degree of the diatonic scale. 2. The tone next above the subdominant. AI. For instance, in the scale of C major the *dominant* is the tone of G.

dominant seventh

MU. 1. The name of a four-tone chord. 2. The barbershop chord. AI. Dominant seventh chords are designated as C7, D7, E7, etc. See SEVENTH CHORDS.

dope sheet

MP. A music cue sheet, particularly one used to cue an animated (cartoon) motion picture. See CUE SHEET.

dot: •

MU. 1. The mark shown above. 2. A small, round mark which is placed after, over or under a note. AI. A dot placed after a note (or rest) means "add 50%" and thus increases its time value by one half. A dot placed over or under a note indicates that the note (tone) is to be played *staccato*.

dotted double bar: (1) ⫶‖ (2) ‖⫶ (3) ⫶‖⫶

MU. 1. A double bar with dots preceding it, as shown above, indicates that the preceding strain is to be repeated. 2. A double bar with dots after it, as shown above, indicates that the following strain is to be repeated. 3. A double bar with dots both before and after it, as shown above, indicates that both the preceding strain and the following strain are to be repeated.

dotted note: 𝅗𝅥. or 𝅘𝅥. or 𝅘𝅥𝅮. etc.

MU. 1. Any of the notes shown above. 8. A note followed by a dot. AI. A dot increases the time value of a note by one half. For instance, the time value of a dotted half note is equal to the combined time values of a half note and a quarter note. The time value of a dotted quarter note is equal to the combined time values of a quarter note and an eighth note, etc.

dotted rest: ▬· or 𝄽· or 𝄾· etc.

MU. 1. Any of the rests shown above. 2. A rest followed by a dot. AI. A dot increases the time value of a rest by one half. For instance, the time value of a dotted half rest is equal to the combined time values of a half rest and a quarter rest. The time value of a dotted quarter rest is equal to the combined time values of a quarter rest and an eighth rest, etc.

108

double

MU. v. 1. To add to any tone or tones of a melody or harmony the higher or lower octave. 2. To play an additional instrument, as a saxophonist might *double* on clarinet, a pianist might *double* on accordion, a guitar player might *double* on banjo, etc. SB. 3. To substitute, as one performer might *double* for another.

double

MU. n. 1. A note or tone one octave higher or lower. AI. For instance, C above middle C is the double of middle C and vice versa. C below middle C is the double of middle C and vice versa, etc. 2. An understudy. See UNDERSTUDY.

double accent: "

RC. The twin marks shown above. AI. In the pronunciations given in this book, secondary stress is indicated by a *double accent* ("). See TWICE ACCENTED.

double bar: (1) ≣ (2) ≣ (3) ≣ (4) ≣

MU. Two parallel vertical lines drawn through the staff, like those shown above. AI. A double bar is used in songwriting to indicate one of four things: (1) Change in key, when followed by a new key signature. (2) Change in time, when followed by a new time signature. (3) The beginning of a section which is to be repeated. (4) The end of a section to be repeated, when preceded by dots as shown, or the end of a song, when shown without dots. See DOTTED DOUBLE BARS. See SCOTCH BAR.

double-barrel hit

MB. 1. A phonograph record with hit songs on both sides. 2. A two-sided hit. 3. A double decker.

double bass

MU. 1. The largest of the stringed instruments. 2. The bass viol, originally called the *double-bass viol*. See CONTRA BASS.

double beam: ▬▬

MU. 1. Two heavy parallel horizontal lines like those shown above. 2. Two parallel beams used to connect sixteenth notes.

double chorus

MU. A group of singers composed of two complete choruses or two complete choirs.

double colon: :

MU. 1. The sign shown above. 2. Four dots, one above the other. AI. A double colon was used as part of a repeat mark in older forms of music. In modern music this has been replaced by the single colon or colons.

doubled

CH. A term applied to the metrical count of a hymn tune to designate *twice as many*. AI. Abbreviated, *D*. For instance, the abbreviation *S.M.D.*, meaning *short meter doubled*, designates a metrical count of 6.6.8.6.6.6.8.6., or twice that of short meter (6.6.8.6.). The abbreviation *C.M.D.*, meaning *common meter doubled*, designates a metrical count of 8.6.8.6.8.6.8.6., or twice that of common meter (8.6.8.6.). The designation 6.5.6.5.*D*. designates a metrical count of 6.5.6.5.6.5.6.5., etc.

double decker

MB. A double-deck hit.

double-deck hit

MB. A phonograph record with hit songs on both sides.

double dot: ··

MU. Two dots, as those shown above, which are written after a note (or rest). AI. This increases its time value by three quarters (one half for the first dot and one quarter for the second dot).

double dotted notes: 𝅘𝅥.. or 𝅘𝅥𝅮.. or 𝅘𝅥𝅯. etc.

MU. Any note followed by two dots, like those shown above. AI. The time value of a double dotted half note is equal to the combined time values of a half note, a quarter note and an eighth note. The time value of a double dotted quarter note is equal to the combined time values of a quarter note, an eighth note and a sixteenth note, etc. See DOUBLE DOT.

110

double dotted rests: ▬·· or 𝄽·· or 𝄾·· etc.

MU. Any rest followed by two dots, like those shown above. AI. The time value of a double dotted half rest is equal to the combined time values of a half rest, a quarter rest and an eighth rest. The time value of a double dotted quarter rest is equal to the combined time values of a quarter rest, an eighth rest and a sixteenth rest, etc. See DOUBLE DOT.

double entendre (dub'l′ ahn-tahn′-d′r)

RC. A word or phrase of double meaning, the less obvious of these two meanings usually being of doubtful propriety, or risque.

double flag: 𝅄

MU. 1. A flag like that shown above. 2. The flag attached to the stem of a sixteenth note. See FLAG.

double flat: ♭♭

MU. The character shown above. AI. When written before a note, a double flat signifies a tone 2 half steps (a full step) lower in pitch. For instance, double-flatted B is the same tone as A, etc. Double flats are not used in songwriting.

double letters

MU. Capital letters used in pairs, as AA, BB, CC, etc. AI. Double letters are used in some music textbooks to indicate tones one octave lower than tones indicated by single letters. For instance the tone indicated by AA is one octave lower than the tone indicated by A, etc. Also called *doubled letters.*

double octave

MU.1. An interval of two octaves. 2. An interval of a fifteenth.

double quartet

MU. 1. A vocal or instrumental group, or choir, composed of two quartets. 2. A musical composition written for such a group.

double rhyme

PY. A feminine rhyme.

double Scotch bar: ≣‖≣

MU. The character shown above, composed of three lines in this order: thin line, thick line, thin line.

double sharp: ×

MU. The character shown above. AI. When written before a note, a double sharp signifies a tone 2 half steps (a full step) higher in pitch. For instance, double-sharped F is the same tone as G, etc. Double sharps are not used in songwriting.

double staff

MU. Two staves connected on the left by a brace. AI. A double staff, itself, is also called a *brace*. This is one form of a *system*. See SYSTEM.

Double-stemmed note: ♩ or ♩ or ♪ etc.

MU. 1. A stemmed note like those shown above. 2. A note with two stems, one up and the other down. AI. Double-stemmed notes are used in harmony to show that two voices, or two instruments, sound the same note (tone) simultaneously.

double stopping

MU. The stopping of two strings, on a stringed instrument as a violin, simultaneously with the fingers. See STOP.

double talk

LC. 1. Meaningless syllables made to sound like words. 2. Gibberish. AI. An example of a song lyric using double talk is the HUT SUT SONG.

double time

MU. 1. Any time that has two beats to the measure as Cut Time, Two-Two Time and Two-Four Time. 2. Doubled Time. 3. A marching cadence of 180 steps a minute, as distinguished from a normal cadence of 120 steps a minute. 4. Double-quickstep.

double track

RG. A tape recording where sound is recorded on the upper half of the tape going in one direction and on the lower half going in the opposite direction. See DUAL TRACK.

down

MU. 1. Low or lower in pitch. 2. Less or lower in volume. 3. Soft or softer in tone. 4. To the left on the piano keyboard. 5. In the direction away from the head of a stringed instrument and toward the instrument's body. AI. The opposite of *up*.

down-beat

MU. 1. The downward stroke of the hand, or baton, in beating time. 2. The opposite of the upbeat. AI. The down-beat marks the primary or first accent in each measure, also the third accent in Four-Four Time.

down-beat

MB. A music publication devoted to jazz, published biweekly. Issued every other Thursday. Cover dated two weeks later than on-sale date. Address: 205 West Monroe Street, Chicago, Illinois 60606.

down-pour

JZ. 1. A brilliant performance, usually at a fast tempo. CM. 2. The big downpour. See BIG DOWNPOUR.

down-river

MN. 1. Designating the city of New Orleans, particularly its early customs and/or anything typical of early New Orleans, as its music, its style of performing music, etc. AI. For instance it might be said of a song or the performance of a song, "That's real down-river," meaning *That's real New Orleans style.*

downstage

TE. 1. A stage direction meaning toward the *front of the stage.* 2. Having to do with the front of the stage. 3. That part of the stage nearest the audience. AI. The opposite of *upstage.*

downstem notes: Γ Γ $\flat$ etc.

MU. 1. Notes like those shown above. 2. Notes with stems going *down* from their heads, as distinguished from upstem notes. AI. In writing lead sheets, notes above the middle line of the staff should be downstem notes. Notes on the middle line can be either downstem or upstem notes, whichever presents the best appearance. (Notes below the middle line should be upstem notes.)

113

down to earth

MN. See EARTHY.

down to the bricks

JZ. 1. Simple, unadorned. 2. Sincere Harlem style, as said of music, usually in a melancholy mood.

draft

WG. 1. A written outline. 2. A preliminary written sketch, as that of a song. AI. For instance, a songwriter might refer to his *rewrites* of a song as the *first draft, second draft,* etc. See REWRITE.

drag

MU. A very slow tempo.

drama

TE. A literary composition that tells a story. AI. Sometimes used to specify a non-musical play.

dramatico-musical composition

LW. Such products as operas, operettas, musical comedies, musical reviews, sketches, recitations, choreographic works of a dramatic character and other presentations with musical interpolations. AI. Application for registration of a claim to copyright a dramatico-musical composition is made on FORM D, obtainable free of charge from the United States copyright office.

dramatic rights

TE. 1. Dramatic performance rights. 2. The legal rights to perform publicly a dramatic composition, or a dramatico-musical composition, as a play, opera, operetta, musical comedy or like production, as granted by the copyright act. AI. Often called *grand rights,* as distinguished from nondramatic performance rights, called *small rights.*

Dramatists Guild, The

TR. An organization which represents composers and writers as well as playwrights in their relations with theater producers. Address: 6 East 39th Street, New York, N. Y. 10016.

114

dramatization rights

TE. 1. The exclusive right granted by the copyright act, "to dramatize it if it be a nondramatic work." 2. The right to portray the story-line of a song in a dramatic fashion, as in a motion picture, stage or television show, etc., using scenery, props and character action to portray the plot of the song.

dramaturgy

TE. The art of writing or producing plays for stage, radio, TV and motion pictures.

draw

SB. 1. Any entertainer, act, show, etc. that normally attracts (draws) a large audience. 2. A box-office attraction. AI. It might be said that a performer (act, show, etc.) is a *big draw*.

draw a blank

MS. To forget, as the lyric or the melody of a song.

dream songs

SW. A classification in songwriting as to subject matter. Typical dream songs are DREAM A LITTLE DREAM OF ME, MY DREAMS ARE GETTING BETTER ALL THE TIME, DREAM, DREAM, DREAM, WHEN I GROW TOO OLD TO DREAM and ALL I HAVE TO DO IS DREAM.

drift

MU. 1. To improvise, as in playing a song. 2. To wander. AI. The opposite of *to stay with the book*.

drive

MB. The enthusiasm, vigor and/or forcefulness with which a song is performed.

Droit d'Auteur, Le (drwah″ d'o-tuer′, lih)

LW. The official publication of the Berne Union. Address: Le Droit d'Auteur, 32, chemin des Colombettes, Geneva, Switzerland.

drone

MU. 1. A continuous, somewhat dull, monotonous tone, as that produced by a bagpipe. 2. A bass voice producing such a tone. 3. A string, of a stringed instrument, producing such a tone. 4. Such a tone.

drone bass

MU. Monotonous bass.

drone string

MU. An unfretted string, on a stringed instrument, as the second and third strings on a dulcimer, which produce a drone when bowed or plucked.

drop

BY. 1. An effect used in barbershop singing in which the bass *drops* an octave, usually at the ending of a song. TE. 2. A theater curtain that can be raised or lowered (dropped).

drum

MU. A percussion instrument consisting of a hollow cylinder with a membrane stretched tightly over the end or ends, played by beating with the hands, sticks, etc.

drum major

MU. A person who leads a marching band, or one who precedes it, often twirling a baton and prancing.

drum majorette

MU. A girl drum major.

dry spell

SW. 1. A period through which all songwriters go, even the most prolific, when ideas will not come and it is impossible to write songs. AI. This is a well-known and accepted occupational hazard in all fields of creative writing. MB. 2. A period during which a music publisher or a record company fails to have a hit.

116

D. S.

MU. Abbreviation, *dal segno*.

dual track

RG. 1. Designating a tape recording where sound is recorded on the upper half of the tape going in one direction and on the lower half going in the opposite direction. 2. A double-track recording. AI. This method of recording makes rewinding unnecessary. At the end of one track, the positions of the reels are merely exchanged on their spindles in order to play the other track from its beginning.

dub

RG. v. To dub in. See DUB IN.

dub

RG. n. 1. A relatively inexpensive, temporary recording, usually cut (by a cutting machine) on an acetate (record) blank. 2. Any recording (other than a master) made from the original sound (voice, music, etc.) or from the sound of another recording, as distinguished from a *pressing*. 3. Loosely, a demonstration record, a demo.

dubber

MP. 1. A ghost singer. 2. One whose voice is used for another person.

dub in

RG. 1. To add additional sound, music, voice, etc. to a recording. AI. For instance, in the recording of TENNESSEE WALTZ, Patti Page sang the song in two-part harmony. The recording process was in two steps. First, the lead voice and accompaniment were recorded. Second, this was played back and the harmony voice was *dubbed in*. 2. To insert (voice, music, etc.) in the sound track of a motion picture. 3. To insert (synchronized dialog or song in another language) in place of the original dialog or song, as in the sound track of a motion picture. 4. To add song, as that of a ghost singer (dubber) to the pantomimed action of an actor, as in a motion picture.

ducat

SB. A ticket of admission, as that to a theatrical entertainment.

dud

MB. 1. A song that is a failure. 2. Any songwriting effort that is a failure. 3. Any promotional effort that is a failure, etc.

duet

MU. 1. A musical combination of two voices or two instruments. 2. A musical composition for such a combination.

dulcimer

MU, FK. There are several instruments called by the name *dulcimer*. The two best known of these are the European dulcimer and the (American) mountain dulcimer. 1. The European dulcimer is a musical instrument having 16 or more strings which are struck with two small hammers by the player. 2. The mountain dulcimer is a musical instrument with only 3 strings which are either plucked with the thumb, index finger and middle finger of the right hand or strummed with a quill or plectrum. The first or melody string is tuned to G (below middle C). The second string is tuned to this same G. The third string is tuned to C (one octave below middle C). Only the melody string is fretted (either by the index finger of the left hand or by use of a short bamboo stick called a *noter*). The other 2 strings are *drone* strings. The mountain dulcimer has played an important part in the authentic folk music of America.

dumb sound

MB. The sound of untrained teen-age voices, usually in a vocal group.

dummy

PG. The skeleton copy, as of sheet music, a song book, etc., upon which the format is planned and laid out. See LAYOUT.

dummy lyric

SW. 1. Syllables and/or words written to fit, or to partially fit, a rhythm pattern, regardless of their meaning. 2. A temporary lyric. AI. Songwriters often use dummy lyrics while shaping and fitting a melody, while fitting words together, while working out a rhyme scheme, or while waiting for an inspiration, etc. A sample dummy

118

lyric, with a suggested rhyme scheme, might look something like this:

> de-dah de-dah de-dah
> de-dah de-dah we're through
> de-dah de-dah de-dah
> Then I'll come back to you

dummy melody

SW. Notes written to fit, or partially fit, a rhythm pattern, without regard to pitch. AI. Actually, because of this disregard for pitch, a dummy melody is not a melody at all. Dummy melodies are used for the same reasons and purposes as are dummy lyrics. All notes of a dummy melody are usually written in the first space of the staff, on the third line of the staff or without a staff, whichever the individual songwriter prefers. A sample dummy melody (the rhythm pattern for MARY HAD A LITTLE LAMB) might look something like this:

duo

MU. 1. Two. 2. Duet.

duodrama

TE. A musical melodrama in which two people act and sing.

duologue

TE. 1. A conversation between two people, especially in a dramatic performance. 2. A form of songwriting. AI. For instance, the lyric for ANYTHING YOU CAN DO is written in duologue.

dupe

RG. 1. A duplicate recording or record. 2. A *dub*.

duple time

MU. Any time that contains an even number of beats to the measure as: Cut Time, Two-Two Time, Two-Four Time, Two-Eight Time, Four-Two Time, Four-Four Time, etc. AI. Cut Time can also be counted as quadruple time. Duple time is also called *two time, two beat* and *two-beat time*.

duration

MU. 1. The length of time that a thing continues or lasts. 2. A continuance in time, as that of a note, a rest, a record, etc. 3. How long or how short something is. See PLAYING TIME.

dynamics

MU. 1. Musical expression that has to do with the loudness and softness in performance. 2. Directions dealing with the third characteristic of a tone, intensity. AI. There are two classifications of dynamics: (1) Those that indicate a steady rate of tone, not louder or softer, as *very soft, soft, half soft, half loud, loud, very loud,* etc. (2) Those that indicate a change in volume, either louder or softer, as *gradually louder, louder, softer, much softer, gradually softer, dying away, fading out,* etc. A songwriter should feel entirely free to use words and phrases of his own invention, whatever he feels is best suited to direct the way he wants his song to be played.

e

E

MU. 1. The fifth letter in the musical alphabet, representing a pitch one whole tone above D. 2. The letter applied to any octave above or below this pitch. 3. The third tone, note or degree in the ascending major scale of C. 4. The major key that has four sharps in its key signature. 5. The caption for an E major triad. 6. The key or string of a musical instrument that produces the tone of E. 7. The first string on the Spanish guitar, called *treble E*. 8. The sixth string on the Spanish guitar, called *bass E*.

E♭

MU. See E FLAT.

Early American

MN. 1. Designating any musical composition, particularly one in the jazz field, that is more than a few months old. AI. An *Early American* song hit can mean a very recent hit. 2. A facetious designation for a musical composition, its performance, or a musician; used to imply something or someone who is not exactly up to date.

ear, the

MU. 1. Anyone who has a good ear for pitch. MB. 2. An executive whose authority it is to decide which songs are to be exploited, as those of a music publisher. RB. 3. One who decides which songs are to be recorded, which song is to be the A side of a phonograph record, etc.

121

earthy

MN. 1. Simple and natural. 2. Hearty and unashamed. AI. As said of music.

ear, to have an

MU. 1. The ability to recognize slight differences in sound, especially in pitch, rhythm, etc. of musical tones. AI. A person can be said to have a good *ear*, a poor *ear*, etc. for music. To *play by ear* means to play a musical instrument without the use of notation, improvising an arrangement. Jazz musicians sometimes say *he's a good ear* meaning *he has a good ear*. MB. 2. The ability to pick songs that are most likely to become hits.

ear training

MU. Instruction designed to develop the sense of hearing as applied to music, as the recognition of absolute or relative pitch, intervals, chords, meter, rhythm patterns, etc. See SOLFEGGIO.

echo

MU. v. 1. To resound with an echo. 2. To repeat.

echo

MU. n. 1. A repeated sound. 2. A repetition of a musical strain or phrase, usually with less intensity. 3. Imitation of a strain or phrase resembling an echo. 4. A repetition of a lyric or, usually, a part of a lyric. AI. In recording, echoes can be produced by electronic and mechanical means. WG. 5. Wording that is very similar to, or the same as something written by someone else, *as red as a rose, teeth like pearls, the golden sun*, etc. MB. 6. A phonograph record intentionally made in imitation of another recording. 7. A mirror.

echo chamber

RG. A device, used in recording and broadcasting, to produce echoes.

echo mill

MB. A phonograph record company that makes a business of producing records in imitation of the hit records produced by others. AI. Also called a *mirror factory*.

122

echo singer

MB. A vocalist who imitates other singers, for the purpose of recording an echo record or records.

edit

WG. 1. To read, correct, revise (as necessary) and make ready for publication, as the manuscript of a song. 2. To work as an editor. 3. To correct, alter and revise recordings, as those on tape.

edition

PG. 1. The size, style or form in which a book is published, as a song book, etc. 2. The total number of copies of a book, sheet music, etc. printed from the same plates, type, etc. and published at about the same time, as the *first edition, second edition,* etc. 3. A single copy of such a printing.

editor

WG. 1. One who reads, corrects, revises (as necessary) and makes ready for publication, as the manuscript of a song. 2. One who edits. 3. One who corrects, revises or alters recordings on tape, known as a *tape editor.* See MUSIC EDITOR.

E flat: E♭

MU. 1. The symbol shown above. 2. The tone on the piano that is one half step below the tone of E. 3. The same tone on the piano as D SHARP. 4. The major key that has three flats in its key signature. 5. The caption for an E FLAT major triad.

E flat major scale

MU. The scale consisting of these eight notes or tones: E♭, F, G, A♭, B♭, C, D, E♭. Also called *the key of E♭.* See KEY SIGNATURE.

e. g.

LW. Abbreviation for the Latin term *exempli gratia,* (pronounced eg-zem′pli grah′she-ah) meaning: 1. To show by example. 2. For example. 3. For instance. GI. This abbreviation is used frequently in law, as in copyright law. Circular 22 of the United States Copyright office says, "A notice of copyright (*e.g.* © John Doe 1959 or Copyright John Doe 1959) on a published work indicates that copyright is claimed on that particular work."

egg
MB. See LAY AN EGG.

ego trade
MB. Those who patronize song sharks.

eight-bar myth, the
GI. See FOUR-BAR MYTH.

eight by ten
PH. 1. A *professional-size* photograph, as that used by singers and other performers. 2. Usually, a *glossy*. AI. So called because it measures eight inches wide by ten inches high.

eighth
MU. 1. The interval between any note (tone) and the eighth note (tone) above it in the diatonic scale. 2. A note (tone) separated by this interval from any other note (tone). 3. The eighth note (tone) above the keynote (keytone). 4. An octave. AI. For instance, the eighth interval, or degree, above C is the tone of C.

eighth note: ♪ or ♪
MU. 1. Either of the notes shown above. 2. A note with a solid head attached to a stem, either up or down, and a single-line flag. AI. An eighth note represents a time value one eighth that of a whole note, one fourth that of a half note or one half that of a quarter note.

eighth rest: ♪
MU. 1. The rest shown above. 2. A rest with one arm attached to a diagonal descending line. AI. An eighth rest represents a time value one eighth that of a whole rest, one fourth that of a half rest or one half that of a quarter rest. The time value of an eighth rest is equal to that of an eighth note.

8va (eight vee-ae)
MU. Abbreviation, *ottava alta*. Also written as *8va alta* and *8*. See OCTAVE MARKS.

124

8vaba (eight vee-ae-bee-ae)

MU. Abbreviation, *ottava bassa*. See OCTAVE MARKS.

eighty-eight

JZ. A piano. AI. So called because the standard piano has 88 keys, 52 white and 36 black.

electraharp

MU. A deluxe console model steel guitar, with foot pedals for raising or lowering the tones produced by any of six or more strings. AI. The instrument gets its name from its self-contained electronic pick-up.

electrical transcription

RG. 1. A recording made by means of electronics. 2. A large, long-playing phonograph record, usually of a radio program for broadcasting. AI. Also called *transcription*. Abbreviated, *E. T.*

electric guitar

MU. See GUITAR.

electronics

SE. The science that deals with the action of electrons in vacuums and gases and with the use of vacuum tubes, as those used in sound-input equipment, amplifiers, sound-reproduction equipment, etc.

eleven-o'clock song

TE. The big song, or hit song of a musical show. AI. So called because this is the song the audience is singing, whistling or humming as they leave the theater at about *eleven o'clock* at night.

elide (e-lide')

RC. 1. To strike out, as a vowel or syllable in a word. 2. To omit a vowel or syllable in pronouncing or writing. 3. To slur over a vowel or syllable in pronouncing. AI. For instance, in the word *'tis* the *i* is *elided*. In *harm'ny* the *o* is *elided,* etc. Songwriters often elide a syllable or vowel in fitting words to music.

elongate

MU. 1. To make longer, as a melody. 2. To spread a melody over more measures than the number in which it was originally written.

elongation

MU. 1. The spreading of a melody. 2. The writing of a melody in more measures than it was originally written. AI. A motive of one measure written to be played twice as slow, over two measures, is an example of elongation. The opposite of *diminution*.

E major scale

MU. The scale consisting of these eight notes or tones: E, F♯, G♯, A, B, C♯, D♯, E. Also called *the key of E*. See KEY SIGNATURE.

embellishment

MU. 1. An addition, as notation, to a melody. 2. A beautiful improvement. 3. An adornment. SA. 4. The luster added to a barbershop arrangement, or a sequence of chords, by adding swipes, harmonies and/or patter. 5. The *embroidery around the edges*, SPEBSQSA style.

embouchure

MU. 1. The mouthpiece of a wind instrument. 2. The way of applying the lips and tongue to the mouthpiece of a wind instrument. 3. The position or adjustment of the lips, tongue and other speech organs in vocalizing. See LIP.

emotional impact

WG. 1. The power, as that of a song, to excite or stir the emotions. 2. The extent to which emotions are aroused, as by a song. AI. The emotional impact was so great, it was necessary to prohibit the broadcasting of the song GLOOMY SUNDAY because of the number of suicides it occasioned.

emotional participation

PS. 1. The act of reacting emotionally (loving, hating, fearing, suffering, etc.), as to a song. 2. An imagined emotional experience, as that suggested in a song. AI. Many songs have become great because of the emotional participation they provide, such as MOOD INDIGO, YOUR CHEATING HEART, and SOLITUDE.

emotional quality

RG. 1. The degree to which emotions are affected, as by a song. 2.

126

The extent to which emotions are aroused, or can be aroused, as by a song. 3. Loosely, the same as *emotional value*.

emotional value

RG. 1. Worth, as that of a song, based on the extent to which the emotions can be aroused. 2. Any element, as of a song, that excites the emotions. 3. Loosely, the same as *emotional quality*.

employee-for-hire contract

MB. A contract, as between a music publisher and a songwriter or arranger, in which the employee waives all rights to the work or works created or prepared during a certain term (of *work for hire*). AI. Such a contract designates the employer as the sole copyright owner.

encore

MU. 1. A demand by an audience, shown by continued applause, for the repetition of a piece of music or for further performance. 2. The piece of music or performance in answer to such a demand.

endings: ⌐1⌐ ⌐2⌐ ⌐1 2 3⌐ ⌐4⌐

MU. 1. The signs shown above. 2. The last measure, or final several measures of a song designated by these or similar signs. See FIRST ENDINGS. See SECOND ENDINGS. See ADDITIONAL ENDINGS.

end rhyme

PY. A rhyme placement where the last (end) word of one line rhymes with the last word of another line, as distinguished from *internal rhyme*. Also called *terminal rhyme*.

end title

SW. A song title which is placed at the end of the first section of the chorus. AI. Also called section-end title. Typical end titles are YOU TOOK ADVANTAGE OF ME, PERSONALITY, MY BLUE HEAVEN and WHEN IT'S SLEEPY TIME DOWN SOUTH.

engagement

SB. 1. An agreement, as that of an entertainer, to perform. 2. A performance or series of performances, as those of an entertainer. AI. For instance, a singer might have a two-week *engagement* at the Sands Hotel, an *engagement* for a recording session on a certain date, a night-club *engagement,* etc.

engineer

BR. A person skilled or occupied in some branch of engineering, as that of electronics, speech input, etc., as a broadcasting engineer, a recording engineer, etc.

English horn

MU. 1. A double-reed instrument of the wood-wind family, similar to the oboe but larger and a fifth lower in pitch. 2. The alto oboe. AI. The English horn is not of English origin, neither is it a horn.

English meter

PY. The four kinds of meter most often used in writing verse, or poetry, in the English language: iambic, trochaic, anapestic, and dactyllic. AI. These four meters are used straight or mixed, as the occasion demands.

engraving

PG. 1. The act or process of cutting or etching designs or letters on metal plates, as is done in an old method of music printing. 2. An engraved plate, as used in the early days of music printing.

enharmonic

MU. 1. Designating tones identical in pitch, as are G SHARP and A FLAT, on the piano, or other keyboard instruments. 2. Designating the black keys on the piano, or other keyboard instruments.

en masse dances (en mas' danses)

DG. Dances that usually are performed by large groups of dancers all together, or *en masse,* as distinguished from dances that can be performed by only a couple. AI. Typical en masse dances are: the cotillion, the tarantella, the Lambeth walk, the big apple, the conga, and the frug.

ensemble

MU. 1. The performance together of all instruments of an orchestra or all the voices in a chorus. 2. A small group of musicians playing and/or singing together. 3. The instruments or voices that make up such a group. TE. 4. The entire company of performers who make up a show. 5. All performers in a show excepting the principals or those featured.

entertain

SB. 1. To afford amusement. 2. To divert. 3. To occupy pleasantly. 4. To present a public performance for these purposes.

entertainer

SB. 1. One whose business is to entertain, as a singer, a musician, an actor, etc. 2. A performer.

entertainment

SB. 1. A diverting performance. 2. A performance for the purpose of entertaining.

entr'acte (ahn-trahkt')

TE. 1. The interval between two acts, as of a musical show, play, opera, etc. 2. The intermission. 3. A musical selection, dance, etc., performed during this interval.

enunciate

RC. 1. To articulate, utter, speak. 2. To sing.

enunciation

RC. The manner of enunciating words, as in a song. AI. For instance, a singer can be said to have good or bad *enunciation*, as to whether or not he pronounces the words of a song distinctly.

E. P.

RB. Abbreviation, *extended play*.

ephemeral (e-fem'er'l)

LW. 1. Anything that is short lived. 2. A record which, by agreement, will be destroyed after a stated period, as at the end of 30 or 60 days. AI. When music is recorded to be used for educational purposes, the educator who uses the recording might agree, because he is permitted to use the recorded material either without charge or at a reduced charge, to use this material only for a limited time period and to destroy the recording on or before a specified date. In this event the recording is called an *ephemeral*.

equal billing

SB. The listing, as of performers' names and song titles, in the same order and same prominence, as in an advertisement. See BILLING.

equalization

SI. The boosting of high or low frequencies, in recording or broadcasting, to emphasize or produce certain sound effects.

equity

TE. Short for *Actors Equity Association*.

E. T.

RB. Abbreviation, *electrical transcription*.

ethnic

MB. Designating or of any of the basic divisions or groups of mankind, as distinguished by customs, characteristics, language, etc., as an *ethnic* folk song.

euphony (u'fo-ne)

PM. 1. The quality of having a pleasing sound. 2. A well-sounding combination of words. 3. A well-sounding word or syllable. 4. A pleasing sound in music. 5. A pleasing combination of sounds in music.

Euterpe (u-ter'pe)

SW. 1. The mythical goddess of songwriting. 2. The muse of music and lyric poetry in Greek mythology.

even tone

SA. A tone of constant pitch, that is without vibrato. AI. A requirement to the unique effect of *ringing* a barbershop chord SPEBSQSA style. A soloist singing with a perfectly *even* tone may sound color-

130

less. Blended with three other voices, however, even tones can produce most satisfying chords.

evergreen

MB. 1. A standard song. 2. A song that continues in popularity, seemingly without end. AI. Examples of well known evergreens are WHITE CHRISTMAS, EASTER PARADE, TEA FOR TWO, DEED I DO and STAR DUST.

Exchange Place

MN. A short passageway located between Canal Street and Bienville Street, New Orleans, famous as the meeting place of the early-day New Orleans musicians. AI. Also known as *Exchange Alley*.

exclusive

SB. Short for *exclusive contract*.

exclusive contract

LW. 1. A formal agreement that binds the services of one person exclusively to another, as a songwriter to a music publisher, a singer to a recording company, etc. 2. The writing containing such an agreement.

exploit

MB. 1. To stir up interest in. 2. To promote, as a song.

exploitation

MB. 1. The act of exploiting. 2. A promotional campaign, as that of a song.

expose

MB. 1. To make known. 2. To cause to be heard, as a song. 3. To exploit, as a song. 4. To bring to the attention of the trade or general public, as a song.

exposure

MB. 1. An exposing or being exposed, as a song. 2. Exploitation, as that of a song. LW. 3. To display and offer for sale, as printed copies of a song.

131

exposure for sale

LW. 1. To place on public display or otherwise offer for sale to the general public, as printed copies of a song. 2. The act of placing several printed copies of a song on a counter, in a window, or elsewhere and making known, by a sign, or other device, that such copies are for sale. AI. This is a technical requirement to establish publication and does not necessarily imply actual commercial selling.

expression

MB. 1. The quality of a musical performance that appeals to the emotions. 2. The taste, the feeling displayed in performing a song.

expression marks

MU. Written directions as to how a song is to be played and sung. AI. Expression marks may refer to one or more of five things: (1) tempo, (2) a change in tempo, (3) dynamics, (4) a change in volume and (5) style. An expression mark may consist of a single word, as *lively* or a phrase, as *softly, slowly, sweetly*, etc.

expression songs

SW. Songs whose titles and/or text are based on a popular expression. AI. Typical expression songs are SEALED WITH A KISS, IN OTHER WORDS and POINT OF NO RETURN.

extemporaneous

GI. Made, done, spoken, sung or played without preparation, as an extemporaneous song or arrangement, etc.

extended chord

MU. 1. Any chord of more than three tones. 2. A triad which has been extended by the addition of a tone or tones. AI. For instance, C6, C7 and C9 each is an *extension* of the C major triad, Cm6, Cm7, and Cm9 each is an *extension* of the Cm triad, etc.

extended-play

RB. Designating a phonograph record of longer playing time than ordinary, usually a 45 rpm microgroove recording.

extender

MU. 1. A line drawn under notes to be sung to one syllable. 2. A line that indicates the time value of a syllable or word that is sung to tied notes. AI. For instance, if the word *you* in the lyric *I love you* were sung to tied notes, it should be followed by an extender continuing to the last of these tied notes, thus *I love you_____*. Also called an *extension line*, or *extender line*. See MARK OF CONTINUATION.

extension

MU. 1. The addition of one or more measures to the regular song structure. AI. This may be a repetition of a previous motive or only a series of additional chords which the songwriter feels is needed for an ending. 2. Any note or notes (tone or tones) that are added to a triad. AI. For instance, the tone of B♭ is the *extension* of C major triad (C-E-G) when it is added to form the chord of C7 (C-E-G-B♭). The tones B♭ and D are the *extensions* of C major triad (C-E-G) when they are added to form the chord of C9 (C-E-G-B♭-D), etc.

extraneous

RC. 1. Not essential. 2. Unrelated. 3. Not belonging. AI. For instance, an *extraneous* note is one that can be omitted without changing or hurting the basic melody.

extravaganza

SB. An elaborate theatrical production, particularly that of a musical show.

extreme parts

MU. 1. The highest and lowest parts in a song. 2. The highest and lowest tones in a song. 3. The highest and lowest voices in a song, as compared with *inner parts*.

eye rhymes

VN. Words that are spelled alike, but whose different sounds prevent rhyme. AI. Typical eye rhymes are love, prove; are, bare; earth, hearth, etc.

134

f

F

MU. 1. The sixth letter in the musical alphabet, representing a half tone above E. 2. The letter applied to any octave above or below this pitch. 3. The fourth tone, note or degree in the ascending major scale of C. 4. The major key that has one flat in its key signature. 5. The caption for an F major triad. 6. The key or string of a musical instrument that produces the tone of F. 7. The name of the bass clef, as *F clef*. 8. The name of the openings in violins, and similar instruments, called *F holes*. 9. The small letter used to designate the syllable *fah* in the English system of tonic sol-fa.

F♯

MU. See F SHARP.

fa: ◁ or ◁

MU. 1. The syllable used in singing the fourth tone of a scale in the sol-fa system. 2. Either of the shape noteheads shown above representing this syllable. AI. The first of the two noteheads shown above is for use with downstems. The second is for use with upstems. Otherwise the two noteheads have identical meaning.

face

PG. See TYPE FACE.

fade

BR. v. 1. To become less distinct, as the volume of sound. 2. To cause sound to become less distinct by decreasing its volume.

fade

BR. n. A device used in recording and broadcasting to increase or decrease the volume of sound. AI. Also called *gain*. The speech-input engineer who operates the fade is said to be *riding gain*.

fade in

BR. 1. To increase gradually the volume of sound as from zero audibility, to a desired level, an effect used in recording and broadcasting. MP. 2. To make to appear gradually, an effect used in motion pictures. 3. To appear gradually.

fade out

BR. 1. To decrease gradually the volume of sound to zero audibility, an effect used in recording and broadcasting. MP. 2. To make to disappear gradually, an effect used in motion pictures. 3. To disappear gradually.

fair use

LW. The privilege to use copyrighted material in a reasonable and equitable manner without consent of the copyright owner. AI. For instance, book reviewers often quote from copyrighted books. The exact limit of fair use is a highly questionable boundary line.

fake

MN. 1. To play without written or printed music. 2. To improvise, as a chorus, a solo passage, a complete song, etc. 3. To play *by ear*.

faker

MN. A musician (usually jazz) who can not read music. AI. The term has nothing to do with playing ability, which may be very excellent. The opposite of *reader*.

false accent

MU. A musical accent that has been removed from the first beat of a measure to the second or fourth beat.

false pitch

MU. 1. Pitched incorrectly. 2. A tone that is not of true pitch. 3. A tone that is other than it should be in sound.

falsetto (fahl-set′o)

MU. 1. An artificial way of singing, used especially by tenors, in which the voice is placed in a register much higher than that of the natural voice. 2. The voice used in such singing, usually characterized by a soft, nasal quality. 3. A person who sings falsetto.

fan

SB. 1. Anyone who is enthusiastic about a performer, a singer, a musician, etc. 2. Anyone who is enthusiastic about a kind of music, as a jazz fan, a country-music fan, etc. 3. A devotee. 4. A buff.

fan club

SB. An organized group of fans who are devoted to the same personality or thing.

fanfare

MU. 1. A trumpet flourish. 2. A noisy or showy display.

fantasia (fan-tae′zha)

MU. 1. A musical composition of no fixed form, with a structure determined only by the composer's fancy. 2. A medley of familiar tunes, or songs. AI. Also called *fantasy*.

fantasy

MU. 1. Same as *fantasia*. SW. 2. A classification in songwriting as to subject matter. AI. Typical fantasy songs are: DREAMER'S HOLIDAY, CATCH A FALLING STAR, IT'S ONLY A PAPER MOON, PAINTING THE CLOUDS WITH SUNSHINE and EAST OF THE SUN.

far out

JZ. 1. Very unusual. 2. Extraordinary.

fasola

MU. An early system of indicating the tones of the scale chiefly by the four syllables fa, sol, la, mi, as follows:

c	d	e	f	g	a	b	c
fa	sol	la	fa	sol	la	mi	fa

137

AI. This system of singing appeared in the Bay Psalm Book, published in Boston in 1700. This same system is in surprisingly wide use today throughout the southern part of the United States, where it is known as Sacred Harp singing. See SACRED HARP.

F clef:

MU. 1. The symbol shown above. 2. The bass clef. 3. The clef sign indicating the bass stave. AI. The head of the bass clef is placed on the fourth line of the staff, as shown above. This means that a note written on the fourth line is called F, and indicates the tone of the first F below middle C.

feature

SB. 1. A prominently displayed or emphasized person or thing, as a *featured player* or a *featured song*, in a show, etc. 2. A full length motion picture, as a *feature* picture.

featured

TE. 1. To make outstanding or prominent, as a *featured* song in a musical. 2. To be given a prominent role, as a *featured* singer or a *featured* performer. 3. A principal. 4. To be advertised or billed prominently.

feed

TE. To give a necessary cue line, as from one performer to another. AI. Songs are often introduced in musical shows in this manner.

feedback

BR. 1. When the source of input (microphone) picks up sound from the source of output (loud speaker) in the same electrical circuit, as that for recording or broadcasting, this is called *feedback*. AI. Feedback results in a howling sound. MN. 2. Back talk, as an argument. MB. 3. Payola.

feeder

TE. 1. A performer who *feeds* a cue line or lines to another or others. 2. A straight man.

feel out

SW. To proceed in writing a song by the trial-and-error method. AI.

A songwriter is said to *feel out* a song when he tries first one bit of melody then another, one set of words then another, and continues in this manner, shaping, altering, fitting, discarding and changing one thing for another.

feminine ending

PY. Ending, of a line of verse, on an unaccented syllable. AI. For instance, appropriately, the word *fe′male*, itself, has a feminine ending.

feminine rhyme

PY. 1. A rhyme in which the primary or secondary accent falls on next to the last syllable. 2. A double rhyme. AI. For instance, typical feminine rhymes are *guess′ing* and *con-fess′ing*.

fermata: ⌢ or ⌣

MU. 1. The holding of a tone or rest for a longer duration than its normal time value, as is sometimes done at the discretion of a performer. 2. The sign, shown above, indicating this. AI. The first of the two signs shown above is written over a note or rest. The second sign is written under a note or rest. Fermatas are sometimes written over or under a double bar to mean *the end* of a musical composition. Also, sometimes, called *bird's eye*, *hold* or *pause*.

f holes

MU. The openings, in the form of an f, which are cut in the table (top) of a violin and other stringed instruments to give greater freedom of vibration. AI. Also called *sound holes*.

fiddle

CM. v. To play a violin.

fiddle

CM. n. 1. A violin. 2. Any instrument of the violin class, as a *bass fiddle*, etc.

fiddler

CM. 1. One who plays the fiddle. 2. A violinist.

fidelity

RG. The trueness of the reproduction of sound, as that of a phonograph record. AI. The truer the reproduced sound is to the original, the higher the fidelity. Also called *quality*. See HI FI.

field

GI. A realm of knowledge or of special work, as the field of songwriting, the field of singing, the field of music, etc.

field label

WG. Identification as to the field of knowledge or special activity in which a word or phrase is used. AI. For instance, the field labels used in this book consist of a combination of two initials, as MU (music), RB (record business), SW (songwriting), etc. See list of FIELD LABELS in introductory pages in front of book.

field music

MU. 1. Military music. 2. Martial music, as that played on fifes, bugles and drums.

fifth

MU. 1. The interval between any note (tone) and the fifth note (tone) above it in the diatonic scale. 2. A note (tone) separated by this interval from any other note (tone). 3. The fifth degree in any diatonic scale. 4. The fifth note above the keynote. 5. The fifth tone above the keytone. 6. The dominant. AI. For instance, the tone of G is the fifth of the chord C-E-G. The tone of G is also the fifth degree, or dominant, in the diatonic scale of C major.

fifth string

MU. 1. The A string on the Spanish guitar. 2. The short string on a five-string banjo, called the *thumb string*, tuned to G, four notes above middle C.

fight song

MU. A school song written to encourage and/or inspire an athletic team, as in football. AI. Typical fight songs are: ON WISCONSIN, FIGHT ON PENNSYLVANIA, GO YOU NORTHWESTERN, etc.

figuration

MU. The use of ornamental passages in the variation of a musical theme.

figure

MU. 1. A series of consecutive tones or chords forming a distinct group which with other similar groups completes a phrase or theme. 2. A motive. 3. The smallest element into which a musical phrase can be divided. 4. A series of steps and movements in dancing.

figure of speech

RC. An expression using words in an unusual or nonliteral sense, to add beauty and/or vividness of style. AI. Examples are the song titles: LET A SMILE BE YOUR UMBRELLA, I'VE GOT YOU UNDER MY SKIN and I'VE GOT THE WORLD ON A STRING.

fill

JZ. A lick. AI. Same as *fill in*.

fill in

MB. v. To substitute, as one musician for another.

fill in

JZ. n. 1. A lick. See LICK. MB. 2. A substitute, as one musician for another.

film

MP. a. Designating the motion picture industry, its people, properties, etc., as *film writer*, *film plays*, etc.

film

MP. n. 1. Cellulose material on which motion pictures are made. 2. A motion picture.

film rights

LW. See MOTION PICTURE RIGHTS.

finale (fih-nahl′e)

MU. 1. The concluding movement or passage of a musical composition. 2. The last scene, usually the feature, of an entertainment, as a musical show. 3. The conclusion, last part, end.

finder

LW. 1. A person, or organization, that finds. 2. A discoverer. AI. For instance, a person might act as an independent agent in bringing a previously unknown singer to the attention of a record company, or a previously unknown song to the attention of a music publisher, and might be paid for their role as a *finder* in doing so.

fine (fee'ne)

MU. 1. The end. 2. The end of a song or other musical composition. 3. A direction marking the close of a repeated song or instrumental passage.

fingerboard

MU. 1. A strip of hardwood in the neck of a stringed instrument, as a violin, guitar, banjo, etc., against which the strings are pressed with the fingers to produce the desired tones. 2. Rarely, the keyboard of a piano, organ, accordion, etc.

fingering

MU. 1. The method and/or act of applying the fingers to the keys, holes, strings, etc. of a musical instrument to produce musical tones. 2. Directions written or printed, as those on a musical score, to guide the performer or student in placing his fingers. AI. For instance, in the English method of fingering, for the piano, the thumb is designated by the letter *x* and the four fingers by the figures *1, 2, 3* and *4*. The figure *1* designates the first or index finger. *2* the middle finger. *3* the ring finger. *4* the little finger. In the German (or continental) method, the thumb is indicated by the figure *1*. The index finger by *2*. The middle finger by *3*. The ring finger by *4*. The little finger by *5*. In a very old method *o* was used to indicate the thumb and *1, 2, 3, 4* to represent the fingers, as in the English system.

finish

SB. The last part, building in interest to the end, as of a song, a monolog, an act or any material.

first

MU. 1. The first note, first tone or first degree of any diatonic scale is called the keynote, keytone, tonic or prime. 2. The first voice, first instrument or first part in any group, combo, choir, ensemble, etc. is the highest in pitch. 3. The first voice or part in any arrange-

142

ment is the highest in pitch. 4. The first string on any stringed instrument is usually the highest in pitch. 5. The first line in any music staff is the line that is the lowest both in position and pitch. 6. The first space in any music staff is the space that is the lowest both in position and pitch. 7. The first chord in any key is the chord that has the keynote, or keytone, for its root. 8. The first note (or tone) in any chord is its root. 9. The first finger is the finger next to the thumb or *index* finger. The finger designated by the figure *1* in the English method of fingering. The finger designated by the figure *2* in the German method of fingering.

first call

MB. Preferred, as a first-call musician. AI. A *first-call* musician is one who is called, for a job, in preference to others.

first-call clause

LW. 1. A clause in a contract which permits one party, as a music publisher, to have *first call* on the products and/or services of another, as a songwriter. AI. Under such a contract, a songwriter is free to offer his songs to other publishers only after they have been submitted to the publisher to whom he is under contract. See FIRST REFUSAL, RIGHT OF.

first-chair

JZ. Designating a highly skilled and capable musician, as a *first-chair sax man*, a *first-chair trombonist*, a *first-chair sideman*, etc.

first ending: ⌐1̶̶̶̶̶̶̶̶⌐

MU. 1. The measure or measures of a song that are designated by the characters shown above. 2. These characters, themselves. 3. The ending of a song that serves to lead back into a repeat of the chorus or a repeat of the last part of the chorus, as distinguished from the second ending, which serves to bring a song to a conclusion. 4. Lead back. AI. The first ending is used only when it is intended to repeat a song either in whole or in part. When a song is to be played or sung only once, the first ending is omitted and the second ending is used instead. See SECOND ENDING. See ADDITIONAL ENDINGS.

first night

SB. 1. The opening night of a play, a musical or other performance. 2. The opening night of a performer, as a singer in a night club, etc.

first nighter

SB. 1. A person who regularly attends the opening performances of plays, musical shows, etc. 2. A member of a first-night audience.

first publication

LW. 1. The original act of bringing a printed property to the attention of the public, as to offer a song for sale. 2. Preceding all other publications, as of the same song. AI. For instance, when a song is given same-day publication in Canada and the United States, Canada is considered to be the country of *first publication*, by the Berne Convention, inasmuch as Canada is a member of the Berne Convention and the United States is not. (The Berne Convention therefore does not recognize the United States.) See SAME-DAY PUBLICATION.

first refusal, right of

MB. 1. The right to refuse or accept something or someone, as a song or the services of an artist, before it is offered to anyone else. 2. The exclusive right to be the first to whom something is offered, with the right to accept or reject. 3. The right to have first choice. See FIRST-CALL CLAUSE.

first string

MU. 1. The treble E string on the Spanish guitar. 2. The B string on the ukulele (tuned A-D-F♯-B). 3. The D string on the five-string banjo (one note above middle C). 4. Usually, the *highest* string in any set.

five: 5 or V

MU. 1. The Arabic numeral used to designate an interval of a fifth. 2. The Arabic numeral used to designate the fifth, or little finger in the German method of fingering. 3. The Roman numeral used to designate the fifth degree, or dominant, in the diatonic scale.

five flats:

MU. The key signature of D♭ major, as shown above.

five-lined octave

MU. The fourth octave, on the piano, above middle C. AI. Keys

144

(tones) in this octave are designated c⁵, d⁵, e⁵, etc. There is only one key in this octave on the standard 88-key piano (c⁵).

five sharps:

MU. The key signature of B major, as shown above.

five string

MN. Short for *five-string banjo*.

five-string banjo

MU. A banjo with five strings, the fifth string being shorter than the other four. AI. The five-string banjo is tuned as follows: 1st string D (one note above middle C), 2nd string B (one note below middle C), 3rd string G (three notes below middle C), fourth string C (one octave below middle C), fifth string G (four notes above middle C). This is the tuning used by Earl Scruggs of Flatt and Scruggs. There are other tunings in popular use.

fixed pitch

MU. The pitch of such instruments as the piano, organ, etc. in which the pitch of the individual tones can not be changed by the performer. Compare with FREE PITCH.

flag: ͵ or ᷆ or ᷅ etc.

MU. 1. Any of the signs shown above. AI. From left to right, these are: single flag, double flag and triple flag. 2. A tapered, curved appendage attached to the stem of a solid-black-headed note to designate its time value. 3. A pennant. 4. A hook. See FLAGGED NOTE.

flagged note: ♪ or ♪ or ♪ etc.

MU. 1. Any of the notes shown above. 2. Any note to which a flag, a double flag, a triple flag, etc. is attached. 3. An eighth note, a sixteenth note, a thirty-second note, etc. AI. An eighth note and a sixteenth note are the only two flagged notes used in songwriting.

flat: ♭

MU. 1. The sign shown above. AI. A flat is written before a note, or on a degree of the staff, to indicate that its pitch is to be lowered one half step. For instance, B♭ is one half step lower than the tone of

145

B and one half step higher than the tone of A. 2. The name of the black keys on a keyboard instrument, as D FLAT, E FLAT, G FLAT, etc.

flat key
MU. 1. Any key (scale) whose key signature is composed of a flat or flats, as the key of F major (one flat), the key of B♭ major (two flats), the key of E♭ major (three flats), etc. 2. A black key on a keyboard instrument, as A FLAT, B FLAT, D FLAT, etc.

flip
RB. a. 1. Designating the other side of a phonograph record. 2. Designating the opposite side of a phonograph record, as the *flip side*. 3. Designating the song on the flip side of a phonograph record, as the *flip song*.

flip
RB. n. 1. The opposite side of a phonograph record, the other side, as the *flip side*. 2. The song on the flip side of a phonograph record, as the *flip*.

floor
SB. 1. A cleared space in a night club, cafe, theater-restaurant, etc., usually in front of a small stage or entranceway, in which entertainment is presented. 2. A dance floor. 3. The area of a night club that is used for dancing and entertainment.

floor plan
SW. The rough outline or framework for a song.

floor show
SB. An entertainment, as singing, dancing, etc., presented in a cleared space, usually on the dance floor, of a restaurant, night club, etc.

flop
SB. A failure, as a song that fails to win public acceptance, a show that fails to attract audiences, etc.

florid
MU. 1. Highly decorated, embellished, ornamented, as a passage in

146

music. SW. 2. Excessively flowery, overly showy, as might be said of the style in which song lyrics are written. AI. An example of ornate style might be *ruby lips as red as rosy wine.*

flower songs

MB. A classification in songwriting as to subject matter. AI. Typical flower songs are GIVE ME ONE DOZEN ROSES, WHITE AZALEAS, ORCHIDS IN THE MOONLIGHT and RED ROSES FOR A BLUE LADY.

flub

SB. Same as *fluff.*

fluff

SB. v. 1. To make a mistake in singing or playing. 2. To make a mistake in reading lines, as an actor, a radio announcer, etc.

fluff

SB. n. A mistake, as in singing, playing, reading lines, etc.

flute

MU. A high-pitched instrument, of the wood wind family, consisting of a long slender tube, played by blowing across a hole near the upper end; by fingering the holes and keys along its length, a player can produce various tones.

flutter

BR. A distortion of recorded sound, as caused by fluctuations in the speed of a turntable.

FM (eff-em)

BD. Abbreviation, *frequency modulation.*

F major scale

MU. The scale consisting of these eight notes or tones: F, G, A, Bb, C, D, E, F. Also called *the key of F.* See KEY SIGNATURE.

folio

PP. 1. A book, as of songs, music, etc., usually paper bound, approxi-

147

mately 9" x 12" in size. See ALBUM. 2. The number of pages in a book, as a song book, a hymnal, etc. 3. A page number, itself.

folio numbers ˙

PP. Page numbers, as those of a song book. AI. Also called *folios*.

folio rights

MB. The rights to publish a song, usually only the lyric, as in a magazine, newspaper, etc. AI. Also called *lyric rights* and *lyric-folio rights*.

folio royalties

MB. The share of proceeds for folio rights paid the copyright owner, author, etc.

folk music

MU. 1. Music made and handed down among the common people. 2. Traditional music of the common people.

folk song

FK. 1. A song made and handed down among the common people. 2. A traditional song of the common people. AI. Folk songs are generally of simple, unaffected character, in ballad form, reflecting the traditions, customs and/or beliefs of the common people. True folk songs are usually of anonymous authorship. Typical folk songs are: LITTLE JOE THE WRANGLER, ON TOP OF OLD SMOKEY, DOWN IN THE VALLEY, THE GIRL WITH THE BLUE VELVET BAND and GREEN GROW THE RASHES-O! Well-known folk songs from other countries are BARBARA ALLEN (English), ALOUETTE (French-Canadian), LONDONDERRY AIR (Irish), SANTA LUCIA (Italian), SONG OF THE VOLGA BOATMEN (Russian), ALL THROUGH THE NIGHT (Welsh), COMIN' THROUGH THE RYE (Scotch) and JUANITA (Spanish).

follow-up

MB. 1. A songwriter's next song after a hit. 2. An artist's next record after a hit. 3. Additional promotion or advertising, as that of a song.

148

follow-up rights

MB. 1. The rights to publish and record subsequent works, as might be granted to a publisher by a songwriter. 2. The right to sell and exploit subsequent recordings, as might be granted to a record company by an artist. AI. See FIRST REFUSAL, RIGHT OF.

font

PG. A complete assortment of printer's type in one style and size.

foot

PY. 1. A group of two or more syllables serving as a unit of meter in verse. 2. A measure of poetic rhythm. AI. The syllables that make up a foot have a specific placement as to accented and unaccented syllables, as dactyl, anapest, trochee and iambic. A foot in verse corresponds to a measure in music. PG. 3. The lowest part, bottom, as at the *foot* of a song sheet or music page, etc.

footnote

PG. One or more paragraphs of comment or reference at the bottom of a page, as on a song sheet, a page in a music book, album or folio. AI. The copyright notice of a song is usually in the form of a *footnote* on the title page. A *footnote* might be added to a song to explain unusual words in the lyric and give pronunciations, etc.

forefinger

MU. See INDEX FINGER.

foreign rights

LW. 1. The rights to which an American song or its American owner is entitled in a country, or countries, other than the United States. 2. The rights granted a song, or its owner, by an international copyright applying to all countries belonging to such conventions as the Universal Copyright Convention, the Berne Union and/or one or more of its four revisions, etc. 3. Rights granted by any country other than one's native land. See INTERNATIONAL COPYRIGHT.

foreign subpublishers

MB. Foreign publishers who act as subpublishers in their own country, or other foreign countries, for American publishers.

foreign work

LW. 1. The work of a writer who is neither a citizen nor a domiciliary of the United States and is first published outside the United States. 2. Likewise, the work of an American writer first published in the United States is a *foreign work* in Canada, England, Mexico, etc.

form

SW. 1. The particular way of being that gives something its nature or character, as the form of a song. 2. A certain combination of qualities that makes something what it is, as a song. 3. The shape or outline on which a song is constructed or written. 4. The shape or outline of a song itself. AI. A song has form just as a suit of clothes has form, as a building has form, etc. Both the words and music of a song must be constructed to form, as a suit is cut to a pattern, as a building is constructed to a plan. Words and music written without regard to plan are shapeless, meaningless, wasted things, because they have no form. By no means can such writing be called a song in the commercially acceptable sense of the word. See SONG FORM.

format

PP. 1. The shape, size, binding, type, paper and general make-up or arrangement of printed matter, or matter to be printed, as a song sheet, a song book, etc. MN. 2. An arrangement, as that of a song.

form E

LW. 1. Class E copyright application form. 2. The form used in applying for registration of a claim to copyright a published or unpublished musical composition, as a song, in the United States. AI. Class E forms may be had on request from the Register of Copyrights.

form I

LW. Canadian Copyright Rules state that application for registration of copyright in a published work shall be in Form I. The Canadian Copyright Office does not furnish printed forms. The following should be preserved to be copied as needed:

APPLICATION FOR REGISTRATION OF COPYRIGHT IN A PUBLISHED WORK

I, ...

150

of the .... of.....................
 (city, town, etc.)
in the .... of.....................
 (province, state)
.... hereby declare
 (country)
that I am the owner of the Copyright in the original
(here insert: literary, dramatic, musical or artistic as the case may be)
work entitled ".."
by .... of ....
 (author's name and address)
and that the said work was first published by the issue of copies
thereof to the public on the ....
day of .... 19...., in the .... of
 (city, town)
.... and I hereby request you
 (province, state, country)
to register the Copyright of the said work in my name in accordance
with the provisions of the Copyright Act.

I forward herewith the fee of $2 for the registration of the said
Copyright and the further fee of $1 for a certificate of such registra-
tion.

Dated at .... the day of .... 19.....
 Signature.................

The Commissioner of Patents,
The Copyright Office,
Ottawa, Canada.
See COPYRIGHT APPLICATION, CANADA

form K

LW. Canadian Copyright Rules state that application for registration of copyright in an unpublished work shall be in Form K. The·
Canadian Copyright Office does not supply printed forms. The following should be preserved to be copied as needed:

APPLICATION FOR REGISTRATION OF COPYRIGHT IN AN UNPUBLISHED
WORK

I, ... of the ....
 (city, town, etc.)
of .... hereby declare that I am
 (province, state, country)
the owner of the Copyright in the original *(here insert: literary, dra-*

151

matic, musical or artistic, as the case may be) work entitled "......
.................." by .... of ....
(author's name and address)
and that the said work has not been published, and I hereby request
you to register the Copyright of the said work in my name, in accordance with the provisions of the Copyright Act.

I forward herewith the fee of $2 for the registration of the said
Copyright, and the further fee of $1 for a certificate of such registra-
tion.

Dated at .... the day of .... 19.....

Signature...............

The Commissioner of Patents,
The Copyright Office,
Ottawa, Canada.
See COPYRIGHT APPLICATION, CANADA

form R

LW. 1. Class R copyright application form. 2. The form used to
apply for the renewal of a copyright, as that of a song, in the United
States. AI. Class R forms may be had on request from the Register
of Copyrights.

form 2976

LW. A small (1¾" x 2½") green label on which is shown the con-
tents, weight and value of a postal shipment which is being sent outside the United States, as songs which are sent to Canada for same-
day publication. AI. Form 2976 is used to clear customs and can be
had from any United States post office.

form U

LW. The form used in giving notice of use of copyrighted music
on mechanical instruments such as phonograph records in the United
States of America. AI. Printed copies of form U may be had on
request from the Register of Copyrights.

four: 4 or IV

MU. 1. The Arabic numeral used as the upper figure in the Four-
Four Time signature, designating four counts (beats) to the
measure. 2. The Arabic numeral used as the lower figure in the Two-
Four, the Three-Four and the Four-Four Time signatures, desig-

nating that the time value of each count is equal to that of a quarter note. 3. The Arabic numeral used to designate an interval of a fourth. 4. The Arabic numeral used to designate the fourth or little finger in the English method of fingering. 5. The Arabic numeral used to designate the third or ring finger in the German method of fingering. 6. The Roman numeral used to designate the fourth degree, or subdominant, in the diatonic scale.

four-bar myth, the

GI. The widespread but completely erroneous belief that a certain number of measures (usually "four bars") of a copyrighted song can be incuded in another song, or otherwise used, without the owner's permission and without penalty. AI. Nothing could be further from the truth. The copyright laws of the United States and other countries make no such provision. Anyone who willfully appropriates the work of another (regardless of extent or limitation) is guilty of infringement! As a songwriter might aptly say in a song title THAT'S WHY THEY BUILD JAILS.

four flats:

MU. The key signature of A major, as shown above.

Four-Four Time:

MU. 1. The time designated by either of the time signatures shown above. 2. The time which has four beats to the measure, with the time value of each beat equal to that of a quarter note.

four-fund system

MB. See SPREADING OF PAYMENTS.

four-lined octave

MU. The third octave, on the piano, above middle C. AI. Keys (tones) in this octave are designated c^4, d^4, e^4, etc.

four-part

MU. 1. Designating music or a song with four parts. 2. Music for four different instruments or voices playing or singing in harmony. 3. Designating a quartet. 4. Designating a popular form of harmony, as *SATB*. See MULTIPLE VOICE ARRANGEMENTS. See BARBERSHOP HARMONY.

153

four properties of a tone, the

MU. Every tone has (1) pitch, (2) duration, (3) intensity and (4) timbre.

four sharps:

MU. The key signature of E major, as shown above.

fourth

MU. 1. The interval between any note (tone) and the fourth note (tone) above it in the diatonic scale. 2. A note (tone) separated by this interval from any other note (tone). 3. The fourth degree in any diatonic scale. 4. The fourth note above the keynote. 5. The fourth tone above the keytone. 6. The subdominant. AI. For instance, in the scale of C major, the fourth degree is the tone of F.

fourth finger

MU. 1. The fourth finger from the thumb on either hand. 2. The *little finger*. 3. The finger designated by the numeral *4* in the English method of fingering. 4. The finger designated by the numeral *5* in the German method of fingering.

Fourth International Conference of American States

LW. See BUENOS AIRES CONVENTION.

fourth string

MU. 1. The D string on the Spanish guitar. 2. The A string on the ukulele (tuned A-D-F♯-B). 3. The C string on the five-string banjo (one octave below middle C).

four-track

RG. Designating a tape recording with four separated paths of sound, as distinguished from *single-track* tapes, *double-track* or *two-track* tapes, etc.

four-track-mona

RG. Short for *four-track-monaural*.

four-track-monaural

RG. Designating a method of recording (and playback) in which

154

four separate tracks are used on the same length of tape to record (and reproduce) sound from a single source. AI. For instance, track one is recorded and played in one direction. Track two is recorded and played in the opposite direction. Track three is recorded and played in the same direction as track one. Track four is recorded and played in the same direction as track two. This makes rewinding unnecessary. At the end of any track, the reels are merely exchanged on their spindles to continue with the next sound track, or to go from track four back to track one. A four-track-monaural tape has four times the capacity of a single-track tape of the same length and twice the capacity of a dual-track-monaural tape of the same length.

four-track-stereo

RG. Short for *four-track-stereophonic.*

four-track-stereophonic

RG. Designating a method of recording (and playback) in which four separate tracks are used on the same length of tape to record (and reproduce) sound from two different sources simultaneously. AI. For instance, track one and track two are recorded and played at the same time and in the same direction. On track one is recorded and played the sound from source one. On track two is recorded and played the sound from source two. Track three and track four are recorded and played at the same time and in the same direction, opposite that of tracks one and two. On track three is recorded and played the sound from source one. On track four is recorded and played the sound from source two. This makes rewinding unnecessary. At the end of each pair of tracks, the reels are merely exchanged on their spindles to continue with the next pair of tracks, or to go from tracks three and four back to tracks one and two. A four-track-stereophonic tape has twice the capacity of a two-track-stereophonic tape of the same length.

Fox, Harry

MB. See HARRY FOX OFFICE, THE

fox trot

MU. 1. A dance in Two-Four Time or Four-Four Time with a variety of steps, both fast and slow. 2. Syncopated music for such a dance. AI. The fox trot is so called because it is said to have been originated by a dancing teacher named Earnest Fox. Typical fox

trots are (slow) AS TIME GOES BY and AMONG MY SOUVE-
NIRS, (medium) CRAZY RHYTHM and AIN'T MISBEHAVIN',
(fast) BEYOND THE BLUE HORIZON and YOU WERE
MEANT FOR ME.

frame

SW. v. To shape, pattern, construct, conceive or compose, according to plan, as a song.

frame

SW. n. Framework.

framework

SW. 1. The basic structure, arrangement of parts or system on which
something is constructed, as a song. 2. Form.

free

MU. Unrestrained by strict rules.

freebie

MB. 1. A free record. 2. A record given as a bonus or sales incentive.
AI. For instance, record distributors might be offered a merchandising deal, by a record company, whereby they are given so many free
records with every 100 records they buy at the regular distributor's
price. These free records are called *freebies*.

freehand

SW. Drawn, sketched or written by hand, as disinguished from
printed. AI. For instance, a music manuscript is done (written)
freehand. A song sheet or song book (if typeset or engraved) is
printed. Below is shown (a) the printed version and (b and c) the
freehand versions of the same character, a quarter rest:

$$\text{(a)} \quad \text{(b)} \quad \text{(c)}$$

free-lance

MB. v. To act as a free lance.

free lance

MB. n. 1. A songwriter who is not under exclusive contract and is

156

free to offer his song to anyone he chooses. AI. The opposite of staff writer. 3. A singer, performer, etc. who is free to offer his services to anyone he chooses.

free music

MB. Music in public domain, for which no performance fees are charged.

freeola (free-o'la)

MB. 1. Anything that is free. 2. A freebie. See FREEBIE.

free pitch

MU. The pitch of such instruments as the guitar, violin, banjo, etc. in which the individual tones can be altered by the performer, as compared with *fixed pitch*.

free ride

MB. Said of an unknown song that is on the same phonograph record with a hit. AI. Because the unknown song (on the B side) earns, for its writer and publishers, royalties in proportion to the hit, for all records sold, it is said to be getting a *free ride*. See HITCHHIKER.

free verse

PY. Verse characterized by much rhythmic variation, irregular or unusual forms, and either no rhyme or a loose rhyme pattern. Also called *vers libre*.

frequency

SE. 1. The number of vibrations, as those of a string on a stringed instrument, per second. AI. For instance, the standard of pitch in the United States gives the tone a^1 (the A above middle C) a *frequency* of 440 vibrations per second. 2. The number of cycles, as those of a broadcasting station, per second. AI. For instance, radio station WOR broadcasts on a frequency of 710 kilocycles, WMAQ on a frequency of 670 kilocycles, KGO on a frequency of 810 kilocycles, etc.

frequency modulation

BD. A static-free method of broadcasting that is more faithful in the reproduction of sound than is the more commonly-used method of *amplitude modulation*, or A.M. AI. Abbreviated, *F.M.*

fret

MU. A ridge of wood, metal, ivory or other material across the fingerboard of a guitar, banjo, mandolin or other similar stringed instrument to regulate the fingering. See FRET NUMBERS.

fret numbers:

MU. The numbers by which the frets on a fretted instrument are known. AI. The fret nearest the nut is always the first fret, the next is the second fret, the next is the third fret, etc. The fingering for an E♭7 chord on the guitar, as shown by the above guitar diagram, is designated as follows: *fourth string-first fret, second string-second fret, first string-third fret, third string-fourth fret.* The sixth string and the fifth string shown above are *unfretted* or *open* strings. See STRING NUMBERS.

fretted instrument

MU. Any musical instrument constructed with frets, as the guitar, ukulele, banjo, mandolin, etc.

front

MU. v. 1. To lead or act as the leader of a band. SB. 2. To act as a representative or business agent for a theatrical organization or theatrical personality.

front

MN. n. 1. A band leader or one who acts as a band leader. SB. 2. A person who serves as a public representative, usually for a theatrical organization or for a theatrical personality. 3. A public-relations or publicity man.

front cover

PP. The first, outside cover, as that of a song, a song book, etc., as distinguished from inside-front cover, inside-back cover and back cover.

front man

MN. 1. Orchestra leader. BS. 2. Anyone who acts as a representative

158

for a person or organization, as a business manager.

front title

SW. A song title which is placed at the very beginning of the chorus. AI. Also called on-the-nose title. Typical front titles are ONCE IN A WHILE, NIGHT AND DAY and TELL ME WHY.

F sharp: F♯

MU. 1. The same tone on the piano as G FLAT. 2. The second string on the ukulele (tuned A-D-F♯-B). See G FLAT.

full

MU. 1. Having clearness, volume and depth, as a *full tone*. 2. Filling the required number, as a *full orchestra*. 3. Having complete volume, as a *full organ*.

full title

MB. 1. The complete title of a song, including both main title and subtitle. LW. 2. Unshared ownership, undivided ownership, as that of a song.

full track

RG. Same as *monaural*.

fundamental

MU. a. 1. Designating the lowest in pitch, as the root of a chord. 2. Designating the harmonic part consisting of the root tone of chords, as the *fundamental bass*.

fundamental

MU. n. 1. The lowest tone in a chord. 2. The root of a chord. 3. The tone on which a chord is built. AI. For instance, the tone of C is the fundamental of the chord C-E-G. The tone of F is the fundamental of the chord F-A-C, etc.

fundamental tones

MU. 1. The first, fourth and fifth tones of any scale or key. 2. The tonic, subdominant and dominant. AI. Expressed in Roman numerals, these are: I, IV and V. Transposed to the key of C, these are: C, F and G. 3. Root tones. See ROOT TONES.

fundamental triad

MU. A triad to which a tone or tones are added to build another chord. AI. For instance, the triad of C major (C-E-G) is the fundamental of the chord Cmaj7 (C-E-G-B), etc. The triad of C major is also the fundamental of the chord C6 (C-E-G-A), etc.

funky

RM. 1. In the groove or solid. 2. Basic. 3. Earthy. 4. Traditionally authentic. 5. Played or sung with deep feeling, usually of a melancholic nature. 6. Of true Negro style and/or origin. 7. Dirty.

fusion

SW. 1. The act of blending. 2. The state of being blended throughout. AI. The lyric and melody of a song are said to have *fusion* when they blend well together. A lyric and melody that do not blend are said not to have *fusion*, etc. One of the greatest all-time examples of fusion is the MUSIC GOES ROUND AND ROUND. Where the lyric says *up*, the melody goes *up*. Where the lyric says *down*, the melody goes *down*. Throughout the song the melody gives the feeling of winding its way 'round and 'round through a horn, just as the lyric describes. Other examples of excellent fusion are the titles listed under jazz songs. For jazz lyrics are not the easiest to fuse. One of the most outstanding of these is Johnny Mercer's G.I. JIVE.

g

G

MU. The seventh letter in the musical alphabet representing a pitch a whole tone higher than F and a whole tone lower than A. 2. The letter applied to any octave above or below this pitch. 3. The fifth tone, note or degree in the ascending major scale of C. 4. The major key that has one sharp in its key signature. 5. The caption for a G major triad. 6. The key or string of a musical instrument that produces the tone of G. 7. The third string on the Spanish guitar. 8. The name of the treble clef, as G clef.

G♭

MU. See G FLAT.

gag

SB. 1. A joke, especially one with an unexpected turn or twist. 2. A brief, humorous story or saying.

gag line

SB. 1. A humorous sentence or phrase climaxing a gag. 2. The pay-off. 3. The line ending a gag. AI. Gag lines often are used in songs such as I HAD SOMEONE ELSE BEFORE I HAD YOU.

gag man

SB. A gag writer.

gag writer

SB. 1. A writer of gags. 2. A writer who specializes in comedy material. 3. One who writes material for comedians.

gain

SN. An increase in volume from one stage to another in an amplifying system, usually expressed in decibels.

galop (gal'uhp)

MU. 1. A rapid and lively dance in Two-Four Time. 2. The music for this dance.

gas

SB. Short for *gasser*.

gaslight

SB. 1. Of or characteristic of the period of gaslight illumination, as a gaslight song, gaslight piano, gaslight melodrama, gaslight performance, etc. 2. A style of performance identified with the gaslight era. 3. Overly emotional. AI. Typical gaslight songs are: MY MOTHER WAS A LADY, SHE IS MORE TO BE PITIED THAN CENSURED, IF JACK WERE ONLY HERE and HEAVEN WILL PROTECT THE WORKING GIRL.

gasser

SB. 1. A success, as a song hit. 2. A big producer of money. AI. Same as *oiler*.

gate

MU. 1. A musician who swings. 2. A fan of swing music. 3. One particularly knowledgeful of and/or adept at swing music. AI. The word *gate* is a complimentary designation. SB. 3. The entranceway, as to an outdoor performance. 4. Therefore, the number of customers attending such a performance. AI. It might be said that a certain show had a *good gate* meaning that it had a large attendance. See BOX OFFICE.

gay nineties

MB. The period between 1890 and 1900, a notable era in songwriting and music publishing. AI. Typical of the many big song hits of the Gay 90's are: AFTER THE BALL, SHE MAY HAVE SEEN BETTER DAYS and THE PICTURE TURNED TOWARD THE WALL.

G clef:

MU. 1. The character shown above. 2. The treble clef. AI. The G clef, when properly positioned, spirals around the second line of the staff. This means that any note written on this second line is called G and designates the tone of one-lined G (g¹), the next G above middle C.

generosity error

PS. 1. The error of rating acquaintances more favorably than strangers. 2. The error of rating the accomplishments and works of acquaintances more favorably than that of strangers. AI. Songwriters, like all other creative people, are in constant danger of accepting and believing the unjustified praise of equally unqualified relatives and friends, unless liberal allowances are made for the *generosity error*. This is an ever-present occupational hazard.

get off

MN. To solo, especially in an emotional, arousing manner.

get-off man

MN. A soloist, especially an instrumentalist featured as such.

get over dirty

MN. A jazz-musical phrase consisting of a two-measure lick, similar to *shave and a hair cut* and *over the fence is out.*

G flat: G♭

MU. 1. The symbol shown above. 2. The tone on the piano that is one half step below the tone of G. 3. The same tone on the piano as F SHARP. 4. The major key that has six flats in its key signature. 5. The caption for a G FLAT major triad.

G flat major scale

MU. The scale consisting of these eight notes or tones: G♭, A♭,

B♭, C♭, D♭, E♭, F, G♭. Also called the *key of G♭*. See KEY SIGNATURE.

ghost singer

MP. A singer whose voice is used for that of someone else, as in a motion picture.

ghost writer

WG. A writer, as a songwriter, who writes for another who professes to be the author.

gibberish song (jib′er-ish)

SW. A song with a lyric wholly or partially composed of incoherent syllables, usually written to be performed at a rapid tempo. AI. Typical gibberish songs are: the HUT-SUT SONG, MAIRZY DOATS, CHICKERY CHICK and THE WITCH DOCTOR.

gig

MN. 1. A date worked by a musician or singer. 2. A paid-for performance by a musician or singer. AI. For instance, a musician might say that he is *booked to work a gig* next Tuesday or that he has a *gig coming up* in Tulsa, etc.

gimmick (gim′ik)

SB. 1. Any effect or device designed or used to attract attention, as a manner of singing or playing, individualized gestures, distinctive wearing apparel, etc. 2. An attention-getting device. GI. For instance, Skitch Henderson and Al Hirt wear beards as gimmicks. Groucho Marx and George Burns use cigars, etc. 3. Among magicians the word is used to mean a trick device that is concealed from the audience. 4. Anything that tricks or mystifies.

girl in the song, the

MB. The central character in a song concerning a girl. AI. For instance, the girl who wore the sweet little ALICE BLUE GOWN, the girl who says MY HEART BELONGS TO DADDY, the girl with the BLUE EYES CRYING IN THE RAIN, the girl called SWEET GEORGIA BROWN and THE GIRL FROM IPANEMA.

girl lyric

MU. 1. A lyric written to be sung by a female singer. 2. A Susie song. See GIRL SONG.

girl-name song

SW. A classification in songwriting as to title. AI. Typical girl-name songs are: CHLOE, MY DIANNE, MARGIE, SWEET SUE and GIGI.

girl song

MU. A song with a girl lyric. AI. Typical girl songs are: DADDY, TEN CENTS A DANCE, IT'S SO NICE TO HAVE A MAN AROUND THE HOUSE, HE'S MY GUY and I ENJOY BEING A GIRL.

gitfiddle

FK. A guitar.

glee

MU. A song for three or more solo voices, usually without accompaniment. AI. The word *glee* is not properly descriptive of its nature, as there can be serious glees as well as merry glees.

glee club

MU. A group of singers organized to sing glees.

glossy

PH. 1. A photograph that has a shiny surface, as distinguished from a photograph with a matte or dull finish. 2. Usually, an 8″ x 10″ high-finished photograph, as that used by singers and other performers for theater lobby displays and other publicity purposes. AI. Also called a *professional*, a *professional photo* or an *eight-by-ten*.

G major scale

MU. The scale consisting of these eight notes or tones: G, A, B, C, D, E, F♯, G. Also called the *key of G*. See KEY SIGNATURE.

Godward

MB. 1. Toward God, as said of a hymn, as distinguished from *man-*

ward. 2. With reference or in relation to God. Compare with MANWARD.

golden age

MB. The period, roughly, from 1894 to 1926. Also called *golden days.* AI. The golden age is so called because of the growth and enormous popularity of the popular song that took place during this period. It was in the *golden age* that many of the leading music publishers came into being and many great songwriters established their immortal names.

golden seventeen, the:

SW. 1. The section of the piano keyboard shown above. 2. The seventeen tones between c^1 (middle C) and e^2 (E an octave above E above middle C). AI. So called because it is in this range of seventeen tones that 99% of all popular songs are written.

gold record

MB. A phonograph record supposedly made of gold, usually gold plated or simulated to resemble gold. AI. It is customary in the phonograph record business to give gold records as awards, to recording artists, songwriters, music publishers, etc., when the sale of a recording reaches a certain high point, as a million copies, a half million copies, etc.

gong

MU. A percussion instrument of Chinese origin, consisting of a large bronze or brass disk, resembling a shallow plate. It is suspended to hang freely and is struck with a bass-drum beater. Also called *tam-tam.*

good gopher

MN. 1. A highly skilled musician, particularly one in the jazz field. 2. A capable performer.

go song

MB. A rhythm song, usually played or sung at a lively tempo. AI. Typical go songs are JEEPERS CREEPERS, DINAH, RICOCHET and the GIRL FRIEND.

166

gospel song

MU. 1. A musical composition written in the form of a personal experience or testimony, with text matter founded on the teachings of the first four books of the New Testament, ascribed to Matthew, Mark, Luke and John. 2. A song written *about* God, as distinguished from a hymn, which is written *to* God. 3. A song written from a *manward* point of view, as distinguished from a song written from a *Godward* point of view. AI. There are two general classifications of gospel songs. These are *inspirational* and *southern-style*. See POPULAR-GOSPEL SONGS.

gospel song, inspirational

MB. A gospel song that lends itself to a smooth, close-harmony performance in moderately slow tempo, as distinguished from a southern-style gospel song. AI. Typical inspirational gospel songs are EACH STEP I TAKE, LONELY ROAD UP CALVARY'S WAY and SOMEONE TO CARE.

gospel song, southern-style

MB. A gospel song that lends itself to a harmony performance in vigorous hand-clapping, foot-stomping rhythm as distinguished from inspirational style. AI. Typical southern-style gospel songs are NEARER TO THEE, SITTIN' AROUND THE TABLE (Of My Lord) and I WAS THERE WHEN IT HAPPENED.

go tune

MB. Same as *go song*. AI. The term *go tune* is applied to either a song or an instrumental composition.

G. P.

MU. Abbreviation, used in orchestral scores meaning *general pause*— a rest for the whole orchestra.

grammy

MB. Any of the statuettes, in the form of miniature gramophones, awarded annually in the United States, by the National Academy of Recording Arts and Sciences, for outstanding contributions to the recording industry.

167

gramophone

MB. 1. The trade-mark for an early phonograph. 2. A phonograph, especially an early model.

grand

MU. a. Full, compete, as a *grand chorus.*

grand

MU. n. 1. A grand piano, as distinguished from a *baby grand* and *concert grand.*

Grand Ole Opry

CM. The greatest of all country-music shows, presented each Friday and Saturday night at The Grand Ole Opry House, 116 Opry Place, Nashville, Tennessee. The *Opry* is the oldest show of its kind and attracts world-wide interest.

grand opera

MU. Opera, generally of a serious theme, in which the entire text is set to music, as distinguished from operetta, light opera and comic opera.

grand piano

MU. A large, flat-type, harp-shaped piano with three legs, in which the strings and soundboard are placed horizontally, as distinguished from an *upright.* AI. The rich *voice* of a grand piano is due to each of its tones being produced by three or more strings. See PIANO-FORTE.

grand rights

TE. See DRAMATIC RIGHTS.

great barrer

MU. See BARRER, GREAT.

great octave

MU. The second octave, on the piano, below middle C. AI. Keys (tones) in this octave are designated C, D, E, etc.

168

great staff

MU. 1. The staff shown at the right. 2. Both treble and bass staves joined by a brace, with space between for middle C. AI. Also called the *grand staff*:

green room

TE. An off-stage waiting room, or reception room, provided by some theaters for the use of performers between performances.

green sticker

LW. See FORM 2976.

groove

RG. 1. A spiraling furrow cut or modeled in the surface of a phonograph in which sound is recorded. 2. The path, on a phonograph record, followed by the needle.

groovy

JZ. 1. Designating a smooth, highly skilled performance, particularly that of jazz music. 2. In the groove.

group

MU. 1. Several short notes tied together. 2. A section of an orchestra or band including instruments of one kind or class, as *string group*, *wood wind group*, *brass group*, etc. MB. 3. A number of musicians and/or singers, as a trio, quartet, chorus, glee club, etc. 4. A combo. 5. Any number of persons gathered closely together and forming a recognized unit, as the employees of a music publisher, the personnel of a record company, etc. 6. Any organization, as AFM, ASCAP, CMA, etc.

G sharp: G♯

MU. 1. The symbol shown above. 2. The tone on the piano that is one half step above the tone of G. 3. The same tone on the piano as the tone of A FLAT.

guitar

MU. A stringed instrument of the lute family, with a fretted keyboard, which is played by plucking or stroking the strings. AI. The

169

two most popular kinds of guitars are the Spanish guitar and the Hawaiian, or steel, guitar. Others are Tenor guitar (tipple), Bass guitar, Rhythm guitar, Electric guitar and Special guitar.

guitar diagram:

MU. 1. A diagram like that above. 2. A diagram showing the fingering of a chord on the (6-string) Spanish guitar. AI. Guitar diagrams are included in the printed copies of many songs and appear just above the melody line on the song sheet. These are added by arrangers who are employed by music publishers and need be no concern of the songwriter.

guitarist

MU. One who plays the guitar.

guitar tuner

MU. A series of six connected pitch pipes whose tones are E-A-d-g-b-e^1, respectively, used to tune a Spanish guitar.

h

H

MU. The capital letter used to designate the word *hand*, as in *RH* (right hand) and *LH* (left hand).

habit

MB. Popular, as a song. AI. To become a habit means to become popular.

hack

MB. v. 1. To write, as a song. 2. To play, as a song. AI. For instance, a songwriter might say he *hacked out* a song, meaning he *wrote* a song. An orchestra leader might say *let's hack it out in the key of G*, meaning *let's play it in the key of G*. WG. 3. To work as a hack writer.

hack

WG. n. Short for *hack writer*.

hackneyed

WG. 1. Made commonplace by frequent use. 2. Overly used. 3. Worn out. AI. For instance, the words *moon, spoon* and *June* are hackneyed song rhymes.

hack writer

WG. 1. A second rate writer. 2. A second rate songwriter. Also called *hack*.

half note: ♩ or ♩

MU. 1. Either of the notes shown above. 2. A note with an outlined, open head attached to a stem, either up or down. AI. A half note represents a time value one half that of a whole note.

half rest: ▬

MU. 1. The rest shown above. 2. A rest in the shape of a solid rectangle that sits on (above) the third line of the staff or on (above) a leger line. AI. A half rest represents a time value of half that of a whole rest. The time value of a half rest is equal to that of a half note.

half step

MU. 1. Half of a whole step, half of a whole tone. 2. The regular chromatic step. 3. A semitone. 4. A half tone. AI. A half step is the smallest interval in the diatonic scale. See DEGREE.

half, the

MN. 1. The beginning of the bridge in a song. 2. The half-way point in a song. AI. For instance, an orchestra leader might say, "Let's go back to the half," meaning *Let's go back to the bridge* or *release.*

half tone

MU. 1. Half of a whole note. 2. A half step. See HALF STEP. PG. 3. A technique of representing shadings by dots produced by photographing an object from behind a fine screen. 4. A photoengraving so made, as that used on the covers of some sheet music and song books.

half-track monaural (haff-trak mon-au'ral)

RG. 1. A method of pickup. 2. A method of recording and sound reproduction. AI. The same as dual track. See DUAL TRACK.

half-track stereophonic

RG. 1. A method of pickup. 2. A method of recording and sound reproduction. AI. The same as two-track stereophonic. See TWO-TRACK STEREOPHONIC.

half-turned v

MU. Same as v-on-its-side. See V-ON-ITS-SIDE.

172

ham

TE. 1. An incompetent actor or performer, especially one who over-acts. 2. A show-off.

ham and egger

SB. 1. A mediocre songwriter, singer or performer. 2. One who writes or performs with little or no feeling. 3. A hack.

ham bone

TE. Ham.

hamburger

MB. A poor melody, especially one that does not move or flow smoothly. AI. The expression comes from such a tune having a *chopped up* effect.

hand

SB. Applause. AI. As, they gave the singer a big *hand*.

hand cue

BR. A signal by a motion of the hand to impart certain information, as to singers, musicians, etc. AI. Hand cues are *thrown* (given) by A and R directors, sound engineers, band leaders, etc. For instance, a downward stroke of the pointed index finger usually means *begin* singing or playing. A clenched fist held at head level usually means *stop at first logical ending*, etc. Hand cues and their meanings vary as to locality.

hand-me-down

MB. A song, melody or lyric supplied by a song shark or by a song mill.

hard

MU. Coarse, rough, harsh, cold, unsympathetic, lacking in feeling, as said of tones or performance.

harmonica (har-mahn´e-kah)

MU. Any one of several musical instruments: 1. A small reed instru-ment, usually called a *mouth harmonica*, which is played by blowing and sucking the air through its reed holes. AI. Also called a *mouth harp*. 2. A xylophone-like instrument with bars of glass. 3. A set of musical drinking glasses tuned to a scale and played by rubbing their edges with the finger tips.

harmonize

MU. 1. To sing, or play in harmony. 2. To add chords to (a melody) so as to form a harmony.

Harmonizer, the

SA. The official publication of the SPEBSQSA. Published at Harmony Hall, 6315 Third Avenue, Kenosha, Wisconsin 53141.

harmony

MU. 1. The combination of two or more tones that are pleasing when sounded together. 2. The performance of two or more agreeable tones at the same time. 3. Concord. AI. Harmony is the Greek word for *system*. Hence, the art of combining tones systematically, according to established rules and patterns.

harmony accuracy

SA. The condition resulting when the tones of a chord are sung in proper pitch, each bearing the correct relationship to the others, as used in the SPEBSQSA style of barbershop singing. AI. When harmony accuracy is achieved, the chord is said to *ring*.

harmony progression

MU. A chord progression. See CHORD PROGRESSION.

harp

MU. 1. A musical instrument with strings which are stretched across an open, nearly-triangular frame, played by being plucked with the fingers. AI. The modern harp has 46 strings and a series of foot pedals which permit the playing of half tones. 2. A mouth harp. 3. A jew's harp. See HARMONICA. See JEW'S HARP.

harpsichord (harp'se-kord)

MU. A keyboard stringed instrument, resembling the piano (in fact, the harpsichord was the forerunner of the piano), the strings being plucked by quills or leather-tipped points fastened to pieces of

174

wood manipulated from the keyboard. GI. The harpsichord has been an effective background instrument for a number of popular recordings, as those of Rosemary Clooney and Lawrence Welk.

Harry Fox Office, The

MB. An organization established by the Music Publishers Protective Association (MPPA) to act as agent-trustee in administering mechanical licenses on their behalf and on behalf of other, non-member publishers who wish to subscribe to this particular service on a fee basis. Address: 460 Park Avenue, New York, N. Y.

Hawaiian guitar

MU. A six-string guitar originally made of Koa wood which is usually held in the lap and its strings stopped with a steel bar held in the left hand while being plucked with picks worn on the thumb and two or three fingers of the right hand. AI. The Hawaiian guitar is usually tuned E-A-e-a-c♯-e¹. Also called *steel guitar*.

head

MU. 1. Notehead. 2. That part of a note, usually oval in shape, which determines its place on the staff. AI. Noteheads were formerly square and diamond shaped. Music written in shaped-note form uses eight different notehead designs. 3. The membrane stretched over a drum, banjo or tambourine. 4. A drumhead. AI. Also called *skin*. 5. That part of a stringed instrument, as a guitar, violin, banjo, etc., at the end of the neck opposite the body, containing the machine head, pegs or keys. 6. The machine head of a guitar or similar instrument. PG. 7. The title of a song at the top or *head* of a printed song sheet or page. 8. The top of a song sheet or song page. 9. A printed heading.

head arrangement

MU. 1. A memorized arrangement that has been made extemporaneously. 2. An offhand arrangement that exists only in the mind. 3. An informally created arrangement that has never been put into writing (notation).

heading

PG. The inscription at the top of a song sheet or song page giving the title, subtitle (if any) and credits.

175

Helicon (hel'e-kahn″)

MY. 1. A mountain in southern Greece, regarded by the ancient Greeks as the home of the muses. AI. It was here, they thought, that the creative impulses of poets and songwriters originated. MU. 2. A tuba designed to encircle the body and rest on the left shoulder, thus making it easier to transport in marching bands. AI. The most modern designed helicon is called the *Sousaphone*.

herd, the

MN. Facetiously, any group of musicians, as a band, an orchestra, etc. AI. Also called the *thundering herd*.

hi-fi

RG. Short for *high fidelity*.

high

MU. 1. Extending upward, as pitch, notes, tones, etc. 2. Loud, as the volume of sound. MB. 3. To be impressed by something, to be enthusiastic about something, to like something. AI. For instance, a publisher might be said to be *high* on a certain song, meaning he is impressed by it, etc.

high fidelity

RG. 1. Exceptional trueness of reproduced sound. 2. Highest quality of reproduced sound. AI. Often abbreviated *hi-fi*.

High Fidelity

MB. A magazine for music listeners. Published monthly. Address: The Publishing House, Great Barrington, Massachusetts 01230.

hillbilly

MB. a. Of or characeristic of hillbillies, as *hillbilly* songs, *hillbilly* music, *hillbilly* performance, etc. AI. The word *hillbilly* is sometimes used as a somewhat contemptuous term and is not to be confused with *country*, *hill* or *mountain* in designating songs, music, performance, etc.

hillbilly

MB. n. 1. A person who lives in or comes from the mountains or

176

backwoods, especially those of the South. 2. Usually, a burlesqued characterization of such a person. 3. A rustic clown. 4. A Toby.

hill folk

MB. 1. People who live in or come from the hills or mountains, especially those of the South. 2. Residents, usually of the Appalachian, Cumberland, Ozark and Smoky Mountains. AI. A more respectful term than *hillbilly*.

hill music

MU. 1. The music and songs of hill folk, in particular those of the Appalachian, Cumberland, Ozark and Smoky Mountains. 2. The true folk music of the hills. 3. Mountain music. AI. Many hill songs are authentic Old English folk songs that have been preserved over the years in the purity, or almost in the purity, of their original forms. Not to be confused with *hillbilly* songs or music. Typical hill songs are THE TWO SISTERS, BARBARA ALLEN and SOURWOOD MOUNTAIN.

hill song

MU. A song of the hills. See HILL MUSIC.

Hindu music

MU. The music of India.

hippie

MB. 1. Anyone who operates, or attempts to operate, a business without an office or desk space, as a would-be music publisher, a would-be performers' agent, etc. AI. The term comes from it being said that such individuals operate out of their *hip pocket*. 2. A *sidewalk operator*. 3. A *curbstone operator*.

hire, works made for

LW. See WORKS MADE FOR HIRE.

hit

MB. 1. A song that sells a million or more phonograph records. 2. A song that is played 10,000 or more times on radio and/or television during its introductory period. 3. A song for which its writer, writers and/or publisher has been awarded a gold record. 4. A gold-record song. 5. Formerly, a song that sold a million or more copies of sheet music. AI. The word *hit* is often used loosely and erroneously to mean any song that enjoys better than average popularity. Many songs that are claimed to be hits fall far short of meeting the necessary requirements. Also called *smash* and *smash hit.*

hitch

MB. Short for *hitchhike* or *hitchhiker.*

hitchhike

MB. A free ride, as that given a song. See FREE RIDE.

hitchhiker

MB. A song that is given a free ride.

hoedown

MU. 1. A lively, rollicking dance, often a square dance. 2. The music for this dance. 3. A party at which hoedowns are danced.

hold

MU. v. To go on sounding (a tone).

hold

MU. n. 1. A pause. 2. A rest. See FERMATA.

holding note

MU. A note that is held (prolonged) while others are in motion.

holding tone

MU. The tone designated by a holding note.

hold over

SB. 1. To extend a booking beyond the original contract. AI. For instance, a performer is engaged to play a theater for two weeks and is then *held over* for a third week.

holidays, legal, Canada

LW. See LEGAL HOLIDAYS.

holidays, legal, United States

LW. See LEGAL HOLIDAYS.

Hollywood

SB. a. 1. Lavish, garish, in the manner of Hollywood. 2. Spectacular. 3. Overly done.

Hollywood

SB. n. 1. A section of Los Angeles, California, regarded as the center of the American motion picture industry, hence: 2. The American motion picture industry, its life, world, etc.

Hollywood song

MB. 1. A song from a motion picture. 2. A song of the kind used in motion pictures. 3. A song written in Hollywood, usually for the motion picture industry.

home songs

MB. 1. A classification in songwriting as to subject matter. AI. Typical home songs are BACK HOME AGAIN IN INDIANA, MY LITTLE GRASS SHACK, SHANTY IN OLD SHANTY TOWN and ISLAND IN THE SUN. 2. Also, songs suitable to being sung and played in the home.

homonym (hahm′a-nim″)

RC. A word with the same pronunciation as another but with a different meaning and, usually, a different spelling. AI. Typical homonyms are *dear* and *deer, one* and *won, vale* and *veil*, etc.

homophonic (hom″a-fahn′ek)

MU. 1. Having a single voice carrying the melody. 2. Formerly, sounding alike, having the same pitch, in unison. AI. The opposite of *polyphonic*.

homophony (ho-mahf′a-nee)

MU. 1. Music in which a single voice carries the melody, often with an accompaniment in chords, as in a lead sheet. 2. Formerly, unison, or music written, sung or played in unison. AI. The opposite of *polyphony*.

179

hone-ya-da (hoh'nae-yah-dah)

MN. Designating a musician or group of musicians who cannot read music as a *hone-ya-da man*, or *hone-ya-da band*. AI. When TIGER RAG was first *written* by the Original Dixie Land Band, only one of its five members could read music. As the composition was first written as an instrumental (words were not added until years later), it was necessary to create a set of dummy lyrics by which the band learned to play and remember the number. The phrase that was later replaced by the words *hold that tiger* was *hone-ya-da*. The designation is by no means derogatory. In fact, it is often used to imply a degree of musical proficiency, particularly in the jazz field.

honky-tonk

RC. a. 1. Showy without elegance. 2. Gaudy, garish, tawdry. 3. Typical of a honky-tonk establishment, as its music, songs and manner of performance. 4. Honky-tonk style.

honky-tonk

RC. n. 1. A cheap, disreputable saloon, usually one that furnishes musical entertainment. 2. A cabaret. 3. A juke joint. 4. A barrel house.

hoof

SB. To dance, usually to tap dance professionally.

hoofer

SB. A dancer, usually a professional tap dancer, male or female.

hook

MU. 1. A flag. 2. A pennant. See FLAG.

hook up

ET. v. 1. To make an electrical connection, as for broadcasting, recording, etc. MB. 2. To become connected or associated with. AI. For instance, it might be said that a songwriter *hooked up* with a certain music publisher, etc.

hook up

ET. n. 1. The arrangement and connection of parts, circuits, etc. in radio recordings, etc. MB. 2. A business connection or association. AI. For instance, it might be said that a music publisher has a *hook up* with a certain record company, etc.

hoot

MB. Short for *hootenanny*.

hootenanny

MB. 1. A gathering of folk singers and folk musicians to sing and play folk songs. 2. A performance of folk songs and music. AI. Originally, *Hootin' Annie*.

hop

MB. 1. Generally, a gathering for the purpose of dancing, as a fraternity hop. 2. Especially, an informal gathering for dancing, usually to phonograph records, as a sock hop.

hope box

SW. 1. An indexed card file of ideas for songs and song writing, kept by some songwriters. 2. A book of ideas kept for the same purpose. AI. Also called *hope book*.

horizontal

MU. Parallel to the plane of the horizon. AI. For instance, the lines that make up the music staff are *horizontal* lines, as distinguished from the *vertical* lines used for bars.

horizontally

MU. In a horizontal manner or direction. AI. For instance, music is written and read in two ways: *horizontally* and *vertically*. A melody is written and read horizontally, from left to right, one note after another. Compare with VERTICALLY.

horn

MU. 1. A metal wind instrument with a long tube bent upon itself and ending in a flare, called a bell. AI. Typical horns are the cornet, trombone, tuba, etc. Incidentally, the English horn is not a horn, nor is it English. MB. 2. One who plays a horn. AI. For instance, it might be said that he is a good *horn*, or that he is the first *horn* in a combo, etc.

hornpipe

MU. 1. An obsolete wind instrument with a bell and mouthpiece made of horn. 2. A lively English dance, formerly performed to the music of the hornpipe, usually by sailors. 3. The music for this dance.

host

SB. 1. Master of ceremonies. 2. Sponsor of a radio or television program.

hot

MU. 1. Designating or of playing jazz characterized by exciting rhythmic and tonal effects, imaginative improvisation and, often, a fast, driving tempo. 2. A fast, unrestrained and intense style of jazz performance, called hot jazz. AI. The term comes from the expression to *burn 'em up*, the result of speed. Among the many truly great performers who popularized hot jazz are Adrian Rollini (vibes), Jelly Roll Morton (piano), and Louis (Satchmo) Armstrong (trumpet).

hot cat

MB. 1. A musician who plays hot jazz. 2. A devotee of hot jazz. See CAT.

hot property

MB. 1. An artist, as a singer, a song, a phonograph record, etc., that is in big demand. 2. A song or any part of a song that has been bought from a song shark or music foundry. 3. A song or any part of a song that has been stolen.

hound-dog guitar

CM. A style of guitar playing that imitates the baying of hunting hounds. AI. Used in Folk and Country music.

house

SB. 1. A theater. 2. The audience in a theater. 3. Loosely used to mean the audience for any performance, in a theater or otherwise.

house band

TE. A pit band or orchestra, as distinguished from *stage band*.

182

house orchestra

TE. Same as *house band*.

hybrid chord

MU. A special chord. See SPECIAL CHORD.

hybrid instrument

MU. Any musical instrument, usually custom made, that combines the features of two or more other musical instruments. AI. For instance, the banjo-ukulele, the slide (trombone) cornet, the mandolin-guitar, etc.

hymn

MU. 1. A song in praise of God, a song in honor of God, usually sung by a congregation or choir. 2. A song written *to* God, as distinguished from a gospel song, which is written *about* God. 3. A song of glorification. 4. A national song of lofty character, as the MARSEILLAISE.

hymnal

MU. 1. A book of hymns. 2. A collection of hymns. 3. A hymnbook.

hymnal arrangement

MU. 1. An arrangement in the style of a hymn. 2. A two-staff, or two-stave arrangement. See TWO-STAFF ARRANGEMENT.

hymnist

MU. A composer of hymns.

hymnodist (hihm′na-dist)

MU. An expert in hymnody.

hymnody (hihm′na-dee)

MU. 1. The study of hymns, their history, use, etc. 2. The singing of hymns. 3. Hymns collectively.

hymnologist (hihm-nal′a-j′st)

MU. 1. A person who composes hymns, usually an expert. 2. An expert in hymnology. AI. The term *hymnologist* is used to imply a greater degree of proficiency and know-how than does *hymnist*.

183

hymnology (hihm-nal'a-jee)

MU. 1. The study of hymns, the writing or composition of hymns, the technique of hymnal writing, the history of hymns, the use of hymns, etc. 2. Hymns collectively. AI. The term *hymnology* usually is used to imply a deeper study of hymns and the writing of hymns than does *hymnody*.

hymn tune

MU. 1. The melody or air of a hymn. 2. Loosely, a hymn. AI. For instance, typical of well-known hymn tunes are the following, with the hymns (in parentheses) that are usually sung to them: ORTON-VILLE (How Sweet the Name of Jesus), HANKEY (I Love to Tell the Story), DENNIS (Blest Be the Tie) and CHAUTAUQUA (Day Is Dying in the West).

hype

MB. 1. To promote and/or advertise, as a song, by false claims. 2. To make false claims.

hyperbole (hi-per'bo-lee)

RC. An exaggeration for effect, not meant to be taken literally. AI. Examples of hyperboles are: *a heart of gold, as old as time, as light as a feather, thanks a million,* etc.

hyphen: -

RC. 1. The punctuation mark shown above. 2. A short dash, or mark, used between the syllables of words, as in song writing.

hyphenate (hi'f'n-ate)

RC. 1. To insert a hyphen, as between the syllables of words in song writing. 2. To connect or separate by a hyphen. 2. To write or print with a hyphen. AI. For instance: *syl-lab-i-fy.*

i

I

RC. The capital letter used in Roman numerals to represent one. GI. For instance, I equals *one*. II equals *two*. III equals *three*. When I is placed *after* another numeral, this means it is to be *added*, as VI equals *six*. When I is placed *before* another numeral, this means it is to be *subtracted*, as IV equals *four*, IX equals *nine*, etc.

iamb (i′amb)

PY. An *iambus*. See IAMBUS.

iambic (i-am′bihk)

PY. a. 1. Of or made up of iambs or iambuses. See IAMBUS.

iambic

PY. n. 1. An iamb. 2. An iambus. 3. Iambic verse. See IAMBUS.

iambus (i-am′b's)

PY. A metrical foot of two syllabes in this order: an unaccented syllable, an accented syllable, or: ◡ — . Example, *a song*. The opposite of trochee. Musical counterpart: Two-Four Time. GI. One of the four kinds of English meter. See ENGLISH METER.

ictus (ihk′t's)

PY. 1. A metrical stress or accent on a word or syllable. MU. 2. A rhythmical stress, as on a note or tone.

idea

SW. 1. A thought, mental conception, mental image, as that of a song. 2. A plan, aim, design, as for writing a song. MU. 3. A unit used in the construction of music, also called a *figure*, a *phrase*, a *subject* or a *theme*.

idealism

WG. 1. Imaginative treatment that seeks to show the writer's conception of perfection. 2. The representation of imagined types or ideals, as opposed to *realism*. 3. A treatment used in song writing, as exemplified by the songs DREAMER'S HOLIDAY, EAST OF THE SUN and PENTHOUSE SERENADE. A song that draws a sharp contrast between idealism and realism is SWINGING ON A STAR.

idiom

RC. 1. The language or dialect of a people, region, class, etc. 2. The usual way in which the words of a language are put together to express a thought. 3. An accepted phrase contrary to the usual patterns of a language, or having a different meaning than the literal. AI. For instance, typical idioms are *high and mighty*, meaning arrogant or haughty. *Eating one's heart out*, meaning to yearn. *Open one's eyes*, meaning to make one aware (of the facts), etc. 4. The style of expression characteristic of an individual, as a songwriter or performer. AI. For instance, one might speak of the idiom (style) of George Gershwin, Sigmund Romberg, or Al Jolson, etc.

idiomatic (ihd″e-o-mat′ek)

RC. 1. Characteristic of a particular language. 2. Using or having idioms. 3. Characteristic of a person, usually his work.

idiot board

SB. Same as IDIOT CARD.

idiot card

SB. A large card on which lines, as those to be spoken, or lyrics, are written. AI. Idiot cards are used in the theater, television and motion pictures. These are held up off-stage or behind the cameras for reference by actors, announcers and singers as a safeguard against their forgetting what is to be spoken or sung. Also called *idiot board*.

illiterate

MB. 1. A person who is unable to read music. 2. A music illiterate. AI. Not necessarily a disparaging term. Also called *illit*.

image

RC. 1. A mental picture of a person or thing. 2. A conception or impression, as the *image* created by a song. 3. A figure of speech, especially a metaphor or simile.

imitation

MU. 1. A musical answer. 2. The repetition of a musical phrase, called the *consequent*, in answer to a questioning phrase, called the *antecedent*. 3. The repetition of a theme in different parts of a musical composition, with or without slight changes in rhythm, intervals, etc. 4. The repetition of a musical phrase by another voice or instrument. 5. Any form of musical repetition, as the repetition of a musical phrase in a different key, etc. MB. 6. A competitive phonograph record made to sound like a record made by another company. 7. A side of such a record. See MIRROR.

imp

PN. Abbreviation, *imprint*.

impact

RC. See EMOTIONAL IMPACT.

impresario (ihm"pre-sah're-o)

MU. The director, manager or organizer of a musical organization, as an opera company, a ballet company, a concert series, etc.

imprint (ihm'print)

PN. A publisher's note on the title page or at the end of a book, giving his name, the time and place of publication, etc.

impromptu (ihm-prahmp'tu)

RC. 1. Without preparation or advance thought, as the performance of a song. 2. Extemporaneous. 3. Unrehearsed. 4. Unplanned.

improvise (ihm'pro-vize)

MU. 1. To play or sing with little or no preparation. 2. To compose on the spur of the moment. 3. To play or sing offhand. 4. To play or sing extemporaneously.

inactive tones

MU. The 1st, 3rd, 5th, and 8th tones of any major or minor scale. AI. For instance, in the key of C major, these are the tones of C, E, G and the octave C.

inches per second

RG. The unit of measure used to tell the rate of speed at which certain recordings, as those on tape, are made and are to be played, as 7½ inches per second, 15 inches per second, etc. AI. Abbreviated, *ips*.

incidental music

MU. 1. Music played in connection with the presentation of a motion picture, play, poem, etc., to heighten the effect on the audience. 2. Mood music. 3. Background music.

inde (ihn'de)

MB. 1. Short for *independent*. 2. An independent phonograph record company. 3. An independent label. 4. An independent agent. 5. A free lance. AI. Also spelled *indie* by some of the music business trade publications.

independent

MB. 1. Free from the control, influence, financing, etc. of others. 2. An independent phonograph record company. 3. A phonograph record company that has no connections with other companies, usually a small company. AI. See INDIE.

independent agent

LW. 1. One who is free of the control of others. 2. One who is not under an exclusive contract, as a songwriter, a singer, musician, etc. 3. A free lance.

index finger

MU. 1. The finger next to the thumb. 2. The forefinger. 3. The finger designated by the numeral *1* in the English method of fingering. **4.** The finger designated by the numeral *2* in the German method of fingering.

inferior numbers: C_1, D_1, E_1, etc.

PG. **1.** Small figures like those shown above. **2.** Small figures that are placed lower than other characters in the same line. AI. In music, inferior numbers are used in connection with capital letters to designate the tones in the third and fourth octaves below middle C. For instance, the three tones shown above designate *contra C, contra D and contra E* respectively (all in the third octave below middle C). A_2 and B_2 designate *sub-contra A* and *sub-contra B* respectively (both in the fourth octave below middle C).

inflection

MU. A change or variation in pitch or tone.

infringe (ihn-frinj′)

LW. **1.** To trespass upon, to encroach upon (the rights of another). **2.** To violate the privileges of another, as to plagiarize a song written by someone else. See PLAGIARIZE.

infringement

LW. **1.** The act of infringing. **2.** An act of trespass without legal license upon the rights secured under a (patent or) copyright by making use of, or selling to another to be used, the thing which is the subject-matter of the (patent or) copyright, as a song. **3.** The wrongful use of another's copyrighted material.

infringer (ihn-frinj′er)

LW. Anyone who violates any of the exclusive rights of a copyright owner.

in group, the

SB. **1.** Those who are employed in show business and are particularly knowledgeful of its functioning, as distinguished from those who are not. MN. **2.** Those who understand and appreciate a subject or activity, as the writing and performance of jazz music, as distinguished from those who do not. AI. Also called *the in crowd*.

injunction

LW. A legal order from a court prohibiting a person or a group of persons from continuing a given action, or ordering that a specified action be carried out. AI. For instance, an injunction might be issued to stop a copyright infringement.

ink

SB. To sign, as a contract.

inner-leger lines

MU. Lines that are added below the treble staff and above the bass staff, on which to write notes. AI. For instance, middle C is written on an inner-leger line.

inner parts

MU. Vocal or insrumental parts that lie between the lowest and highest parts in a musical composition. AI. Also called *inner voices*. See EXTREME PARTS.

inside back cover

PG. 1. The page immediately preceding the outside back cover, as of a song sheet, song book, etc. 2. The page that is back to back with the back cover. AI. Also called *third cover*.

inside front cover

PG. 1. The page immediately following the outside front cover, as of a song sheet, song book, etc. 2. The page that is back to back with the front cover. AI. Also called *second cover*.

inside job

SW. A song written by a staff songwriter or songwriters, as distinguished from a song written by a free lance. AI. The opposite of *outside job*. Also called *inside song* as distinguished from an *outside song*.

instrument

MU. A mechanical contrivance for producing musical sounds. AI. Musical instruments are usually classified in four categories: string, wood wind, brass and percussion.

instrumental

MU. 1. Designating music that is performed on an instrument or

190

instruments, as distinguished from that which is sung. 2. The opposite of vocal. AI. Typical instrumental numbers are: DIZZY FINGERS, JAZZ PIZZICATO, SLEIGH RIDE, COUNTRY GENTLEMAN and KITTEN ON THE KEYS.

instrumentation

MU. The number and kind of instruments that are combined to make up a combo, an orchestra, a band or a section of an orchestra or band. See ORCHESTRATION.

intellectual property

LW. An original idea, as for a song, a play, a motion picture, etc. AI. The term is usually used to imply something that is not as yet in completed or more tangible form, as a song or a play in manuscript form, a motion picture in scenario form, etc.

intensity

MU. 1. The loudness or softness of a tone or tones. 2. Volume. AI. Intensity is one of the four characteristics of a tone. See TONE. See DYNAMICS.

internal rhyme

SW. 1. A rhyme within a line of verse or poetry. 2. A rhyme within a lyric line. 3. An inner-line rhyme, as used in songwriting. AI. For instance, in the following couplet, the words *dashing* and *splashing* are internal rhymes (or *internal-rhyme* words), the syllables *rain* and *pane* are *terminal* rhymes (or *terminal-rhyme* words):

> The *dashing, splashing* rain
> Falling on my windowpane

A good example of internal rhyming is to be found in the song CAROLINA IN THE MORNING. See TERMINAL RHYME.

international copyright

LW. See COPYRIGHT, INTERNATIONAL.

International Copyright Union

LW. Another name for the *Berne Convention* or *Berne Union.*

191

International Musician, The

MB. The official journal of the American Federation of Musicians of the United States and Canada. Address: 39 Division Street, Newark, New Jersey 07102.

International Union for the Protection of Literary and Artistic Work

LW. *Bureau de l'Union Internationale pour le Protection des Oeuvres Littéraires et Artistiques,* better known as the *Berne Convention* or *Berne Union.* Address: 32, chemin des Colombettes, Geneva, Switzerland.

interpolate (ihn-ter'po-late″)

MU. To alter by combining one thing with another, as to combine one song with another song, in an arrangement, in a performance, etc.

interpolation (ihn-tur″po-lae'shun)

MU. 1. The act of interpolating. 2. The combining of one or more songs in a musical show. 3. The combining of one song with another, usually in the following manner: first song, in whole or in part, second song, in whole or in part, first song repeated, in whole or in part. 4. The *second song,* as that in the foregoing example. AI. The two songs combined in this manner usually are of similar subject matter. For instance, UNTIL THE REAL THING COMES ALONG might be interpolated with HONEST AND TRULY. YOU MUST HAVE BEEN A BEAUTIFUL BABY might be interpolated with TOO MARVELOUS FOR WORDS. SING, SING, SING might be interpolated with I FEEL A SONG COMING ON, etc.

interval

MU. The difference in pitch between two tones. AI. The name of an interval is determined by the number of letters (tones) included. This includes both the letter with which an interval begins and the letter with which it ends. For instance, the interval between C and E is a *third,* as it includes *three* letters (C, D, and E). The interval between C and G is a *fifth,* as it includes *five* letters (C, D, E, F, and G), etc.

in the can

MB. A song, or other musical composition, that has been recorded and is being held for future release is said to be *in the can.*

in the groove

JZ. 1. Performing or performed with a high degree of skill, in a smooth, seemingly effortless manner, as originally said of jazz musicians and/or jazz music. AI. The expression comes from the needle on a phonograph being *correctly* in the groove of the record, *just as it should be for correct playing.* See GROOVY. MB. 2. Designating *as it should be,* as a commercial song, a commercial recording of a song, a commercial sound, etc., is said to be *in the groove.*

in the racks

MB. Same as *on the shelves,* as applied to rack dealers and/or rack locations. See ON THE SHELVES.

intone (ihn-tone')

MU. 1. To speak or recite in a singing tone. 2. To sound a tone, usually vocally.

INTRO.

MU. The abbreviation used on popular sheet music to mean *introduction.*

introduction

MU. The preliminary musical phrase or division, as that of a song, intended to set the mood and prepare the ear for the composition that is to follow. AI. The introduction for a song is usually short, consisting of only a phrase or a few measures. However, there is no set rule as to how long or how short an introduction should be. Often called *intro.*

inventory

MD. 1. An itemized list of goods or items of merchandise that are on hand, unsold, as copies of sheet music, phonograph records, etc. 2. Unsold merchandise as distinguished from merchandise that has been sold. AI. It is customary for a record company to pay mechanical-license royalties on the recordings that are sold, rather than the number of recordings in inventory (that have been manufactured but remain unsold).

inversion (ihn-ver'zhun)

MU. 1. A change in the order of chord tones, the lower tones being placed above and the upper tones being placed below. For instance, E-G-C and G-C-E are *inversions* of the chord C-E-G. SW. 2. A reversal of the normal order of words, as *came the dawn* instead of *the dawn came*. AI. Another example of inversion is the phrase *drove she ducklets* in the song CLEMENTINE.

inverted chord

MU. A chord whose fundamental tone, or root, is not its lowest tone. AI. For instance, when the chord F-A-C (F major) is inverted, it becomes either the *inverted chord* A-C-F or the *inverted chord* C-F-A. Compare with ROOT POSITION.

inverted v: ∧

MU. 1. The accent mark shown above. AI. Also called *upside-down v*. 2. Caret. See CARET.

ips (i-pee-ess)

RG. Abbreviation, *inches per second*.

irregular rhythm

MU. Syncopation. See SYNCOPATION.

island

MU. 1. Designating any island in the West Indies, as that of Trinidad. 2. Typical of such an island, as *island* music, *island* beat, etc.

island beat

MU. Rhythm typical of the West Indies particularly that of Trinidad. AI. Songs with an island beat are DON'T WANT NO PEAS AND RICE AND COCOANUT OIL, MARY ANN, ROW THE BOAT ASHORE, YELLOW BIRD and MATHILDA, MATHILDA!

isolation board

BR. A screen-like partition used to divide a broadcasting or recording studio in order to isolate one source of sound from another, so that each source might be controlled individually. AI. For instance, a singer might be screened off from the musicians who are accompanying him. A violin section might be screened off from the other instruments of an orchestra, etc.

194

issue

MB. 1. To release, to offer for sale, as a song, in the form of sheet music or a phonograph record. 2. To provide, as a music publisher might *issue* a contract to a songwriter, etc.

ital

PG. 1. Abbreviation, *italics*. 2. A proof reader's mark meaning *set in italics*, as certain words of a song. See ITALICS.

italics

PG. A style of type in which the letters slant. AI. *These seven words are set in italics*. Italics often are used in printing songs to *emphasize* certain words, for foreign-language words, etc. AI. Abbreviated *ital*.

j

J

jacket

RB. The open-end envelope used to contain a phonograph record.

jam

MN. 1. To improvise musically. 2. To play or sing *as the spirit moves*. 3. To play *ad lib*. See JAM SESSION.

jamboree

CM. 1. A gay, merry and boisterous party that usually includes music, singing and dancing. 2. A country-music jam session.

jam session

MN. 1. A gathering of jazz performers to play and/or sing extemporaneously. 2. A jam performance. AI. Because of the crowded conditions under which these gatherings were originally held, they became known as jam, for *jammed in*, sessions. AI. Typical jam-session numbers are TIGER RAG, HONEYSUCKLE ROSE, RAMPART STREET PARADE and WHEN THE SAINTS GO MARCHING IN (usually called *Saints* by jazz devotees).

jazz

MN. A type of driving, syncopated music based on an intricate rhythmic and melodic structure, created by the Original Dixieland

(Jazz) Band, under the direction of Nick LaRocca. See DIXIE-LAND. See PROGRESSIVE JAZZ.

jazzman

MN. 1. A jazz musician. 2. A jazz devotee. 3. A cat.

jazz songs

MB. A classification in songwriting as to musical treatment. AI. Typical jazz songs are DARKTOWN STRUTTERS BALL, MISSISSIPPI MUD, G.I. JIVE and JERSEY BOUNCE.

jew's harp or jews' harp

MU. A small musical instrument made of metal or metal and plastic, which is held between the teeth and played by plucking a projected bent piece with the finger to produce twanging tones. AI. It is possible that the word *jew* is a mispronunciation of the word *jaw* and that the instrument was originally called a *jaw harp*.

jig

MU. 1. A light, gay dance to a rapid-moving tune. 2. The music for this dance. AI. Typical jigs are IRISH WASHERWOMAN, GARY OWEN and THE WIND THAT SHAKES THE BARLEY.

jingle

MB. 1. An advertising message, a promotional or public service announcement, on radio or television, containing musical material (with or without words), originally written for this purpose. 2. A musical work, originally written for other purposes, with lyrics replaced or changed for advertising, promotional or public service announcement purposes. 3. The performance of the foregoing material. AI. This is one of the categories used by performing-rights societies in establishing credit values. PY. 4. Any two-line rhymed verse. 5. A rhymed advertising, promotional, or public service message, with or without music. See JINGLES.

jingle notes: 𝄐 𝄐

MU. Notes like those shown above. AI. In music written for the tambourine, jingles and other such percussion instruments, notes with short vertical strokes over them call for the same number of *jingles* or *shakes* as there are lines. AI. Also called *shaker notes*. See WAVY-STEM NOTES.

jingles

MU. 1. Metal disks affixed to a stick, the rim of a tambourine or other device, which produce a jingling tone when shaken. 2. A percussion instrument consisting of a stick to which jingles are affixed, which is shaken to produce jingling tones.

jive

MU. A general term originally used to describe or designate improvised jazz, usually played at a fast tempo.

job

MB. v. To do or work odd jobs, as a musician who is not steadily employed.

job

SW. n. 1. A song. 2. A musical composition. AI. For instance, a songwriter might speak of a song as a *country job*, a *sixteen-measure job*, a *rhythm-and-blues job*, etc. MN. 3. A piece of work, an assignment, as a recording session, a dance, etc. AI. For instance, a musician might be said to be working a theater *job*, a *night-club job*, a *TV job*, etc.

jobber

MB. 1. Anyone who sells merchandise, as phonograph records, sheet music, etc., to retailers. 2. A middleman. 3. A distributor.

jobbing musician

MB. Any musician who is not exclusively employed and who is open to accept free-lance jobs. 2. A musician who *jobs*. AI. Many excellent musicians are *jobbing musicians* by preference.

jock

MB. Short for *jockey*, meaning *disk jockey*.

jockey

MB. Short for *disk jockey*.

joint

JB. 1. A saloon. 2. A restaurant or cafe, usually where drinks are served. 3. A juke joint.

joint authorship

SW. A collaboration, as that on a song, of two or more writers, usually in which the contribution of any one writer is not distinct from the contribution of the other writer or writers.

joint ownership

LW. Owned by two or more persons, as a song.

journeyman

MN. A worker who has learned his trade, as a musician, stage hand, recording engineer, etc., as distinguished from an *apprentice* or *amateur*. AI. The word usually implies a member of a trade union.

jubilee

GI. 1. An ancient celebration which was an occasion of great rejoicing. 2. A gathering at which rejoiceful songs are sung. AI. Hence, a joyful and triumphant song is known as a *jubilee song*. One who sings such songs is called a *jubilee singer*, etc.

jug

HM. 1. An earthenware container for liquids, usually with a small opening and handle, used to amplify bass tones which are blown into the opening from different formations of the blower's mouth. 2. A hill-music bass instrument.

jug band

HM. Any combination of musicians using one or more jugs as instruments.

juke box

JB. 1. A coin-operated machine which plays phonograph records. 2. A play-for-pay phonograph.

juke joint

JB. 1. A saloon, restaurant, cafe, etc., in which a juke box is installed. 2. A honky tonk which has a juke box. 3. A (juke box) *location*.

200

jump

MN. v. 1. To *jump* or *jump over* is to omit or leave out (not to play or sing) one or more notes or measures of music, either in error or intentionally. AI. For instance, an orchestra leader might tell a trumpet player to jump the sixth and seventh measures, so that the trombone player can fill in, etc. SB. 2. To travel. AI. For instance, a booking agent might tell an act, "Then the following week, you *jump* from Chicago to Omaha for three days," etc.

jump

MU. n. 1. A quick, lively beat. 2. Bounce or bounce tempo. 3. Skip. SB. 4. Travel. AI. For instance, a singer might say, "I jumped from Las Vegas to Reno." A performer might say, "It's only an overnight jump from New Orleans to Houston," etc.

jump tune

MU. 1. A tune usually characterized by a constant repetition of riffs and a pronounced steady beat. 2. A lively, bouncy tune. 3. An up tune.

jurat

LW. A statement added to an affidavit telling *when* and *before whom* the affidavit was made. AI. For instance, in establishing proof of existence, as for a song, an affidavit might be made on oath *of a certain date* before a *notary public*.

k

K

kettledrum

MU. A timpano. See TIMPANO.

kettledrummer

MU. A timpanist. See TIMPANIST.

key

MU. 1. A scale. 2. A series of related notes or tones that make up a given scale, based on and named after a certain note or tone, which is the keynote or keytone respectively. 3. The main tonality of a musical composition. AI. For instance, in the key of C, the keynote is C. In the key of D, the keynote is D, etc. 3. A lever on certain musical instruments which produces a tone when pressed, as a key on a piano, an accordion, a celesta, etc. 4. The padded disk operated by a lever that opens and closes the sound holes in such instruments as a flute, oboe, clarinet, saxophone, etc. 5. The peg-like part on which a string of a stringed instrument is wound and which, when turned, serves to tune the string. See KEYED.

keyboard

MU. The row, or rows of black and white keys on a piano, organ, accordion, etc. AI. Instruments with keyboards are called *keyboard* instruments. The keyboard of an organ is also called a *manual*.

keyed

MU. 1. Pitched in a certain key, as a song might be *keyed* in the key of C. 2. Having keys, as do certain musical instruments. AI. The term usually applies to instruments, like the guitar, ukulele, banjo, etc., which are *tuned* by keys rather than *played* by keys, as the piano. For instance, the guitar is a *keyed* instrument. The piano is a *keyboard* instrument. See KEYBOARD.

key name

MU. The identification by which a key (scale) is known. AI. A key is named after its keynote, as C, F, G, etc.

keynote

MU. 1. The lowest, basic note of a musical scale. 2. The first note of any scale. 3. The note designating the keytone. 4. The tonic.

key signature

MU. One or more sharps or flats placed at the beginning of a staff, immediately following the clef sign. AI. The number of sharps or flats and the formation in which these signs appear designates the key to be used. For instance, one sharp, on the fifth line of the treble staff designates the key of G major. Two flats, one on the third line and one in the fourth space of the treble staff designate the key of B♭, etc. When no sharps or flats are shown following the clef sign, this means that the composition is to be played in the key of C major. See C MAJOR SCALE.

keytone

MN. The tone designated by the keynote.

kick

MB. 1. An inclination to move or act in a particular direction and/or way, usually excessively so. 2. Biased actions, seemingly in excessive and/or unreasonable proportions. AI. For instance, it might be said that a certain disk jockey is *on a rhythm-and-blues kick* meaning that he is *playing a large number of rhythm-and-blues records*.

kick around

SW. To think about and/or to discuss, as two or more songwriters might *kick around* the idea for a song, etc.

kick off

MN. To begin playing, as a song. AI. For instance, in explaining an arrangement, an orchestra leader might say, "The piano kicks off and is then joined by the drums, bass and guitar, in that order."

kid songs

MB. A classification in songwriting, as to subject matter. AI. Kid songs are of two kinds: those about kids and those in which a kid is the narrator. Typical kid songs in the first category are DIRTY HANDS DIRTY FACE, SMALL FRY and LITTLE MAN YOU'VE HAD A BUSY DAY. Typical songs in the second category are GIMME A LITTLE KISS, WILL YA HUH, I FAW DOWN AND GO BOOM and I SAW MOMMIE KISSING SANTA CLAUS.

kilocycle

BD. One thousand cycles per second, as used to express the frequency of a broadcast station.

knock off

SW. v. 1. To write or compose quickly, and usually roughly, as a song. MB. 2. To copy illegally, in whole or in part, a melody, a lyric or a complete song. 3. To steal a song or part of a song.

knock off

MB. n. 1. A melody, a lyric or a complete song that has been illegally copied from another melody, lyric or song. 2. A song that is a duplicate, in whole or in part, of another song, intentionally or otherwise. AI. For instance, a publisher might say, "I've never seen these words before but the melody is a *knock off*," meaning that the melody is the same as that of another musical composition.

1

L

MU. 1. The capital letter used to designate the word *left* or *on* or *at the left hand*. AI. For instance, in the German method of fingering, *L1* means the thumb of the *left* hand. 2. The Roman numeral meaning 50. 3. The small letter used to designate the syllable *lah* in the English system of tonic sol-fa.

la: ▢

MU. 1. The syllable used in singing the sixth note (tone) of a scale in the sol-fa system. 2. The shape notehead shown above designating this syllable.

label

RB. 1. The label on a phonograph record. 2. Hence, the trade-mark or name of its manufacturer. 3. The name of a phonograph record manufacturing company. AI. For instance, when a song is said to be on the RCA Victor *label*, this means that it has been recorded by the RCA Victor *Company*. Or it might be said that an artist records for the Capitol *label*, meaning he is under contract to Capitol Records.

labor union

MS. An association of workers to promote and protect the welfare, interests and rights of its members, as AFTRA, AF of M, etc.

lacquer

RG. A high quality blank disk on which master recordings are made.

lacy

MS. 1. A delicate arrangement or performance of a musical composition, as a song. 2. Thin, as applied to harmony. AI. The opposite of *solid*.

lament

MU. 1. A song mourning some loss or calamity. 2. A blues song. 3. The blues.

lap

MN. One playing of a complete musical composition, as a song. AI. For instance, a band leader might say, "Let's take it in three laps" meaning *let's play it three times*. Two and a half laps means twice through completely and once from the bridge.

lap dissolve

MP. 1. A dissolving view, used in motion pictures, in which one scene fades in, overlapping and blending with a scene that is fading out. MN. 2. This same effect in musical performance, in which one musical composition, as a song, fades in to overlap one that is being faded out.

large

MN. Fulsome, loud, vigorously, with a pronounced beat, as applied to the performance of music. AI. For instance, a band leader might say, "Let's play it large."

lark

MB. A female singer. AI. Same as *canary*.

Latin

MB. Latin-American. AI. A term used to designate songs and music from south of the United States southern border. Typical Latin rhythms are the *calypso, conga, meringue, rumba, samba, bossa nova,* etc.

lay

MU. A melody or tune. See ROUNDELAY.

lay a bomb

MB. 1. To fail, usually in a big way. 2. To succeed, usually in a big way. GI. Strangely, this expression is used to mean either of two directly opposite things.

208

lay an egg

SB. 1. To fail, as a song that fails to gain public acceptance, a show that fails, etc. 2. To fail after trying to succeed.

layman

GI. 1. A person not belonging to a given profession or trade. 2. A person not skilled or knowledgeful of a certain business, as that of songwriting, or the music business.

lay out

MN. v. 1. Not to play, as a musician. 2. To tacet. AI. For instance, a certain musical arrangement for an orchestra might call for the trumpet player to *lay out* while others are playing. SW. 3. To suggest in rough or incomplete form, as a song or an idea for a song. AT. 4. To suggest by a rough or incomplete drawing, as the idea for a front cover for sheet music, a song book, etc.

layout

AT. n. 1. A rough drawing, as for a printed song sheet, an advertisement, as that for a song, etc. 2. A plan, as for the make-up of a song sheet, a song book, etc.

l. c.

TE. 1. A stage direction meaning *left center* of stage. PG. 2. A proofreader's mark meaning *lower case*.

lead

MU. v. 1. To direct others in playing or singing. 2. To play or sing the leading part, as a *leader* or *lead* singer.

lead

MU. n. 1. A leading melody. 2. A lead melody. 3. The singer that sings this melody, as distinguished from tenor, bass, etc., as in a quartet.

lead back

SW. See FIRST ENDING.

leader

MU. 1. The leader of any instrumental group, as a combo, orchestra, band, etc. 2. The leader of any vocal group, as a quartet, choir, etc. 3. A conductor. 4. A director.

leading melody

MU. 1. The principal melody in a musical composition of several parts. 2. The lead. 3. The theme. 4. The leading melody. 5. The melody sung by the lead singer. AI. For instance, a trio of harmony singers sing three different melodies. The lead singer sings the *leading melody*. The other two singers sing high and low harmonizing melodies respectively.

leading note

MU. The note that indicates the leading tone.

leading tone

MU. 1. The major seventh of any scale. 2. The tone next below the (octave) tonic, or keytone. 3. The tone next above the submediant. 4. The tone called the *subtonic*. AI. For instance, in the scale of C major the leading tone is the tone of B.

lead sheet

MU. The manuscript of a song showing the lyric, the melody and the harmony (as designated by chord captions). AI. This is the form in which most songwriters write songs. A lead sheet is not complete, or correctly written, without chord captions written above the melody line to show the desired harmony progressions.

lean

MN. 1. Thin in tone. 2. Lacking in volume. 3. Lacking in fullness. 4. Weak. AI. As said of a musical performance.

lean on

MN. To accent, stress or emphasize, as a note, a chord or a passage of music in singing or playing.

leap

MU. 1. A jump or spring, usually suddenly, from one note to another note or from one chord to another chord, as in playing the piano. 2. A skip, as in harmony.

ledger

MU. The original spelling of the more often used word *leger*. AI. While *leger* is preferred, both spellings are in general use. See LEGER SPACES. See LEGER LINES.

210

legal holidays

LW. In applying for same-day publication in the United States and Canada, the following U. S. legal holidays and Canadian public days (as well as all Saturdays and Sundays) are to be avoided when choosing a date of publication:

January 1	New Year's Day	U.S. Canada
January 20 (Approximately)	Inauguration Day (Every Four Years)	U.S.
February 12	Lincoln's Birthday	U.S.
February 22	Washington's Birthday	U.S.
1st Friday Before Easter	Good Friday	U.S.
1st Monday After Easter	Easter Monday	Canada
1st Monday Before May 25	Victoria Day	Canada
May 30	Memorial Day	U.S.
July 1	Dominion Day	Canada
July 4	Independence Day	U.S.
1st Monday In August	Civic Holiday	Canada
1st Monday In September	Labor Day	U.S. Canada
2nd Monday In October	Thanksgiving Day	Canada
October 12	Columbus Day	U.S.
1st Tuesday After 1st Monday in Nov.	General Election Day	U.S.
November 11	Armistice Day Remembrance Day	U.S. Canada
4th Thursday In November	Thanksgiving Day	U.S.
December 25	Christmas Day	U.S. Canada

AI. When statutory holidays fall on Sunday, it is possible that the following day will be observed.

legato: ⎯⎯⎯⎯⎯⎯⎯

MU. 1. In a smooth and connected manner. 2. Notes played without a break between the tones. AI. Legato is indicated by a slur, a slightly-curved line, like that shown above, which is written over or under the notes to be played in this manner.

leger lines

MU. 1. The short parallel lines that are added above or below the regular music staff lines. 2. Lines that form a continuation of the staff above or below. AI. On these lines are written the notes that are too high or too low in pitch to be written on the staff. Leger lines are counted away from the staff. The line nearest the staff is the *first* leger line, next is the *second*, etc., either up or down. Sometimes spelled *ledger* lines. Also called *added lines.*

leger spaces

MU. The spaces between leger lines. AI. Leger spaces are counted away from the staff, in the same manner as leger lines. Also called *added spaces.* See LEGER LINES.

legitimate

BS. 1. Genuine. 2. Lawful. TE. 3. Stage plays, as distinguished from other forms of theatrical entertainment. MB. 4. The *legitimate* music business, as distinguished from the make-believe world of song sharks and others who prey on would-be songwriters.

letter notation

MU. The letters used to designate a note, a tone, a key or a staff degree, as C, D, E, etc. AI. Also called *letter names.* See PITCH NAMES. See NUMERAL NAMES.

letter of submission

SW. Same as *letter of transmittal.*

letter of transmittal

SW. A written message that accompanies a song which is submitted to a music publisher, a record company, a singer, etc. AI. A letter of transmittal states what is enclosed and the terms on which it is submitted. Also called *letter of submission.*

212

letterpress

PG. A process of printing, occasionally used in printing music, which prints directly from an inked surface upon which the paper is impressed. See OFFSET.

level

BR. The degree of volume at which a sound is heard. AI. For instance, it might be said that a phonograph record is made at a *low level*, meaning *low in volume*. It might be said that a song has been recorded at a *very high* level, meaning *very loud*. Also called *sound level, voice level, tone level*, etc.

level of comprehension

PS. Point of understanding. AI. For instance, it might be said that the lyric of a fairly sophisticated song is written at a *level of comprehension* equal to that of Reader's Digest, or that the lyric for a children's song is written at the *level of comprehension* of that of Mother Goose.

L.H.

MU. Abbreviation, *left hand*. AI. Where this appears on music, it means that the left hand is to be used to play the part indicated. Opposite of *R.H.*

liberty, at

SB. See AT LIBERTY.

librarian

MB. One in charge of a music library, as that of a radio or television station, a band, an orchestra, etc. AI. Such librarians are often called *station librarian, band librarian, orchestra librarian, music librarian*, etc.

library

MB. A collection of printed music and/or phonograph records, as those maintained by radio and television stations, bands, orchestras, etc. AI. Also called *music library, record library*, etc.

librettist

MU. The writer of a *libretto*.

213

libretto

MU. 1. The story of an opera. 2. The story of a musical play. 3. The *book*.

license

LW. A formal, usually written, permission to do something, as a license to perform a song, a license to record a song, etc.

licensee

LW. A person or organization to whom a license is granted, as a phonograph record company, a radio station, etc. AI. Also spelled *licencee*.

licensor

LW. 1. A person or organization with the authority to grant a license, as a songwriter, a music publisher or any other owner of a copyrighted song or songs. 2. An agent authorized to act for the owner of copyrighted material, as a clearance society.

lick

MU. 1. An improvised musical phrase, hot or cool. 2. A fill in. AI. A lick is often used to *fill in* a break. A lick is often erroneously called a *break*. A lick is something you *hear*. A break is a period of *silence* (something you *don't* hear).

ligature

MU. 1. The group of notes connected by a slur. 2. Formerly, the slur itself. AI. Notes thus connected are called ligature notes. PG. 3. A printing character containing two or more united letters. AI. These are ligatures: *æ, fi, fl,* etc.

light face

PG. 1. Light face printers' type. 2. Printing type that has thin, light lines, as distinguished from *medium face, bold face,* etc.

light opera

TE. 1. A musical play with humorous situations and a happy ending. 2. An operetta.

214

line

MU. 1. Any one of the five lines that make up the music staff. 2. A leger line. 3. The music staff itself, composed of five lines and four spaces. MT. 4. A row of written or printed words extending across a page, as a line of lyric in a song. 5. A *lyric* line. SB. 6. The group of girls composing a chorus, as in a musical show. 7. A *chorus* line, as that of a musical show.

line note

MU. Any musical note that is written on a staff line or on a leger line.

line out

FK, HM. To call out the words of a song, a line at a time, to a group of singers, as a choir, a congregation, etc. AI. In the early days of community singing, printed songs and song books were scarce items. So that everyone might join in the singing, the system of *lining out* was invented. The leader would read and call out the first line of a song, the congregation would sing it. The leader would then read and call out the second line, the congregation would sing it, and so on. The leader was often called the *liner* or the *liner out*. See RESPONSE.

liner

FK, HM. 1. One who *lines out*. 2. A *liner out*. See LINE OUT.

lip

MU. 1. The art or faculty of adjusting the lips to the mouthpiece of a wind instrument, as a horn, to produce artistic effects of tone. 2. Embouchure. AI. An exceptionally good horn player is sometimes called a *lip, the lip* or is said to have a *good lip*, etc.

lip sinc

MP. Short for *lip synchronization*.

lip synchronization (lihp sihn″kro-nih-zae′shun)

MP. Vocal sounds fitted to the movement of lips, as is done in making a motion picture. AI. For instance, a singer might be photographed singing in pantomime. Later, the singer's voice, or the voice of another, might be added to the film in *lip synchronization*, often called *lip sinc*.

listener

RO. 1. A member of the radio audience. MB. 2. One who hears a song sung or played. 3. A member of the song audience.

listener point of view

SW. 1. The way in which the listener considers himself in relation to a song. 2. The listener's mental attitude toward a song. AI. For instance, a listener to the song I LOVE YOU might identify himself either as (a) *the one who loves*, (b) *the one who is loved* or he might feel that he is merely (c) *a bystander*, who hears the song being sung to someone else. See POINT OF VIEW.

listener reaction

RO. See REACTION.

listening audience

RO. 1. Those who listen to radio. MB. 2. Those who listen to musical compositions, as songs.

literal

SW. 1. Based on the actual words in their ordinary meaning. 2. Not figurative or symbolical.

litotes (lih′to-teez″)

SW. A figure of speech in which a meaning is expressed by a negation of something to the contrary. AI. For instance, *no little help* meaning of *much help, no sad affair* meaning a *happy occasion, no fair day* meaning *bad weather*, etc.

little finger

MU. 1. The finger farthest from the thumb. 2. The smallest finger. 3. The finger designated by the figure *4* in the English method of fingering. 4. The finger designated by the figure *5* in the German method of fingering.

live

RT. 1. A term used to designate a performance that takes place at

216

the same time it is being broadcast or telecast, as distinguished from one that is broadcast or telecast, at a later time, by means of tape or transcription. 2. Designating a performance that is seen and/or heard at the time it takes place, as that of *live* music.

live microphone

BR. A microphone that is turned on and is in working order. AI. Also called *live mike*.

live music

MB. Music that is heard at the same time it is being played by musicians, as distinguished from music that has been recorded. AI. The opposite of *canned music*.

living speech

SW. 1. The words, idioms and figures of speech that are currently being used. 2. The speech of today. 3. Speech that lives, as opposed to words, expressions, etc., that are dead or have been discarded, etc. 4. The vocabulary used in the modern way of talking.

L.M.

CH. Abbreviation, *long meter*, as applied to hymn tunes.

local

GI. 1. Pertaining to a limited area, as distinguished from *regional* and/or *national*. MB. 2. A song popular in a certain town or city is said to have *local* appeal. RT. 3. A single radio and/or television station of limited power is said to have only *local* coverage. MB. A chapter of the AF of M, usually called *the local*.

local boy

MN. A male member of the local (AF of M) union.

local color

SW. Customs and other features characteristic of a certain region or time introduced in song lyrics to supply realism. AI. An outstanding example of local color is the lyric of the great Hank Williams song JAMBALAYA.

localism

SW. 1. A mode of speaking peculiar to a place or location. 2. A local idiom. 3. A manner of speaking peculiar to a location. AI. An example of a localism is the song title Y'ALL COME.

local lyrics

MB. Lyrics written to suit a locality, as to subject matter and/or language as, for instance, a Spanish lyric for an American song for use in a Latin country.

location

MP. An outdoor set, away from the studio, where a scene or scenes for a motion picture are enacted and photographed.

loco

MU. Place. AI. Following *8va* or *8vaba*, *loco* means *perform the notes as written.*

log

MB. 1. A record kept, usually daily, to show the titles of musical compositions played during a certain period of time, as the station log kept by a broadcasting station. 2. A log book. 3. The record kept by performance-rights societies, as ASCAP, BMI and SESAC, to ascertain the frequency of *plays* given the works under their control.

logo (lo′go)

PG. Abbreviation, *logotype.*

logotype (lo′go-tipe″)

PG. A trade-mark, as that of a music publishing company, a phonograph record company, etc.

long hair

MN. 1. Originally, a term applied to classical music, classical musicians and devotees of classical music. 2. Originally, a *square*, the opposite of *cat*. AI. See CAT. 3. More recently, a rhythm-and-blues musician, or singer who wears his hair long. 4. An English rhythm-and-blues musician or singer.

long meter

CH. Designating a metrical count of 8.8.8.8., as that of a hymn tune. AI. Abbreviated, *L.M.*

long play

RB. 1. A *long-playing* phonograph record. 2. A microgroove phonograph record which plays at the speed of 33⅓ RPM. AI. Abbreviation, *LP.*

long syllable

SW. 1. An accented syllable. 2. The opposite of *short syllable*. See ACCENTED SYLLABLE.

long v-on-its-side: (a) ◁ (b) ▷

MU. The signs shown above, used to indicate (a) *crescendo* and (b) *decrescendo* or *diminuendo*. AI. Not to be confused with the much shorter v-on-its-side used to indicate an accent. Also called *long half-turned v*. See ACCENT MARKS.

loud-speaker

ET. A device for converting electrical energy to sound and for amplifying this sound to the desired volume. AI. Also called *speaker*.

love songs

MB. A classification in songwriting, as to subject matter. AI. This is, by far, the largest classification of all. Typical love songs are LET ME CALL YOU SWEETHEART, I LOVE YOU and I'M IN THE MOOD FOR LOVE.

low

MN. 1. Extending downward, as to pitch, notes and tones. 2. Soft, as to volume.

lower case

PG. In printing, used to designate and distinguish from capital letters (upper case). AI. For instance, *these eight words are set in lower case*. THESE SEVEN WORDS ARE SET IN CAPITALS. Abbreviated, *lc* or *l.c.*

lows

SW. The blues.

LP (ell-pee)

RB. Abbreviation, *long play*.

lullaby

MU. A cradle song, as BRAHMS' LULLABY. AI. Typical popular-song lullabies are LULLABY OF THE LEAVES, RUSSIAN LULLABY and LULLABY OF BROADWAY.

lute

MU. A stringed instrument related to the guitar, with a body shaped like a half of a pear, from which extends a fretted fingerboard strung (usually) with six strings tuned G-c-f-a-d^1-g^1. The lute is played by plucking its strings. AI. Music for the lute is notated, not on a staff, but by various systems employing letters and/or figures to indicate the frets. See TABLATURE.

lute player

MU. 1. One who plays the lute. MN. 2. A facetious name for a guitar player.

lyric

MU. 1. The words of a song, as distinguished from the music. 2. The text of a song. AI. A song is said to have *one lyric, one set of lyrics, two sets of lyrics, three sets of lyrics,* etc. See LYRIC LINE.

lyricist

MB. 1. One who writes the words of a song. 2. Author. See SONG-WRITER.

lyric line

MU. 1. A row of words extending from one side of a song page to the other. 2. One line of lyric (words). AI. Where more than one line of lyrics appears in a song, the uppermost line is called the *top line*, the *top lyric line*, the *top line of lyric*, the *first lyric line* or the *first line of lyrics*. The second lyric line is called the *second lyric line*, the *second line of lyrics*, etc.

m

M

MU. 1. The capital letter used to designate *manual*, as on an organ.
2. The capital letter used to designate *metronome*. 3. In Roman numerals, the capital letter used to mean *1,000*. 4. The small letter used
to designate the syllable *me* in the English system of tonic sol-fa. 5.
The small letter used to designate *minor*, in chord captions, as *Cm* (C
minor), *Cm7* (C minor seventh), etc.

machine head

MU. 1. A rack-and-pinion adjustment, used in place of the ordinary
tuning-pegs, on the double-bass, the guitar and other stringed instruments, used to tighten or loosen the tension of the strings. See PEG.

macron (mae'krahn) : —

PY. The short, straight mark shown above which is placed over (or
under) a vowel or syllable to show that it is long. AI. A macron is
the opposite of *breve*.

maestro (mies'tro)

MN. 1. Master. 2. Leader. 3. A highly skilled composer or conductor. 4. An artist of renown. AI. MN. 5. The title is also used facetiously among musicians, particularly those in the popular field.

magnetic tape

ET. A thin strip of metal, plastic or other material coated with a magnetic substance on which sound, television images, etc. can be recorded. AI. The tape is then used to reproduce the recorded sound, images, etc.

mailing list

MB. A list of names and addresses to which mail is sent. AI. For instance, a music publisher might have a *mailing list* of performers to whom he sends professional copies of his songs. A phonograph record manufacturer might have a *mailing list* of disk jockeys to whom he sends records, etc.

main title

MB. 1. The main title of a song, as distinguished from a *subtitle*, or *secondary title*. AI. For instance, in the following song title the main title is set in capital letters, the subtitle in parentheses: IT'LL HAPPEN TO YOU (Just Like It Happened To Me). MP, TE. 2. The title of a musical composition, as a song, which is the same as the motion picture or musical show in which it is played and/or sung. 3. The musical composition by this title. 4. A title song.

maj

MU. The symbol meaning *major*, used in chord captions, thus: Cmaj7, Dmaj7, Emaj7, etc.

major

MU. 1. Greater, as used in reference to chords, intervals and scales. RB. 2. Leading, large, as used to designate an important phonograph record company, as a *major* label.

major chords

MU. Major triads and major seventh chords, as distinguished from *minor* chords, *augmented* chords and *diminished* chords. See MAJOR TRIAD. See MAJOR SEVENTH.

majorette

MN. 1. A girl drum major. 2. A girl who leads a marching band, or one, usually of several, who precedes it, often twirling a baton and prancing.

222

major intervals

MU. The major intervals of a major scale are the *second, third, sixth,* and *seventh.* AI. For instance, in the major scale of C these are the tones of D, E, A and B. See PERFECT INTERVALS.

major label

RB. 1. The label, or trade-mark, of a large phonograph record company, as distinguished from that of a smaller company. 2. A large phonograph record company, itself.

major scale

MU. The diatonic scale of eight tones with a *half step* between the third and fourth intervals and a *half step* between the seventh and eighth intervals. Between the first and second intervals, between the second and third intervals, between the fourth and fifth intervals, between the fifth and sixth intervals, between the sixth and seventh intervals are *whole steps.* AI. The steps of the major scale are the same ascending as descending. For instance, the major scale of C is made up of these eight tones: C=D=E−F=G=A=B−C. The symbol = represents a *whole* step. The symbol − represents a *half* step.

major seventh

MU. 1. The name of a particular kind of chord. 2. A chord composed of four tones, consisting of a major triad to which a major seventh has been added. For instance, the C major seventh chord (abbreviated Cmaj7) is composed of these four tones: C-E-G-B.

major triad

MU. 1. The name of a particular kind of chord. 2. A chord composed of these three tones: a root, its major third and its perfect fifth. AI. For instance, the C major triad is composed of these three tones: C-E-G. Major triads have no additional symbols other than the letter name of their root. For instance, a C major triad is simply designated as *C.* A D major triad is designated as *D.* An E major triad is designated as *E,* etc. See SEVENTH CHORDS.

make up

TE. v. 1. To put on cosmetics, as a singer for a stage appearance. 2. To put on a costume, as an actor. PG. 3. To compose, or put together, as type for printing, as for a song sheet.

make-up

TE. n. 1. The way in which a performer is costumed, painted with cosmetics, etc. 2. The costumes, cosmetics, etc. used by performers in making up. PG. 3. The arrangement of printing type, illustrations, etc., as for printing sheet music, song books, etc.

manager

SB. 1. Anyone who, by agreement, manages the affairs, business interests, expenditures, etc. of another or others, as for singers, musicians and other performers. AI. Also called *business manager*. 2. One who manages a business, as a theater, etc.

mandolin

MU. A stringed instrument of the lute family, with eight strings tuned in pairs. Tuning and fretting of a mandolin is the same as that of a violin. The mandolin, however, has a fretted fingerboard and is played with a plectrum.

man in the song, the

MB. The central character in a song concerning a man. AI. For instance, the man whose name is Harry in I'M JUST WILD ABOUT HARRY, the man who says I'M JUST BIDING MY TIME, THE UMBRELLA MAN, PUDDIN' HEAD JONES and the man who wears PINK SHOE LACES.

man in the street

BS. 1. The average man. 2. The ordinary person. 3. One typical of many. 4. The average buyer of sheet music, phonograph records, etc. 5. The average radio listener. 6. The average television viewer. AI. The male counterpart of *Mrs. Lady Next Door, the lady across the street, Mrs. Average Housewife*, etc.

manual

MU. A keyboard, especially that of an organ, to be played by the hands, as opposed to *pedals* or a *pedal keyboard*, played by the feet.

manuscript

SW. A handwritten or typewritten composition, as that of a song. AI. The original copy of a song often is a combination of both, the

224

notation being handwritten and the lyric being typed on a typewriter. AI. Abbreviated, *MS* (singular), *MSS* (plural).

manuscript paper

MU. Music manuscript paper. See MUSIC MANUSCRIPT PAPER.

manward

MB. 1. Toward man, as said of a gospel song, as distinguished from a hymn, which is *Godward*. 2. In relation to or toward man. AI. A sacred song that is written *about* God, rather than *to* God, is said to be *manward*. By no means does the term imply impiety. A manward song can be every bit as religious as a Godward song.

maracas

MU. A Cuban percussion instrument consisting of a dry gourd filled with a small amount of shot, pebbles or dried seed, which is shaken to produce a rattling or swishing sound.

march

MU. A musical composition of well-marked rhythm designed to keep a group of marching people in step. AI. Marches are usually written in Four-Four Time. Typical marches are the STEIN SONG, STARS AND STRIPES FOREVER, ANCHORS AWEIGH, MAC NAMARA'S BAND and SEVENTY-SIX TROMBONES.

marimba (mah-rihm′bah)

MU. A percussion instrument similar to the xylophone, of larger size (usually five to six octaves), consisting of a series of wooden bars, graduated in length, with resonators beneath, which are played by being struck with small mallets or hammers.

market

BS. v. 1. To sell, as song sheets, song books, phonograph records, etc. 2. To vend. 3. To merchandise.

market

BS. n. The source for buying articles of merchandise, as song sheets, song books, phonograph records, etc.

225

mark of continuation

MU. Any line or lines indicating that something which has been established is to be continued. AI. Examples of marks of continuation are as follows: the wavy line following the designation for a trill. The broken or dotted line following the designation *8va* or *8vaba*. The extender line used in writing lyrics. The bracket or line that designates first ending, second ending, etc.

marshmallow

MN. 1. An overly sentimental song or melody. 2. An all-too-sweet performance in playing a musical composition, as a song. AI. Also called *cream puff*.

masculine ending

PY. Ending on an accented syllable. AI. For instance, the word *a-lone'* has a masculine ending.

masculine rhyme

PY. 1. A single rhyme. 2. A one-syllable rhyme. 3. A rhyme word in which the rhyme falls on the last syllable. AI. For instance, *night* and *de-light* are two masculine rhyme words.

master

RG. 1. An original recording (tape or lacquer) from which other recordings can be made. 2. The die from which phonograph records are pressed. MT. 3. A camera-ready image from which printing plates are made, as those for printing music, usually called a *camera-ready master*.

mastering

RB. The act of editing an original recording (master).

master of ceremonies

SB. A person who presides over an entertainment, as on a stage, radio, television, in a night club, etc., introducing other performers, filling in intervals with jokes, songs, etc. AI. Also called *m.c.* or *host*.

material

SW. 1. Subject matter for a song or songs. 2. Song text matter. 3.

Collected ideas, as for songwriting, or the notes containing them.
4. A song or songs, as *artist's* material, *special* material, etc. TE.
5. Written matter, as a monolog, dialog, patter, special songs, etc.
used by performers in the make-up of an act.

material object

LW. Something that can be seen or touched. Something that occupies space, as a sheet of music, a song book, a phonograph record, etc., as distinguished from a *privilege*, as a copyright. AI. Transfer of ownership of any material object, as a phonograph record, in which a work, as a song, is fixed, does not of itself convey any exclusive rights in the copyright work embodied in the object. Likewise, the transfer of ownership of a copyright does not convey property rights in any material object. A *song*, as it is printed on a sheet of music or recorded on a phonograph record, and the *copyright* of the same song are two entirely different things, to be dealt with separately.

matrix (mae´trihks)

RB. 1. A mold used in the manufacturing of phonograph records. 2. The die used to press phonograph records, which in turn are called *pressings*.

maxim

SW. A brief statement of self-evident truth, as used in songwriting. AI. Typical maxims are: *Fools rush in where angels fear to tread. Great oaks from little acorns grow. We never know how much we loved till what we loved is lost.*

MBS (emm-bee-ess)

RO. Abbreviation, *Mutual Broadcasting System.*

m. c.

SB. Abbreviation, *master of ceremonies.*

measure:

MU. 1. The space between one bar and the next bar, including the notation contained therein, as shown above. 2. A division of time in music by which movements are regulated. 3. The unit by which the length of a song is measured. AI. Erroneously called a *bar*. See BAR.

mechanical instruments

MU. 1. Appliances designed to produce music mechanically, without an actual performer. AI. Well-known mechanical instruments are the barrel organ (erroneously called the hurdy-gurdy), the music box, the player piano, the phonograph, the tape recorder (and playback), the juke box, etc.

mechanical license

MB. A written permit by a copyright owner, as a music publisher, authorizing the addressee, as a phonograph record manufacturer, to make records of one particular recording of a particular musical composition, as a song. AI. A mechanical license states the rights which are granted as well as the obligations, as royalties to the copyright owner, which are imposed.

mechanical rights

LW. The rights to reproduce a musical composition by mechanical means, as tapes, records, etc. AI. These are among the rights under copyright, granted a music publisher by a songwriter. The publisher, in turn, gives a mechanical license to a record company, when a recording is secured.

mechanical royalties

MB. Payments for permission to record a musical composition for performance by mechanical instruments.

mediant

MU. 1. The third degree of the scale. 2. The tone next above the supertonic. AI. For instance, in the scale of C the mediant is the tone of E.

medium

LW. 1. The mechanical or physical agent by which music is performed. AI. For instance, a juke box is a *mechanical* agent. A singer is a *physical* agent. Each is a *medium*. GI. 2. Any agency, means, or something intermediate, as radio is a *medium* for popularizing songs, newspapers and trade publications are *media* for publicity and advertising. Plural, *media*.

medium face

PG. A printer's type that is between light face and bold face in heaviness of characters. Abbreviation, *m.f.*

medley

MU. 1. A musical arrangement made up of several different tunes, or parts of tunes, to be used for continuous performance. 2. A mixture of songs played as a continuous whole.

melodic

MU. 1. Pertaining to melody. 2. Having the nature of a melody.

melodics

MU. The department of musical science which deals with the laws, principles and construction of melody and to the pitch of tones.

melodist

MU. 1. A composer of melodies. 2. A singer.

melodize

MU. 1. To construct melodies. 2. To compose melodies.

melody

MU. 1. A succession of single musical tones, one following the other, written according to definite rules to produce a pleasing effect. 2. An air. 3. A tune. 4. The element in music most readily remembered. LW. 5. The musical idea around which a composition is constructed. AI. A melody consists of one tone at a time. Whereas harmony is the performance of two or more tones at the same time.

melody guitar

MU. 1. A style of guitar playing in which the melody is played, as distinguished from rhythm guitar. 2. Solo guitar.

melody line

MU. 1. A lead sheet. 2. The staff line on which the melody of a song is written. 3. The top staff in a 3-staves-to-the-system, piano-and-

229

vocal, arrangement. 4. The staff line that appears immediately above the lyric line on printed sheet music.

melody properties

MU. The characteristic qualities that make up a melody. AI. A melody has six properties. These are: (a) Rhythm, (b) Range, (c) Register, (d) Direction (whether predominantly up or down the scale), (e) Progression (whether movement is by long or short intervals) and (f) Length.

melody staff

MU. The staff on which the melody is written or printed, as distinguished from the *treble staff* and *bass staff* accompaniment in a 3-staves-to-the-system, piano-and-vocal, arrangement.

menagerie (meh-naj″r-ee)

MN. Facetiously, an orchestra or a band, as the *house* or *pit* band in a theater, the *staff* band at a broadcasting station, etc.

mental effects

PS. 1. The reaction or reactions produced within a person by music. 2. The effect that music has on attitude and thought.

metaphor (meht′a-for)

SW. A figure of speech in which one object is likened to another, as used in songwriting. AI. A metaphor is distinguished from a *simile* by not using any word of comparison, as *like* or *as*. Typical of songs using metaphoric titles are: YOU'RE THE CREAM IN MY COFFEE, LIFE IS JUST A BOWL OF CHERRIES and I'M ALWAYS CHASING RAINBOWS.

meter

SW. 1. A measured verbal rhythm, the structure of verse, as used in songwriting. 2. A definite arrangement of groups of syllables. MU. 3. In a musical composition or section, the basic grouping of beats and accents as found in each measure and as indicated by the time signature, as Two-Four meter (or Two-Four Time), Four-Four meter (or Four-Four Time), Three-Four meter (or Three-Four Time), etc.

metonymy (meh-tahn´a-me)

SW. A figure of speech that uses the name of one thing to mean another which is associated with it, as used in songwriting. AI. For instance, *blue eyes* to mean an actual *girl*, *Lazybones* to mean a *person*, *Scatterbrain* to mean a *person*, etc.

metrical

SW. 1. Related to meter. 2. Composed in poetical measures. 3. Rhythmical.

metrical numbers

CH. 1. The group of numbers used to designate the metrical count of a hymn tune. 2. The group of numbers which usually follow the name of a hymn tune, as Marietta *7.6.7.6.*, Snowdon *8.7.8.7.*, etc. AI. Metrical numbers are used in fitting words to a hymn tune and vice versa. Each group of numbers tells two things: (a) the number of lyric lines to the musical phrase and (b) the number of syllables in each line. For instance, the metrical count for Merrial (the hymn tune to which NOW THE DAY IS DONE is usually sung) is *6.5.6.5.* This means there are *four* poetic lines to the stanza (one for each of the *four* figures). The first figure (*6*) designates that there are *six* syllables in the first line. The second figure (*5*) designates that there are *five* syllables in the second line, etc.

metrics

PY. 1. The art of writing in meter. 2. The characteristics and details of poetry or verse.

metronome

MU. 1. An instrument for indicating and marking exact time in music. 2. A mechanical device for beating exact time. AI. The metronome was invented by John Maelzel in 1815.

metronome marks

MU. Directions for setting the metronome, which appear as figures on music, referring to corresponding figures on the metronome. AI. For instance, the metronome marks M.M. ♩=112 means that the metronome is to be set at 112. As each click of the metronome represents the time value of a quarter note, (♩) this means a speed of 112 quarter notes a minute. See M. M.

mezzo (met'soh)

MU. 1. Medium. 2. Moderate. 3. Half.

mezzo soprano

MU. 1. The female voice between *soprano* and *contralto*. 2. A person having such a voice. 3. The part written for such a voice. AI. Also called *second soprano*.

mi (mee): ◊

MU. 1. The syllable used in singing the third note (tone) of the scale in the sol-fa system. 2. The shape notehead shown above representing this syllable.

microgroove

RG. Small grooves that are spaced closely together on a phonograph record to give a longer playing time for the same surface area. AI. For instance, all 33⅓ rpm records and all 45 rpm records are microgrooved as distinguished from 78 rpm records, which have *conventional* grooves.

microphone

BR. An instrument that picks up sound and transmits it in the form of electric impulses. AI. Often called *mike*.

middle

SW. 1. The so-called *middle* part or *middle* section of a song chorus. 2. The bridge or release. 3. The B section of a song chorus written in AABA form. AI. Also called the *half*. See BRIDGE.

middle C

MU. 1. The C midway between the treble and the bass staves. AI. Middle C is written on the first leger line below the treble staff. Or, middle C is written on the first leger line above the bass staff, which is the same leger line. 2. The fourth C from the left on the keyboard of a standard 88-key piano. 3. The fourth C from the right on the keyboard of a standard 88-key piano.

middle finger

MU. 1. The finger between the index finger and the ring finger.

2. Usually, the longest finger on the hand. 3. The finger designated by the figure 2 in the English method of fingering. 4. The finger designated by the figure *3* in the German method of fingering.

middle note

MU. The note designating the middle tone.

middle tone

MU. The tone halfway between the highest tone and the lowest tone of a vocal or instrumental range. AI. Each voice, as soprano, alto, tenor, bass, etc., has a middle tone. The average voice has a range of from about one octave higher to about one octave lower than this middle tone.

mike

BR. Short for *microphone.*

miked-up

BR. To have a microphone or microphones properly connected, properly placed and in working order, ready to be used. AI. For instance, a director or A-and-R man might ask an engineer, "Are you miked up?" This means *are you ready to start broadcasting or recording.*

mill

WR. A writer's term for his *typewriter.*

min

MU. The symbol meaning *minor.* AI. For instance, a C *minor triad* is designated as *Cmin.* A C *minor seventh chord* is designated as *Cmin7*, etc.

miniature score

PP. A small, usually pocket-size, full score, designed chiefly for the student who wishes to read music while listening to it being performed.

minor

MU. 1. Smaller. 2. Less by a semitone. 3. A term used in reference to chords, intervals and scales. 4. A term used to name a certain kind of chord, as *Cmin* (C minor), *Dmin* (D minor), etc. AI. A song written in a minor key has a pathetic theme or quality.

minor chords

MU. Minor triads and minor sevenths, as distinguished from *major* chords, *augmented* chords and *diminished* chords. See MINOR TRIAD. See MINOR SEVENTH.

minor interval

MU. An interval a half step smaller than a *major* interval. AI. For instance, in the major scale of C these are the tones of Db, Eb, Ab and Bb.

minor scale

MU. There are two kinds of minor diatonic scales (keys): 1. In the *harmonic minor scale* the semitones fall between the second and third and between the seventh and eighth intervals, ascending or descending. 2. In the *melodic minor scale* the semitones fall between the second and third and between the seventh and eighth intervals *ascending;* and between the sixth and fifth and between the third and second intervals *descending.* Between all other intervals are whole tones. AI. For instance:

HARMONIC	C D Eb F G Ab B C
MELODIC ASCENDING	C D Eb F G A B C
MELODIC DESCENDING	C D Eb F G Ab Bb C

minor seventh chord

MU. A chord composed of these four tones: a minor triad with a minor seventh added. For instance, the *C minor seventh* chord is composed of the tones C-Eb-G-Bb. Minor seventh chords are usually captioned Cm7, Dm7, Em7, etc.

minor triad

MU. A chord consisting of these three tones: a root, its minor third and its perfect fifth. For instance, the *C minor triad* is composed of the tones C-Eb-G. Minor triads are usually captioned Cm, Dm, Em, etc., or Cmin, Dmin, Emin, etc.

minstrels

MU. 1. Originally, professional musicians, singers and poets of the middle ages, who traveled from place to place to entertain. 2. In modern usage, entertainers, especially comedians who perform in black face (Negro make-up). 3. Modern folk singers and musicians. AI. The black-face minstrels played an important part in the history of the music business. Among those who were truly great are Bert Swor, Sugarfoot Gaffney and Dan Emmett, the writer of DIXIE.

minus sign: —

MU. 1. The short, horizontal mark shown above. 2. Sometimes called the *negative sign*. AI. The minus sign is sometimes used to designate *minor*, as C- (C minor), D- (D minor), E- (E minor), etc.

mirror

MB. 1. A recording that is an imitation of another recording, usually that of a competitive label. 2. A cover that is very similar to the original record it covers. 3. A phonograph record that is an intentional imitation of another record. See COPY CAT.

misprint

PG. An error in printing, as that in a song.

mix

BR. To blend sounds, as is done in broadcasting and recording.

mixed chorus

MU. A chorus of both male and female voices. AI. Also called *mixed voices*.

mixer

BR. 1. An electrical device for combining the sounds emanating from several different sources. 2. One who operates this device, as a control-room engineer, at a broadcasting station or recording studio.

M. M.

MU. Abbreviation, *Maelzel's Metronome*.

MOA (em-oh-ae)

MB. Abbreviation, *Music Operators of America*.

mode

MU. A key or a scale, as a *major* mode or a *minor* mode.

modulation

MU. 1. The musical process of passing from one key to another. 2. A series of chords or tones arranged according to certain rules, progressing from one key to another.

monaural (mahn-au′ral)

RG. The method of picking up and/or reproducing sound from one source of origin only. AI. A monaural record or tape has only one sound track. Also known as *full track* or *single track* recording. Compare with STEREOPHONIC, DUAL-TRACK and FOUR-TRACK.

money song

MB. 1. A song of assured or proven commercial worth. SW. 2. A sugar stick.

monochord (mahn′a-kord″)

MU. A musical instrument of the Middle Ages consisting of a sound box with graduated markings indicated by letters of the alphabet, over which was stretched a single string. AI. This was the beginning of the use of the letters A, B, C, D, E, F, and G to indicate the tones of a scale.

monolog (mahn′a-lawg″)

TE. 1. That which is spoken by a performer, as distinguished from that which is sung. 2. The patter chorus of a song. 3. A recitation. 4. A part in a play in which one person speaks alone.

monologuist (mahn′a-lawg″est)

TE. One who performs a monolog.

monometer (mahn″o-me′ter)

SW. One metric foot, as in verse or poetry. AI. Musical counterpart, a one-measure phrase.

monophonic (mahn″a-fahn′ek)

RG. Designating sound reproduction using a single channel to carry

236

and reproduce sounds, through one or more speakers. See MONAURAL.

monophony (ma-nahf′o-ne)

MU. Music having a single melody without accompaniment or harmonizing parts, as distinguished from *polyphony*. See HOMO-PHONY.

monosyllable (mahn′a-sihl″a-b'l)

PY. A word of one syllable, as *boy, girl, love,* etc.

monotone

MU. 1. Continuous repetition of the same tone. 2. Chanting or singing in such a tone.

montage (mahn-tahj′)

MP. 1. The process of producing a rapid sequence of very short motion-picture or TV scenes to show a rapid succession of associated ideas. 2. The part of a motion picture, or TV play, in which this is used. RO. 3. A radio sequence, usually dramatic, in which voices and other sounds are used to break in on one another or blend to suggest a progression of thought. MU. 4. A progression of brief musical themes blended together to suggest a progression of thought. AI. Montage is used in dramaturgy to change scenes from one location to another, to indicate a lapse in time, to indicate general confusion, to change moods, as from sadness to hope, from happiness to dismay, etc.

montage music

MP. Music written or arranged to be played behind montage, as in a motion picture, on radio or TV, etc.

mood

PS. A particular state of mind or feeling, humor or temper. AI. Music has a strong influence on the mood of a person.

mood music

MU. 1. Music designed to affect a person's mood. 2. Generally, incidental music. See INCIDENTAL MUSIC.

237

moonlighter

MN. One who *moonlights*.

moonlighting

MN. The practice of holding a second job in addition to one's regular job, as said of musicians, performers, etc.

moon songs

MB. A classification in songwriting, as to subject matter. AI. Typical moon songs are CAROLINA MOON, OH YOU CRAZY MOON, ALLEGHENY MOON and WABASH MOON.

mosaic rhyme

SW. A rhyme consisting of more than one word. AI. Typical mosaic rhymes are: enfold me, hold me; dream away, scheme away; oh, man, oh, go, man, go, etc.

mother

RB. The female mold from which (record) stampers are made.

mother songs

MB. A classification in songwriting, as to subject matter. AI. Typical mother songs are M-O-T-H-E-R, MY MOM, MAMMY and MY YIDDISHA MOMME.

motif (moh-teef')

MU. 1. An idea. 2. A motive. 3. A figure.

motion

MU. Progression of a melody or a part of a melody.

motion-picture rights

LW. Two rights are necessary to the performance of music in a motion picture: the synchronization right, which is the right to record music in timed relation to the action shown, and the right to perform publicly the music that is recorded under the synchronization right. Also called *film rights*.

238

motivation (moh"te-vae'shuhn)

PS. 1. The force that causes action. 2. The reason why a person does something. AI. For instance, a song might be written with the purposeful motivation to cause listeners to cry.

motive (moh'teev)

MU. 1. A musical theme. 2. A musical figure. GI. The motive is the smallest part of a melody, usually the pattern by which a melody is written. The motive, or variations of the motive, occur and reoccur throughout a melody. As an example, the *da da da dah* (V theme) in Beethoven's Fifth Symphony occurs more than sixty times in the first movement of this piece.

mountain music

MB. Hill music. See HILL MUSIC.

mouth harmonica

MU. A musical instrument made of a series of graduated metal reeds in a narrow frame, which is blown or sucked to produce different tones. AI. Also called a *mouth harp.*

mouth organ

MU. 1. A mouth harmonica. 2. A mouth harp.

mouthpiece

MU. 1. That part of a wind instrument which is held between the lips, as a clarinet, or applied to the lips, as a cornet. AI. There are different kinds of mouthpieces and these form the chief distinction between the various families of wind instruments. MN. 2. A singer.

movement

MU. 1. A section of a musical composition. 2. A strain.

movie work

MB. A complete musical work originally written for and performed in full in a full-length feature motion picture shown in motion picture theaters in the United States prior to the television releases, as defined by BMI. AI. Also called *motion-picture work.*

MPPS (em-pe-pe-ess)

MB. Abbreviation, *Music Publishers Protective Association.*

MS or ms (em-ess)

GI. Abbreviation, *manuscript*, as that of a song.

MSS or mss (em-ess-ess)

GI. Abbreviation, *manuscripts* (plural), as those of songs.

multiple-voice

MU. A designation applied to vocal arrangements which are for more than one voice. AI. The most popular *multiple-voice* arrangements are classified in music publishers' catalogs as: SA, SSA, SSAA, SAB, SATB, TTBB, SSCB, (each combination pronounced as a set of initials). S means *soprano*. A means *alto*. T means *tenor*. B means either *baritone* or *bass*. C means (choir) *boys' voices*. For instance, SSAA means first soprano, second soprano, first alto and second alto, the four voices that make up the usual girls' quartet. TTBB means first tenor, second tenor, baritone and bass, the four voices that make up the usual male quartet. SA means a girls' duo. SSA means a girls' trio. SAB means a mixed trio. SSCB means a mixed quartet, of higher voices than SATB.

multiplex

RO. A system of broadcasting both sound channels of a stereo program, usually by FM, over the same frequency. AI. Also called *stereo FM.*

music

MU. 1. The art and science of combining tones in a pleasing manner. 2. A rhythmical succession or combination of sounds that are pleasing to the ear. 3. A written or printed musical composition. 4. The melody and/or harmony of a song, as distinguished from the lyric or words.

musical

TE. 1. A musical show, as is typical of those produced on Broadway. 2. A musical motion picture. 3. A musical comedy.

240

musical comedy

TE. 1. An elaborate theatrical production containing song and dance numbers, humorous skits, centered on some semblance of a plot, usually having a colorful costuming and staging. 2. A musical. AI. Typical musical comedies are: *No, No, Nanette* (which included the song hit TEA FOR TWO), *Girl Crazy* (which included the song hit I GOT RHYTHM) and *On Your Toes* (which included the song hit THERE'S A SMALL HOTEL).

musical composition

LW. The United States Copyright Office says, "The term 'musical composition' includes compositions consisting of music alone, or of words and music combined. It also includes arrangements and other versions of earlier compositions, if new copyrightable work of authorship has been added." The term *musical composition* does not include so-called "song poems" and other works consisting of words without music.

musical image

PS. 1. The idea, thought or feeling that is caused by listening to music. 2. The emotions aroused by music. 3. What one experiences in feeling while listening to music.

musical play

TE. A theatrical production consisting of a play of somewhat more serious plot situations than a musical comedy, with special-written musical material. AI. Typical musical plays are: *Carousel* (including the song hit JUNE IS BUSTIN' OUT ALL OVER), *Kismet* (including the song hit STRANGER IN PARADISE) and *Brigadoon* (including the song hit ALMOST LIKE BEING IN LOVE).

musical sound

MU. Tone. See TONE.

musical theater

TE. Musicals, musical plays and plays with which music is performed, as distinguished from the dramatic field and/or the *legitimate theater*.

musical work

MB. A musical composition, as a song.

music business

MB. Those organizations and individuals who are *legitimately* in business to create, promote and sell songs and other forms of musical works. AI. Unfortunately, it is necessary to make the above distinction due to the misleading statements of song sharks and others who advertise profusely, falsely claiming to be part of the *real* music business.

music center

MB. 1. A city in which is located active music publishers, recording studios, phonograph record companies and allied concerns. 2. Any locality which is particularly active in the performance and/or study of music. AI. Important music centers in the United States are New York City, Nashville, Los Angeles and Chicago.

music city

MB. Nashville, Tennessee. AI. Also called *Music City, U.S.A.*

music contractor

MB. One who selects and assembles musicians for a job, as a recording session. AI. The fee for this service, as regulated by the American Federation of Musicians, is paid by the person or company—as a record company—employing the musicians, not by the musicians themselves.

music copyist

MB. See COPYIST.

music director

MB. An employee of a radio station, television station, or other organization, who is in charge of music.

music engraver

PG. A person or organization who engraves plates to be used for printing music, a somewhat outmoded process. AI. The major portion of modern music is *set*, for printing, by *music typographers*.

music foundry

SS. 1. A company or individual that sells melodies and/or lyrics to

242

would-be songwriters. 2. Those who advertise for so-called *song poems*. See SONG SHARK.

music hall

TE. 1. An auditorium for musical and other theatrical productions. 2. A British vaudeville theater.

musician

MB. 1. Generally, any person skilled in music. 2. Specifically, a professional (union) musician. AI. Actually there are three kinds of musicians: (1) Those who write or compose music. (2) Those who perform music. (3) Those who listen to music with knowledge and understanding.

musicians' lounge

TE, RT. Quarters, provided by some theaters, night clubs, broadcasting stations, ballrooms, etc., for staff musicians.

musicians' union

MB. The American Federation of Musicians.

musicians' war cry:

MN. The above little melody. AI. The war cry is used to call members of an orchestra back to the band stand after an intermission, by uually being played with one finger on the piano. It is whistled by a musician to attract the attention of another musician or musicians, to identify one's self as a musician, etc.

music illiterate

MN. A person who cannot read music. AI. The term is not necessarily one of disparagement. Also, *music illit*.

music man

MB. Anyone in the music business, as a songwriter, musician, singer, music publisher's representative, employee of a phonograph record company, disk jockey, etc. AI. The title is complimentary and often used to mean a *dedicated* person.

music manuscript

MB. A handwritten or handwritten-and-typewritten musical compo-

243

sition, as that submitted to a music publisher by a songwriter. AI. The word *manuscript* usually implies the author's original copy.

music-manuscript paper

MB. Specially prepared paper, on which staves are printed, for writing music, as a song. AI. Music manuscript paper comes in a variety of sizes and forms, as to the length of the staves and the number of staves to a page. The kind most often used by songwriters is folded once and has four pages, each approximately 9½″ wide x 12½″ high, with 12 staves printed on each page.

musicologist (mu″zih-kahl′a-jihst)

MU. An expert in musicology.

musicology (mu″zih-kahl′a-je)

MU. The scholarly study of music, its science, history, forms and methods.

musicomedy

TE. Same as *musical comedy*.

Music Operators of America

JB. A national organization of juke box operators. Abbreviated, MOA. Address: 228 North La Salle Street, Chicago, Illinois 60601.

music page

PG. A page on which music is printed, as distinguished from pages that do not contain music, as those of a song sheet, a book, a manuscript. AI. For instance, a song book might be made up of a number of music pages as well as a number of pages that contain conventional printed matter (called non-music pages). If a song is printed on two pages of a folded song sheet, these two inside pages are *music pages*. The front cover and the back cover are *not* music pages, or *non-music pages*.

Music Publishers Protective Association

MB. A national organization whose purpose is stated in its name. Abbreviated, MPPA. Address: 460 Park Avenue, New York, N.Y. 10022.

music typographer

PG. A person or organization skilled in setting type (both words and notation) from which music is printed.

music typography

PG. 1. The art of printing music (and words) with type. 2. The setting and arranging of type for printing music notation and words. 3. The arrangement, style, or general appearance of music and words printed from type. AI. Music typography is by far a more modern process than engraving and is rapidly becoming much more used.

mute

MU. A device for softening or diminishing the tone of certain musical instruments, as a violin, trumpet, trombone, etc. AI. A mute performs the same functions as the *soft pedal* on the piano.

muted

MU. 1. A *muted* instrument is one played *with a mute*, to produce a modified tone. 2. A *muted* tone is a *softer* tone.

Mutual Broadcasting System

RO. A network of radio broadcasting stations. Abbreviated, MBS. Address: 135 West 50th Street, New York, N.Y. 10019.

n

N

name band

MB. 1. A band whose name is widely and favorably known. 2. A band of importance.

name songs

MB. A classification in songwriting, as to subject matter. AI. Name songs are usually further classified as to *girl* name songs and *boy* name songs. Typical girl-name songs are MARGIE, SWEET ROSIE O'GRADY and GIGI. Typical boy-name songs are CHARLIE MY BOY, HAPPINESS IS A THING CALLED JOE and BILL.

name writer

MB. A songwriter whose name is widely and favorably known, as one with important songs to his credit.

NAMM (en-ae-em-em)

MB. Abbreviation, *National Association of Music Merchants.*

NARAS (en-ae-ahr-ae-ess)

MB. Abbreviation, *National Academy of Recording Arts and Sciences.*

narrate

SW. To tell or relate, as the story told in a song.

narrator

SW. The person who tells or relates a story, as that in a song. AI. For instance, the narrator of OL' MAN RIVER is a downtrodden Mississippi-river roustabout. The narrator of MY BLUE HEAVEN is a happily-married young man. The narrator of I WENT TO YOUR WEDDING is a rejected sweetheart. The narrator of KING OF THE ROAD is a hobo.

NARRD (en-ae-ahr-ahr-dee)

MB. Abbreviation, *National Association of Retail Record Dealers.*

nasal

SG. 1. A vocal effect produced by singers. 2. An effect produced by stopping all or part of the breath in the mouth and permitting it to pass through the nose, particuarly when sounding the letters *m, n* and *ng.* 3. A vocal effect produced by *singing through the nose.* MU. 4. For instance, the clarinet is less nasal than the oboe.

Nashville sound, the

MB. The obvious but difficult-to-describe quality peculiar to the majority of songs and song arrangements that are recorded in Nashville, Tennessee. AI. An entire book could well be written on the evolution of the Nashville sound. A list of those who have contributed to its being would fill many pages. The first Nashville recordings to attract nation-wide attention were NEAR YOU, by Francis Craig's Orchestra, featuring Bob Lamm as vocalist, and the recordings of Hank Williams, beginning with COLD, COLD HEART, recorded under the A-and-R direction of Fred Rose.

national

BS. 1. Of a nation or the nation. 2. Nation-wide, as distinguished from *local* or *regional.* 3. Restricted to the one nation, as distinguished from international.

National Academy of Recording Arts and Sciences

MB. An organization whose purpose it is to encourage and acknowledge outstanding achievements in the creative fields of the phonograph record industry. Awards are given each year in the form of miniature old-fashioned gramaphones called *Grammies.* Abbreviated, NARAS. Western Chapter address: 9034 Sunset Boulevard, Suite 206, Los Angeles, California 90069. Eastern Chapter address: 21 West 58th Street, New York, N.Y. 10019.

national anthem

MU. A song adopted by a nation to be played at all official functions, as THE STAR SPANGLED BANNER.

National Association of Music Merchants

MB. An organization of retailers in any facet of the music business. AI. Abbreviation, NAMM. Address: 222 West Adams Street, Chicago, Illinois 60606.

National Association of Record Merchandisers

MB. An organization of rack jobbers, which record manufacturers and rack jobber equipment manufacturers and suppliers are eligible to join as associate members. AI. Also called NARM (pronounced as a word as well as separate initials). Address: 112 Beverly Road, Philadelphia, Pennsylvania.

National Association of Retail Record Dealers

MB. An organization of retail record dealers. AI. Also called NARRD (pronounced as a word as well as separate initials). Address: 327 Jackson Avenue, Jersey City, New Jersey.

National Better Business Bureau, Inc.

BS. See BETTER BUSINESS BUREAU.

National Broadcasting Company

RT. A radio and television broadcasting network, usually called NBC. Address: 30 Rockefeller Plaza, New York, N.Y. 10020.

national country music month

MB. A month, usually in the fall of the year, during which country music is honored. AI. Country music month varies from year to year.

nationalism

MU. 1. The rhythmic and melodic characteristics peculiar to the music of a country that enables us to recognize the nationality of a musical composition. 2. The individuality of a nation's music. 3. The style of a country's music. 4. The national traits of a country's music.

249

national music

MU. Music which is peculiarly characteristic of its own country, as distinguished from that of other countries.

national usage

SW. 1. A word, phrase or expression is said to be *in national usage* when it is in present, reputable and general use throughout a nation. 2. Widely used. 3. Understood. AI. Compare with provincialism.

natural: ♮

MU. 1. The sign shown above. AI. A natural is written before a note to cancel the effect of a sharp or flat. Also called a *cancel*. 2. A note (tone) that is neither sharped nor flatted. 3. A white key on a keyboard instrument, as the piano, accordion, etc. MB. 4. A song that is particularly suited to a certain artist is said to be a natural for that artist. 5. A song that has good reasons to become popular.

natural chords

MU. Any chord that can be written or played without the use of sharps and flats. AI. There are seven natural triads. These are: CEG, DFA, EGB, FAC, GBD, ACE, and BDF. There are seven natural seventh chords. These are: CEGB, DFAC, EGBD, FACE, CBDF, ACEG, and BDFA.

natural key

MU. 1. A key (or scale) having no sharps and no flats. 2. Therefore, a key (or scale) having no key signature, as the major scale of C.

natural scale

MU. The same as *natural key*.

nature songs

MB. A classification in songwriting, as to subject matter. AI. Typical nature songs are WINTER WONDERLAND, JUNE IS BUSTIN' OUT ALL OVER, TUMBLING TUMBLE WEEDS and THEY CALL THE WIND MARIA.

NBC (en-bee-see)

RT. Abbreviation, The *National Broadcasting Company*.

neck

MU. That part of a stringed instrument, as a violin, guitar, etc., that extends from the body to the head and on which the fingerboard is fixed.

negative

PG. A photograph, usually on film, which has the light and shade reversed. What is light on a *positive* is dark on a negative and vice versa. When camera-ready copy is photographed, a negative is produced. From this negative a printing plate is made, as that used in printing music.

negative sign: —

MU. 1. The sign shown above. 2. A minus sign. See MINUS SIGN.

Negro music

MU. The American Negro has contributed far more to songwriting and the music business as a whole than has any other race. Without this tremendous influence, the music business would be much different from what it is today. It is doubtful that it would be as great. Entire volumes have been written on each of the forms of music originated by the American Negro, as spiritual, gospel, ragtime, rhythm, blues, hot jazz, cool jazz, bop, re bop, be bop, rock and roll, progressive jazz, etc. It would be impossible to give adequate description of any one of these forms within the limited pages of a book such as this.

neo (nee-o)

GI. 1. New. 2. Young. 3. Recent. See NEOFOLK MUSIC.

neofolk music

FK. 1. A recently written musical composition in the folk style, as distinguished from *authentic* folk music. 2. An imitation of folk music.

network

RT. 1. A number of radio or television stations connected in series, thus providing national or regional listener or viewer coverage, as distinguished from the *local* coverage of a single station. 2. An organization such as the American Broadcasting Company (ABC), the Columbia Broadcasting System (CBS), the National Broadcasting Company (NBC), and the Mutual Broadcasting System (MBS). AI. Also called *hookup*.

251

neume (noom): ▔▜ ▪ ◆ •

MU. 1. Any of the signs shown above. 2. The tone designated by one of these signs. AI. Neumes were used in the Middle Ages in writing church music to designate melody and the manner in which it is performed. Reading from left to right, the signs shown above are the *long*, the *double-long*, the *breve*, the *semi-breve* and the *minim*.

new version

LW. 1. A different form or variation of a previous work, as a new arrangement or translation of a song. 2. The republication of a musical composition, as a song with new matter or material added. AI. The copyright that may be secured in a *new version* is entirely independent of any and all copyright protection that may have been secured earlier. The only *authors* of the new version, recognized by the United States copyright law, are those who contributed copyrightable matter or material to the new version. A new version of a copyrighted work cannot legally be made without the consent of the copyright owner. Also called *revision*.

New York sound

MB. A soft, sweet blend of feminine Negro voices, conspicuously with a New York accent, as used by a number of vocal groups.

night club

SB. A place of entertainment that is open at night for eating, drinking, etc., often having a floor show. AI. Sometimes called a *supper club*.

night people

SB. 1. People who work at night, either by choice or of necessity, as musicians, entertainers and others employed in show business, as distinguished from *day people*. 2. Those who work better at night than day, as do some songwriters. 3. Those who prefer to work at night.

nine-by-twelve

MB. A standard song sheet with a piano-and-vocal arrangement, the usual form in which popular songs are printed for sale, as distinguished from *professional copies* (which are smaller in size). AI. So called because the page size is approximately nine inches by twelve inches.

252

nine rights, the

LW. The nine rights of the owner of a copyrighted musical composition, as a song, as prescribed by the United States Copyright Act of 1909, are these: 1. The right to print and reprint. 2. The right to publish. 3. The right to copy. 4. The right to sell or vend. 5. The right to arrange. 6. The right to adapt. 7. The right to publicly perform for profit. 8. The right to make any arrangement or setting in any system of notation. 9. The right to produce mechanically, as by means of phonograph records, music rolls for player pianos, films, tapes, etc. AI. There are certain limitations to some of these rights. Any one of these rights can be assigned or transferred to another, without affecting or including any other right, unless so agreed.

nine-to-five life, the

SB. 1. The life lived by the average person who is not connected with show business. 2. The normal, natural life of normal people. 3. The life and world outside of show business. 4. Sometimes, a prosaic life.

ninth

MU. 1. An interval of nine degrees. 2. A kind of chord.

ninth chord

MU. Any seventh chord with its ninth added. AI. For instance, C7 (C dominant seventh), comprised of the tones C-E-G-B♭, becomes C9 (C dominant ninth) when the tone of D is added, thus: C-E-G-B♭-D. Captions or symbols for other ninth chords are: Cmaj7(9), Dmaj7(9), etc. Cm7(9), Dm7(9), etc. Caug7(9), Daug7(9), etc. Cdim7(9), Ddim7(9), etc. Sixth chords can become ninth chords in the same manner as seventh chords. Captions for these are: C6(9), D6(9), etc. Cm6(9), Dm6(9), etc. Also called *a chord of the ninth*.

nocturne (nahk′tern)

MU. a. Pertaining to the night, as a night song.

nocturne

MU. n. 1. A night song. 2. A dreamy, romantic song about the night. 3. A musical composition that suggests the night. 4. A serenade. 5. A song or instrumental for evening performance. AI. Typical nocturnes are GOOD NIGHT SWEETHEART, SLEEP, CLOUDS, THE NIGHT IS FILLED WITH MUSIC and I'LL SEE YOU IN MY DREAMS.

noel (no-ell′)

MB. 1. A Christmas carol. 2. A hymn of good tidings pertaining to Christmas. 3. A joyous song particularly suited to be sung on Christmas Eve. Typical noels are: O COME ALL YE FAITHFUL, O LITTLE TOWN OF BETHLEHEM, THE FIRST NOEL, and IT CAME UPON THE MIDNIGHT CLEAR.

noise

MU. A sound produced by irregular vibrations, as distinguished from tone. See TONE.

nom de plume (nahm′ d′ ploom′)

WR. 1. A pen name. 2. A pseudonym, as that of a songwriter.

non-Berne country

LW. Any country that does not subscribe to the Berne Convention of 1886 or to any of its four successive revisions, Paris 1896, Berlin 1908, Rome 1928, and Brussels 1948. AI. The Berne Convention is established to give automatic copyright, without compulsory requirements, to all authors in its member countries. The United States copyright law requires compulsory registration in order to secure copyright. For this reason the United States can not belong to the Berne Convention. The United States, therefore, is a *non-Berne country*.

nonchurch music

MB. Musical compositions that are not necessarily written to be performed in a church, as distinguished from church music. AI. By no means does the term necessarily imply impiety or music of a secular nature. Nonchurch music can be just as religious in character as church music.

nondramatic rights

TE. 1. Nondramatic performance rights. 2. The rights to perform a nondramatic composition, as a song or other musical work in which there is no plot depicted by action, as granted by the copyright act. AI. Often called *small rights* as distinguished from *dramatic performance rights*, called *grand rights*.

nonliturgical music

MU. Music of a serious religious nature but which is composed for

254

concert purposes rather than for a specific function in church cere-
mony, as distinguished from liturgical music. AI. Almost any hymn
tune is an example of a nonliturgical musical composition. Typical
of nonliturgical music are ABIDE WITH ME, NEARER MY
GOD TO THEE, NOW THE DAY IS OVER and AVE MARIA.

non-qualifying work

MB. 1. A work, as a musical composition, that is not copyrightable.
2. A work, as a musical composition, that does not meet the requirements of a performance rights society. See QUALIFYING WORK.

nonsense songs

MB. A classification in songwriting, as to subject matter, handling
and/or treatment. Typical nonsense songs are I'M JUST WILD
ABOUT ANIMAL CRACKERS, I SAID MY PAJAMAS, SHUT
THE DOOR THEY'RE COMING THROUGH THE WIN-
DOW, CHI-BABA CHI-BABA and THE PURPLE PEOPLE
EATER.

noodle

MN. 1. To play extemporaneously and at random. 2. To improvise.
3. To play no particularly recognizable tune. 4. To compose on the
spur of the moment. 6. To improvise a phrase or lick. See LICK.

notary public

LW. An official authorized to certify or attest documents, affidavits,
etc., as those stating the date of existence of a musical composition,
as a song.

notation

MU. 1. The system by which the symbols for musical sounds are
put on paper. 2. The writing of music. 3. Written music, as distinguished from words. AI. The usual notation generally uses a staff of
5 lines with a clef, a time signature and a key signature, on which
are written notes, rests, accidentals, ties, slurs, dots, bars, etc. See
TONIC SOL-FA. See TABLATURE.

note

MU. A character used to designate the pitch and duration of a tone.

AI. There are two classifications of notes: (a) round notes and (b) shape notes. See NOTE VALUES.

note count

MU. The number of notes (tones) in a given section of a musical composition, as in a specified number of measures of a song, as in the *first A section*, in the *second A section*, in the *release*, etc. AI. A note count is made in fitting a lyric to a melody and vice versa. A note count is made by music typographers in laying out music pages.

notehead: o •

MU. 1. Usually, an oval character like those shown above, for round notation. 2. The *head* or principal part of a note, as distinguished from note *stems* and *flags*. AI. There are two kinds of round noteheads: (1) those formed in outline and (2) those that are solid black. See SHAPE NOTES.

note holder

MB. 1. A singer who sings in a sustained-tone style. 2. A singer who prolongs tones. 3. A singer capable of sounding a continuous tone for unusually long duration. 4. A musician who can do likewise.

note values

MU. The relative duration a tone is to be sounded as designated by a note. AI. For instance, a tone designated by a half note is to be sounded half as long as a tone designated by a whole note. The five notes used in songwriting are shown below. Each note designates a time value one half as long as the note preceding it, as:

WHOLE NOTE	o = ♩ ♩
HALF NOTE	♩ = ♩ ♩
QUARTER NOTE	♩ = ♪ ♪
EIGHTH NOTE	♪ = ♬ ♬
SIXTEENTH NOTE	♬ = ♬ ♬

For each note there is a corresponding rest. All notes shown above are *round* notes. See SHAPE NOTES. See REST.

256

notice

AP. 1. A story or an article, usually brief, in a newspaper or other publication, about a song, a play, a singer, a performer, etc. 2. A press notice. SB. 3. An advance written statement terminating a contract, as that of a staff musician, etc. AI. A notice of this kind is required by the American Federation of Musicians and other unions. When the contract of a musician, an actor, a singer, etc., has been terminated in this manner, he is said to have been *given notice*.

notice of copyright

LW. Copyright notice. See COPYRIGHT NOTICE.

notice of reservation

LW. A written or printed statement indicating that property rights, as those to a song, are withheld by the owner and are not granted to others. AI. The Buenos Aires Convention requires that a notice of reservation be used. In compliance with this, the following three words are usually added to a copyright notice: ALL RIGHTS RESERVED.

notice of use

LW. The notice required to be filed in the United States Copyright Office by the owner of a copyright in a musical composition when he has recorded his work, or licensed his work to be recorded by another, on mechanical instruments, as on a phonograph record, a music roll for player pianos, etc. AI. Information concerning *notice-of-use-requirements* may be found on page 4 of form U. See FORM U.

novelty songs

MB. A classification in songwriting, as to subject matter and treatment. AI. Typical novelty songs are RAG MOP, SHOE FLY PIE AND APPLE PANDOWDY, WITCH DOCTOR and ITSY BITSY TEENIE WEENIE YELLOW POLKA DOT BIKINI.

number

MB. 1. A song, as a *fast* number, a *show* number, a *rhythm-and-blues number*, etc. 2. A musical composition, as an *instrumental* number. 3. One of the parts of a musical composition. 4. One of the divisions of a piece of music. TE. 5. One of the divisions of a dance program, as a ballet.

257

number one plug

MB. 1. Designating a particular song chosen by a music publisher, over his other songs, to be given preferred promotion and advertising. 2. Designating a song that is to be given the most extensive promotion and sales effort.

numeral

MU, SW. A character, figure, letter or word used to express a number. AI. Two kinds of numerals are used in the study of music and songwriting. These are *Arabic* and *Roman* numerals:

Arabic numerals:	1	2	3	4	5	6	7	8	9	10
Roman numerals:	I	II	III	IV	V	VI	VII	VIII	IX	X

numeral names

MU. 1. The Roman numerals used to name the degrees of a scale, as: I tonic, II supertonic, III mediant, IV subdominant, V dominant, VI submediant, VII leading tone and VIII octave. 2. The Arabic numerals used to designate a staff degree, as: 1st line, 2nd line, etc., 1st space, 2nd space, etc., 1st leger line below the staff, 2nd leger line above the staff, 1st leger space above the staff, 2nd leger space below the staff, etc. See LETTER NAMES.

nut

SB, MB. 1. An investment, as that which a theatrical producer might have in a show, a music publisher might have in a song, a record company might have in a record, etc. 2. The cost necessary to doing business, as the *daily nut*, the *weekly nut*, etc. MU. 3. A slightly projecting ridge at the upper end of the neck of a stringed instrument, over which the strings pass, to prevent them from touching the finger board. See FRET NUMBERS.

O

O

MU. 1. The small letter sometimes used in guitar diagrams to designate an open string. 2. The small letter sometimes used in organ music to designate *heel.*

Oakley, Annie

SB. See ANNIE OAKLEY.

objective

SW. 1. Designating a type of song treatment that has to do with the subject in a detached, impersonal manner. 2. Without bias or prejudice. 3. Impersonal. AI. For instance, in a song written objectively, the narrator might tell what happened to someone else (not to himself). Typical of songs written objectively are: THE LADY IS A TRAMP, MISS OTIS REGRETS and KAW-LIGA. Compare with SUBJECTIVE.

oboe (o′bo)

MU. A flute-like, double-reed, soprano instrument of the woodwind family. AI. The tenor oboe is called the *English horn.*

ocarina (ahk″a-re′na)

MU. A small musical instrument, usually made of terra-cotta, with a mouthpiece and finger holes. The ocarina is made in several sizes to provide a variety of tones. AI. Also called the *sweet potato.*

occasional song

HM, FK, SW. A song written about a particular occasion, happening, or event, fancied or real. AI. Typical occasional songs are: THE WRECK OF THE OLD 97, THE SINKING OF THE TITANIC, THE BALLAD OF FLOYD COLLINS, WAITING FOR THE ROBERT E. LEE and THE LAST TIME I SAW PARIS.

octave

MU. 1. The eighth degree of the diatonic scale. 2. The tone eight steps above, or below, the key tone. 3. An interval of eight diatonic degrees. 4. The interval formed by a tone and the eighth tone above or below it. AI. For instance, C is the octave of C, D is the octave of D, etc.

octave marks

MU. 1. Abbreviations (marks) written above notes to designate that they are to be played an octave higher. 2. Abbreviations (marks) written below notes to designate that they are to be played an octave lower. AI. For instance, any one of these three abbreviations, *8va*, *8va alta* or *8*, followed by a dotted or broken line, indicates that the notes over which this is written are to be *played one octave higher*. The abbreviation *8vaba*, followed by a dotted or broken line, indicates that the notes under which this is written are to be *played one octave lower*. Any of the above four abbreviations are called an *octave mark*.

octave string

MU. The fifth string on a five-string banjo. See FIVE STRING.

octavo

PG. 1. A certain page size of a book, as a song book or music book. 2. A book consisting of pages this size. AI. The word octavo indicates a page size arrived at by folding a large sheet of printing paper into eight leaves, or pages. As the size of these large sheets varies, as to the kind of paper and its manufacturer, the size of the resulting pages varies accordingly. This means that an octavo page measures from about 5″ x 8″ to about 7¼″ x 10½″. The term *choral size* is often used to mean *octavo*.

offbeat

MU. 1. An unaccented beat. GI. 2. Anything that is unusual. SW.

2. For instance, a song that does not conform to the accepted order is said to be an *offbeat*.

off Broadway

TE. Any theater or theatrical activity in New York City that is not in the vicinity of the theatrical district called *Broadway*.

off camera

MP, TV. 1. In a position not to be photographed. 2. Outside of camera range. AI. For instance, in filming a motion picture, cue cards might be held up, for actors to see, *off camera*. The same as *offstage* in the theater.

off center

RG. 1. Designating a phonograph record in which the hole is not exactly centered. 2. Designating the wobbling effect produced by such a record, either in motion or in sound. TE. 3. Off-color. See OFF-COLOR.

off-color

GI. 1. Improper. 2. Indecent. 3. Risque, as an *off-color* song, *off-color* material, etc. AI. Also called *blue material*, not to be confused with *blues*, a type of song that can be perfectly proper and decent. See BLUES. See OFF NOTE.

off key

MU. 1. Not on pitch. 2. Not in the right key. AI. For instance, a singer might be said to be *off key* when he is not singing in the same key as the accompaniment is being played. The opposite of *on key*.

off mike

RO, MP, TV. 1. Not in range of the microphone. 2. Outside of the area in which the microphone can pick up sound. 3. At some distance from the microphone, so as to be heard as from far away. AI. The opposite of *on mike*.

off note

MU. a. Same as *off key*.

off note

MT, SW. n. 1. Any note that is not properly centered, *on* a line or *in* a space of the staff. 2. Any note that is written or printed in an incorrect position on the staff. AI. Off notes are also said to be *off center* and are sometimes called *off-center notes.*

offset

PG. A process or method of printing in which the inked impression is first made on a rubber or plastic roller and then transferred to the paper. AI. The major portion of all music printed is printed by this process. See LETTERPRESS.

off-staff

MT. 1. Designating any note or rest that is written or printed on a leger line or in a leger space, as *off-staff notes* and *off-staff rests.* 2. Any notation for which leger lines are used, as *off-staff notation.*

off-stage

TE. 1. The part of a stage, as in a theater, that is not in view of the audience. 2. Backstage. 3. Unseen by the audience.

off the air

RG. 1. A recording made from a broadcast as heard through a receiving set. 2. The method of making such a recording.

off the cuff

MN. 1. Extemporaneously, as to play or sing in this manner. 2. Unrehearsed. 3. Without preparation.

off the ground

MB. A song is said to get *off the ground* when it begins to attract attention and gain popularity.

O.K. (o-kae)

PG. A proof reader's, printer's and editor's mark meaning *all right, correct* or *approved.* When this is written on a proof, as that of a song, followed by the writer's initials, it means that the page is ready to be printed as is. AI. Songwriters often use this mark, with their initials, to indicate that a proof or an arrangement submitted to them by a music publisher, meets with their satisfaction.

O.K. with

PG. A proof reader's, printer's and editor's mark meaning *O.K. with corrections* (or revisions), which have been marked on the proof. AI. Actually, this is saying, *this is ready to be printed after corrections and revisions have been made.*

old number three

MB. An easily-recognized, hackneyed melody that has been sold and resold by song sharks since, as it is said, *the year One.* It is possible for one music publisher to receive *old number three* dozens of times in the same mail, each submission from a different, unwitting would-be songwriter.

one: 1 or I

MU. 1. The Arabic numeral used to designate the *prime* or *unison* (interval). 2. The Arabic numeral used to designate voices or instruments of the same class which are the highest, as *1st soprano, 1st violin,* etc. 3. The Arabic numeral used to designate the lowest line in the staff. 4. The Arabic numeral used to designate the lowest space in the staff. 5. The Arabic numeral used to designate the *first* string on a stringed instrument. 6. The Roman numeral used to designate the first degree, or tonic, in the diatonic scale.

one-finger

MU. A style of playing the piano by sounding only one tone at a time.

one-finger composer

SW. A songwriter who plays the piano with but one finger or, at most, with but two or three fingers. AI. There are many such songwriters who are highly successful.

one flat:

MU. The key signature of *F major*, shown above.

one-lined octave

MU. The octave, on the piano, beginning with middle C and ending

263

with the first B above middle C. AI. The keys (tones) in this octave are designated thus: c^1, d^1, e^1, etc.

one-liner

SB. A short, usually fast, gag.

one nighter

SB. An engagement, as that for a performer, an act, a band, etc., for *one evening only.*

one sharp:
MU. The key signature of *G major*, shown above.

one-shot

MB. A phonograph record, usually made with limited finances, released by an individual, or organization, with the hope of selling this property to an established phonograph record company. AI. Such an individual is known as a *one-shot operator*. This method of doing business is known as a *one-shot operation.*

one-shot label

MB. The label designating a phonograph record exploited in a one-shot operation. See ONE-SHOT.

one-staff arrangement

MU. 1. Occasionally used to mean *lead sheet.* 2. A written or printed melody.

one step

MU. 1. A ballroom dance characterized by quick walking steps, in TWO-FOUR TIME. 2. The music for this dance.

one stop

JB. A phonograph record distributing business that caters to juke box operators by carrying a full line of juke box supplies.

one-syllable rhyme

SW. A masculine rhyme. See MASCULINE RHYME.

264

one-way song

SW. 1. A song lyric that can be sung only by a boy or man. 2. A song lyric that can only be sung by a girl or a woman. AI. Typical one-way songs are: FIVE FEET TWO EYES OF BLUE, MY BEAUTIFUL LADY, THE GIRL THAT I MARRY, THE MAN I LOVE, MY HEART BELONGS TO DADDY and PAPA WON'T YOU DANCE WITH ME.

on mike

RO, MP, TV. 1. Within the area from which a microphone can pick up sound. 2. In range of the microphone. AI. The opposite of *off mike*.

on note

MU. Same as *on key*.

on stage

TE. 1. On the stage, as that of a theater, in view of the audience. 2. The words used by a call boy to tell an actor that it is time to make his entrance (appearance) *on stage*. AI. The opposite of *off-stage*.

on the air

RT. 1. The wording used in radio and television stations to warn that broadcasting is in process. 2. Anyone who is heard via radio or seen on television is said to be *on the air*.

on the beat

MU. In tempo.

on the shelves

MB. 1. In stock. 2. Available. AI. For instance, it might be said that the sheet music of a certain song is *on the shelves* of all music stores in Chicago. Or it might be said that a certain record will be *on the shelves* of distributors by the end of the week, etc. Similar to *in the racks*.

op

JB. Short for *operator*.

open

SB. 1. To begin a series of performances at one location, as a singer might be said to *open* at a certain night club or theater. 2. To *open* (for business)`, as a new night club or theater might begin operations.

open date

SB. 1. A date, as a night, a week, etc., for which a performer has not scheduled a performance or performances. 2. A date on which a performer is not working.

open mike

BR. 1. A microphone that has been turned on and is in working condition. 2. A live mike. AI. The opposite of *dead mike*.

open note

MU. A note that is played on an *open* string of a stringed instrument. See OPEN STRING.

open string

MU. A string on a stringed instrument that is played without being stopped. See STOPPED STRING.

open syllable

SW. A sound ending with a vowel. AI. For instance, the word *dearie* is an open-syllable word.

open tone

MU. The tone produced by playing an *open* string on a stringed instrument. See OPEN STRING.

opera

MU. A dramatic play that has all or most of its text set to music, as arias, recitatives, choruses, duets, trios, etc., which are sung to an orchestral accompaniment. AI. The term *opera* usually means *grand opera*. There are also *light opera* and *comic opera,* which are in a lighter vein.

operator

JB. 1. The operator of a juke-box route or routes. RB. 2. A rack operator, one who services a number of racks. AI. Also called *op.*

opry (ohp'ree)

CM. See GRAND OLE OPRY.

option

LW. The, usually written, right to renew a contract, as that of a songwriter with a music publisher, upon its expiration, and under certain stated terms and conditions.

optional note

MU. An alternate note. See ALTERNATE NOTE.

opus (o'puhs)

MU. 1. A musical work. 2. A musical composition, usually of a serious nature. AI. The term *opus* is sometimes used facetiously to mean a popular *song*.

orchestra

MU. 1. A group of musicians organized to play as a group. 2. A band.

orchestrate (or'kes-traet")

MU. 1. To compose music to be played by an orchestra. 2. To arrange music to be played by an orchestra.

orchestration

MU. 1. Music written for an orchestra. 2. Music arranged for an orchestra. 3. An arrangement of music for an orchestra.

original

MB. 1. A musical composition, as a song, no part of which has been copied or taken from any other musical composition. 2. The first recording of a musical composition, as a song, as distinguished from a *cover*. See COVER.

ork

MN. 1. Short for *orchestra*. 2. Short for *orchestration*.

Oscar

MP. A statuette awarded annually in the United States, by the

267

Academy of Motion Picture Arts and Sciences, for outstanding contributions to the motion-picture industry. AI. In 1934 the Academy instituted a category for screen songs among its other awards. The first recipient of this Oscar was Con Conrad for his song THE CONTINENTAL, from *The Gay Divorcee*.

ottava (a-tah′va)

MU. Octave.

ottava alta (a-tah′va ahl′ta)

MU. An octave higher. AI. Abbreviated, *8va*, *8va alta* or *8*. See OCTAVE MARKS.

ottava bassa (a-tah′va bahs′sa)

MU. An octave lower. AI. Abbreviated, *8vaba*. See OCTAVE MARKS.

outdoor show business

SB. That segment of show business which operates generally outside of a building, in the open air, as amusement parks, fairs, carnivals, etc.

outer leger lines

MU. 1. Leger lines that are above the treble staff. 2. Leger lines that are below the bass staff. AI. For instance, C two octaves above middle C is written on the second *outer* leger line above the treble staff. See INNER LEGER LINES.

outing

MB. A phonograph record, single or album, that has just been released. AI. The term is most often used by music-business trade journals.

outlet

MB. A store, as one that sells sheet music and/or phonograph records. AI. Outlets are designated as to *retail* and *wholesale*.

outlook

PY. See POINT OF VIEW.

268

out of sinc

MP, TV. Not in synchronization, as a motion picture. This means that the sound of a motion picture, as words and music, does not coincide with the action. One is ahead of the other. AI. For instance, we might see a motion picture of a singer. However, the words we hear are the words her lips formed several seconds previous. Or they may be the words her lips form several seconds later.

outside job

SW. 1. A song written by a songwriter or songwriters who are not on the staff of its publisher. 2. Any published song written by a free lance songwriter or songwriters. AI. Also called an *outside song*. The opposite of *inside job*.

outside label

MB. A phonograph record company that is not owned by the record club through which its records are sold.

out take

RG. 1. A recording that is not acceptable. 2. A rejected take. AI. Also called *throw away* or *reject*. See TAKE.

overage

SB. The money paid a performer, an act, a band, etc., in addition to a minimum guarantee, as by a night club, a theater, etc.

over dub

RG. Dub in. See DUB IN.

overture

MU. An instrumental musical introduction, as to an opera, a musical show, etc.

owl

MN. 1. A night-working musician. 2. A night person. 3. Anyone who stays up late.

p

P

MU. Abbreviation, *piano*.

PA (pe-ae)

SB. 1. Abbreviation, *personal appearance*. 2. Abbreviation, *press agent*. 3. Abbreviation, *public-address* system.

package

SB. 1. A group of related things and/or persons that combine to make a complete whole, as the acts, master of ceremonies, band, etc., that make up a musical show. 2. Everything necessary for a complete theatrical performance, as might be offered by a booking agency. AI. Also called *package production, package deal*.

pact

SB. 1. An agreement, usually written, as that between a songwriter and a music publisher. 2. A contract.

padding

SW. 1. A word, or words, obviously inserted in a song lyric solely to fill out a rhythmic pattern. AI. For example, the word *do* in the following sentence: When flowers *do* bloom. 2. Notes obviously inserted in a melody solely for this same reason. 3. Any extension, words or music, that is added to a musical composition, solely to increase its playing time.

271

page

PP. 1. One side (only) of a leaf, as that of a book, a song sheet, a magazine, a newspaper, etc. 2. The printed matter, as that for a song, that appears in such an area. 3. The type for such printed matter. AI. The term page is all too often erroneously used to mean *leaf*, as that in a book. Actually, a leaf has a *page* on each of its two sides. The size of a page is its *trim size*, as distinguished from the size of the *printing area* on the page.

pagination

PP. The arrangement and number of pages, as those of a song book, a hymnal, etc.

pah

MU. The syllable used to represent an unaccented note or tone, usually as played by the tuba. AI. For instance, um-*pah*-um-*pah*, um-*pah*-um-*pah* in Four-Four Time and um-*pah*-*pah*, um-*pah*-*pah* in Three-Four Time.

pain killer

MN. A song, an arrangement, an act, a gag, etc., that is very good is said to be a *pain killer* or a *real pain killer*. AI. The designation is complimentary.

pancake

RB. A phonograph record.

paper

TE. v. To distribute a large number of free tickets to a theatrical performance, usually with the purpose of making it appear that a theatrical production is more successful than it actually is.

paper

TE. n. A free ticket, or free tickets, as those to a theatrical performance.

paper jobber

WR. 1. A writer. 2. A songwriter. AI. The term comes from the

272

fact that a writer buys paper, puts words or words and music on it, and then resells it.

paraphrase

MU. To rearrange a musical composition, as a song, usually with more elaboration.

parody

MU. 1. A humorous imitation of a song. 2. A travesty. 3. A caricature.

part

MU. 1. In ensemble works, the melody for one voice or one instrument, as the *soprano* part, the *piano* part, etc. 2. The melody for a group of voices or a group of instruments. 3. A section of a song.

part song

MU. A song for two or more voices (parts) in harmony.

party

LW. Either of the persons or sides concerned in an action, proceeding, contract, legal matter, etc., as the *party* of the first part and the *party* of the second part. AI. For instance, in a contract, a music publisher might be designated as the *party* of the first part and a songwriter might be designated as the *party* of the second part, etc.

party song

SB. A risque song.

pass

SB. 1. A free ticket, as that to a theatrical performance. 2. A complimentary ticket, or *comp*.

passage

MU. 1. A term loosely used to mean a *short section* of a musical composition. 2. A musical phrase. 3. A figure. 4. Any division of a musical composition.

passing notes

MU. Notes that represent passing tones. See PASSING TONES.

passing tones

MU. Tones that are foreign (not harmonious) to the immediate chords which they accompany, but which connect the tones which are essential. 2. Discordant tones passing from one tone to another. Compare with CHORD TONES.

patriotic songs

MB. A classification in songwriting, as to subject matter. AI. Typical patriotic songs are YOU'RE A GRAND OLD FLAG, THE MAPLE LEAF FOREVER, THERE WILL ALWAYS BE AN ENGLAND and GOD BLESS AMERICA.

patter

SW. A recitation set to music. AI. Patter is spoken whereas lyrics are sung. Songs, especially those written for special material, sometimes have a patter chorus in addition to the usual lyric. The term patter sometimes refers to a lyric or lyrics that are written to be performed at a fast tempo, half spoken and half sung.

pause: ⌒

MU. 1. The sign shown above, which indicates that the note (or rest) over which it is written or printed should be prolonged. 2. A rest. 3. A hold. See FERMATA.

pay-me

MB. 1. A pay-me song, pay-me melody or pay-me tune designates a song, a melody or a tune bought from a song shark or song mill. 2. A pay-me record is one which a songwriter, singer or musician has paid to have recorded solely for self-satisfaction. AI. Not to be confused with a demonstration record, demo or dub.

pay-off

SB. 1. A punch line, gag line, climax, as that of a song. 2. Payola.

payola

MB. Unethical payments, as money or gifts given a disk jockey, or

274

other broadcasting station personnel, for playing a song.

PD or p.d. (pe-de)

MB. Abbreviation, *public domain.*

peculiar meter

CH. Designating an unusual metrical count, of no established form, as that of a hymn tune. AI. Abbreviated, *P.M.*

pedal

MU. A mechanism moved by the foot, as that on a piano. AI. Also called *foot pedal.*

peg

MU. 1. A movable pin, made of wood, metal, plastic or other material, set in the head of a stringed instrument of the violin family, and used to tighten or loosen the tension of a string. 2. A tuning pin. See MACHINE HEAD.

peg box

MU. The hollow part of a violin-head in which the pegs are inserted.

peghead

MU. The head of a stringed instrument. See HEAD.

pencil-in

SB. 1. To agree *tentatively*, as to pencil-in an agreement. 2. To note, in writing or verbally, a provisional fact, as a date, sum of money or agreement. AI. To *pencil-in* a booking date means that the agreement to play the particular date is a tentative one, usually subject to future conditions and circumstances.

pen name

WR. 1. A name used by an author, as a songwriter, in place of his true name. 2. A nom de plume. 3. A pseudonym. AI. The counterpart of *stage name*, as used by singers and other performers.

pennant

MU. 1. A flag. 2. A hook. See FLAG.

pen-pal

MB. a. Designating a song that has been written, in whole or in part, by a song shark, as a *pen-pal* song.

pen pal

MB. n. 1. A song shark. 2. A ghost writer.

penult (pe-nuhlt')

SW. The syllable next to the last syllable in a word. AI. For instance, the syllable *pe* is the penult of the word *penult, sweet* is the penult of the word *sweetheart,* etc.

percussion

MU. Designating a musical instrument in which tone is produced by striking or by causing two or more things to strike against each other, as a *percussion instrument.* AI. Percussion instruments that are struck are the drum, bells, cymbals, gong, chimes, clog box, etc. *Percussion instruments* that are shaken are the tambourine, maracas, rattle, etc. Although the keys of a piano are struck to produce tones, the piano is not a percussion instrument.

percussionist

MU. 1. One who plays percussion instruments. 2. A drummer.

percussion melody instruments

MU. Percussion instruments which have numerous tones of definite pitch, on which melody parts are played. AI. Typical percussion melody instruments are the orchestra bells, chimes, marimba-xylophone, vibraphone, etc.

perfect

MU. A term applied to certain intervals and chords to mean that they have not been altered by inversion. See PERFECT INTERVALS. See PERFECT TRIAD.

perfect intervals

MU. 1. The perfect intervals of the major scale are the first, the fourth, the fifth and the eighth. AI. In the scale of C, these are the tones: C, F, G, and C. See MAJOR INTERVALS.

276

perfect period

MU. A complete termination of a melody, or part of a melody, that is satisfactory and agreeable to the ear.

perfect pitch

MU. See ABSOLUTE PITCH.

perfect rhyme

SW. A rhyme in which the accented vowel of one word and the consonant that follows are identical in sound with the accented vowel and the consonant that follows of another word, but with a difference in the consonant before the accented vowel. AI. For instance, the words *late, date* and *mate* are perfect rhyme words. Each has the same accented vowel (a) followed by the same consonant (t). However, each has a different consonant before the accented vowel (a). *Late* has *l. Date* has *d. Mate* has *m.*

perfect triad

MU. A chord of these three tones: a root, its major third and its perfect fifth. AI. For instance, the C perfect triad is composed of these tones: C-E-G.

perforated rolls

MU. The rolls of paper on which music is recorded, by perforations, for the player piano. AI. The counterpart of a phonograph record.

perform

SB. 1. To execute, to render, as to sing or play a song. 2. To entertain publicly.

performance

SB. 1. Anything done for the entertainment of an audience, as singing or playing a song, the enactment of a play, etc. 2. A play, a musical, a variety show, an act, etc.

performance rights

LW. The rights to perform (sing and/or play) a musical composition, as a song, publicly, usually for profit. AI. Also called *performing rights*. See NINE RIGHTS, THE.

277

performance rights societies

MB. Organizations which license the performance rights of their members for their members. AI. Such organizations, operating in the United States, are ASCAP, BMI and SESAC.

performance royalties

MB. The money paid and received for the rights to perform a musical composition, as a song.

performer

SB. 1. One who performs. 2. Specifically, one who takes part in public entertainment, as an entertainer, a singer, an actor, a musician, etc.

period

MU. A complete musical sentence.

personal appearance

SB. Any public appearance such as that of a singer or an actor in a theater, etc. AI. Abbreviation, *PA*.

personal manager

SB. 1. A manager of talent, as a singer, whose services extend to the management of *personal*, often confidential, matters, as distinguished from a (general) manager, whose services are usually more generalized and extended to more clients.

personal representative

SB. A business representative of talent, as an agent or manager.

personification

SW. 1. A person or thing thought of as representing some quality, thing or idea. 2. A figure of speech in which a thing, quality or idea is represented by a person, as *Jezebel* represents *wickedness*, *Venus* represents *beauty* and *Cupid* represents *love*.

philosophical songs

MB. A classification in songwriting, as to subject matter and/or

278

treatment. AI. Typical philosophical songs are OPEN UP YOUR HEART AND LET THE SUNSHINE IN, OLD MAN RIVER, WHAT WILL BE, WILL BE and LOOK FOR THE SILVER LINING.

phonetics (fo-net′eks)

SW. 1. The study of a language dealing with speech sounds, their productions and combinations. 2. Also, the study of representing these sounds by written symbols.

phono

RB. Short for *phonograph.*

phonofilm

MP. Film on which sound is recorded photographically, as for motion pictures.

phonograph

RB. An instrument that reproduces the sounds that are recorded on phonograph records. AI. Also called *phono.*

phonograph record

RB. A flat disk or, formerly, a cylinder, on which sound has been recorded to be reproduced or *played* on a phonograph. AI. Also called *phonorecord.*

phonorecord

LW. 1. Phonograph records, as distinguished from *record,* which can be a tape recording, etc. LW. 2. The Copyright Law Revision Bill, introduced in Congress in 1964, states: "Phonorecords are material objects in which sounds, other than those accompanying a motion picture, are fixed or reproduced by any method now known or later developed, or otherwise communicated, either directly or with the aid of a machine or device."

photocopy

PG. A photographic reproduction, as that of a song, made by a photocopying machine, often called an *office copying machine.* AI. Songwriters often use this method to make reasonably inexpensive

279

copies of their manuscripts for submission to music publishers. Companies who supply photocopies are listed in the yellow pages of telephone directories. See PHOTOSTAT.

photostat

PG. A relatively inexpensive reproduction, as that of a song manuscript, made by the photostatic process. AI. Photostats are usually supplied by companies who make *blueprints*. See PHOTOCOPY.

phrase

MU. v. 1. To mark off or divide notes in phrases. SG. 2. To stylize a song by the manner in which it is sung, especially as to the timing and accenting of the lyric. AI. Frank Sinatra and Peggy Lee are among the truly greats in this respect.

phrase

MU. n. 1. A short musical sentence. 2. A musical idea. 3. A brief thought expressed musically. SW. 4. A group of two or more words, not containing a subject or predicate, as used in songwriting.

phrasing

MU. 1. The act of making phrases, as in arranging or performing a musical composition, as a song. 2. The manner in which melodic phrasing is made, often referred to as *style*, as that of a singer.

pianist (pe-an'ihst)

MU. One who plays the piano.

piano

MU. A large stringed instrument, played from a keyboard, each key of which operates a small hammer that strikes a string, causing it to vibrate and thus produce a tone. The standard piano has 88 keys ranging over seven octaves. The most familiar styles of piano are the *concert grand*, the *grand*, the *baby grand*, and the *upright*. AI. Also called the *pianoforte*.

piano accordion (pe-an'o a-kor'd'yun)

MU. An accordion with a keyboard, like that of a piano. See ACCORDION.

piano-and-vocal

MU. 1. Designating an arrangement for voice and piano. 2. Designating the arrangement most often used for popular sheet music. 3. A 3-staves-to-the-system arrangement, the first (top) stave being used for the melody to be sung, the second (middle) stave being used for the piano treble and the third (bottom) stave being used for the piano bass. AI. Abbreviated, *p-and-v.*

piano arrangement

MU. 1. A two-stave score for piano. 2. A lead sheet. 3. The arrangement on a lead sheet. 4. Sometimes, incorrectly, used to mean a piano-and-vocal arrangement. AI. Same as *piano copy.* AI. In designating a lead sheet as a piano arrangement, the assumption is that any good pianist should be able to play a fully-harmonized arrangement of a song from a correctly written lead sheet.

pianoforte (p'yan"a-for'te)

MU. The original name for a piano.

pianola

MU. A player piano.

piano man

MN. A pianist, usually one who plays popular music.

piano rolls

MU. Same as player-piano rolls.

pick

MU. v. 1. To pluck, as the strings of a guitar, with the fingers or a plectrum. 2. To play, as a guitar. 3. To use a plectrum in playing a stringed instrument. MB. 4. To choose or select, as a song most likely to become popular, as is done by music trade publications.

pick

MU. n. 1. A plectrum. MB. 2. A song chosen as one that is most likely to become popular, or become a hit, as is done by music-trade publications.

pick up

BR. 1. To *capture* sound, as is done for broadcasting and recording, through the use of *pick-up equipment*, consisting of microphones and companion equipment. MU. 2. To start playing or singing. AI. For instance, an orchestra leader might say, "I want the trumpet to *pick up* the melody at the seventh measure," meaning that the trumpet player is to *start playing* at the seventh measure.

pick-up band

MN. 1. A temporarily organized band, as distinguished from a well established band or orchestra. 2. A band consisting of musicians who have been *picked up* for a limited engagement. AI. Pick-up bands are used by such traveling organizations as some musical shows, ballets, circuses, etc.

pick-up notes

MU. Not all songs start at the beginning of a complete measure. The same is true of choruses of songs and other musical compositions. Some start with only part of a measure. The notes contained in this part-measure are called *pick-up* notes.

pick-up words

SW. Words written to be sung to *pick-up* notes.

picture song

MP. 1. A song that is used in a motion picture. 2. A song typical and worthy of being included in a motion picture. AI. For instance, a motion-picture producer might say, "I think this is a real *picture song*."

piece

MU. 1. A musical composition. 2. A song. 3. A musical instrument. AI. For instance, an instrumental quartet might be called a *four-piece combo*. Or you might say a *sixteen-piece orchestra* or a *forty-piece band*, etc.

pile driver

MN. 1. A forcefully played, resounding chord. 2. A musician who plays, or is capable of playing, with great force, usually a pianist. 3. A forcefully played musical composition.

282

pinkie

MU. 1. The fifth, or smallest finger. 2. The little finger.

pipe

MN. 1. Any tube, usually made of metal, which produces sound when blown into at one end. 2. Facetiously, a horn.

pirate

LW. 1. To appropriate without permission and/or to publish without permission, as a song. 2. To steal, as a song.

piratical copies

LW. 1. Copies, as those of a musical composition, that have been pirated. 2. Copies, as those of a phonograph record, that have been pirated. 3. Copies of a copyrighted work that have been made without the consent of the copyright owner.

pit

TE. The small, often depressed, section of a theater immediately in front of the stage, where the orchestra sits.

pit band

TE. 1. An orchestra that plays in the pit of a theater, usually to accompany the performance on the stage. 2. A pit orchestra. 3. A house orchestra. 4. A house band.

pitch

MU. v. 1. To determine or to set the key of a musical composition, a voice or an instrument. AI. For instance, an orchestra leader might say, "Let's *pitch* it in the key of G," meaning let's *play* it in the key of G. MB. 2. To make a verbal sales effort. 3. To give a sales talk, as to *make a pitch*.

pitch

MU. n. 1. The highness or lowness of a musical sound (tone). 2. How high or how low a tone is. AI. Musical sounds are caused by vibrations. The greater the number of vibrations, the greater the frequency. The greater the frequency, the higher the pitch. The higher the pitch, the higher the tone. To the contrary, the fewer the

283

vibrations, the lower the frequency. The lower the frequency, the lower the pitch. The lower the pitch, the lower the tone. Pitch is one of the four characteristics of a tone. The United States standard of pitch assigns 440 vibrations to the tone of a¹ (the A immediately above middle C). See TONE. MB. 3. A sales talk. 4. An effort to sell or exploit, as a song. AI. An extensive verbal sales effort is called *making a pitch*.

pitch pipe

MU. 1. A small reed instrument. AI. When blown into, a pitch pipe produces one or more tones of fixed pitch, to which a musical instrument may be tuned. 2. A small pipe, or pipes, used to tune musical instruments, also to give vocalists the right key.

Pitch Pipe, The

MS. The official publication of the Sweet Adelines, Inc. Published at 3560 West McLean Avenue, Chicago, Illinois 60647.

pit orchestra

TE. Same as *pit band*.

pizz (pihtz)

MN. Short for *pizzicato*, an expression often used by musicians in this abbreviated form.

pizzicato (piht"zih-kah'to)

MU. A direction for musicians who play bowed instruments, like the violin, to pluck the strings with their fingers, instead of bowing.

place

SW. To *place* a song means to have a song accepted, as for publication by a music publisher, or to be recorded by a phonograph record company, performed by a certain singer, etc.

place of publication

LW. The country in which copies of a song are first placed on sale, offered for sale, sold and otherwise publicly distributed.

place songs

MB. A classification in songwriting, as to subject matter. AI. Typical

284

place songs are DO YOU KNOW WHAT IT MEANS TO MISS NEW ORLEANS, CHICAGO, OLD CAPE COD, ABILENE and I LEFT MY HEART IN SAN FRANCISCO.

plagiarize (pla′ja-riz″)

LW. 1. To steal and claim as one's own the literary and/or musical work of another. 2. To pirate, as a song.

plastic

RB. A phonograph record, which usually is made from plastic.

plate

PG. See PRINTING PLATE.

platitude (plat′e-tood″)

SW. 1. A commonplace or trite remark or statement, especially one that is used as if it were fresh and original. 2. A commonplace, flat, dull remark.

platter

RB. A phonograph record. AI. So called because of its disk-like (platter) shape.

play

SB. v. To perform in any manner for entertainment. AI. For instance, a musician might *play* a trombone and *play* in a band. He might also *play* a job or *play* a recording date. A singer might *play* the Palace Theater. A dance band might *play* Houston, Texas. A disk jockey might *play* a phonograph record or a tape recording. An actor might *play* a part in a motion picture. A musical show might *play* a one-night stand, etc.

play

SB. n. 1. A dramatic composition. 2. The performance of such a composition, as on the stage of a theater, usually without music. AI. However, there are musical plays for which incidental music is used as a background, etc.

playback

RB. When a recording is made, as of a song, it is then played for the

285

criticism, suggestions, approval, acceptance or rejection of those conducting the recording session. This is called the *playback*.

playbill

TE. 1. The printed program of a theatrical performance. 2. A poster or circular advertising such a performance.

play by ear

MU. To play a musical instrument without the use of notation, improvising the arrangement, or playing an arrangement from remembered sound.

player piano

MU. 1. A piano that plays automatically, the hammers being made to strike against the strings by air pressure, which passes through perforations in a roll of paper, which moves over a device containing slits, like the mouth of a mouth harmonica; there is a slit for each hammer (key or tone). LW. 2. A mechanical, piano-like instrument.

player-piano roll

MU. A perforated paper roll on which musical compositions, as songs, are recorded for player pianos. AI. Also called *piano rolls* and *player rolls*.

playing time

MB. The time it takes to play a phonograph record. AI. The playing time of a record usually is shown on its label, such as: *2:15* (meaning *two minutes and fifteen seconds*) or *1:45* (meaning *one minute and forty-five seconds*), etc.

play list

RT. A list of songs currently being played by a radio or television broadcasting station.

playoff

TE. v. To play an accompaniment for a stage exit, as that of a performer.

playoff

TE. n. 1. The music played for a stage exit. 2. Exit music. 3. Exit coda.

286

playon

TE. v. To play an accompaniment for a stage entrance, as that of a performer.

playon

TE. n. 1. The music played for a stage entrance, as that of a performer. 2. Come-on music. 3. Entrance music.

play-or-pay

LW. 1. Designating a clause in a booking contract by which the performer agrees that he will pay an agreed-on forfeit if he fails to appear at a certain location, at a certain date and time, in order to play a specified booking. AI. Sometimes called *pay-or-play*.

playwright

TE. 1. A person who writes plays. 2. A dramatist.

plectrum (plehk'tr'm)

MU. 1. A small device, usually made of bone, shell, ivory, wood, felt, metal or plastic, used to pluck the strings of a stringed instrument. 2. A pick, as used to play a guitar or banjo.

plot

WR. 1. The plan of action, as that of a play, musical play, musical comedy, poem, story, song, etc. 2. The story of a play, etc.

plot song

SW. 1. A situation song. 2. A plot number. See SITUATION SONG.

pluck

MU. 1. To twitch or pull at, as at the strings of a stringed instrument. 2. To pick, as the strings of a stringed instrument, with the fingers or with a plectrum.

plug

MB. v. 1. To promote, as a song. 2. To attempt to popularize.

plug

MB. n. 1. A song chosen by its publisher to be *promoted*. AI. Also called a *plug song, the plug song, plug number*, etc. 2. The performance of a song, as on a radio station. AI. For instance, a disk jockey might say to a music publisher, "I gave your song a plug," meaning *I played your song*.

plus sign: +

MU. 1. The sign shown above. 2. The symbol meaning *augmented*. AI. Also called the *positive sign*. See AUG.

P.M.

CH. Abbreviation, *peculiar meter*, as applied to a hymn tune.

poet

PY. 1. A person who writes poetry or verse. 2. A person who writes with imaginative power and beauty of language and thought, as do some songwriters.

poetaster (po′et-aes″ter)

PY. 1. A writer of mediocre verse. 2. A would-be poet.

poetess (po′et-ess)

PY. A female poet.

poetic license

PY. The right to, for artistic effect, deviate from strict fact and the rules of form, as grammar, etc. AI. A right that the true artist uses sparingly and within good judgment.

poetize (po′et-iz″)

PY. 1. To make poetic. 2. To write poetically.

poetry

PY. A form of writing that embraces beautiful thought and deep feeling in rhythmical, and often metrical, language.

point

MU. 1. A dot. 2. A staccato mark.

point of view

PS. The relative position from which one sees a person, an object, a proposition, or a situation, as that expressed or stated in a song. AI. For instance, the point of view expressed in SOLITUDE, GLOOMY SUNDAY and YOUR CHEATING HEART is that of utter despair. The point of view expressed in APRIL SHOWERS, POWDER YOUR FACE WITH SUNSHINE and HAPPY DAYS ARE HERE AGAIN is that of optimism. The two songs JEZEBEL and MY MAN each picture the same situation, one from the woman's point of view, the other from the man's.

polka (pohl′ka)

MU. 1. A lively Bohemian dance in Four-Four Time. 2. The music for this dance. 3. A song written in *polka* style. AI. Typical polkas are THE BEER BARREL POLKA, the PENNSYLVANIA POLKA and the LIECHTENSTEINER POLKA.

polyphonic (pahl″e-fon′-ek)

MU. 1. Having or producing many sounds. 2. Having two or more harmonizing melodies, as a harmony arrangement of a song. 3. Contrapuntal.

polyphony (pah-lihf′a-nee)

MU. 1. A combined number of sounds, as in an echo. 2. A combining of two or more individual but harmonizing melodies, as distinguished from monophony. AI. The opposite of *homophony*. The song YOU'RE JUST IN LOVE is a *polyphonic* song.

pop

MB. Abbreviation for popular, as applied to pop song, pop music, pop songwriter, pop artist, pop arrangement, pop orchestra, pop orchestration, pop audience, etc. However, the term pop is restricted to a more specific meaning than the word popular. Pop is a particular type, a definite style, a well-defined classification. AI. For instance, a pop song is a song written according to certain formulas, to meet specific requirements and tastes, as distinguished from a production song, a country song, a rhythm-and-blues song, etc. It is possible for a pop song to be an *unpopular* song. Whereas, it is possible for a production song, a country song, a rhythm-and-blues to be a *popular* song. Typical pop songs are SOMEBODY STOLE MY GAL,

289

ANGRY, HALF AS MUCH, NOBODY'S SWEETHEART NOW and DEED I DO. See POPULAR.

popular

MB. 1. Widely liked. 2. Suited to the tastes of most people. 3. Easily understood and generally liked. 4. Intended for the greatest number of people, as popular music, a popular song, etc. 5. Designating almost any music and/or song that is not *classical*.

popular classic

MB. A song consisting of a modern-day lyric fitted to a classical melody. AI. Typical popular classics are TONIGHT WE LOVE (melody: *Tchaikovsky's First Piano Concerto*), MY MOON-LIGHT MADONNA (melody: *Fibich's Poem*), TILL THE END OF TIME (melody: *Chopin's Polonaise in A Flat*), I'D CLIMB THE HIGHEST MOUNTAIN (melody: *Anton Dvorak's Humoresque*), LOVLIEST NIGHT OF THE YEAR (melody: *Ivanovici's Over The Waves*) and KISS OF FIRE (melody: *Vollol-do's El Choclo*).

popular-gospel songs

MB. A classification in music publishing designating (contemporary) gospel songs whose popularity extends far beyond that of the general gospel-song field. AI. Popular-gospel songs are not written as such, they become such by popular acceptance. Typical popular-gospel songs are HE'S GOT THE WHOLE WORLD IN HIS HANDS, HE, I BELIEVE and CRYING IN THE CHAPEL.

position

MU. 1. The arrangement of the notes of a chord. 2. The place taken by the hands or hand in playing a musical instrument, as the *position* of the left hand on the fingerboard of a violin. 3. The places taken by the fingers of the left hand on the fingerboard of a stringed instrument, as a guitar, as shown by chord diagrams.

position marks

MU. Inlaid markings, in the form of dots or other designs, on the fingerboard of a stringed instrument, as the guitar, by which positions might be quickly located.

290

positive sign

MU. The *plus sign.* See PLUS SIGN.

potato man

MN. 1. Anyone who does not know music but who pretends to do so. 2. Anyone who pretends to play a musical instrument. 3. A poor musician. AI. In the early days of New Orleans jazz, the demand for marching bands exceeded the supply of musicians. To overcome this situation, band leaders often employed marchers who were non-musicians but who carried instruments, which they pretended to play. Thus a band composed of 20 marchers might have only 6 or 8 actual musicians who did the playing. To prevent a non-musician from inadvertently blowing a sour note, the horns they carried were stuffed with potatoes (or rags). So, those who carried such instruments became known as *potato men.* Even today, non-musicians, as singers, who pretend to lead orchestras are known by this designation.

power house

MN. 1. The rhythm section of an orchestra. AI. Also called the *power-house gang.* The term is complimentary, usually implying *solidity.*

prelude

MU. 1. An opening strain or introduction at the beginning of a musical composition. 2. A short introductory musical composition.

press

RB. v. To mold a phonograph record by pressure.

press

SB. n. 1. Newspapers, magazines, etc., in general. 2. Reporters, columnists, critics and others who write for newspapers, magazines, etc. 3. Journalism and journalists in general. 4. Printed or published publicity, as a press release. RB. 5. A machine, somewhat on the order of a waffle iron, for pressing phonograph records. PG. 6. A printing press.

press agent, press agency

SB. A person or organization whose business it is to obtain publicity, as for a song, a singer, a phonograph record, etc. AI. Abbreviated, PA.

pressing

RB. A phonograph record *pressed* or stamped from master dies. AI. All ordinary records sold to the public are made by this process.

pressing plant

RB. A factory where phonograph records are made (pressed).

press notice

JM. A newspaper or magazine story, as that concerning a song, a singer, an actor, a play, etc., usually brief.

press release

JM. 1. A news story written to be given (released) to newspapers, magazines, etc., as a story about a singer, a song, etc. 2. A publicity story.

prima donna (pree′ma dahn′a)

TE. 1. The principal female singer, as in an opera. SB. 2. Anyone, male or female, who acts overly important and/or is given to temperamental outbursts. 3. A temperamental person.

prima-facie (pri′mah faesh′ee)

LW. 1. At first sight. 2. A presumption of fact unless refuted, as said of legal evidence. AI. For instance, a registration of copyright is usually considered to be *prima facie* evidence, admissible in courts, without further proof or production of other evidence.

primary accent

MU. 1. The accent at the beginning of a measure. 2. The first accent in a measure. 3. The accent designating the down-beat. SW. 4. The heaviest accent, or stress, in pronouncing a word, as the *prime accent*. 5. The mark used to designate this accent. See PRIME ACCENT.

primary chord

MU. 1. The common chord. 2. The first chord.

292

prime

MU. 1. The first note (tone) of a scale. 2. The keynote, or keytone. 3. The tonic.

prime accent

WE. 1. The heaviest accent, or stress, in pronouncing a word. 2. The principal accent. 3. The primary accent, as distinguished from the *secondary accent*. 4. The mark (') used to designate this accent. AI. In the pronunciations given in this book, both *prime accent* and *secondary accent* are used. In the writing, arranging and editing of songs, the term *prime accent* usually is used to apply to *words*. The term *primary accent* usually is used to apply to *music*. See SECONDARY ACCENT.

principal

MU. 1. The first player of a division of orchestral instruments, except the first-violin section. SB. 2. A main actor or performer. 3. A featured player, as in a musical show.

principal chords

MU. 1. The five principal forms of chords are: major triad, dominant seventh chord, minor chord, augmented chord and diminished chord. AI. Built on the tone of C these are, in the above order: C, C7, Cm, Caug and Cdim. 2. The three principal chords in any key are the (a) chords built on the first tone (tonic), the (b) chords built on the fourth tone (subdominant) and the (c) chords built on the fifth tone (dominant). The first two of these (a) and (b) are triads. The third (c) is either a triad or a dominant seventh chord. AI. For instance, the principal chords in the key of C are: C, F, and G or G7. Also called *primary chords*. Compare with SECONDARY CHORDS.

printing area

PP. That part of a page, as that of a song sheet or song book, allotted to or for printed matter, as distinguished from *trim size*.

printing plate

PG. 1. A plate made of metal, plastic or other material, from which printed copies, as song sheets, are reproduced. AI. Basically, there are two kinds of printing plates, each for a different process of printing: *offset plates* and *letterpress plates*.

priority

LW. 1. The quality of being prior. 2. The condition of being previous or earlier. 3. The right to be recognized as being prior or earlier than (someone else or something else).

priority of existence

LW. 1. The right to claim earliest existence, as that of a song. AI. For instance, if two songs are exactly alike, the one that is proven to have existed first has *priority of existence*.

pro

MB. Short for *professional*, as a songwriter, a singer, a musician, etc. AI. A complimentary term, as, "He's a real pro."

producer

SB. 1. Anyone who produces. 2. A person who is in charge of the production of a play, musical show, a motion picture, television program, radio program, etc.

production

SB. 1. Something that is produced, as a work of art, literature, music, the theater, motion pictures, radio and television, etc. 2. A theatrical performance.

production number

TE. 1. An elaborate scene in a musical show (stage, screen or television). 2. The song written for such a scene. AI. Also called a *production song*, or *production music*. Typical production numbers are: A PRETTY GIRL IS LIKE A MELODY, WEDDING OF THE PAINTED DOLL and I'M IN LOVE WITH THE GIRL ON A MAGAZINE COVER.

profession

SB. 1. Show business. 2. Any of the many fields that make up show business, as the theatrical, radio, motion-picture, circus, etc. 3. Any field allied with show business, as the music business. AI. Spoken of as *the* profession.

professional

SB. 1. One who is engaged in or worthy of the high standards of a profession, particularly that of show business or any of its allied fields. 2. One who is skilled and knowledgeful of his profession, as a songwriter, as distinguished from a beginner or amateur. 3. One who conducts himself according to the ethics of his profession, particularly that of show business or its allied fields. 4. A person of high standards and skills. 5. Anyone in the entertainment business, who depends upon this business for a living.

professional copy

MB. A small-size sheet of music, or song sheet, usually about 9" x 12" before being folded once, which music publishers distribute free of charge to members of the *profession*, as singers, band leaders, musicians, program directors, music librarians, etc. AI. This is one of the most important media by which songs are popularized.

professional courtesy

SB. 1. Any courtesy extended by someone in show business to someone else in show business, in recognition of his being in show business. 2. Usually, the giving of free tickets or admission to a theatrical performance, by one professional to another. AI. Also called *professional recognition*.

professional man

MB. 1. A music publisher's representative who contacts the *profession*, as singers, band leaders, musicians, disk jockeys, etc., to distribute and promote his company's songs. 2. A contact man. 3. A song plugger.

professional material

MB. 1. Song sheets, usually professional size, and/or phonograph records which are distributed (to the profession), free of charge, for the sole purpose of exploiting a musical composition, as a song. SB. 2. Written matter, as dialog, monolog, songs, etc., that make up a professional performance, or act, as distinguished from that which is amateurish.

professional name

SB. 1. A name used for professional purposes, as distinguished from one's legal name. 2. A stage name. 3. A nom de plume. 4. A pseudonym.

program

MB. v. 1. To include in a program, as that for a show. 2. To add to a performance, as one for entertainment. AI. For instance, when a disk jockey agrees to *program* a song, this means that he has agreed to *play* it on his show.

program

SB. n. 1. A list of events, acts, songs, dances, performers, etc., that make up a theatrical performance or any entertainment. 2. A list giving the entertainment to be offered and the order in which it is to be seen and/or heard, as that for a musical show, a radio show, a stage play, etc. 3. Entertainment, and other events, that are seen and/or heard, as a radio or TV program. 4. The order in which events follow one another, particularly those connected with the entertainment. 5. These events, themselves.

program credit

MB. When a song is scheduled or *programmed* to be played on a radio or television station, and is so played, it is said to be given (that much) *program credit*.

program director

RT. An executive employed by a radio or television station who is in charge of the program or programs that are offered.

program music

MU. Descriptive music that is intended to suggest a series of moods, scenes and/or incidents. AI. Typical of program music is George Gershwin's RHAPSODY IN BLUE, Leroy Anderson's THE SYNCOPATED CLOCK and Ferde Grofe's GRAND CANYON SUITE.

progress (pro-gres')

MU. To advance or move on, as from one tone to another tone, or one chord to another chord.

296

progression (pro-gresh″n)

MU. 1. A movement forward. 2. Advancement. AI. A *harmonic progression* means advancing from one chord to another chord. A *melodic progression* means advancing from one tone to another tone. A harmonic progression is also called a *chord progression.*

progressive jazz

MU. A complex form of jazz that borrows from serious, modern music. AI. Progressive jazz is intended for listening, not dancing. Among early exponents of progressive jazz are sax man Boyd Albert and pianists Newcomb (Stan) Kenton and David Brubeck.

prolog (pro′laug)

MU. 1. The preface to a musical composition. 2. The introduction to a musical composition. 3. The preface or introduction to a performance, usually of a musical nature. 4. A prelude.

promo (prohm′o)

SB. Short for *promotion,* as a publicity release, a sales letter, a promotional stunt, etc.

promo man

SB. Short for *promotion man.*

promote

SB, MB. 1. To work actively and attempt to create interest for something, as a song. 2. To sell. 3. To exploit.

promoter

SB, MB, TE. 1. One who promotes. 2. A person who furthers the interest of a new undertaking (as a musical show) by selling its stock, as a *theatrical promoter.*

promotion

MB. 1. The effort to popularize and sell, as a song. 2. The material used in the effort, as publicity releases, sales letters, etc. AI. Also called *sales promotion.*

promotion man

MB. 1. An employee of a music publisher or record company whose duties include the promotion of songs and/or records. 2. A professional man. 3. A song plugger. AI. Also called *promo man.*

promotion program

MB. 1. A plan for promotion, as that of a song. 2. A detailed promotional campaign, usually in writing.

proof

PG. 1. A printed sheet showing the typographical composition of matter to be printed, as the page of a song. 2. Or a sheet on which the image is produced photographically, showing the same thing, for the same purpose. AI. There are two kinds of printers' proofs: *Editors' proofs* which are used to check against the original manuscript in order to find errors, if any. *Reproduction proofs,* which are used for making printing plates. PH. 3. A trial photographic print from a photograph, as that of a performer.

proof marks

PG. 1. Printers' marks used in editing proofs. 2. Proof readers' marks. 2. Typographical Signs. See TYPOGRAPHICAL SIGNS.

proof of access

LW. See ACCESS.

proof of existence

LW. Any document, or other evidence, by which a work, as a song, can be established as having been written, or as having existed, as of a specified date. AI. In order to claim common-law copyright, it is always advisable to establish proof of existence as and when a song is written. For this purpose, several devices are used: (a) A notarized copy of the song. (b) A copy of the song that is dated and signed by several witnesses. (c) A copy of the song that is sealed in an envelope, usually with sealing wax, which the author addresses and mails to himself. The envelope is then stored away for safekeeping, not to be opened by anyone other than a duly authorized officer of a court, as and when the occasion may arise. As the postmark on the envelope (showing the date) is the important evidence, most songwriters take their songs to the post office in person and request that the envelope be stamped with the dated postmark *several times and plainly so.* Sending a mailing of this kind by registered mail provides an additional record of mailing.

298

proofread

PG. To read and mark errors in proofs, as those of songs. AI. Music publishers sometimes send proofs to songwriters for this purpose. Usually, however, proofreading is done by a staff arranger.

proof reader

PG. One who reads proofs. AI. Uusually an employee of a printing company. However, large publishers do have their own proof readers.

proof-readers' marks

PG. See TYPOGRAPHICAL SIGNS.

proof sheets

PG. Same as *proofs*.

prop

TE, MP. Short for property, meaning a *stage prop*.

property

LW. 1. Anything that might be owned, as a song. 2. A part of a song, as the lyric, the music, the arrangement. AI. Except under unusual circumstances, song titles cannot be owned and are therefore not a property. MP, TE. 3. Any movable object or article, as a telephone, a chair, a table, a pencil, a letter, etc., that is used as part of the setting or action of a play, or in a piece of stage business, not including actors' costumes, backdrops (the farthest backstage curtains), etc. AI. Also called *prop* or *props*.

property man

MP, TE. The stagehand who has charge of all props or properties.

property rights

LW. See NINE RIGHTS, THE

proprietor

LW. One who has legal title or legal right to a property, as a song. AI. The owner of a copyright is designated by United States Copyright Law as the *proprietor* thereof.

props

MP, TE. A name used for a *property man.*

prose (prohs)

RC. The ordinary form of written or spoken language, without rhyme or meter, as distinguished from poetry, verse or song lyrics.

prosodist (prohs'a-d'st)

PY. 1. A person skilled in prosody. 2. A skilled lyricist.

prosody (prohs'a-de)

PY. The science or art of versification, including the study of metrical composition, structure, rhyme, form, etc.

protected song, a

LW. 1. A song for which formal copyright has been secured, either domestically or both domestically and internationally. 2. A song protected by common-law copyright, for which proof of existence has been established. AI. Also called *protected material.* For instance, a songwriter might put the following notice on the manuscript of a song: *This is protected material,* or *protected material.*

protection

SW. Anything that shields against loss, as that of a song. AI. A formally copyrighted song has copyright protection. An unpublished, uncopyrighted song has common-law protection. A song for which proof of existence has been established has proof-of-existence protection.

protection notice

SW. 1. A briefly stated notice warning that an unpublished, uncopyrighted literary or musical work has been protected as of a certain date (by proof of existence). AI. The usual form of a protection notice is as follows: PROTECTED MATERIAL, FEBRUARY 15, 1965. See COPYRIGHT NOTICE.

proverb

WR. A short saying in common use that strikingly expresses some

300

obvious truth or familiar experience. AI. For instance, *all that glitters is not gold* was a proverb of long standing before it finally became a song title. *The best is the cheapest* is an ancient German proverb that could have inspired the song THE BEST THINGS IN LIFE ARE FREE. The great essayist and poet Ralph Waldo Emerson once wrote, *All mankind loves a lover.* Many years later, a songwriter wrote the hit song EVERYBODY LOVES A LOVER. A very old Italian proverb says, *Lovers are fools.* EVERBODY'S SOMEBODY'S FOOL became a 1962 song hit.

provincialism

SW. A word, phrase or expression that is peculiar to a certain part of the country and not used by the nation as a whole.

pseudo (soo'do)

WR. Closely or deceptively similar to the real thing, as a *pseudo topical song*, a *pseudo folk song*, etc.

pseudonym (soo'do-nihm")

LW. 1. A fictitious name, as might be assumed by a songwriter, fiction writer, etc. 2. A pen name. AI. The opposite of *square name*, or *legal name*. The United States Copyright Law requires that both legal name and pseudonym (if any) be given in an application for registration of a copyright.

pseudonymous work (soo-dohn'e-mas w'rk)

LW. 1. Any work, as a musical composition, which is written by a writer or composer using a pseudonym. 2. Any work, as a musical composition, of which the writer or composer is identified under a fictitious name.

psychological songs (si"kih-laj'e-k'l saungs)

MB. A classification in songwriting, as to subject matter and treatment. Typical psychological songs are DON'T FENCE ME IN, FUNNY WHAT LOVE CAN DO, SMOKE GETS IN YOUR EYES and YOU ALWAYS HURT THE ONE YOU LOVE.

psychology (si-kahl'ih-gee)

PS. 1. The science dealing with the mind and mental processes, feelings, emotions, desires, etc. 2. The study of human behavior, actions

301

and reactions. 3. The sum of human actions, traits, thoughts, attitudes, etc.

pub (puhb)

MB. Short for *pubbery*.

pubbery

MB. A music publishing firm. AI. Also called *pub*.

public

MB. 1. The radio listening audience. 2. The television viewing-and-listening audience. 3. The theater-and-show-going audience. 4. The record-buying audience. 5. The printed-music buying audience. 6. All those who buy at retail. 7. The people as a whole. 8. A community at large. 9. The potential customers of the music business. GI. Also called *the general public*.

public acceptance

MB. 1. Favorable reaction as demonstrated by the public, as to a song. 2. A willingness to purchase, as a song, by the public. 3. General and favorable response, as to a song.

public-address system

ET. An electronic system for the amplification of sound, as used in theaters, auditoriums, at open-air gatherings, etc., so that speech, music, etc. can be heard by a large audience. AI. A simple public-address system consists of a microphone (for picking up sound), an amplifier (for increasing the volume of the sound) and one or more loud-speakers (for reproducing the amplified sound). Commonly called a *PA system*.

public domain

LW. 1. The condition of being unprotected by copyright or patent. 2. The condition of never having had copyright secured. 3. The condition of having had copyright protection expire. AI. A song without copyright is said to be *in public domain*, or to be *public domain*. A song in public domain may be copied, altered, printed and performed without obligation or penalty. Abbreviated, PD. See STRAY DOG.

302

public days

LW. The term by which legal holidays are known in Canada. See LEGAL HOLIDAYS.

public reaction

MB. See REACTION.

publish

LW. 1. To print and publicly place on sale for distribution to any and all persons and to sell, as a song or other musical composition. 2. To print, circulate, promote, advertise, widely make known, offer for sale and sell. AI. The United States Copyright Office says, "Publication, generally, means the sale, placing on sale, or public distribution of copies. Limited distribution of so-called 'professional' copies ordinarily would not constitute publication. However, since the dividing line between a preliminary distribution and actual publication may be difficult to determine, it is wise for the author to affix notice of copyright to copies that are circulated beyond his control." Obviously, in order for the author to be eligible to affix this notice, the work first must be copyrighted as an *unpublished work*. All too often the word *publish* is confused with the word *print*, and vice versa. A publisher is not necessarily a printer. A printer is not necessarily a publisher. While printing is a highly important step in publishing, it is but *one* step in an operation composed of many. It costs comparatively little to print a song. What is done *after* a song is printed can spell its success or failure.

publisher

MB. 1. A person or firm that publishes. 2. A music publisher. 3. A person or firm that publishes music in any and all forms. 4. A song publisher. See PUBLISH.

publishing house

MB. A publishing company, as one that publishes music.

pullman

MB. A sleeper. See SLEEPER.

pulsation (puhl-sae'sh'n)

MU. 1. A rhythmical beating. 2. A beat. 3. A vibration.

pulse (puhlss)

MU. Any beat that is regular or rhythmical.

punch line

SW. Any lyric sentence or phrase, in a song, designated to evoke the greatest emotional reaction.

push

MB. a. Designating a song, a record or the side of a record to be exploited, promoted, or *pushed*, as the *push song*, the *push side*, etc.

push

MB. v. 1. To promote or exploit, as a song, a record or one side of a record. 2. To plug.

push

MB. n. 1. A plug song. 2. The act of promoting a song, as "the big *push* is on," etc.

push side

MB. 1. The side of a phonograph record chosen to be promoted, exploited or plugged. 2. The A side of a phonograph record. 3. The song on this side of a phonograph record. 4. The *plug side*.

push song

MB. 1. A song chosen to be promoted, exploited or plugged. 2. The song on the push side (A side) of a phonograph record. 4. A plug song.

pyramid (pihr′a-mihd)

SA. A bell chord running from bass to bari, from bari to lead and from lead to tenor, as used by SPEBSQSA quartets.

pyrrhic

PY. A metrical foot or two unaccented syllables, or ⌣ ⌣. Example, *of the*. Musical counterpart, Two-Four Time.

q

IIIII

Q

quadrat: ♮

MU. 1. The sign shown above. 2. A *natural*. 3. A *cancel*. 4. The natural sign. 5. The cancel sign. 5. The sign meaning these things. See NATURAL.

quadrille (kwau-drihl')

MU. 1. A square dance for four or more couples. 2. The music for such a dance.

quadruple time (kwad'roo-p'l)

MU. Any time in which the number of beats in a measure can be evenly divided by four, as CUT Time, FOUR-FOUR Time and FOUR-EIGHT Time. AI. Even so, CUT TIME is more often counted as *duple* time. Quadruple time is also called *four time, four beat* and *four-beat time*.

qualifying work

MB. 1. A term used by performance-rights societies to distinguish a musical composition, as a song, which meets certain stated requirements necessary to being given credit value for its performance. LW. 2. A term used to designate a musical work, as a song, that meets the requirements for protection by common-law copyright, domestic copyright or international copyright. AI. The opposite of *non-qualifying work*.

305

quality

MU. 1. The characteristic of a tone, apart from pitch and intensity or volume, that enables us to recognize one voice from another, one musical instrument from another, etc. 2. Timbre. AI. Also called *tone color*. Quality is one of the four characteristics of a tone. See TONE. RG. 3. The *fidelity* of reproduced sound, as that recorded on a phonograph record, a tape, etc. See FIDELITY. MB. 4. The degree of excellence which something possesses, as an idea for a song, the lyric for a song, the music for a song, a complete musical composition, as a song, etc.

quantity

MU. 1. The relative length of a note (tone). 2. The relative duration of a tone. SW. 3. The relative length or duration of a vowel, consonant or syllable, as to the time it takes to utter it.

quarter

MU. 1. Any of the four parts of a whole. 2. A fourth. 3. Pertaining to four, as a *quarter* note, a *quarter* rest, three-*quarter* time, etc.

quarter note: ♩ or ♩

MU. 1. Either of the two notes shown above. 2. A note with a solid head attached to a stem, either up or down. AI. A quarter note represents a time value of one fourth that of a whole note, one half that of a half note, etc.

quarter rest: (a) ¿ (b) ⅊ or (c) ⅊

MU. 1. Any one of the three rests shown above. AI. The (a) first of these is a printed quarter rest. The (b) second and (c) third are free-hand quarter rests, as usually written on manuscripts by songwriters and arrangers. 2. The printed-rest resembling two wings of unequal lengths. AI. A quarter rest represents a time value of one fourth that of a whole rest, one half that of a half rest, etc. A quarter rest represents a time value equal to that of a quarter note.

quarter-track

RG. 1. A method of pick up and/or recording on tape. 2. Four track. See FOUR TRACK.

quartet

MU. 1. A group of four singers or four instrumentalists who sing

306

and/or play together. 2. A four-piece combo. 3. A four-voice vocal group. 4. A musical composition for four voices or four instruments.

quatrain (kwaut'raen)

PY. A stanza or poem of four lines, written to either of the following rhyme schemes. 1. The first line rhyming with the third line and the second line rhyming with the fourth line, as *abab*. 2. The first line rhyming with the fourth line and the second line rhyming with the third line, as *abba*.

quaver

MU. 1. To sing or play with a tremulous effect. 2. To sing or play with trills.

question

MU. The musical question phrase is called the *antecedent*. See ANTECEDENT.

question songs

MB. 1. A classification in songwriting as to treatment. 2. The opposite of statement songs. AI. For instance, the song LOVE IS A MANY SPLENDORED THING makes a statement. The song WHAT IS THIS THING CALLED LOVE asks a question. Both deal with the same subject matter. Typical question songs are WHO'S SORRY NOW, HOW DEEP IS THE OCEAN, BROWN EYES WHY ARE YOU BLUE and DOES YOUR HEART BEAT FOR ME.

quickstep

MB. a. 1. Designating *marching*. 2. Pertaining to *marching*, quickstep music (as is printed), quickstep cards (on which quickstep music is printed), etc. AI. Also *quick-step*.

quickstep

MU. n. 1. A lively march in quick steps, usually at the rate of about 108 to the minute, as performed by marching bands. 2. The music for such a march, usually written in SIX-EIGHT Time. 3. A dance in which the dancers take short, fast (quick) steps. 4. The music for such a dance. AI. Also *quick-step*.

quickstep music

PP. 1. Music printed on small-size, heavy-weight paper, or card stock, for use by marching bands. MU. 2. Music for *quickstep* marching or *quickstep* dancing.

quick time

MU. 1. The rate of movement in playing quickstep music. 2. The rate of marching to quickstep music. AI. For marching in quick time (quickstep), the United States Army marches at the rate of 120 (30-inch) paces per minute.

quintet

MU. 1. A group of five singers or five instrumentalists who sing and/or play together. 2. A five-piece combo. 3. A five-voice vocal group. 4. A musical composition for five voices or five instruments.

quire

PG, SW. 1. A quantity of paper, of the same kind and size, usually consisting of 24 sheets. 2. Sometimes, 25 sheets of paper of the same kind and size. 3. The twentieth part of a ream. AI. Music manuscript paper is often bought and sold by the quire. See REAM.

r

R

MU. 1. The capital letter used to designate the word *right, on* or *at the right hand*. **AI.** For instance, in the German method of fingering *R1* means the thumb of the *right hand*. 2. The small letter used to designate the syllable *ray* in the English system of tonic sol-fa. 3. The capital letter used to designate the word *refrain*.

race

MB. 1. Designating a category in songwriting and/or song performance. 2. Of, by or for the Negro race. 3. Usually a style of song performance typical of that of the Negro race, as a race song, a race record, etc. **AI.** The term is not used as frequently as it once was. The classification indicated is now included in the category of *rhythm and blues*.

rack

MB. 1. A framework, stand, case, grating, etc., for holding and displaying various articles of merchandise, which are for sale by retail. 2. Particularly, a device for displaying sheet music and/or phonograph records.

rack dealer

MB. A retail merchant, as a store owner, who displays and sells sheet music and/or phonograph records from racks.

rack jobber

MB. 1. A wholesaler who supplies racks and rack merchandise, as sheet music and/or phonograph records, to retailers. 2. A middle-man catering to rack dealers.

rag

MU. v. 1. To compose ragtime music. 2. To play or sing in ragtime style. AI. Also called *ragging*. Examples of ragging are RAGTIME VIOLIN, RAGGING THE SCALES and PIANO ROLL BLUES.

rag

MU. n. A musical composition, as a song, written in ragtime style.

ragtime

MU. An early form of New Orleans music in which a pronounced syncopated treble is played against a rigid, even-rhythm bass. AI. Typical *rags* are ALEXANDER'S RAGTIME BAND, HELLO MA BABY, OCEANA ROLL, KITTEN ON THE KEYS, DIZZY FINGERS and MAPLE LEAF RAG.

R and B (ahr and bee)

MB. Abbreviation, *rhythm and blues*.

R and R (ahr and ahr)

MB. Abbreviation, *rock and roll*.

range

MU. 1. The difference between the highest and lowest tones of a voice or an instrument. 2. Compass.

rating

MB. 1. The rank and/or class of a song, as in popularity and/or sales. 2. The evaluation of a song, as to its popularity, its estimated appeal, its sales, etc. 3. The charts appearing in music-business trade publications, which show or purport to show the relative evaluations of songs and/or phonograph records.

rattle

MU. 1. A percussion instrument, usually consisting of a cog-wheel

310

which revolves against a flexible spring, of wood or metal, which produces a rattling sound, as *maracas, cabaca, chocolo, guiro,* etc. AI. Also called *shaker.*

re: ◡

MU. 1. The syllable used in singing the second note (tone) of the scale in the sol-fa system. 2. The shape notehead, shown above, representing this syllable.

reaction

MB. 1. The response, favorable or unfavorable, as to a song. 2. The expression or lack of expression as to whether or not a song is liked. AI. Also called *audience reaction, public reaction, listener reaction,* etc.

read

MN. To read music. AI. If a musician is said to *read,* this means that he can read and understand written or printed music. AI. To play without reading is to *fake.*

reader

MN. A musician who can read music, as distinguished from one who can not. AI. The opposite of *faker.*

reading

MU. 1. The performance of a song. AI. For instance, it might be said that a singer gave a highly-emotional *reading* of a song. 2. A recitation. 3. The performance of a recitation.

realism

SW. 1. Subject matter and/or text, as of a song, that deals with facts, as distinguished from imaginary or visionary subject matter and/or text. 2. The act of picturing or describing people and things as they actually are. AI. For instance, the song JUST A COTTAGE SMALL BY A WATERFALL pictures a *realistic* abode, as compared with the *fanciful* residence of THE COUPLE IN THE CASTLE IN THE AIR. Folk songs, as a rule, deal entirely with realism.

realist

SW. 1. A person concerned with realism. 2. A songwriter whose work is characterized by being *realistic*.

ream

PG. A quantity of paper of the same kind and size, usually consisting of 500 sheets, sometimes 480. AI. Music manuscript paper is sold by the ream (480 to 500 sheets), the half ream (240 to 250 sheets), the quarter ream (120 to 125 sheets) and by the quire (24 or 25 sheets).

recapture rights

LW. 1. The rights to recapture. 2. The rights to regain something, as certain foreign rights to a song, that has been assigned away for a limited period. AI. The rights to recapture are entirely subject to contractural agreement. The rights to recapture are *not* included in the rights granted by copyright.

recital

MU. 1. A musical performance given by a vocal or instrumental soloist or several soloists. 2. A musical performance given by a small vocal or instrumental ensemble or combo. AI. While the term is sometimes used to designate a performance given by a small group, a performance given by a group, small or large, is actually a *concert*.

recitation

SW. A piece of prose or verse that is written to be spoken, not sung, as those sometimes used in connection with a song. AI. Examples of songs that use recitations are MAMA SING A SONG, WHAT KIND OF BIRD IS THAT and HANK WILLIAMS GUITAR.

record (re-kord')

RG. v. 1. To capture and preserve sound, so that it may be heard again, as to *make* or *cut* a phonograph record, a tape, etc. 2. To make a record of. 3. To make or cut a phonograph record.

record (rehk'ord)

RB. n. 1. A phonograph record, as the familiar disk popularly known

312

by this name. 2. A disk. 3. A platter. 4. Any flat disk, cylinder, paper roll, tape, film, etc. on which sound has been recorded and from which this same sound can be reproduced. AI. Records are used to preserve and reproduce *musical compositions, the spoken word, sounds other than music and/or words, educational material*, etc.

record club

RB. A mail-order organization that sells phonograph records by various *club* plans, as *record-of-the-month, special-discount-to-members-only, buy-two-and-get-one-free* plan, etc.

record company

RB. 1. A phonograph record company. 2. Any company whose business it is to make and sell phonograph records. MN. 2. A diskery. 3. A pancake factory.

recorder

RG. 1. A machine that records sound, as on phonograph records, tape, etc. 2. Usually, a tape recorder. MU. 3. An old-style, flute-like instrument which is blown at the end, instead of at the side. AI. Recorder music was popular at the Globe Theater when Shakespeare's plays were originally produced.

record hop

GI. A party to which people come to dance, usually without shoes, to recorded music. AI. Also called *sock hop, record hop*, etc.

Record Industry Association of America, Inc.

RB. An organization of phonograph record manufacturers for the betterment of recorded music and literature. Also called RIAA, pronounced both as a word and as separate initials. Address: One East 57th Street, New York, N. Y. 10022.

recording

RB. 1. Any sound, music, etc. that is recorded, as on a phonograph record. 2. The record itself. 3. The act of recording, as *making* or *cutting*, a record. 4. Anything on which sound has been recorded, as a disk-shaped phonograph record, a perforated-paper piano roll, a plastic or metal tape, wire, etc.

recording artist

RB. 1. Any performer, as a singer, musician, monologuist, etc., whose performance is recorded on phonograph records. 2. Anyone whose performance is recorded and who is so featured, as distinguished from an accompanist or sideman.

recording blank

RG. 1. A phonograph record, usually made of acetate, on which no sound has been recorded. 2. An *un-cut* record. AI. Also called *record blank, blank, blank acetate* or *acetate blank*.

recording center

RB. Any locality where a large number of recordings are made by various recording artists and record companies, as New York, Nashville, Los Angeles and Chicago.

recording company

RG. 1. Any company that makes recordings of any kind. 2. Usually, a company that makes custom recordings as distinguished from a record company.

recording date

MB. 1. An appointment to record at a specified time and day of the month, as that given a singer, a musician, an A-and-R man, etc. 2. An assignment or job to make a phonograph record or records on a certain day. 3. A booking to make a record or records.

recording session

MB. A gathering of various personnel to record, as to make or cut a record or records, a recording or recordings. AI. The AFM designates a recording session as a period of three hours' time, in which members may rehearse and record not more than four 10-inch sides, nor more than three 12-inch sides. A session may be extended by additional 30-minute overtime periods. AFM members are restricted to rehearsing and recording not more than one additional side, regardless of size, for each additional 30-minute overtime period.

record man

RB. 1. Anyone connected with the phonograph record business,

314

particularly one who is *dedicated* to his work. 2. Specifically, a record-promotion man.

Record One Stop Association

RB. An organization of one-stop proprietors and operators. AI. Also called, ROSA, pronounced as a word and as separate initials. Address: 511 North Broad Street, Philadelphia, Pennsylvania.

record-promotion man

RB. 1. An employee of a phonograph record company whose duties are to promote his company's records. 2. The counterpart of a *professional man* with a music publisher. AI. Also called *promo man*.

record speed

RB. The speed at which phonograph records are recorded and played. AI. For instance, the speed at which phonograph records are made to turn in playing might be: 16⅔ rpm, 33⅓ rpm, 45 rpm, 78 rpm, etc. See RPM.

Record World

MB. A music-business trade publication. Published weekly. Issued every Monday. Dated the Saturday following date of issuance. Address: 200 West 57th Street, New York, N. Y. 10019.

recto (rehk´to)

PP. 1. Any right-hand page, as that of a song book, hymnal, etc. 2. The front side of a leaf, in a book. AI. The opposite of *verso*.

reed

MU. A thin strip of cane, wood, metal, plastic, or other material, which produces musical tones when it is set in vibration by a current of air, as used in reed instruments like the clarinet. AI. A *free* reed vibrates within the aperture without striking the edges. A *beating* reed strikes the edges. *Double* reeds are two beating reeds that strike against each other.

reed instrument

MU. 1. A musical instrument that uses a reed or reeds to produce tones. 2. One whose tone is produced by the vibration of a reed, or reeds, in its mouthpiece. AI. The clarinet and saxophone are *single-reed* instruments. The oboe and English horn are *double-reed* instruments.

reel

MU. 1. A lively Scotch and Irish dance. 2. The music for this dance, usually in Four-Four Time or Six-Eight Time. AI. Typical reels are the VIRGINIA REEL, the SAILOR'S HORNPIPE and CHICKEN REEL.

refrain

MU. A musical phrase or strain that is repeated at intervals. AI. A refrain usually recurs at the end of a stanza (or verse) as in old-style ballads and hymn tunes. A refrain is shorter than the usual chorus of a song. The term is sometimes erroneously used to mean *verse*.

refrain form

MU. A song form that has several verses followed by a refrain. AI. These verses are used to tell the story and the refrain, which repeats a brief thought set to a musical signature, is of secondary importance story-wise. Typical songs written according to the refrain form are MAÑANA, HAIR OF GOLD EYES OF BLUE, FOUR WALLS and A LITTLE BITTY TEAR LET ME DOWN.

regional

MB. 1. Of a whole region or district, larger than that called local. 2. A portion of territory, a district, as distinguished from national. AI. The term is used in speaking of the *regional* popularity of a song or record, the *regional* sale of sheet music or phonograph records, the *regional* distribution of sheet music or phonograph records, the *regional* coverage provided by radio and/or television stations. For instance, the Yankee Network (covering the New England states) and the Texas Network are *regional* networks, as distinguished from ABC, CBS and NBC, which are *national* networks. The sales territory covered by a sheet-music or record jobber is usually *regional*, compared to the *local* territory of a dealer.

register

MU. 1. A musical range or compass. 2. A particular portion of the compass of a voice or instrument, of which all the tones are pro-

316

duced in the same manner or are similar in quality, as the *head* register, the *upper* register, the *lower* register, etc. PG. 3. The exact and correct placement of printed matter, as wordage and colors, on a printed page, as that of a song sheet, or the cover for a song sheet. LW. 4. The official in charge of the United States Copyright Office, called the *Register of Copyrights*.

register of copyrights, the

LW. The official, appointed by the Librarian of Congress, who is in charge of the United States Copyright Office. See COPYRIGHT OFFICE, U.S.A.

rehearse

MU. 1. To perform in preparation for performance. 2. To repeat for practice or improvement, as the *rehearsal* of a song by a singer and/or musicians.

reject (re-jehkt′)

MB. v. To refuse to accept, as a song.

reject (ree′jekt)

MB. n. 1. Something that is or has been rejected, as a song. 2. A rejection.

rejection

MB. Something rejected, as a song by a music publisher.

rejection slip

MB. 1. A form, usually printed or typewritten, used by music publishers to notify songwriters that their submissions have been rejected. 2. A letter of rejection, used for the same purpose. AI. A rejection slip is usually enclosed with songs that are returned to the sender.

related

MU. 1. Designating tones, chords, etc. that are closely connected melodically or harmonically. 2. Belonging to the same family, group or series. 3. Connected in some manner. 4. Akin. AI. For instance, the tones C, E and G are *related* because they belong to the family of seven tones that make up the key of C.

relative

MU. 1. As regarded in relation to something else. 2. Depending on connection or relationship. 3. Depending on being akin.

relative pitch

MU. 1. The pitch of one tone in relation to the pitch of another tone, usually indicated by an interval, as the interval between the tone of E to the tone of C, the interval between the tone of F to the tone of A, etc. 2. The ability to recognize and identify a related tone as, for instance, to be able to sing *the tone of E* when called upon to identify *the major third (interval) above* C. AI. Relative pitch is by far a more valuable asset to a singer or musician than absolute pitch. See ABSOLUTE PITCH.

release

LW. v. 1. To give up, to surrender, as certain rights. 2. To permit the performance of a song without penalty or liability. 3. To cancel, as a contract or a part of a contract. MB. 4. To issue and offer for sale, as a song. RB. 5. To issue and offer for sale, as a phonograph record. AP. 6. To issue a publicity story, as a press release.

release

LW. n. 1. A written statement granting freedom from liability and/or obligation. AI. A release is sometimes sent to a music publisher by a songwriter in connection with the submission of a work, as a song. A release might be demanded by a radio station before they will agree to play a song, etc. 2. The cancellation of a contract, usually in writing. MU. 3. The bridge of a song. See BRIDGE. MB. 4. A song that is put on the market or offered for sale, as in the form of sheet music or on a phonograph record. RB. 5. A phonograph record that is offered for sale. See PRESS RELEASE.

release date

MB. 1. The date on which something is first issued or distributed to the public, as the sheet music of a song, a phonograph record, etc. AP. 2. The earliest date on which a press release may be printed. AI. When the same press release is sent to a number of publications, a

318

release date is specified, so that all those receiving the release will be treated equally. (Thus, no one publication can print the release in advance of the others.)

religious music

MB. Musical compositions that are of a devout nature, usually pertaining to the Christian faith. AI. While the term is sometimes loosely used to mean nonliturgical music, religious music can also be liturgical. Also, religious music can be either church music or nonchurch music.

repeat

MU. A certain measure or measures that are designated to be sung and/or played twice. AI. A repeat is designated by *repeat signs*.

repeat marks: or or

MU. Characters consisting of dots placed in the spaces of the staff, preceding and/or following double bars, like those shown above. AI. Repeat marks on the left side of a double bar mean, *go back to the repeat marks on the right of the double bar and play (or sing) it over again.* Repeat marks on both sides of a double bar mean, *both the preceding and following strains are to be repeated.* In older music, four dots were used, one in each space in the staff. Modern music uses but two dots, one in the second space and one in the third space in the staff. Also called *repeat signs*.

repertoire (rep′er-twahr″)

SB. 1. A list of musical compositions, as songs, that a singer, a combo, a band, an orchestra, etc. is prepared to perform. 2. A list of material, as songs, stories, jokes, etc. that a performer is prepared to perform. 3. A list of plays, musical shows and/or other presentations that an organization, as a theatrical company, is prepared to perform.

repertory company (rep′er-tor″ee kuhm′p′nee)

TE. 1. A traveling organization of actors, singers, comedians and other performers, which is prepared to offer a variety of entertainment, as plays, musical shows, etc. 2. Originally, a company of actors which presented only dramatic plays.

repetition

MU. The singing or playing of the same musical passage over again. AI. A device used in melody writing.

replay (re-plae′)

MB. v. 1. To play again, as a phonograph record. 2. To repeat.

replay (ree′plae)

MB. n. A repeated hearing, as that of a phonograph record.

request

MB. v. 1. To express a desire for, to ask. 2. To ask that a certain song be played.

request

MB. n. Any musical composition that has been requested to be played. AI. Also *request song* or *request number*.

reservation notice

LW. See NOTICE OF RESERVATION.

residual (r′sihd′joo-′l)

RT. The payment or payments made for each repeated broadcast of a recorded performance, on radio or television, as that of a singer or other performer whose voice and/or likeness is used, as in a commercial.

resolution

MU. To pass from one tone, or chord, to another that is more satisfying.

resolve

MU. To cause, a tone or chord, to undergo resolution, as in the writing or performing of music.

resonance (rehs′o-n′ns)

MU. 1. The quality of being resonant. 2. A resonant sound.

320

resonant (rehs'o-n'nt)

MU. 1. Having the quality of sending back or prolonging sound. 2. Resounding. 3. Re-echoing. 4. Full of or intensified by resonance, as a resonant sound or a resonant voice.

resonator (rehs'o-nae-ter)

MU. A mechanical or electrical device for prolonging sound as used in connection with certain musical instruments.

response

MU. 1. A musical reply, as one musical phrase that answers another. 2. The vocal reply made by a choir or congregation, in answer to an officiating clergyman or priest. 3. The vocal repetition, by a choir or group of singers, of the words called out by a *liner*, in *lining out* a song.

rest

MU. A character used to designate a period of silence (between tones). See REST VALUES.

rest tones

MU. Inactive tones. See INACTIVE TONES.

rest values

MU. The relative duration silence is to be maintained, as designated by a rest. AI. For instance, the period of silence designated by a half rest is one half as long as that designated by a whole rest. The five rests used in songwriting are shown below. Each of these designates a rest value one half as long as the rest preceding it, as:

WHOLE REST	▬ = ▬ ▬
HALF REST	▬ = ⌇ ⌇
QUARTER REST	⌇ = 𝄾 𝄾
EIGHTH REST	𝄾 = 𝄿 𝄿
SIXTEENTH REST	𝄿 = 𝄿 𝄿

For each rest there is a corresponding note. See NOTE VALUES.

321

return clause

LW. A clause in a songwriter-music publisher contract which states that all rights to a song will be returned to the songwriter if the publisher fails to get a regulation phonograph record made of the song by a specified date.

reversion right

LW. The right, as that of a recording artist, to the ownership of the masters of his recordings after a specified time. AI. Reversion right is secured only by contractural agreement.

review

NM. v. 1. To examine, inspect. 2. To write a critical discussion, as that of a song, its performance, etc., as might appear in newspapers, music-business trade publications, etc.

review

MB. n. 1. A written description and/or opinion of songs, records, etc., as those newly released, as might appear in newspapers, music-trade publications and other media. RT. 2. A verbal description and/or opinion for the same purpose, as that given on some radio and television shows. TE. 3. A revue. See REVUE.

review board

MB. A group of people, as those employed by a music publishing company or phonograph record company, whose business it is to review song submissions and to decide which are to be accepted or rejected. AI. Also called *board of review* or *reviewing board*.

review copy

MB. A phonograph record, which is sent free of charge to a newspaper, magazine, trade publication or other media, for the purpose of being reviewed. AI. Also called *reviewer*.

reviewer

NM. 1. One who writes reviews, as those of music and/or phonograph records. MB. 2. A phonograph record sent as a *review copy*.

revision

LW. A new version of a musical composition, as a song. See NEW VERSION.

revue

TE. A type of musical show consisting of a series of loosely connected skits or brief scenes, songs and dances, often parodying or satirizing current events, recent plays, prominent personages, etc. AI. Also spelled *review*, which has another and different meaning. The spelling *revue* has only the one.

rewrite

SW. v. To write again, usually with some changes and/or improvements, as a song.

rewrite

SW. n. A version, a draft, as that of a song, that has been rewritten. AI. Songwriters use the designations *rewrite number one, rewrite number two* or *first rewrite, second rewrite,* etc.

R. H.

MU. Abbreviation, *right hand.* AI. Where this appears on music it means that the right hand is to be used to play the part indicated. Opposite of *L. H.*

rhapsody

MU. 1. A free, irregular form of musical composition that follows the fancy of the composer. 2. In many instances, a fanciful arrangement of folk songs. AI. Typical of modern rhapsodies is George Gershwin's immortal RHAPSODY IN BLUE.

rhetoric (reht''r-ihk)

RC. 1. The art and science of using words effectively in speaking or writing, as in writing song lyrics. 2. The art and science of literary composition.

rhyme

PY. v. 1. To correspond in sound. 2. To fit a word to another word, or words, that correspond in sound, as *rhyme* and *time.*

rhyme

PY. n. A word, or words, that corresponds in sound with another word, or words, as *girl* and *curl*. AI. The correct spelling of the word is *rime*. However, the spelling *rhyme* has been commonly used since the sixteenth century.

rhyme scheme

PY. The order or pattern in which lines, as those of verse, are rhymed, as in songwriting. AI. Rhyme schemes are designated by small letters, using *a* to designate the first rhyme, *b* to designate the second rhyme, *c* to designate the third rhyme, etc. The five rhyme schemes most often used in songwriting are these: The *couplet*, in which each two successive lines are rhymed, as *aa, bb, cc*, etc. The *quatrain* in which every other line is rhymed, as *abab*, or in which the first line is rhymed with the fourth line and the second line is rhymed with the third line, as *abba*, or in which the second line is rhymed with the fourth line and the first line and the third line are left unrhymed, as *abcb*. (Actually, however, this third form is the form of the couplet, with longer lines.) The *dead-end rhyme*, or *three-line rhyme*, in which the first three lines are rhymed and the fourth (dead-end) line is left unrhymed, as *aaab*. See TERMINAL RHYME.

rhyming dictionary

PY. 1. A book containing the words of a language, as English, arranged in groups according to the similarity of their sounds. 2. A rhyme book.

rhythm

MU. 1. The measured movement of similar groupings of tones, as to the pattern in which their strong and weak beats (heavy and light accents) occur, as the *rhythm of a beating heart*, the *rhythm of clicking train wheels*, the *rhythm of the surf*, etc. 2. Musical movements marked by regularity, as *rhumba rhythm, triple rhythm*, etc. PY. 3. The measured movement of groupings of words, as to the pattern in which their heavily-accented, lightly-accented or unaccented syllables occur, as the rhythm of verse or poetry, as used in songwriting.

rhythm and blues

MB. A category in songwriting, as to subject matter, text and treatment. AI. Formerly called *race* songs, *race* records, *race* style, etc. Typical rhythm-and-blues songs are JUMPIN' JIVE, I CRIED A TEAR, QUARTER TO THREE and GREEN ONIONS.

rhythm ballad

MB. 1. A beat ballad. 2. A ballad with a beat. See BEAT BALLAD.

rhythm guitar

MU. 1. A style of guitar playing consisting of a series of chords played as a rhythmic accompaniment, as distinguished from *melody guitar* or *solo guitar*. 2. A four-string guitar is usually used for this purpose.

rhythm instruments

MU. 1. Any one of the musical instruments usually included in the rhythm section of an orchestra or dance band. 2. Any instrument that is used to play a rhythm accompaniment, as a four-string guitar.

rhythm section

MU. The section of an orchestra, particularly that of a dance band, which plays the rhythm accompaniment. AI. A rhythm section usually includes such instruments as piano, guitar, string bass, drums, etc.

rhythm song

MB. Any song with a strongly pronounced rhythm and accent, both in the melody line and in the background accompaniment. AI. Typical rhythm songs are AIN'T MISBEHAVIN', THAT OLD BLACK MAGIC, HONEY and AFTER YOU'VE GONE.

rhythm step

DG. 1. A short, quick dance step done in rhythm. 2. Any dance step done in time to a rhythmic melody.

rhythm sticks

MU. See CLAVES.

RIAA (ahr-i-ae-ae)

MB. Abbreviation, *Record Industry Association of America, Inc.*

ricky-tick

MN. 1. Designating a tin-panny style of playing, usually the piano.

325

2. Honky-tonk style. 3. A country style of playing, typified by the Hoosier Hot Shots.

ride

MU. v. 1. To play a somewhat difficult passage or complete musical composition in a fast-moving, skillful manner. ET. 2. To control the volume of speech-input equipment, as to *ride gain.*

ride

MU. n. The performance of a passage or complete musical composition that is given a *ride,* as by a trumpet player, pianist, guitarist, etc.

ride gain

BR. 1. To control volume, as in recording or broadcasting. AI. The audio engineer who controls the *level* of volume used in recording or broadcasting is said to *ride gain.*

riff

MU. A simple musical phrase, characteristic of Dixieland jazz, usually of two-measures duration, that is repeated for an entire chorus as a background for an instrumental solo.

riffle

MU. A skillfully manipulated, fast strumming effect, in playing the guitar, which gives the melodic impression of riffling (shuffling) cards or thumbing (riffling) the pages of a book.

right

LW. 1. That which belongs to a person by law or by custom, as the right to ownership, the right to copyright, etc. 2. A claim. 3. A title to. 4. An interest in. AI. See NINE RIGHTS, THE.

rime

PY. The correct spelling of *rhyme.* See RHYME.

ring

SA. The sensation which occurs when four tones are rendered in perfect pitch, according to the overtone series of *true,* not *tempered* tones. An important feature in SPEBSQSA style barbershop singing.

326

river-boat

MN. 1. Designating the kind of songs sung on the old Mississippi river boats, as a river-boat song. 2. Designating the style in which these songs were played and/or sung, as a "real *river-boat* performance." AI. Same as *Dixieland*.

river songs

MB. A classification in songwriting, as to subject matter. Typical river songs are UP A LAZY RIVER, RIVER STAY 'WAY FROM MY DOOR, FOGGY RIVER and MOON RIVER.

road, on the

SB. 1. In tour, on tour, en tour. 2. En route. 3. Traveling. AI. Performers are said to be *on the road* when they are traveling from place to place giving performances.

rock and roll

MB. A song and/or music category which, actually, is a division of the rhythm-and-blues category. Typical rock-and-roll songs are ROCK AROUND THE CLOCK, ALL SHOOK UP and HOUND DOG.

role

TE. A part, as a character or characterization, that an actor plays in a play, a musical comedy, etc.

roll

MU. 1. The rapid beating of a drum to make it sound continuous. 2. A trill or tremolo on the drum. 3. The rapid and repeated hither-and-thither stroke on the tambourine.

roll notes

MU. Notes designating a roll, as on the drum or tambourine. AI. See WAVY-STEM NOTES.

Roman numerals

MU. The letters used by the ancient Romans to express numbers, as: I=1, II=2, III=3, etc. AI. Roman numerals are used in music to represent the degrees of the diatonic scale. Some publishers use Roman numerals to designate the year in which a song is copyrighted. For instance, MCMLIX meaning 1959, MCMXLIII meaning 1943, etc. See NUMERALS. See NUMERAL NAMES.

room

SB. 1. A dining room that offers entertainment, as in a hotel. 2. A supper club. 3. A dinner club. 4. A night club, usually of the intimate variety.

root

MU. 1. The fundamental note (tone) of a chord. 2. The note (tone) on which a chord is built. AI. For instance, the note (tone) C is the *root* of the C major chord C-E-G. The note (tone) G is the *root* of the G7 chord G-B-D-F, etc.

root position

MU. If the root of a chord is the *lowest* note (tone) in a chord, the chord is said to be in *root position*. AI. For instance, the C major chord played C-E-G is in root position. The same C major chord played E-G-C or G-C-E is *not* in root position and is said to be *inverted*.

root tones

MU. Any of the seven tones: A, B, C, D, E, F, and G. AI. Also called *fundamental tones*.

round

MU. A song, usually short, that is repeated several times, the musical phrases of which are of equal length and harmonize with one another. AI. In singing a round, one singer, or the first group of singers, begins the song. Then when this singer, or group, is starting on the second phrase, a second singer, or group of singers, joins in by starting at the first phrase, and so on.

round dance

DG. 1. Any dance in which the dancers, performing as couples, revolve and dance a circular movement, as the waltz, fox trot, one step, polka, etc., as distinguished from square dance.

roundelay

MU. 1. A simple little song in which some phrase or line is continuously repeated. 2. The music for such a song. DG. 3. A dance in which couples move in circles.

round notes

MU. 1. Musical notes that are constructed with round and/or oval noteheads, as distinguished from shape notes. 2. The notes most commonly used, particularly for printed popular music. See SHAPE NOTES.

route

SB. 1. The course traveled, as by a band, a singer or other performer, in going from one place to another to give performances. JB. 2. A *juke-box* route. 3. A number of juke boxes which have been installed in various locations, as restaurants, bars, etc., which are serviced by an individual or by an organization. MB. 4. A rack route. 5. A number of locations, as supermarkets, drug stores, etc., where racks are installed.

route man

JB. 1. An individual who owns and/or services a juke-box route. 2. A (juke-box) operator. 3. A (juke-box) collector. 4. A (juke-box) service man. 5. A (rack) operator. 6. A (rack) service man.

route sheet

SB. A written outline designating the route to be followed by a band, a singer or other entertainers who are on the road. AI. For instance, a booking agency usually furnishes its clients with *route sheets*.

routine

SB. 1. A prepared performance that follows an established (usually written) and rehearsed procedure, as that of an act, a singer or other performers. 2. The written outline for such a performance. 3. What an entertainer does, the manner and order in which it is done.

royalties

MB. A share of proceeds owed or paid to the writer, or copyright owner, of a song by those doing business under some right or rights belonging to him.

RB. Abbreviation, *revolutions per minute*, as used to designate the speed at which a phonograph record is to be played. See RECORD SPEED.

rubato (roo-bah′toh)

MU. 1. Designating a performance of a musical composition, as a song, which intentionally, and temporarily, deviates from a strict tempo, as in jazz music. 2. Having some notes (tones) intentionally lengthened and/or shortened in a musical performance.

ruffle

MU. 1. A low, continuous beating of a drum, not as loud as a *roll*. 2. The same effect on a tambourine or other percussion instrument.

run

MU. 1. A rapid succession of notes. 2. The tones played or sung in this manner. AI. In vocal music, a run is usually sung to one syllable.

run over

MN. v. To rehearse, as a musical composition. AI. For instance, an orchestra leader might say, "Let's run over the first two songs," meaning, let's *rehearse* the first two songs.

run-over

PP. n. That part of a musical composition, as a printed song, which is continued from a preceding page, as in a song book. AI. For instance, if a hymn is printed on a page and a half in a hymnal, the second page contains the *run-over*.

S

S

S

MU. 1. The capital letter used to designate *soprano* in multiple-voice arrangements, as in SATB. 2. The small letter used to designate the syllable *soh* in the English system of tonic sol-fa.

sacred-harp

GM. Designating a method of unaccompanied congregational-gospel singing that goes back to the days of Shakespeare, which is in use in the southern United States today. AI. Sacred-harp singing uses the fasola system. The singers sit in four groups, as to voice (melody, bass, alto and treble). Each group faces one side of an open square and the leader stands in the center of this square. It is not unusual for sacred-harp singers to travel from one state to another to attend a sacred-harp sing.

sacred music

CH. 1. Religious music and/or songs. 2. Music and/or songs for devotional purposes. 3. Religious music and/or songs that are most devout, pious and Godly.

safety

RG. A duplicate or extra master recording. AI. A safety is made as *insurance* against the original master's being damaged or lost.

saga

GI. 1. A story, usually of adventure. MB. 2. A song that tells a usually detailed story. AI. Also called *saga song.*

saga songs

MB. A classification in songwriting, as to treatment. Typical saga songs are THE MIRACLE OF THE BELLS, JAMBOREE JONES, THE SAGA OF JENNY and THREE BELLS.

Saint Cecilia

RN. The patron saint of music. See SAINT CISSIE.

Saint Cissie

SW. Saint Cecilia, the *adopted* patron saint of songwriters, who is affectionately called *Saint Cissie* and *Saint Cis* by singers and musicians, as well as by songwriters. See SAINT CECILIA.

sales chart

MB. A list of song titles in the order of their respective sales, as those of sheet music and phonograph records, that might be made confidentially or as might appear in a music-business trade publication.

saloon

PF. Facetiously, night club or supper club.

same-day publication

LW. 1. The act of bringing a printed property, as a song, to the attention of the public in two, or more, countries on the same day. 2. Publication in two or more countries simultaneously. AI. In order to secure international copyright in the countries belonging to the Berne Convention, authors of the United States (which is not a Berne member) can secure the rights granted by the Berne Convention "but only if they publish their works *first or simultaneously* in a country of the Union" (Berne Convention). It is generally accepted that publication means the distribution and offering of printed copies for sale to the public. Canada is the nearest Berne-member country to the United States. Because of this, and because there is no language difference, most American publishers arrange to have printed copies of a song placed on sale in Canada the *same day* that printed copies are placed on sale in the United States, the date specified as *date of publication* in FORM E. (See LEGAL HOLIDAYS.) The act of placing copies on sale in Canada is usually arranged through Canadian agents who are established to furnish this service. Later, these agents furnish their American clients with a *certificate of publication*, attesting the fact that simultaneous (same day) publication was effected. See COUNTRY OF ORIGIN. See BRUSSELS AMENDMENT. See FIRST PUBLICATION.

sardine

MB. One of a number of small music publishers who share limited office or desk space.

Sarrusophone

MU. A brass wind instrument, like the saxophone in construction and appearance, but with a double reed (like the oboe and bassoon). AI. The Sarrusophone was invented by the French bandmaster Sarrus in 1856.

S.A.T.B. or SATB

MB. Abbreviation, *soprano, alto, tenor, bass,* as appears on the title page of a vocal score designating that it has been *arranged for these particular voices*. AI. The SATB arrangement is the most-often-used in multiple-voice arrangement. See MULTIPLE VOICE.

Saturday-night song

JB. 1. The song played the most often on a juke box, or juke boxes, on Saturday night. 2. A song that is popular on juke boxes (Saturday night being the night that juke boxes are usually played the most).

saw

SW. A saying, a maxim, a proverb, as *a miss is as good as a mile, two wrongs do not make a right, seeing is believing,* etc. Usually used with the word *old* as *old saw.*

sax

MU. Short for *saxophone.*

saxhorn

MU. A brass wind instrument of the bugle family, having valves instead of keys, which was invented by the inventor of the saxophone but not to be confused with the saxophone.

sax man

MU. A saxophone player.

saxophone

MU. A brass wind instrument that has a single reed and is keyed like the clarinet but which has a deeper, mellower tone. The saxophone was invented by Adoph Sax, the inventor of the saxhorn, about 1840. The saxophone is popularly made in twelve sizes, as soprano, tenor, alto, etc.

saying

SW. 1. Something popularly said, especially a well-known adage, proverb or maxim. 2. A simple, direct truth. 3. A brief expression of wisdom, as might be used in songwriting, as *love makes the world go 'round, misery loves company* and *absence makes the heart grow fonder.*

scale

MU. 1. A succession of tones in an established order. 2. A tone ladder. 3. All tones (or notes) of a key in regular (ascending or descending) order. MB. 4. The rates of pay designated by a labor union, as AFM or AFTRA, as for a musician, singer or other performer, also called *union scale.*

scan

SW. 1. To analyze, as verse, poetry or a song lyric, and separate into metrical feet. 2. To determine the rhythmic structure of verse.

scansion

SW. The act of scanning verse to determine its metrical parts.

scat

MU. 1. Designating a style of jazz singing which uses meaningless, nonsensical syllables. 2. Pertaining to *scat singing* or *scatting.* AI. Scat singing was popularized (if not invented) by Cab Calloway, with his *hi-de-ho, hi-de-hi* in his famous song MINNIE THE MOOCHER. Typical scat syllables might be *be-reet be-reet be-reet be-reet* or *sha-baba sha-baba sha-wawa sha-wah.* Scat syllables are also called *vocables.* See VOCABLE.

334

scenario

MP. 1. The outline of a motion picture, indicating the action in order of its development, the scenes as reveiwed by the camera, the characters, dialog, music and/or songs, etc. 2. A manuscript or type-written copy of a *screen play*. 3. The *script* for a motion picture. TE. 4. An outline or synopsis of the plot, scenes, characters, dialog, (music) etc. for an opera, drama or musical show.

scenarist

MP. 1. One who writes scenarios, usually for motion pictures. 2. A motion-picture writer. 3. A movie writer.

scene

TE. 1. A division of a theatrical performance, as *scene one* of a musical play. 2. The surroundings, depicting a location, in which a theatrical performance takes place.

schmaltz

MN. Anything overly sentimental, as a song or its performance in this manner. AI. Typical *schmaltzy* songs are the old tear-jerkers HEARTS AND FLOWERS, A BIRD IN A GILDED CAGE and THE FATAL WEDDING.

score

MU. v. 1. To orchestrate, to arrange, as a musical composition. 2. To write out, as in the form of a score. MP. 3. To add music to, as to score a motion picture. MB. 4. To achieve credit for a hit song as *to score a hit*.

score

MU. n. 1. The notation for a musical composition, in manuscript or printed form, showing the part to be played by each instrument and/or the part to be sung by each voice. See the various kinds of scores, as SCORE, PIANO; SCORE, ORCHESTRAL, etc. 2. The music for a theatrical performance, as a musical, a musical comedy, etc., and/or for a motion picture, as distinguished from lyrics and dialog. 3. Incorrectly but sometimes used to mean a *system* (part of a score). See SYSTEM. MB. 4. A hit song or a hit record, as to *chalk up a score*, to *register a score*, etc.

335

score, four-part

MU. 1. A four-part score, as that for four instruments that make up a combo. 2. Usually, an arrangement for four voices in which no accompaniment is included. AI. A four-part vocal score is usually written or printed on a system consisting of two staves. Notation for the two higher voices appears on the upper staff. Notation for the two lower voices appears on the lower staff. Upstem notes on the upper staff are for the highest voice. Downstem notes on the upper staff are for the second highest voice. Upstem notes on the lower staff are for the second lowest voice. Downstem notes on the lower staff are for the lowest voice. Also called *quartet arrangement, four-part harmony arrangement, four-part harmony score, short score, hymn-style* or *hymnal-style* score. See MULTIPLE-VOICE.

score, full

MU. A full score is one in which each vocal and/or instrumental part is written or printed on a separate staff. There are instances, however, when two parts are written on the same staff, as that for the piccolo on the same staff with that for the flute, that for the second trombone on the same staff with that for the third trombone, etc. AI. This score is used by the conductor, or orchestra leader, while the performers use copies of individual *parts.* Also called *band score, open score* or *orchestral score.*

score, orchestral

MU. See SCORE, FULL.

score, piano

MU. 1. A piano score is usually considered to be an arrangement of any musical composition for piano alone. 2. However, a piano arrangement of an orchestral score might have the words for any or all vocal parts, either with notation written or printed on individual staves for each vocal part or without such notation, above the two-stave system, on which the piano arrangement appears. See SCORE, PIANO-AND-VOCAL.

score, piano-and-vocal

MU. A piano-and-vocal score is written or printed on a three-stave system. The top stave, same as that on a lead sheet, is used for the melody line, or vocal notation. Below this is the lyric. Below the

336

lyric are the two staves containing the piano arrangement, the treble on the upper of these two staves, the bass on the lower. AI. This is the score used for popular-song sheet music. Chord captions and/or guitar diagrams are usually included above the top stave in each system. Also called *p-and-v arrangement*, or *p-and-v score*.

score reading

MU. The act of grasping the essential details, as harmony, leading melodies, etc., of a score and reproducing them on the piano.

score, short

MU. 1. A short score is any abridged arrangement, any skeleton transcript or abbreviated version, as one for later embellishment. 2. Also, a 4-part vocal score written on a 2-stave system. Also called *closed score*, or *compressed score*.

score, supplementary

MU. A supplementary score is any additional scoring attached to the original score, when all parts can not be written on one page. AI. Also called *additional score* or *ad score*.

score, vocal

MU. 1. A vocal score is that of an a cappella composition, or a score in which the vocal parts are written out in full (usually using a separate stave for each part) above the 2-stave system on which the piano accompaniment appears.

scoring

MU. 1. Instrumentation. 2. Arrangement. 3. Orchestration.

Scotch bar: (a) (b)

MU. 1. Either of the double bars shown above. 2. A double bar composed of one thin line and one thick line, in this order or vice versa. AI. A *left-hand* Scotch bar (a) has the thick line at the left of the thin line. A *right-hand* Scotch bar (b) has the thick line at the right of the thin line. See DOUBLE SCOTCH BAR.

scratch

MB. 1. To write by hand, as a song in manuscript form. 2. To write a manuscript.

scratch arrangement

MB. 1.The original copy of a handwritten arrangement, as that of a musical composition. 2. A printed (or otherwise reproduced) copy of a handwritten arrangement, as distinguished from one that has been *type-set* or *engraved*. 3. A facsimile of a handwritten arrangement.

scratch copy

MB. 1. The original copy of a handwritten manuscript, as that of a song. 2. A printed (or otherwise reproduced) copy of a handwritten manuscript, as that of a song. 3. A facsimile of a handwritten song.

screamer

MB. 1. A singer, usually female, with a powerful voice. AP. 2. A sensational headline, as for a publicity story. SB. 3. A very funny gag, gag line or story.

screen

MP. 1. The surface on which motion pictures are projected. 2. Therefore, motion pictures collectively. 3. The motion-picture industry, its people, its properties, as *screen* writer, *screenplay*, etc. See FILM.

screen credit

MP. Acknowledgement given for work done on a motion picture, any contribution made to a motion picture, etc. AI. For instance, a writer might have *screen credit* for writing a certain motion picture, a songwriter might be given screen credit for the song he wrote for a certain motion picture, etc.

screw

MU. 1. Peg. 2. Machine head. See MACHINE HEAD.

scribe

WE. 1. A writer. 2. An author. MB. 3. A songwriter, as a *song scribe*. AP. 4. A reporter, as a newspaper writer. 5. A journalist, as a magazine writer.

script

MB. 1. A manuscript or typewritten copy of a song, as a song

338

script. 2. A manuscript or typewritten copy of a play, radio show, television show, motion picture, etc. See SCENARIO.

season songs

MB. A classification in songwriting as to subject matter. AI. Typical season songs are AUTUMN LEAVES, BLACKBERRY WINTER, WINTER WONDERLAND and INDIAN SUMMER.

second

MU. a. Designating a voice, instrument or part that is lower in pitch than the first, as *second tenor, second violin,* etc.

second

MU. n. 1. An interval between any note (tone) and the next note, above or below it, in the diatonic scale. 2. The second note above the keynote. AI. For instance, in the scale of C major, the second note (or degree) is the note (tone) of D. 3. The supertonic.

secondary accent

WE. 1. The weaker accent, or stress, in pronouncing a word. 2. The accent that is weaker than the *prime* accent or *primary* accent. 3. The mark (″) used to designate this accent. In the pronunciations given in this book, both *prime accent* and *secondary accent* are used. See PRIME ACCENT.

secondary chords

MU. 1. The four secondary (or less important) forms of chords are: major seventh, minor seventh, sixth and ninth. Built on the tone of C, these are: Cmaj7, Cm7, C6 and C9. 2. The four secondary chords in a key are chords built on the second (supertonic), third (mediant), sixth (submediant) and seventh (leading tone) of any scale (or key). Secondary triads in the key of C major are: Dm, Em, Am and Bdim. AI. Secondary chords may be triads or any seventh chord other than dominant seventh, as Cmaj7, Cm7, Caug7 and Cdim7. Also called *subordinate chords.* Compare with PRINCIPAL CHORDS.

secondary label

RB. The label of a phonograph record company that is second in importance to its first label.

339

second cover

PP. 1. The inside front cover of a song sheet, song book, etc. 2. The second page of a 4-page folder, as a song sheet.

second ending: ⌐2̄‾‾‾‾‾‾¬

MU. 1. The measure or measures of a song that are designated by the characters shown above. 2. These characters themselves. 3. The ending of a song that serves to bring it to a conclusion, as distinguished from the first ending, which serves to lead back into a repeat. AI. After a song has been played or sung, using the first ending, and has been repeated either in whole or in part, the first ending is then omitted and the second ending is used to bring the song to a conclusion. See FIRST ENDING. See ADDITIONAL ENDINGS.

second finger

MU. 1. The middle finger. 2. The finger between the first or index finger and the third or ring finger. 3. The finger designated by the numeral 2 in the English method of fingering. 4. The finger designated by the figure *3* in the German method of fingering.

second string

MU. 1. The B string on the Spanish guitar. The F-SHARP string on a ukulele (tuned A-D-F♯-B). 3. The B string on a five-string banjo that is one tone below middle C.

section

MU. 1. A short division of a musical composition that has distinct rhythmic and harmonic boundaries, as the *A section* of a song. 2. A dependent musical idea. AI. Although a section actually is *half a phrase*, the term is often loosely used to mean almost any division of a song.

secular

MU. 1. Of or belonging to the world, as distinguished from those things belonging to the church, as *secular music*. 2. Worldly, not religious or sacred. AI. The term does not necessarily imply sinful or wicked. The term *secular music* usually is used simply to designate any music that is *not church music*.

340

segno (sa′nyo): % or ♐

MU. 1. One of several signs, as those above. 2. A sign. AI. A segno is used in writing music to designate the beginning or ending of a section that is to be repeated. See DAL SEGNO.

segue

MU. A musical direction meaning *continue without a break or interruption into the next section, song, piece,* etc.

Select Editions of Standard Catalogs

MB. Usually called SESAC, pronounced as a 2-syllable word: *see′sak.* See SESAC, INC.

sell

MB. 1. To give up or part with for a payment or price, as a song. 2. To exchange for money, as a song. 3. To establish confidence, belief or faith in, as a song. AI. While the term *sell* usually implies a transfer of ownership, this is not always the case. For instance, a songwriter might say he is going to try to *sell* a singer on his song, or *sell* his song to a singer, meaning that he is going to try to *interest* a singer in using his song. 4. To arouse and inspire liking, approval and/or acclaim for, as a singer who *sells* a song to a theater audience, an action called *selling out.*

semitone

MU. 1. An interval equal to half a major tone on the scale. 2. A half tone. 3. A half step.

sentence

MU. 1. A musical phrase. 2. A musical division. RC. 3. A related group of words containing a subject and a predicate and expressing a complete thought, as used in song lyrics.

sentimental songs

MB. A classification in songwriting, as to subject matter and handling. AI. Sentimental songs are those that express sentimental attachments other than for a member of the opposite sex (as is expressed in *love songs*). Typical sentimental songs are THE WHIFFENPOOF SONG, DEAR HEARTS AND GENTLE PEOPLE, SWEET LEILANI and THE LAST TIME I SAW PARIS.

sequence

MU. The repetition of a musical progression at regular intervals. AI. A melodic sequence is the repetition of a melodic phrase. A harmonic sequence is the repetition of a harmonic (or chord) progression.

serenade

MU. 1. An evening song. 2. A song about the evening or to be sung at evening time. 3. A concert in the open air at night, especially under the window of the one to be entertained. AI. Typical popular-song serenades are SERENADE IN THE NIGHT, SLEEPY SERENADE, SERENADE IN BLUE and GOODNIGHT SWEETHEART.

serious music

MU. Music of a more serious nature than the popular song.

SESAC, INC. (see'sak, ihnk)

MB. Abbreviation, Select Editions of Standard Catalogs, Inc. A privately-owned performance rights licensing organization. Address: SESAC, Inc. The Coliseum Tower, 10 Columbus Circle, New York, N. Y. 10019.

session

MB. 1. A period of time devoted, usually intensively, to an activity, as recording, songwriting, arranging, etc. 2. Short for *recording session*. AI. For instance, a music publisher might have a (recording) *session* scheduled for Tuesday. A songwriter might put in an all-night *session* (of songwriting), etc. See WOODSHED. See RECORDING SESSION.

set

MN. 1. A group of musical numbers, as songs played by a dance band. 2. A group of strings, as those used on a stringed instrument. AI. For instance, a Spanish guitar uses a *set* of six strings, a ukulele uses a *set* of four strings, etc. TE. 3. The arrangement of scenery and properties, as on a theater stage for a play, a musical, a TV show, a motion picture, etc. 4. The location of such a scene, as for a motion picture.

342

seven: 7 or VII

MU. 1. The Arabic numeral, used to designate a *seventh* chord, as C7, Dmaj7, Em7, etc. 2. The Roman numeral used to designate the leading note (tone), subtonic or *seventh* degree of the major scale.

seventh

MU. 1. The interval between any note and the seventh note above it on the diatonic scale. 2. Any note separated by this interval from any other note. 3. The seventh note above the keynote. AI. For instance, in the scale of C major, the seventh degree is the tone of B. 4. The leading tone. 5. The subtonic. 6. A kind of chord. See SEVENTH CHORDS.

seventh chords

MU. A seventh chord is composed of a root, its third, its fifth, and its seventh. There are five kinds of seventh chords. These are: The dominant seventh, abbreviated C7, D7, E7, etc. The major seventh, abbreviated Cmaj7, Dmaj7, Emaj7, etc. The minor seventh, abbreviated Cm7, Dm7, Em7, etc. The augmented seventh, abbreviated Caug7, Daug7, Eaug7, etc. The diminshed seventh, abbreviated Cdim7, Ddim7, Edim7, etc. AI. Seventh chords built on the root of C are composed of the tones that follow: C7: C-E-G-B♭. Cmaj7: C-E-G-B. Cm7: C-E♭-G-B♭. Caug7: C-E-A♭-B♭. Cdim7: C-E♭-G♭-A. A seventh chord is also called *a chord of the seventh*.

sextet

MU. 1. A group of six singers or six instrumentalists. 2. A six-piece combo. 3. A musical composition for six voices or for six instruments. 4. An arrangement for six voices. 5. An arrangement for six instruments. 6. A six-part score.

sforzando (sfohr-tsahn′doh): *sfz sf* > ∧ —

MU. 1. Any one of the two abbreviations or three signs shown above. 2. A direction applied to a single tone or chord, indicating that it is to be performed with marked and sudden emphasis or sudden stress.

sfz (ess-eff-zee)

MU. Abbreviation, *sforzando*. AI. Same as *sf*.

shade

MU. 1. To give expression to, as to a tone, a chord, a measure, etc., in its performance. 2. To vary slightly.

shake

MU. Same as *trill*. See TRILL.

shaker notes

MU. Same as *jingle notes*.

shakers

MU. Any percussion instrument that produces sound when shaken. See MARACAS.

shape note

MU. A kind of notation that uses notes with eight differently shaped noteheads to indicate the different degrees of the scale. GI. Shape notes are largely used by publishers of gospel songs in the southeastern part of the United States. Special arrangers are used by these publishers to arrange songs in shape-note form. This need be no concern of songwriters. Shape notes with noteheads in four designs, representing the tones of *fa, sol, la, mi*, first appeared in a book titled *The Easy Instructor*, by William Little, published in 1802. See FASOLA. Compare with ROUND NOTES.

shape noteheads

MU. 1. The noteheads used in shaped-note notation. 2. The following noteheads:

△	▽	◇	◁ or ▷	⊘	□	▽
do	re	mi	fa	sol	la	si(ti)

AI. The syllable *fa* has two shapes. The first is for downstem notes. The second is for upstem notes. Thus:

shape-note publisher

MB. 1. A music publisher who prints all or most of his songs in shape-note form. 2. Generally, a music publisher in the contemporary gospel field, whose publications are printed in shape-note form.

344

sharp

MU. v. 1. To sing or play *sharp*. 2. To sing or play too high, usually by a half step.

sharp: ♯

MN. n. 1. The sign shown above. AI. A sharp is written before a note or on a degree of the staff to indicate that its pitch is to be raised one half step. For instance, F SHARP is a tone one half step higher than F (and one half step lower than G). 2. The name of a black key on any keyboard instrument, as F SHARP, G SHARP, A SHARP, etc.

sharp keys

MU. 1. Those keys (scales) for which the key signature is composed of a sharp or sharps. AI. For instance, the key of G major (one sharp), the key of D major (two sharps), the key of A major (three sharps), etc. are called *sharp keys* or, sometimes, *sharped keys*. 2. The black keys on a keyboard instrument, as the piano, organ, accordion, etc.

sheet music

MB. 1. Music printed on unbound sheets of paper, usually 9″ x 12″ page size. 2. The usual 4-page (9″ x 12″), folded-once, song sheet on which songs are printed in piano-and-vocal score form. 3. The form in which most popular songs are offered for sale. See PROFESSIONAL COPIES.

shindig

FM. 1. Formerly, a jovial kick in the shin or shins. 2. Hence, a merry dance. 3. A spirited social affair or dance. 4. Spirited musical and/or vocal entertainment. AI. Also called *shindy*.

shindy

FM. A shindig.

shirt-sleeve

WR. 1. Designating an easy-to-understand, informal style of writing that uses everyday words and phrases that most people understand. SW. 2. Designating song lyrics written in this style, as *shirt-sleeve lyrics*.

short

PY. 1. As used in this book, an abbreviation. AI. For instance, *sub* is short for *substitute*. *Mike* is short for *microphone*. PY. 2. A short syllable or sound, as distinguished from one that is *long*. MP. 3. A motion-picture *short subject*. 4. A motion-picture presentation that is shorter than a feature picture. AI. Shorts in which music is included, other than for background, are called *musical shorts*.

short meter

CH. Designating a metrical count of 6.6.8.6., as that of a hymn tune. Abbreviated, *S.M.*

short score

MU. See SCORE, SHORT.

short syllable

PY. 1. An unaccented syllable. 2. The opposite of *long syllable*. AI. Also called *short*. See ACCENTED SYLLABLE.

show

SB. A presentation of entertainment, especially of a theatrical nature, as a musical show, a stage show, a radio show, a television show, a tent show, etc.

show business

SB. 1. The theater, motion pictures, radio, television, circuses, carnivals, outdoor entertainment, etc. as a business or industry. 2. The entire entertainment business as a whole.

showcase

SB. Any place where a performer, particularly those just starting in show business, as a beginning singer, can display their talents to the public and to the *right* executives in show business. AI. For instance, a certain radio and/or television show might be said to be a *good showcase* for new talent, meaning a good place to get a start.

showman

SB. 1. A person who makes a business of producing or managing shows. 2. Anyone who is skilled at this or at presenting a perform-

346

ance in an exceptionally interesting and/or highly dramatic manner, male or female. AI. For instance, it might be said of a female singer, "She is a real showman."

showmanship

SB. 1. The art of being a successful showman. 2. Exceptional skill as a showman. AI. A classic compliment to one's showmanship is a saying in the circus world, "Give him a monkey and an umbrella and he will play to capacity."

show music

MB. "A song from an original score written for and performed for the run of the show, musical comedy, revue or operetta in a first-class, legitimate Broadway theater," as defined by BMI.

show song

MB. A song written especially for a musical show. Typical show songs are GET ME TO THE CHURCH ON TIME (from *My Fair Lady*), HEY LOOK ME OVER (from *Wildcat*) and MACK THE KNIFE (from *The Three-Penny Opera*).

show stopper

SB. A performer, act, song, etc. that has a reputation for *stopping* shows. See STOP THE SHOW.

shuffle

DG. 1. A dance, or step used in such a dance, where the dancer pushes his feet along the floor, raising them just as little as possible. MU. 2. The music for such a dance.

shuffle rhythm

MU. A rhythm that produces a *shuffling* effect, as that popularized by Henry Busse. AI. Typical of shuffle rhythm is Busse's arrangement of his theme song HOT LIPS.

si (see): ◇

MU. 1. The syllable used in singing the seventh note (tone) of a scale in the sol-fa system. 2. The shape notehead shown above representing this syllable. See TI.

side

RB. 1. The playing surface of a phonograph record. 2. One of the two *sides* of a phonograph record. 3. The song recorded on a *side*. MU. 4. A *part* of an orchestration. AI. For instance, the part written for the trombone is a *side*, the part written for the saxophone is a *side*, etc. TE. 5. A part or role, as that taken by an actor in a musical play. 6. Particularly, such a part or role, as it appears in manuscript, written or printed form. 7. Each such written or printed *page*.

sideman

MB. 1. An accompanist. 2. A member of a band, orchestra, combo, etc. 3. Any musician who plays a *side*.

side wheeler

MN. Any jazz or Dixieland style musical composition arranged or played in a highly spirited tempo.

side-wheeling

MN. Designating a highly spirited tempo, in jazz or Dixieland style.

sight reading

MU. The ability to read, interpret and/or perform music *at first reading* or *first sight*.

sign

MB. v. 1. To write one's name or signature, as on a contract. 2. Hence, to agree to the terms of a contract. 3. Or, to acquire by contract, as a music publisher might *sign* a songwriter to his staff. 4. Therefore, to place under contract.

sign

MU. n. Any symbol or mark that has a specified meaning, as a *repeat sign*. 2. A musical symbol, as a note, rest, sharp, flat, etc. 3. Segno. PP. 4. Any of the typographical or printers' signs used in marking a proof sheet, as the sign *x* meaning *broken letter*.

signature

MU. 1. The signs (sharps or flats) placed at the beginning of a musical composition to designate the key, called *key signature*. 2. The sign (somewhat resembling a fraction, etc.) placed at the beginning of a musical composition to designate the meter, called the *time signature*. MB. 3. The opening or closing *theme song* or *instrumental signature*, as that of a band, orchestra, radio or television show, etc.

sign off

MB. 1. The musical signature used to end a performance, as that of a dance band, particularly on radio or television. RT. 2. The musical signature used by a radio or television station to designate the end of its daily broadcasting. 3. The announcement made by a radio or television station that broadcasting will cease for the day.

simile (sihm′e-lee″): ⁒

MU. 1. The character shown above. AI. When this character is written on the staff, it means that the previous measure is to be repeated. 2. In the same manner. 3. Similarly. RC. 4. A lyrical statement, as used in song lyrics, that a person, a thing or a fact is like another, as *kisses sweet as wine, tears like rain* or *lonely as the moon*. AI. A simile differs from a metaphor in that it uses words of comparison, as *like* or *as*. A metaphor does not. See METAPHOR.

simple measure

MU. A measure with only one accent. AI. For instance, a measure in Two-Four Time, a measure in Three-Four Time or a measure in Cut Time.

simple percussion instruments

MU. Percussion instruments having a single tone of indefinite pitch, as drums, cymbals, triangle, etc., as distinguished from percussion melody instruments.

simultaneous publication

LW. Same as *same-day publication*. See SAME-DAY PUBLICATION.

singdown

FK. A singing contest in which the winning singer or group is said to *sing down* all other contestants. Also called *sing-off*.

single

RB. 1. A phonograph record with only one song recorded on each side, as distinguished from an album. 2. Usually, a 45 rpm record. SB. 3. An act performed by only one person, as distinguished from a *duo* or *trio*, etc.

single accent

WE. The prime accent, as distinguished from secondary or *double* accent. See PRIME.

single colon

MU. See COLON.

single-track

MU. 1. Designating a method of sound recording, pick-up and/or playback, as that on tape. 2. Same as *monaural*.

sing-off

FK. Same as *singdown*.

sit down

FK. A community sing.

sit in

MN. A musician is said to *sit in* with other musicians when he joins them in playing, usually informally, as in a jam session.

situation comedian

SB. A comedian who develops and exploits humorous situations, as those in a musical comedy, as distinguished from a stand-up comedian. AI. Typical situation comedians are Jackie Gleason, Jack Benny and Dick Van Dyke.

situation comedienne

SB. Lucille Ball.

situation song

MB. 1. A song that grows inevitably from a plot, as that of a musi-

350

cal show. 2. A song that contributes to a *situation* in the plot of a musical show, musical comedy, light opera, etc. AI. A correctly-written situation song does one or more of these things: (a) states a plot situation, (b) explains a plot situation, (c) explores the possibilities that may arise from a plot situation, (d) questions a plot situation, (e) advances a plot situation, usually by adding some new element or channel of thought. Typical situation songs are BE-WITCHED, BOTHERED AND BEWILDERED (from *Pal Joey*), THE LADY IS A TRAMP (from *Babes in Arms*), and I MARRIED AN ANGEL (from *The Boys from Syracuse*). Also called *situation number, plot song or plot number.*

six: 6 or VI

MU. 1. The Arabic numeral used to designate an interval of a sixth. 2. The Arabic numeral used to designate a chord of the sixth or a sixth chord, as C6, D6, E6, etc. 3. The Roman numeral used to designate the sixth degree, or submediant, in the diatonic scale.

six-string guitar

MU. 1. A guitar strung with six strings, as distinguished from a *four-string guitar*, or a *twelve-string guitar*. 2. Usually, the Spanish guitar. AI. The Hawaiian guitar and/or steel guitar both have six strings.

sixteenth

MU. 1. Any of the sixteen parts of a whole. 2. A sixteenth, as a *sixteenth* note or *sixteenth* rest.

sixteenth note: ♪ or 𝅘𝅥𝅯

MU. 1. Either of the two notes shown above. 2. A note with a solid head attached to a stem, either up or down, with a double flag. AI. A sixteenth note represents a time value of one sixteenth that of a whole note, one half that of an eighth note, etc.

sixteenth rest: 𝄿

MU. 1. The rest shown above. 2. A character with two arms attached to a descending line slightly at a slant. AI. A sixteenth rest represents a time value of one sixteenth that of a whole rest, one eighth that of a half rest, etc. The time value of a sixteenth rest is equal to that of a sixteenth note.

sixth

MU. 1. The interval between any note (tone) and the sixth note (tone) above it in the diatonic scale. 2. A note (tone) separated by this interval from any other note (tone). 3. The sixth degree in the diatonic scale. 4. The sixth note above the keynote. 5. The submediant. AI. For instance, in the scale of C major, the sixth degree is the tone of A. 6. A kind of a chord, as C6, D6, E6, etc.

sixth chords

MU. 1. Chords of the sixth. 2. A chord composed of a root, its third, its fifth and its sixth. AI. There are two kinds of sixth chords, *major sixth* (abbreviated C6, D6, E6, etc.) and *minor sixth* (abbreviated Cm6, Dm6, Em6, etc.) For instance, sixth chords built on the root of C are made up of the following tones: C6: C-E-G-A. Cm6: C-Eb-G-A.

sixth string

MU. 1. The bass E string on a six-string guitar. 2. The lowest string on a six-string guitar.

sketch

TE. 1. A short theatrical scene. 2. A playlet. 3. A brief theatrical performance, as a *musical sketch*. See SKIT.

skip

MU. 1. A melodic progression by an interval of more than a whole tone. 2. Sometimes called a *jump*.

skirt

AP. A paper extension, or flap, pasted on the bottom of a (publicity) photograph, on which is written or printed information concerning the photograph, as its title, the name or names of person or persons in the photograph, etc.

skit

TE. 1. A brief theatrical performance, as a musical skit in a revue. 2. A brief sketch. AI. A skit is usually shorter than a *sketch*.

sleeper

MB. 1. A song that becomes a hit quite some time after it is published. 2. A Pullman. 3. A Rip Van Winkle. 4. A snoozer. AI. Examples of songs that were sleepers are PAPER DOLL, APRIL IN PARIS, BEGIN THE BEGUINE and STAR DUST.

slide

MU. 1. A rapid run of two or more notes (tones). 2. The movable, U-shaped tube of a trombone which slides in and out to alter pitch.

slur: ⌒ **or** ⌣

MU. 1. Either of the curved lines shown above. AI. The one at the left is drawn or printed *over* notes, and is called a *down slur*. The one on the right is drawn or printed *under* notes and is called an *up slur*. 2. A curved line that is written, drawn or printed over or under two or more notes of *different pitch*. AI. This designates that notes (tones) thus indicated are to be played or sung *legato*. In songwriting, the slur is used to unite two or more notes that are to be sung to the same syllable and in one breath. 3. The notes so designated are also called a *slur*. Compare with TIE. See LEGATO.

slurred melody

MU. A melody in which two or more tones are sung to one syllable. AI. The opposite of *syllabic melody*.

S.M.

CH. Abbreviation, *short meter*, as applied to a hymn tune.

small barrer

MU. See BARRER, SMALL.

small octave

MU. The first octave, on the piano, below middle C. AI. The keys (tones) in this octave are designated by small (lower-case) letters, thus: c, d, e, f, g, a, b.

small rights

TE. See NONDRAMATIC RIGHTS.

small time

SB. Designating something that is minor, limited, second-class, second-rate, as distinguished from *big time*. AI. Formerly used to designate *small time vaudeville*. For instance, on the old Pantages Circuit, which was *small time*, acts played five shows a day. On the Orpheum Circuit, which was *big time*, acts played only two shows a day. (While there was also a difference in the overall quality of the acts and the prices paid them, not all acts which played small time were necessarily of small-time quality. In fact, some of the highest-regarded, big-time acts in vaudeville played small time on occasion for limited engagements.)

smash

MB. 1. A song that achieves exceptional popularity and sales. 2. A song that is more popular than a *hit*. AI. Also called a *smash hit*.

smooth music

MU. 1. Music in which the rhythms are very simple. 2. Music with rhythms that are not complicated or complex. 3. Ballad-style music.

snare drum

MU. A small drum with two heads and with snares. AI. Snares consist of one or more lengths of wire or gut which are strung across the lower head to increase resonance. It is possible that this was originally thought to snare (capture or *trap*) the sound, thus leading to the name *trap drum*.

Society for the Preservation and Encouragement of Barber Shop Quartet Singing in America, Incorporated

SG. An organization whose purpose is stated in its name. AI. Also called SPEBSQSA (each initial pronounced separately). Address: (International Headquarters): Harmony Hall, 6315 Third Avenue, Kenosha, Wisconsin 53141.

Society of Record Dealers

RB. An organization of record dealers. AI. Also called SORD, pronounced both as a word and as separate initials. Address: 327 Jackson Avenue, Jersey City, New Jersey.

sol: ○

MU. 1. The syllable used in singing the fifth note (tone) of a scale

354

in the sol-fa system. The shape notehead, shown above, representing this syllable.

sol-fa or solfa (sohl-fah)

MU. 1. The syllables used to designate the tones of a scale, regardless of key. 2. The use of these syllables, as they are sung in vocal exercises. AI. In the United States these syllables are: *do, re, mi, fa, sol, la, ti.* (Formerly, *ut* was used for *do* and *si* was used for *ti.*) In England the following syllables are used: *doh, ray, me, fah, sol, lah, ti.* These appear on much of the sheet music printed in Great Britain (just as chord captions are used in the United States) in the following abbreviated form: *d, r, m, f, s, l, t.* The song hit DO RE MI (from *The Sound of Music*) is based on the *sol-fa* method of singing.

sol-feg-gio (sol-fehj′ee-oh)

MU. 1. The use of sol-fa syllables in singing. 2. Vocal exercises in which sol-fa syllables are used, as in singing the scale. 3. Solmization.

solid

MU. 1. Designating a well-blended togetherness in musical performance, as that of an orchestra. 2. Very good. 3. Excellent. 4. Skillfully performed.

solid chord

MU. A chord, the tones of which are performed (sounded) simultaneously, as distinguished from a *broken chord.*

solid sound

MU. Well-blended sound.

solid South

JZ. 1. Well blended, skillfully performed New Orleans jazz. 2. Excellently played Dixieland music.

solmization

MU. 1. The act of using a set of syllables, particularly the sol-fa syllables, to sing the tones of a scale. 2. The practice of using dummy lyrics to represent the tones of a scale, as in vocal practice.

solo

MU. 1. A musical composition composed or arranged for a single instrument or a single voice. 2. A passage or part of a musical composition written, arranged or performed in the same manner. 3. A performance by one singer or one instrumentalist. 4. Alone.

solo guitar

MU. 1. Usually the Spanish guitar, as used to play solos. 2. The playing of solos, solo parts or the playing of the melody, as distinguished from *rhythm guitar*. 3. Any guitar used for playing solos or melody.

soloist

MU. 1. A singer who performs a solo. 2. An instrumentalist who performs a solo.

song

MU. 1. A musical composition for the voice, or for several voices, usually with an instrumental accompaniment. 2. Usually the generally-accepted popular-type song, as that in AABA form, including both words *and music*. AI. The United States Copyright Office says, "The term 'musical composition' *does not include song poems* and other work consisting of words without music. Works of that type are not registrable for copyright in unpublished form." All of which means that *words without music are not a song*. The word *song*, as used throughout this book, means the kind of song described above. It should not necessarily be assumed that this term applies to other kinds of songs as, for instance, hymns. See POPULAR SONG. See FORM.

song and dance

TE. 1. Designating one who sings and dances, as a *song-and-dance man*. 2. Designating entertainment in which singing and dancing is featured, as a *song-and-dance act*. 3. Designating the nature of a performance, or a part of a performance, as a *song-and-dance routine*.

songbird

MB. 1. A female singer. 2. Thrush.

song credit

MB. The recognition of having written a song, as listed by a per-

356

formance-rights society, as included in a motion picture, as stated on the program of a musical show, as stated on a song sheet, as stated on a phonograph record label, etc. See CREDITS.

song cycle

MB. See CYCLE OF SONGS.

songfest

MU. 1. A festival in which singing is the featured activity and/or attraction. 2. A community sing. 3. A festival of songs.

song folio

MB. A song book, usually paper covered and approximately 9″ x 12″ in size.

song form

SW. The pattern to which a song is written, as the AABA form, the ABAB form, etc. AI. Typical examples of songs written in the four most-used song forms are as follows: Songs in the AABA form: BIRTH OF THE BLUES and SEPTEMBER IN THE RAIN. Songs in the ABAB form: WHEN I TAKE MY SUGAR TO TEA and I'LL GET BY. Songs in the ABAC form: WITH A SONG IN MY HEART and WHEN DAY IS DONE. Songs in the ABCA form: IF YOU KNEW SUSIE and ME AND MY SHADOW.

song mill

SW. 1. Any individual or company whose business it is to write music for so-called song poems and/or words to music for would-be songwriters. 2. Music mill. 3. Music foundry. 4. Song foundry.

"song poem"

SS. A song-shark term meaning anything that anyone may care to send them, no matter the form, no matter how terrible. The term definitely is not used in the *legitimate* music business.

song request

MB. A song that is requested to be played and/or sung, as on radio, by a dance band, a night-club singer, etc.

song scribe

MB. Songwriter.

song service

SS. 1. Any individual or organization whose business it is to offer so-called *services* to would-be songwriters. 2. Song mill. 3. Song shark. 4. Also called *songwriters' service*. AI. Established songwriters do not require such services, nor did they get where they are by using them.

song shark

MB. 1. A term created by Ashby Deering, of the New York Morning Telegram, to mean any indivdual or organization whose business it is to sell a variety of so-called services, by questionable advertising and misleading promotion, to would-be songwriters. 2. A song mill that uses questionable advertising and promotion. 3. A songwriters' service which uses misleading advertising, in publications and/or by direct mail. 4. One who preys on would-be songwriters. AI. The song shark is not a part of the actual music business. He operates in a make-believe twilight zone of his own. The music business has no place for anyone who has dealings with song sharks.

song sheet

MB. 1. A printed copy of a song. 2. A sheet on which several songs are printed. 3. The standard folded-once, 9″ x 12″ page-size sheet music. 4. Professional-size printed music.

songsmith

MB. A songwriter, male or female.

songster

MB. 1. A singer, male or female. 2. A songwriter.

song story

SW. The story told in a song. AI. For instance, the story told in TENNESSEE WALTZ is that of losing a sweetheart to a best friend. See STORY SONGS.

songstress

MB. 1. A female singer. 2. A female songwriter.

song survey

MB. The examination of songs in order to learn their current popularity, as those most requested by radio listeners, those most played by disk jockeys, those selling the most records, those selling the most sheet music, etc. AI. Song surveys are usually made by some newspapers, music trade publications, radio stations, television stations, etc. See SURVEY SONG.

song words

SW. 1. Words that are suited to songwriting, as distinguished from words which, because of their harshness of sound, unsingability, connotation, meaning, etc., are not. 2. Words that are particularly suited to songwriting. 3. The words of a song.

songwriter

MB. 1. One who writes either the words or the music for a song. 2. One who writes both the words and the music for a song. 3. A lyricist. 4. A composer. AI. ASCAP designates the writer of *lyrics* as an *author*, the writer of *music* as a *composer*. The United States Copyright Office says, "Authors include composers of music, authors of words, arrangers, compilers, etc." All of these are *songwriters*.

songwriting range

SW. 1. The compass within which popular songs are written. 2. The vocal range most suitable to the greatest number of average singing voices. AI. See GOLDEN SEVENTEEN, THE.

sonorous

MU. 1. Producing sound. 2. Capable of producing sound. 3. Sounding. 4. Resounding. 5. Loud, full, rich, deep, as said of sound. 6. Resonant.

soprano

MU. 1. The highest female singing voice. 2. The original (unchanged) voice of a boy, as those in a boys choir. 3. Any voice in the soprano range, usually two octaves or more up from middle C. 4. Anyone having a voice in this range. 5. The part for such a voice. 6. Any instrument with a compass in this range, as a *soprano* sax. AI. Soprano vocalists are classified *coloratura* soprano, *lyric* soprano and *dramatic* soprano, according to tone quality and range.

359

SORD (sord) or (ess-oh-ahr-dee)

RB. Abbreviation, *Society of Record Dealers.*

sotto voce (saht'oh voh'che)

MU. 1. *Under the voice*, therefore in an *undertone*. 2. Softer than the normal voice. 3. Not as loud. 4. Sung or spoken in a semi-whispered, confidential manner. 5. Played softly.

soul solid

MN. 1. From the soul, as said of a musical or vocal performance. 2. Well played or sung with deep feeling.

sound

AS. 1. The sensation that is produced through the organs of hearing. 2. Anything that is or can be heard. See TONE. See NOISE.

sound board

MU. A thin plate of wood placed below the strings of a stringed instrument to reinforce the tone. AI. Also called a *sounding board.*

sound engineer

BR. 1. A technician who operates the audio equipment for recording or broadcasting. 2. Audio engineer. 3. Speech input engineer.

sound input

BR. Same as *speech input.*

sound level

BR. See LEVEL.

sound lock

BR. The, usually small, vestibule immediately outside a broadcasting or recording studio, through which it is necessary to pass in going from the studio to the control room, or vice versa.

sound track

RG. The space in which sound is recorded, as on a phonograph record, a tape, motion-picture film, etc. AI. For instance, the groove on a phonograph record contains the sound track. The area along one side of a motion-picture film *carries* the sound track, etc.

sour

MN. Discordant, unpleasant, as a *sour* note (tone).

Sousaphone

MU. *A helicon.* AI. Named in honor of the great band leader John Philip Sousa, who suggested it.

space

MU. 1. The interval between two lines of the staff. 2. The interval between two leger lines, called *leger space.*

space note

MU. Any note written in the space between two staff lines or between two leger lines, as distinguished from a *line note.*

Spanish guitar

MU. The modern Spanish guitar has six strings, the three highest are made of gut, the three lowest are made of a silk core wound with fine silver wire, usually tuned E-A-d-g-b-e[1]. AI. Used as a solo instrument or for accompanying songs, as distinguished from *rhythm* guitar.

speaker

ET. Same as *loud-speaker.* See LOUD-SPEAKER.

SPEBSQSA (pronounced as separate initials)

SG. The Society for the Preservation and Encouragement of Barber Shop Quartet Singing in America, Inc.

SPEBSQSA categories of judging

SG. The five categories of judging barbershop-harmony quartets used by the SPEBSQSA are as follows: (a) arrangement, (b) balance, (c) blend, (d) harmony accuracy and (e) stage presence.

spec (spehk)

SB. Short for *spectacular.*

special chord

MU. 1. Any chord that has been altered or especially built to fit a particular harmony need. 2. A hybrid chord. AI. Typical special chords are G7susC, Cm7♭5, etc.

special material

SW. 1. Any song written for a special purpose or occasion. 2. Any song written for limited or restricted use, as for performance exclusively by one particular singer. SB. 3. Monolog, dialog, etc. written for special purposes or occasions, or for limited or restricted use.

specialty

TE. 1. A specialized and/or featured performance. 2. Any additional entertainment, as the performance of songs, dances, patter, etc. between the acts of a play. 3. The material, as songs, for such performance. AI. Also called *specialty material, specialty songs,* etc.

spectacular

SB. Any performance, as on stage, screen, television or outdoors, that is exceptionally unusual and usually characterized by being large and/or elaborate.

speech input

ET. Designating the science of picking up sound (speech) by a microphone or microphones, for the purpose of recording or broadcasting.

speech input equipment

ET. 1. The equipment used in speech input, as microphones, volume controls, amplifiers, etc. 2. That part of recording or broadcasting equipment that has to do with picking up sound.

spell

MU. 1. To name, write, print or play the notes that make up a chord or a melody. 2. To *spell out* musically. AI. For instance, just as the word *boy* is spelled b-o-y, the chord of C major is spelled *C-E-G*. The chord of C minor is spelled *C-E♭-G*. The chord of C dominant seventh is spelled *C-E-G-B♭*. The melody of JINGLE BELLS is spelled out *A-A-A, A-A-A, A-C-F-G-A*, etc. Songwriters often use this kind of musical shorthand to jot down melody ideas.

spin

MB. To play a phonograph record. AI. For instance, a songwriter might thank a disk jockey for the *spin* given his latest song.

spinner

MB. 1. One who plays (spins) records, as for a public performance. 2. Specifically, a disk jockey, who is not necessarily connected with a broadcasting station, who works on location, as in a tavern, a saloon, a night club, etc. and whose records and voice are heard over a public address system. 3. A discothèque disk jockey.

spiritual

MU. A religious folk song of the kind originated by the American Negro during slavery days, employing a refrain and forceful rhythm. AI. Typical spirituals are NOBODY KNOWS THE TROUBLE I'VE SEEN, SWING LOW SWEET CHARIOT, HEAV'N HEAV'N (*All God's Children*) and GET ON BOARD LITTLE CHILDREN.

split copyright

MB. 1. A jointly owned copyright. 2. A copyright owned by two or more proprietors. AI. There is some question as to the validity of a *split copyright*, as a copyright is legally considered to be *indivisible*.

split record

MB. 1. A phonograph record whose two sides share equal popularity. 2. A phonograph record whose popularity (is limited and) is divided more-or-less equally between the songs on each of its sides. 3. A phonograph record whose A side and B side has not been determined by the moderate amount of plays it has been given by disk jockeys. See TWO-WAY RECORD.

spoken word

RB. 1. Designating a recording or a performance, as that of a monolog, a speech, a lecture, a sermon, a poem or song lyrics, etc., in which no music is used. 2. Designating a performance by a speaker or speakers, without music in any form.

spondee (spahn′dee)

PY. A metrical foot containing two accented syllables, or — —. Example, *Swa′nee′*. The opposite of pyrrhic. Musical counterpart, Two-Four Time.

spreading payments

MB. Designating a method of payment used by ASCAP designed to give steadier incomes to writer members, as compared with payments based on current-performance computation. AI. Songwriters who are ASCAP members have their choice of either of these two methods of payment. Also called *four-fund system*.

square

MU. a. 1. Designating anything that is conservative, as music, the performance of music, etc. 2. Conservative, as a musical composition, the singing or playing of music, etc.

square

MN. n. 1. A conservative person, as distinguished from a *cat* or one of the *in crowd*. AI. The opposite of being *far out*.

square dance

CM. 1. A dance in which couples form sets in squares. 2. A breakdown. 3. The music for such a dance. AI. There are three basic styles of square dancing: (a) The shuffle. (b) The clog. (c) The stomp. Some dancers combine the shuffle and the clog in one style of dancing, which they call by either name or by *shuffle-clog*.

square name

SB, MN. 1. The legal name of someone, as a songwriter, who uses a nom de plume. 2. The legal name of someone, as a performer, who uses a stage name or pseudonym.

sro or SRO (ess-ahr-oh)

SB. Abbreviation, *standing room only*.

364

staccato

MU. 1. Played, or to be played, in an abrupt, disconnected manner. 2. Marked by an abrupt, sharp emphasis, as opposed to *tenuto*.

staccato mark: · ,

MU. Either of the accent marks shown above. AI. The first is called a *dot*. The second is called a *dash*.

staff:

MU. 1. The combined 5 lines and 4 spaces shown above, used to designate the pitch of notes, and on which notation is written. AI. Also called *stave*. The plural for both *staff* and *stave* is *staves*. The designation *single staff* is used to distinguish the staff shown above from a *double staff*. See DOUBLE STAFF. MB. 2. The personnel of a company, as that of a music publisher, a phonograph record company, a radio station, etc.

staffer

MB. 1. A staff songwriter. 2. A staff musician. 3. Anyone who is a member of a staff, as that of a music publisher, a phonograph record company, a music trade publication, etc.

staffless notation

MU. Music notation that does not employ, or require, the use of a staff or staves. AI. For instance, the tonic sol-fa letters, figures and other symbols used in *tablature*. See TABLATURE.

staff line

MU. 1. A single staff (composed of 5 lines and 4 spaces) that extends from one side of a page to the other, as those printed on music manuscript paper. MT. 2. Also called *line*. AI. For instance, a music typographer might say that a song manuscript contains so many *lines* of copy, meaning so many *staff lines* of notation.

staff musician

MB. 1. A musician who is regularly employed by one employer. 2. A musician who is under contract. AI. For instance, a music publisher might employ a *staff pianist* or a *staff arranger*. A broadcasting station might employ a *staff band* made up of a number of *staff musicians*, etc.

staff notation

MU. Music notation which is written or printed on a staff or staves, as distinguished from *staffless notation*.

staff writer

MB. A songwriter who is under exclusive contract, as to a music publisher, as distinguished from *free lance*.

stage

TE. v. 1. To plan, arrange, produce and/or present a performance, as that on the stage of a theater. 2. To produce entertainment, as that in a theater or on an open-air stage.

stage

TE. n. 1. The entire area in a theater which is back of the footlights. 2. The theater, its people, its world, drama, acting, singing, dancing, music or any other form of entertainment that is *staged*, as a profession. SB. 3. Any platform, or designated area, indoors or out, on which entertainment is performed.

stage band

MB. A band, or orchestra, that performs on the stage of a theater, as distinguished from a pit band. AI. A typical stage band is that of Lawrence Welk.

stagecraft

SB. The art and skill of *staging* performances, as those that might be given on a stage, as writing, directing, producing, etc. thereof.

stage door

TE. The outside backdoor leading to the backstage of a theater, auditorium, arena, night club, etc.

stage effect

TE. Any impression created by a device, as lighting, scenery, etc. to give an *effect* on the stage, as rain, fog, lightning, thunder, etc.

stagehand

TE. Anyone who does manual labor in connection with producing or presenting a play, musical or other kinds of stage performances, as the arrangement of the scenery and properties, operating the curtains, lights, etc.

stage left

TE. 1. At an actor's left, as he stands facing the audience. 2. The same as *audience right*. 3. The opposite of *stage right*, or *audience left*.

stage name

TE. A fictitious name, as that used by an actor, singer or other performer.

stage presence

TE. 1. The image or impression one gives while appearing on a stage. SA. 2. The art of appearing natural, original and self-confident while on the stage. AI. This is one of the five categories for judging by the SPEBSQSA.

stage right

TE. 1. At an actor's right, as he stands facing the audience. 3. The same as *audience left*. 3. The opposite of *stage left* or *audience right*.

stamper

RB. A metal die used to stamp or press phonograph records.

stand

SB. 1. A performance or series of performances, as a singer might play a *one-night stand* or a *week's stand*. MB. 2. A *bandstand*, as the platform on which a dance band performs. 3. A *music stand*, as the metal rack, or other device, used by musicians to hold sheet music.

standard

MB. 1. A standard repertory song. 2. Any song that continues to be sung and played over a period of many years. 3. An evergreen. AI. Typical standards are TAKE ME OUT TO THE BALL GAME,

367

EASTER PARADE, ST. LOUIS BLUES and WHITE CHRIST-
MAS.

standby

MB. 1. A musician, as a pianist, who is employed by a broadcasting
station to *fill in* in case of program failure RB. 2. A cue meaning *get
ready*. AI. For instance, an A and R man might give a singer a *standby* meaning *get ready to start singing*.

standee

TE, SB. A paying customer who stands to see a show (after all seats
are sold).

standing room

TE. That portion of a theater or auditorium, immediately back of
the last row of downstairs seats, where patrons may stand to watch
a performance (after all seats are sold). AI. Standing room is limited
by the fire ordinances of all major cities.

standing room only

TE. The notice posted by a theater, when all seats are sold, meaning
that only admissions to the standing-room area are available. AI. Post-
ing such a notice is called *hanging out the SRO sign*.

stand-up

SB. 1. A stand-up comedian or comic. 2. A one-liner comic.

stand-up comedian

SB. 1. A comedian who stands up, alone, before an audience and
delivers, usually fast, pointed gags, as distinguished from a situation
comedian. 2. A one-liner comic. AI. For instance, Bob Hope works
as a stand-up comedian when he works alone. He works as a situation comedian when he appears in motion pictures. Typical stand-up
comedians are Alan King, Shelly Berman, Buddy Hackett and Henny
Youngman.

stanza

PY. 1. A certain number of lines of verse grouped in a definite
scheme of meter and sequence. 2. A metrical division of a poem, often

368

incorrectly called *verse*. MU. 3. The verse of a song, particularly that of a hymn.

star

SB. 1. A prominent performer, as a singer in a musical show, especially one who is assigned a leading role. 2. The featured performer in a show.

state

LW. 1. One of the territorial and political units constituting a federal government, as the United States. 2. The District of Columbia and any other territory to which this title is made applicable by an act of Congress, as Alabama, Alaska, Arizona, etc.

statement songs

MB. 1. A classification in songwriting as to treatment. 2. The opposite of question songs. AI. For instance, the song WHY DO I LOVE YOU asks a question. The song I LOVE YOU makes a statement. Both deal with the same subject matter. Typical statement songs are YOU'RE THE TOP, ALL I DO IS DREAM OF YOU, THERE'LL BE NO TEARDROPS TONIGHT and I LOVE YOU AND DON'T YOU FORGET IT.

State Street

JZ. 1. A main thoroughfare that featured in Chicago's early jazz history. 2. Therefore, anything typical of that era, as *State-Street music*, *State-Street rhythm*, *State-Street style*, etc. AI. It was in Chicago that the Original Dixieland (Jazz) Band first introduced jazz. The term *State Street* usually designates the style of music and its performance thus introduced. State Street is the street designated as that *great street* in the song hit CHICAGO.

station

BD. 1. A radio or television station. 2. A place equipped to transmit radio and/or television programs. 3. The studios, offices, technical equipment, etc. collectively of such an establishment.

statute law

LW. A law established by a legislative body, as the copyright law, as distinguished from *common law*.

369

statutory

LW. 1. Fixed or authorized by an established rule of law. 2. Conforming to a law passed by a legislative body, as a *statutory copyright*, as distinguished from *common law literary property*.

stave

MU. A staff. AI. The plural of either staff or stave is staves.

stay with the book

MN. 1. To play or sing a musical composition, as a song, as it is written, without improvising. 2. To perform as directed. AI. The opposite of *ad libbing, drifting* or *wandering*.

steal

SW. 1. A song that is very similar to another song. 2. Any part of a song that is very similar to a part of another song. AI. The term *steal* does not necessarily imply *intentional theft*.

steal the show

SB. A performer, act, etc. who attracts the large majority of audience attention and acclaim is said to *steal the show* (from other performers, acts, etc.).

steel

MU. 1. A steel bar, made in a variety of shapes and sizes, used to fret a guitar played Hawaiian style. 2. A guitar played in this fashion.

steel drum

MU. A drum, originally made of an empty oil drum, which is played by being struck with padded mallets or hammers. AI. The steel drum is a percussion instrument of West Indies origin. The head of a steel drum is marked off in areas. Then each of these areas is tuned to a different tone of the scale by being hammered (with a carpenter's hammer) into tune. Some steel drums have a range of an octave or more. Steel drums are made in a variety of registers, as *tenor, alto, baritone* and *bass*.

steel drum band

MU. A band composed of steel drums, in a variety of registers.

370

steel guitar

MU. 1. A 6-string guitar that is played face up and fretted with a steel bar called a *steel*. 2. A guitar played Hawaiian style. 3. A guitar made for this purpose. AI. Steel guitars are made in the conventional Spanish-guitar style and in *console* style, mounted on legs or a base.

steel man

MN. 1. A steel guitar player. 2. A musician who plays the guitar Hawaiian style.

stem: |

MU. The vertical line shown above. AI. A stem is attached to a notehead to construct an ascending or descending *stemmed note*.

stemmed note

MU. Any note that has a stem, ascending or descending, as a *half note*, a *quarter note*, a *sixteenth note*, etc.

step

MU. 1. An interval measuring a difference in pitch. 2. A degree on the staff. 3. A degree on the scale. See DEGREE.

stepwise

MU. From one step to the next step. AI. For instance, a melody that moves from C to D, from D to E and from E to D is said to proceed *stepwise*, as distinguished from one that *skips*. See SKIP.

stereo (stehr′e-oh)

RG. a. Short for *stereophonic*.

stereo

PG. n. Short for *stereotype*.

stereo FM

RO. See MULTIPLEX

stereophonic (stehr″e-oh-fahn′ihk)

BR. Designating a method of picking up sound by two microphones, each placed in a different location, and reproducing it from two speakers, each placed in a different location, in imitation of the way sound is picked up and heard by a person's two ears. AI. The object is to achieve greater naturalness. A stereophonic record, tape or film has two separate sound tracks that are played simultaneously. Compare with *monaural*.

stereotype

MB. 1. Anything that has no individuality, as though cast from a mold, as a hackneyed or trite song. PG. 2. A one-piece printing plate, made from a mold, as is sometimes used in printing music by the letterpress process.

stern wheeler

JZ. Designating a powerful, moving, musical performance in Dixieland style.

stet (steht)

PG. 1. A typographical sign meaning *let it stand as originally written or printed*. 2. A printers' term, used in marking proof sheets, as those of a song, which means *disregard* a (previously made) alteration or correction. AI. For instance, if a word is marked to be *deleted*, the printer would follow instructions by omitting this word from the finished printing. However, if a word is marked to be *deleted* and then the term *stet* is written by it, the printer would disregard the instructions to delete and the word would appear in the finished printing. It is facetiously said among printers that the term *stet* was created for people who cannot make up their minds.

stick

MN. 1. A drumstick. 2. The slender baton used by orchestra leaders. 3. Facetiously, an orchestra leader (one who wields the stick). 4. Likewise, *the head man* in any organization, as a music publishing company. See SUGAR STICK.

stick beat

MN. 1. The rhythm or sound of drumsticks beating on a surface, as that of a drumhead, on a clog box, etc. or one drumstick beating against another. 2. The motions (rise and fall) of an orchestra leader's baton.

stick man

MN. An orchestra leader (the man who wields the stick). AI. Also called *the stick*.

sticks

MN. 1. Drumsticks. 2. A name used for a *percussionist*.

sting

MN. To play sharply, quickly and with emphasis, as in an emphasized staccato style.

stinger

MN. 1. A note (tone), chord, passage or section played in emphasized staccato style. 2. A musician who plays in this style.

stomp

DG. 1. A dance, or the step or steps used in it, in which the dancer brings down his feet quickly, heavily and noisily. MU. 2. The music for such a dance. JZ. 3. In the early days of jazz, New Orleans bands originated a double-time (twice-as-fast) jazz march known as the *stomp* (which has no direct connection with the previously described dance or the music for it). AI. Early exponents of the stomp were Joe "King" Oliver, trumpet player; "Kid" Ory, trombone player, and "Jelly Roll" Morton, pianist. Typical stomps are KING POR-TER STOMP, SUGAR FOOT STOMP and THE PEARLS.

stomper

DG, CM. 1. A stomp dancer, male or female. 2. One whose dancing style is accentuated by *stomping*. 3. A square-dancer who stomps, as distinguished from one who *shuffles* or *clogs*. 4. One who dances a *stomp-type* breakdown or square dance.

stop

MU. v. 1. To press down a string on the fingerboard of a stringed instrument, in order to vary its pitch. 2. To change the pitch of a string by the action of stopping. AI. *Double stopping* means to press down two strings at the same time with the same finger.

stop

MU. n. The mechanism on a pipe organ that admits and/or *stops* the flow of air to the pipes.

stopped note

MU. Any note designating a tone to be played by stopping a string on a stringed instrument, as distinguished from *open note*.

stopped string

MU. Any string on a stringed instrument that is played while being pressed down (stopped), as distinguished from an *open string*.

stopped tone

MU. 1. Any tone that is designated by a *stopped note*. 2. The tone produced by playing a *stopped string*.

stop the show

SB. A performer is said to *stop the show* when he so pleases an audience that he is awarded unusually-prolonged, enthusiastic applause, thus *stopping* other entertainment on the program from taking place, at least for the time being.

stop watch

RG. A watch with a mechanism that can be stopped and started at will and which shows an accumulation of time. AI. Stop watches are used as by A and R men, to time the making of phonograph records, by directors to time radio and television shows, by orchestra leaders to time orchestral numbers, etc.

story

SW. 1. A series of events. 2. A short tale, as that told in a *story song*. See SONG STORY.

story line

SW. The series of events, in the order of their occurrence, that make up a story, as that in a story song. See STORY SONG.

story song

MB. A category in songwriting, as to material used and the manner in which it is used. Typical story songs are BALLERINA, I FOUND A MILLION DOLLAR BABY, THE SWEETHEART TREE, RUDOLPH THE RED NOSED REINDEER and TENNESSEE WALTZ.

374

straight

TE. Short for *straight man.*

straight man

TE. An actor who serves as a foil for a comedian, as in a musical show. AI. Also called a *feeder* (one who feeds lines, as to a comedian).

strain

MU. 1. A particular portion of a melody of peculiar interest. 2. A well-defined musical passage. 3. A motive. 4. A theme.

stray

MB. Short for *stray dog.*

stray dog

MB. 1. An uncopyrighted song. 2. A song in public domain. AI. A term usually applied to a song that never has been legally copyrighted, as distinguished from a song whose copyright has expired.

strictly-from-Dixie

MN, SW. Corny.

string

MU. A slender cord, usually of gut, wire, silk, nylon or a combination of materials, etc. stretched on a musical instrument, as a piano, harp, violin, guitar, double bass, etc., which is struck, plucked, or bowed to produce a musical sound.

string band

MU. A band, or orchestra, composed of stringed instruments.

string bass

MU. The *double bass*, also known as the *bass viol*, as distinguished from the *bass horn.*

stringed instruments

MU. All musical instruments whose tones are produced by strings, which are struck, strummed, plucked or bowed. AI. Typical stringed instruments are the piano, guitar, banjo, mandolin, violin, etc. Also called *strings*. For instance, it might be said that the instrumentation of a certain orchestra includes *ten strings*, meaning *ten stringed instruments.*

string numbers:

MU. The numerals by which the strings on a stringed instrument are known, designated, and identified. AI. The diagram shown above is for the 6-string guitar. The string furthest from the player, when the instrument is held in playing position, is the *first string*.

strings

MU. 1. Stringed instruments, as *the strings* of an orchestra, designating the *string section*. 2. The musicians who play stringed instruments, as in an orchestra. See STRINGED INSTRUMENTS.

string section

MU. That part of an orchestra, or band, which is composed of stringed instruments, as distinguished from *brass section, wood wind section,* etc.

strip show

RT. 1. Originally, a radio show or television show that is presented 5 times a week, Monday through Friday. 2. More recently, any radio or television show that is presented more than twice a week.

structure

SW. 1. That which is constructed, as a song. 2. The arrangement and organized union of relative parts, as the *structure* of a song.

strum

GI. 1. Originally, to pluck a stringed musical instrument in an unskilled or careless manner. 2. More generally accepted, to pluck a stringed musical instrument softly, smoothly and in a *seemingly* unstudied style (which can be the result of skill and practice).

stub

SB. 1. The stub end of a ticket of admission, as to a theater, a ball-

376

room, a show, etc. 2. That portion of a ticket which is returned to the customer. 3. A paid admission.

stub holder

SB. 1. A ticket buyer, as to a theatrical performance. 2. A patron. 3. A member of a paying audience. 4. A paid customer, as to a show.

studio

RB. An acoustically constructed room, equipped with microphones and other speech-input equipment used for recording and/or broadcasting.

study

SB. v. To apply the mind in order to acquire knowledge, as to *study* songwriting, or to *study* a song in order to sing or play it.

study

SB. n. Any performer, as a singer, musician, actor, etc., with reference to his ability to learn. AI. For instance, it might be said that a singer is a *quick study*, meaning that he has the ability to learn quickly to sing a song. A musician who is a *quick study* needs little time for rehearsing. An actor who is a *quick study* has no trouble learning the roles he plays, as in musical shows, etc.

style

MU. 1. The individuality, originality, personality, character and excellence expressed in a work, as a musical composition, or its performance, as the style of Johnny Mercer, the style of Peggy Lee, etc. 2. Style often refers to the fourth characteristic of a tone, *quality*. AI. The *style* in which a song is to be performed is written at its beginning. For instance this might be *lively, affectionately, well-accented, briskly, with feeling, simply, caressingly, in church style, with fire, sweetly,* etc. See EXPRESSION MARKS. RB. 3. A phonograph needle.

stylist

MU. 1. A songwriter whose songs have a particular and distinctive flavor, personality, character or *style*, as Cole Porter, Victor Herbert and Duke Ellington. 2. A singer or performer, whose performance is marked by a particular and distinctive *flavor*, personality, character

377

or *style* as Frank Sinatra, Fats Waller, Mel Torme and Peggy Lee. 3. Anyone who expresses distinctiveness or *style*.

stylus

RG. 1. A sharp, pointed device, usually made of metal, for cutting the grooves (sound track) in a phonograph record. 2. The needle used for recording sound in a (record) blank. 3. A needle used on a phonograph for reproducing sound. 4. A phonograph needle. 5. A style.

sub

MB. v. 1. Abbreviation, *substitute*. 2. To fill in, as one musician might *sub* for another.

sub

MU. p. 1. A prefix meaning below, under, secondary, to a lesser degree than, as *subdominant, subtone*, etc. MB. 2. Secondary, as *subpublish, subpublisher*, etc.

sub

MB. n. Abbreviation, *substitute*, as one musician who *subs* for another.

sub-contra octave

MU. The fourth octave, on the piano, below middle C. AI. The keys (tones) in this octave are designated C_2, D_2, E_2, etc. There are only two keys in this octave on the standard 88-key piano. These are A_2, and B_2.

subdominant

MU. 1. The fourth degree of the scale. 2. The tone next below the dominant. AI. For instance, in the scale of C major the subdominant is the tone of *F*.

subject

SW. 1. The general idea of a song. 2. The thing that a song is written about. MU. 3. The melodic phrase on which a musical composition, or part of a musical composition, is based.

378

subjective

SW. A type of song treatment that has to do with the subject in a manner that states or reflects the ideas, thoughts and/or feelings of the narrator. Typical of songs written subjectively are I CAN'T BELIEVE THAT YOU'RE IN LOVE WITH ME, I COULD HAVE DANCED ALL NIGHT and I CAN DREAM CAN'T I? Compare with OBJECTIVE.

subject matter

SW. 1. The things that make up a song. 2. The materials used to construct a song.

submediant

MU. 1. The sixth degree of the scale. 2. The tone next below the leading tone. AI. For instance, in the scale of C major the submediant is the tone of *A*. Also called the *superdominant*.

submission

SW. 1. The act of submitting or offering something to another, as a songwriter might send a song to a music publisher or record company for their consideration. 2. Anything thus submitted, as a song in manuscript or recorded form. AI. Such a submission is usually accompanied by a *letter of transmittal*.

submission, letter of

SW. See LETTER OF TRANSMITTAL.

submit

SW. To offer, as a song (to a music publisher for his consideration).

subordinate chords

MU. Same as *secondary chords*.

subpublish

MB. 1. To publish further, as a song, (after previous or original publication) by a publisher other than the original publisher. 2. To republish, as a song, by a publisher other than the original publisher. AI. For instance, a song that was originally published by an American publisher in the United States, might be *subpublished* (by agreement with the copyright owner) by a different publisher in another country, possibly with the lyrics in a language other than English.

subpublisher

MB. 1. A music publisher who subpublishes. 2. One who republishes the publications of another publisher, by agreement.

subsidiary rights

LW. 1. Secondary rights, as those in a musical, a musical show, a revue, etc. 2. Those rights that are entirely aside from the *main rights* in a musical show, as *radio, television and motion picture rights, touring-company rights, stock rights, amateur rights, concert rights, grand-opera rights,* etc.

subtitle

MB. 1. The secondary title of a song. 2. Additional wording to that of the *main title* of a song, either before or after the main title. AI. Subtitles are used to distinguish one song from another song having the same main title. For instance, in the following *full titles,* the *subtitles* are enclosed in parentheses: I CAN'T HELP IT (If I'm Still In Love With You), LOVER MAN (Oh, Where Can You Be?), (All of a Sudden) MY HEART SINGS and (Look Over Your Shoulder) I'M WALKING BEHIND YOU.

sub-tone

MU. a. 1. Designating a register or compass low in pitch. 2. Designating a register or compass lower in pitch than comparative registers. AI. For instance, the term *sub-tone clarinet* means a clarinet lower in register, or played lower in pitch, than that of accompanying instruments.

subtone

MU. n. 1. A tone or tones of lower pitch and/or less volume than the accompanying tones with which it is played or sung. 2. Comparatively a lower tone. 3. An *undertone.*

subtonic

MU. 1. The seventh degree of the scale. 2. The tone next below the tonic. AI. For instance, in the scale of C major, the subtonic is the tone of *B.* Also called the *leading tone.*

success

MB. 1. Any song that shows a profit for its publisher, no matter how small. AI. Also called *song success*. RB. 2. Any record that shows a profit for its manufacturer.

succession

GI. 1. The act of following in uninterrupted order. 2. A group of things that follow in order. 3. A series.

sucker

SS. Anyone who patronizes song sharks.

sucker list

SS. 1. The list of potential customers maintained by a song shark. 2. The list of those to whom a song shark sends his direct-by-mail advertising. 3. A song shark's list of customers.

sucker song

SS. A song written in whole or in part by a song shark. AI. Also, *sucker melody, sucker tune and sucker lyrics*.

sugar band

MN. An orchestra or band that plays noticeably *sweetly*, or *overly sweet*.

sugar stick

SW. 1. A song that is particularly successful over an extended period of time. 2. The most successful song in a group, a catalog, etc. 3. An evergreen. AI. For instance, a songwriter might refer to his biggest money-making song as his *sugar stick*. MN. 4. Figuratively, the baton of a leader whose band plays exceptionally sweet music. 5. Hence, exceptionally sweet music. AI. Also called *sugar-stick* music, *sugar-stick band*, etc.

summer is icumen in

MU. 1. The title of a song written sometime during or about the year 1300 A.D. AI. Because of its folk-like melody, its full-bodied harmony, its title and text (all very unusual at the time), this is prob-

381

ably *the first popular song*. 2. The smash hit of 1300 (and for many years that followed).

super

MU. A prefix meaning above, over, as superdominant, supertonic, superoctave, etc.

superdominant

MU. 1. The sixth degree of the scale. 2. The tone next above the dominant. AI. For instance, in the scale of C major the superdominant is the tone of *A*. Also called the *submediant*.

superior numbers: c^3, d^3, e^3, etc.

PG. 1. Small figures like those shown above. 2. Small figures that are placed higher than other characters in the same line. AI. In music, superior numbers are used in connection with lower case letters to designate all treble tones (middle C and all tones above). For instance, c^1 designates *middle C*. c^2 designates two-lined C (one octave above middle C). The three tones shown above designate three-lined C, three-lined D and three-lined E respectively (all in the second octave above middle C), etc.

superoctave

MU. The octave above the given tone.

supertonic

MU. 1. The second degree of the scale. 2. The tone next above the tonic. AI. For instance, in the scale of C the supertonic is the tone of D.

supper club

SB. 1. Same as *dinner club*. 2. A night club. See NIGHT CLUB.

survey (ser-vae')

MB. To examine carefully and evaluate as to relative position of standing, in respect to popularity, sales, etc., as a list of songs. See SONG SURVEY.

survey city

MB. A city in which a survey, as that of songs, is made.

382

survey song

MB. A song that is ranked among those most currently popular, as *the top forty*, those most frequently requested, those most frequently played, as on radio, those selling the most records or those selling the most sheet music, etc.

sus (suhs)

MU. 1. Abbreviation, *suspended.* 2. A designation used in the captions for certain special chords to specify a *suspended* tone. AI. For instance, the special chord caption G7susC means a G7 chord with the suspended tone of C. D7susG means a D7 chord with suspended tone of G, etc. See SUSPENDED TONE.

susie song

SW. Any song with a girl's name for a title. AI. Typical susie songs are MARGIE, ROSE MARIE, DIANE and MARY.

suspended tone

MU. A tone that has been held over from a previous chord. AI. For instance, the special chord G7susC is composed of the tones G-B-D-F (which normally make up the G7 chord) plus the tone of C, which has been *suspended* or held over from a preceding chord. The tone of C is called the suspended tone.

suspension

MU. The holding-over of a tone of a preceding chord to be played with a chord that follows. See SUSPENDED TONE.

sustain

MU. 1. To hold a tone. See TENUTO. RT. 2. To maintain, keep in existence, as a radio or television program that is financially supported solely by a station or network.

sustained chords

SA. A style of singing in which each note (tone) is given full value and connected to the succeeding note (tone), creating a smooth, legato effect, as used in SPEBSQSA barbershop style singing. AI. The opposite of *staccato.*

sustaining program

RT. A radio or television program that is sustained (produced and paid for) by a station or network (and on which no outside commercial advertising is used), as distinguished from a *commercial program*.

sw (ess-dub'l'yu)

MU. Abbreviation, *swell*.

sweet

JZ. 1. Designating a style of playing which is characterized by adherence to the melody, a soothing smoothness and a relatively moderate tempo, as distinguished from *hot*. 2. Designating music played in this manner. 3. Designating music written or arranged to be played in this manner.

Sweet Adelines, Inc., the

BY. An organization of female barbershop harmony singers. The feminine counterpart of the SPEBSQSA. International headquarters: 3321 East 30th Street, Tulsa, Oklahoma.

sweet potato

MU. The ocarina. AI. So called because its shape resembles that of a sweet potato of the *Nancy Hall* variety. See OCARINA.

swell

MU. A gradual increase in sound.

swing

MU. A style of Dixieland jazz originated by clarinetist and bandleader Benny Goodman. AI. Swing was introduced by Goodman at the Congress Hotel in Chicago, November 6, 1935. Among those identified with popularizing swing are band leaders Tommy Dorsey, Artie Shaw and Woody Herman.

swing bass

MU. A method of accompaniment, in Four-Four Time or Cut Time, that consists of playing a bass note (tone), or an octave, on the first and third beats of a measure and playing a solid chord on

384

the second and fourth beats. (The root of this chord is the note that is played as the single note or octave.) AI. For instance, the chord of C major would be played in this manner: C, C-E-G, C, C-E-G or C-C, C-E-G, C-C, C-E-G.

swipe

SA. A progression of two or more chords sung on a single word syllable. A hallmark of the SPEBSQSA barbershop style. AI. For instance, in barbershop harmony, a chord is usually sung for each melody note. Sometimes, however, for a special effect, several chords are sung for a particular single note (word or syllable). This is called a *swipe*. An example of a swipe is singing the word *girl* to four different chords, in this manner: *dear old gir-r-r-rl*.

syllabic melody

MU. A melody in which each tone is sung to a separate syllable. AI. The opposite of *slurred melody*.

syllabification

PY, SW. The division of a word or words into syllables, as is done in fitting lyrics to music and vice versa. AI. Also *syllabication*.

syllabify

PY, SW. 1. To divide a word or words into syllables. 2. To *syllabicate*.

syllable

PY. 1. A single vocal sound. 2. The characters or letters which represent such a sound. 3. A word or part of a word that must be sung with only one movement of the tongue or jaw. AI. For instance, the word *syllable* is composed of three syllables, thus: *syl'la-ble*.

syllable count

SW. The number of syllables in a given section of a song lyric, as in a *word*, a *phrase*, a *line*, etc. AI. For instance, the song title COLD, COLD HEART has a syllable count of *three*. The song title OH, LONESOME ME has a syllable count of *four*. The song title DID YOU EVER SEE A DREAM WALKING has a syllable count of *nine*. Syllable counts are used in fitting words to music and vice versa.

syllable names

MU. 1. The names of the syllables which identify the tones of the scale, as used in the sol-fa system. 2. These names are: *do, re, mi, fa, sol, la, ti, do*. AI. In the English system of tonic sol-fa, these syllables are spelled *doh, ray, me, fah, soh, lah, te, doh*.

symbol

MU. 1. A character, mark, sign, abbreviation or letter indicating something, as a music note, a clef sign, a flat, chord captions, etc. SW. 2. Something used to represent something else. See SYMBOLIC.

symbolic

SW. Of or expressed by a symbol, as in songwriting, as a dove is symbolic of *peace*, heart is symbolic of *love*, a plain gold band is symbolic of *marriage*, etc.

symbolism

SW. The use of symbols, as in songwriting.

sympathetic string

MU. A string adjusted so that it is affected by the vibrations of other strings or resonant bodies, and not by being struck, plucked or bowed. AI. Also called *octave strings*.

symphonic-jazz

MU. Designating a style that borrows both from symphonic techniques and the complexities of modern jazz. AI. Typical of popular pieces done in symphonic-jazz style are BLUE TANGO, SLEIGH RIDE, FIDDLE FADDLE, THE SYNCOPATED CLOCK and THE TYPEWRITER.

sync (sihnk)

MP. Short for *synchronization*.

synchronization (sihn″kr'-nih-zae′shun)

MP, RG. 1. The act of synchronizing. 2. Something that is synchronized.

synchronization license

MB. A written agreement granting the rights to record a specified

386

musical composition in a motion picture, or television film, and stating the use to which such recording is limited, if any, and the territorial limits in which the motion picture, or television film, can be distributed for showing, if any.

synchronization rights

LW. 1. The exclusive rights to synchronize a property, as a musical composition, as a song. MP. 2. The rights to use a song or other musical composition in a motion picture. RG. 3. Also called *dubbing rights*.

synchronization royalties

MB. The money paid for the transfer of synchronization rights.

synchronize

MP. 1. To add and or adjust sound to the movements in a motion picture, as to add the vocal performance of a song adjusted to the pantomimed lip movements of a singer. RG. 2. To add and adjust additional sound, as a song, to previously recorded sound, as on a phonograph record or tape, etc. AI. For instance, in the recording of TENNESSEE WALTZ, Patti Page sang a duet with herself. This was done by recording the lead voice and then synchronizing the harmony voice with this.

syncopation

MU. The tying-over of a weak beat to the next strong beat. 2. The beginning of a tone on an unaccented beat and continuing it through the next accented beat. 3. The beginning of a tone on the last half of a beat and continuing it through the first half of the next beat. 4. The shifting of normal musical accents.

synonym

PY, SW. A word that has the same or nearly the same meaning in one or more senses as another in the same language, as is used in songwriting. AI. For instance, examples of synonyms are these: *love* and *adore*, *desire* and *crave*, and *merry* and *gay*. The opposite of *antonym*.

system

MU. Two or more connected staves, one above the other, extending from one side of the page to the other. AI. For instance, a piano-and-vocal score, the form in which most popular songs are printed, uses systems composed of three staves each. See SCORE.

T.

MU. 1. The capital letter used to designate *tenor* in multiple-voice arrangements, as SATB. 2. The small letter used to designate *tempo*. 3. The small letter used to designate *time*. 4. The small letter used to designate the syllable *te* in the English system of sol-fa.

tab

SB. Short for *tab show, tabloid show* or *tabloid*.

tablature

MU. A general name for various systems of notation in which the tones are indicated by letters, figures, symbols, diagrams, etc., other than notes placed on a staff. AI. Examples of tablature are the guitar and ukulele chord captions and/or diagrams that appear just above the melody line on printed song sheets in the United States, the tonic sol-fa system that appears in a similar position on song sheets printed in England. Music that is written for the lute is written in *tablature*. Music written for the dulcimer combines staff notation with *tablature*. There are various methods of notation for instruments, as the guitar, which use a combination of numerals and letters to designate strings, frets and fingers. Any of these is called *tablature*.

tab show

SB. 1. An abbreviated musical show. 2. A tabloid show. 3. A tabloid. AI. The usual tab show consists of an abbreviated version of a musical comedy or of a series of brief comedy sketches, blackouts and crossovers, interspersed with songs and dances.

tacet

MU. v. 1. To remain silent. 2. To lay out. MN. 3. *Shut up* or *hush* (the equivalent of *pipe down*).

tacet

MU. n. A musical instruction designating that an instrumental or vocal part is to be omitted for the period indicated. AI. For instance, on sheet music which includes guitar diagrams, the words *guitar tacet* might appear, meaning that the guitar is to be silent for the period indicated, usually by a broken line.

tag

MU. 1. An extra ending that is attached to a song or other musical composition, also called *tag ending*. 2. An additional ending, as that of a song, usually especially arranged for use by a particular orchestra and/or singer, called a *personalized tag*. 3. Music, as that of a song in whole or in part, used as an identifying theme or signature, usually at the closing of a performance. 4. A *sign off*.

tag it

MN. Instructions, as might be given to musicians by an orchestra leader, a producer, etc., meaning *play the tag*. AI. There are various hand signals (cues) meaning *tag it*.

tail

MU. 1. Tag. 2. Erroneously used to mean *flag*, as that on a note.

tailgate

GI. 1. The hinged board that forms the back end of a wagon, which can be swung down for loading or unloading. JZ. 2. A style of trombone counterpoint playing characteristic of Dixieland jazz, which originated in New Orleans. 3. A New Orleans-style trombone performance. AI. In the early days of jazz, New Orleans bands were often transported in wagons. On such occasions, the trombone players were always seated at the back, facing the rear. This was done so that the slides of their instruments would not interfere with the other musicians. Thus, as trombones literally were played *over the tailgate*, the style of playing then in vogue became known as *tailgate trombone*, or *tailgate*. Many trombonists are proud of being able to play authentic *tailgate*.

390

take

RG. 1. The material, as the vocal and/or instrumental performance of a song, that is recorded or to be recorded during an uninterrupted period of time. 2. The process of recording such material. AI. In recording a song, it is often necessary to make several *takes* before one is satisfactory. These are designated as *take one, take two, take three*, etc.

talent

MB. 1. A performer or performers. 2. Anyone who sings and/or plays a musical instrument, regardless of ability. AI. Talent can be professional or amateur. Either can be good or bad.

talent rep

SB. Short for *talent representative*.

talent representative

SB. 1. One who represents talent, as singers and other performers. 2. A general or personal manager. 3. A booking agent.

talk-back

BR. A communication system, consisting of a microphone, located in the control room of a recording company or broadcasting station, wired to a loud-speaker, located in the studio. AI. The talk-back is used to give directions and instructions during rehearsals or previous to recording or broadcasting. Also called *talk-back system*.

tambourine

MU. A percussion instrument constructed like the head of a drum, with jingles in the rim, played by shaking and/or striking with the hand.

tam tam

MU. Same as *gong*. AI. Not to be confused with *tom tom*. See GONG.

tap

DG. 1. To execute a rhythm step in tap-dance style. 2. To tap dance.

tap dance

DG. 1. A dance characterized by the sharp, resounding taps of the toe, the heel or entire foot at each step. MU. 2. The music for this dance.

tape

RG. v. To record on tape, as to *tape* a song.

tape

RG. n. 1. A narrow strip of metal, plastic or other material or a wire on which sound is or can be recorded. 2. A magnetic recording tape.

tape record

RG. 1. Tape on which sound has been recorded. 2. The sound thus recorded. 2. A tape recording.

tape recorder

RG. 1. A device for recording and playing back sound. AI. Similar to a *wire recorder*, which uses wire instead of tape, or a film recorder, which uses film.

tape speed

RG. The speed at which tape is recorded and played. AI. For instance, home tape recorders (and players) run at speeds of 3¾ ips and 7½ ips. Professional machines record and play at 7½ ips and 15 ips. See IPS.

tape worm

MB. 1. Facetiously, an editor who edits tape recordings. 2. Anyone who makes a hobby of recording on tape.

tap room

MU. Designating a bouncy, jazz-style rhythm, as that typical of Adrian Rollini, as *tap room rhythm, tap room style*, etc.

tear jerker

MB. 1. An overly sentimental song. 2. An overly sentimental performance, as of a song. See SCHMALTZ.

technician

MB. 1. Any person exceptionally skilled in the intricate details of a subject as, specifically, an artist, writer, songwriter, musician, etc. 2. One who has technical skill and/or knowledge far above the average. AI. As it can be said that *Peggy Lee is a great technician.* 3. Also, less accurately, used to mean any recording or broadcasting engineer.

technique

MU. 1. The method of procedure in skillfully rendering an artistic or musical work, as the manner in which a song is composed, played or sung. 2. The knowledgeful proficiency with which the details of songwriting are used. 3. The knowledgeful proficiency with which a musical composition is performed.

teen

PY. A suffix used to form the cardinal numbers *thirteen* to *nineteen* and to designate the stage of life these numbers represent, as *teen-age.*

teen-age

MB. 1. Those between the ages of thirteen to nineteen. 2. Young people in general. Also *teen-ager* or *teen-agers.* AI. Used to designate the *teen-age record buying market,* the *teen-age song audience,* etc.

teen beat

MB. Any tempo suited to any currently popular style of dancing enjoyed by the *teen-age* audience.

telecast

TV. v. 1. To transmit by television, usually over a wide area. 2. To broadcast by television.

telecast

TV. n. 1. A television program. 2. That which is seen on television.

telecourse

TV. 1. A progressive series of studies broadcast by television, as *a telecourse in music,* etc. 2. A course of televised lectures, usually offered for credit by a university or college.

temple blocks

MU. Same as *Chinese blocks.*

tempo

MU. The speed at which a musical composition, as a song, is played and/or sung.

tempo mark

MU. A word or phrase used to designate the speed at which a musical composition is to be sung and/or played. AI. There are three classifications of tempo marks: 1. Those which designate a steady rate of speed, as *slow, lively, briskly, fast,* etc. 2. Those which designate an increase in speed, as *gradually faster, faster, suddenly faster, twice as fast,* etc. 3. Those which designate a decrease in speed, as *gradually slower, slower, suddenly slower, much slower,* etc. AI. Originally, all tempo marks were in Italian as *lento, andante, allegro, veloce,* etc. However, for a long time, American songwriters have justly felt that the instructions for performing their songs should be given in the same language in which their lyrics are written. By no means is a songwriter restricted to the use of so-called established tempo marks. He is entirely free to use any word or phrase his fancy dictates and which he feels best describes the feeling he wishes to convey.

ten

MU. 1. Abbreviation, *tenuto.* 2. Abbreviation, sometimes used to mean, *tenor.* See TENUTO.

tenor

MU. 1. The highest natural adult male voice, usually ranging from about an octave below middle C to an octave above. 3. A musical instrument having such a compass, as a *tenor trombone, tenor saxophone,* etc. AI. While the term *tenor* is ordinarily used to mean a male voice, *tenors* are used in female barbershop quartets and are called such.

tenor guitar

MU. A stringed instrument in the guitar family, usually about three-quarters as large as a Spanish guitar, having four strings, which are the same as to pitch and position as the first four strings on a Spanish guitar.

ten per

SB. Short for *ten per cent* or *ten percenter*.

ten per cent

SB. The usual commission charged by a booking agent, artists' representative, etc.

ten percenter

SB. A booking agent or artists' representative. AI. So called because the commission charged by booking agents is usually ten per cent of the client's salary or booking price.

tenth

MU. An interval of ten diatonic degrees. AI. A tenth is equal to a diatonic octave plus two degrees.

tenuto

MU. 1. Sustained. 2. Held for the full time value, as opposed to *staccato*. See STACCATO. See TENUTO MARK.

tenuto mark: –

MU. The horizontal stroke shown above. AI. A tenuto mark is written over or under a note to designate that it is to be held for its full time value. Tenuto is also designated by the symbol *ten.*

terminal rhyme

PY. A rhyme scheme in which the last (terminal) word of a line is rhymed with the last word of another line, as:

> Little Miss Muffet
> Sat on a tuffet

AI. In the above couplet, the last words in each line, *Muffet* and *tuffet*, form a *terminal rhyme*. Also called *end rhyme*. Compare with INTERNAL RHYME.

terminal word

PY. The last word in a line of verse, as:

> I wait in despair
> For your step on the stair

AI. In the above couplet the words *despair* and *stair* are *terminal words*.

tetrachord (tet′ra-kord″)

MU. A scale of four tones arranged in this manner:

> Between the 1st and the 2nd tones is a *whole* step.
> Between the 2nd and the 3rd tones is a *whole* step.
> Between the 3rd and the 4th tones is a *half* step.

AI. It was to this pattern that the ancient Greek four-string lyre was tuned. The tetrachord is the smallest scale used in songwriting. For instance, the major scale is composed of two tetrachords, one following the other, with a whole step in between.

tetrameter (te-tram′e-ter)

PY. A line of verse having four metric feet. AI. Musical counterpart, a four-measure phrase.

text

SW. 1. The words of a song. 2. Lyric. 3. A subject. 4. A theme. 5. A topic.

text book

PB. A book used as a standard work in studying a subject, as music.

tf (te-eff)

MB. Short for *top forty*, as a tf song, meaning *a song in the top forty*.

T-forty or T-40

MB. Abbreviation, *top forty*.

theater

TE. 1. A place where plays, musicals, operas, motion pictures, etc.

are presented and performed. 2. The theatrical world, the people engaged in theater activities. 3. Theatrical technique, showmanship, as it might be said, "Her singing was good *theater*."

theater manager

TE. One who is in charge of a theater.

theme

MU. 1. The topic, or subject matter, developed in the lyric of a song is called the *lyrical theme*. 2. The melodic subject developed in a musical composition is called the *melodic theme*. 3. A division of a song is called a theme. AI. For instance, in a song written to the AABA pattern, the letter A represents the *primary theme*, the letter B represents the *secondary theme*. 4. A musical work used as an identifying signature for a performer, an orchestra or band, a radio or television program, etc. is called a *theme song* or *theme. Theme* (song) is one of the categories used by performance-rights societies in establishing credit values for their members.

theme out

MU. 1. A direction, usually given in the form of a hand cue by an orchestra leader, program producer, etc., meaning *continue playing the theme until the end of the program*, as on a radio or television show. AI. When a band *themes out* in his manner, the control operator fades the music down and out at the proper time for the program to end (although the band may continue playing at normal volume well beyond this point). RT. 2. A direction, as given in a radio or television script, meaning *discontinue theme*.

theme song

RT. 1. A song used to identify a performer, an orchestra or band, a radio or television program, etc. 2. A musical signature. AI. For instance, among the famous theme songs that have become known to audiences the world over are: Ted Lewis' WHEN MY BABY SMILES AT ME, Bing Crosby's WHERE THE BLUE OF THE NIGHT MEETS THE GOLD OF THE DAY, Bob Hope's THANKS FOR THE MEMORY, Al Hirt's JAVA and the all-time great theme for baseball broadcasts wherever baseball is played, TAKE ME OUT TO THE BALL GAME.

397

theory

MU. 1. A systematic explanation of the principles involved in a subject, as that of music. 2. A plan for procedure based on proven principles, as the science of songwriting as distinguished from the art of execution. 3. The knowledge of principles and methods, as distinguished from practice. AI. For instance, it is possible to fully understand the theory of music without necessarily being able to play a musical instrument.

thesis

PY. 1. Originally, the *accented* part of a foot of verse or poetry. 2. Now, the *unaccented* part of a foot of verse or poetry. AI. This sense is due to a misunderstanding of the original Greek. MU. 3. The *accented* part of a measure. 4. The downbeat. See ARSIS.

thimble

CM. A small, pitted metal cap or cup, of the kind worn on the end of the finger as a protection in sewing, which is used to *play* the washboard. AI. Washboard players wear several such thimbles on the thumbs and fingers of both hands.

third

MU. 1. The interval between any note (tone) and the next note (tone) but one above it in the diatonic scale. 2. A note (tone) separated by this interval from any other note (tone). 3. The third degree in any diatonic scale. 4. The third note above the keynote. 5. The mediant. AI. For instance, in the scale of C major, the third degree is the tone of E. The tone of E is also the third in the chord of C major (C-E-G).

third cover

PP. The inside back cover of a song sheet, song book, etc.

third finger

MU. 1. The third finger from the thumb on either hand. 2. The *ring finger*. 3. The finger designated by the numeral *3* in the English method of fingering. 4. The finger designated by the numeral *4* in the German method of fingering.

third-stream music

MU. An advanced style of music that is neither jazz nor classical but which borrows from both of these styles and fields. AI. Sometimes incorrectly called *half-and-half music*.

third string

MU. 1. The G string on the Spanish guitar. 2. The D string on the ukulele (tuned A-D-F♯-B). 3. The G string on the five-string banjo (three notes below middle C).

thirty-day publication

LW. The act of bringing a printed property, as a song, to the attention of the public, in a country other than the United States, *within thirty days* of its original publication in the United States. AI. In order to secure international copyright in all countries belonging to the Berne Convention, it is necessary for authors of the United States either (a) to secure *same-day publication* in any Berne Convention country or (b) to secure *thirty-day publication* in a Berne Convention country which subscribes to the Brussels Convention (amendment of the original Berne Convention). Thirty-day publication is usually arranged through agents, residing in the country where publication is to be made, who are established to furnish this service, and who later furnish a *certificate of publication*, attesting the fact that such publication has been effected. At the time this is written, both England and France had subscribed to the Brussels Convention. Canada had not. See BRUSSELS CONVENTION. See SAME-DAY PUBLICATION.

three: 3 or III

MU. 1. The Arabic numeral used as the upper figure in the Three-Four Time signature, designating three counts (beats) to the measure. 2. The Arabic numeral used to designate a triplet. 3. The Arabic numeral used to designate an interval of a third. 4. The Arabic numeral used to designate the ring finger in the English method of fingering. 5. The Arabic numeral used to designate the middle finger in the German method of fingering. 6. The Roman numeral used to designate the third degree, or mediant, in the diatonic scale.

three beat

MU. See TRIPLE TIME.

three-color

PP. Designating the use of three colors (black + two other colors), as used in printing, as the cover of a song sheet, song book, advertisement, etc.

three flats:

MU. The key signature of E♭ major, as shown above.

Three-Four Time: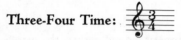

MU. 1. The time designated by the time signature shown above. 2. The time that has three counts (beats) to the measure, with each beat being equal to a quarter note in time value. 3. Three-Quarter Time. 4. Often called *waltz time.*

three-lined octave

MU. The second octave, on the piano, above middle C. AI. The keys (tones) in this octave are designated c^3, d^3, e^3, etc.

three-part

MU. 1. Designating a musical composition, as a song written in three parts, as three-part harmony. 2. Designating a musical composition written or arranged for three voices and/or three instruments. 3. Designating an arrangement for a vocal or instrumental trio. See MULTIPLE-VOICE ARRANGEMENTS.

Three-Quarter Time

MU. Same as *Three-Four Time.*

three sharps: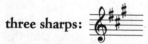

MU. The key signature of A major, as shown above.

three-staff arrangement

MU. Usually a piano-and-vocal arrangement, as that of a song. AI. Also used for instrumental arrangements, as organ, violin, etc.

three-syllable rhyme

PY. Same as *triple rhyme.*

throw

MB. 1. Anything that prevents a singer from singing, a musician from playing, etc., as difficult-to-pronounce words, a difficult-to-play arrangement, etc., is said to *throw* them. AI. Or a performer might be *thrown* by a fit of laughter, by suddenly forgetting the words or notes he is to perform, etc. 2. To *throw* a cue means to give a hand signal. See HAND CUE.

thrush

MB. 1. A female singer. 2. Also called a *canary*, a *lark*.

thumb string

MU. The melody string, or fifth string, on a five-string banjo. AI. The thumb string is shorter than the other four strings and is tuned to G, four notes above middle C.

ti (tee) : ◇

MU. 1. The syllable sometimes used (in place of *si*) in singing the seventh note (tone) of a scale in the sol-fa system. 2. The shape notehead shown above representing this syllable.

tie: ⌣ or ⌢

MU. A short, curved line, like either of those shown above, written over or under and connecting *two notes of the same pitch*. AI. This means that the connected notes are to be sung or played as one continuous tone having the combined time values of both notes. Compare with SLUR.

timbre

MU. 1. The characteristic quality of a tone. 2. Quality. AI. Timbre is one of the four properties of a tone. See QUALITY. See TONE.

time

MU. 1. The combining of rhythmic beats into groups of equal duration, as those contained in a measure. 2. The rhythmic accent of a musical composition as characterized by this grouping, as *waltz time, march time*, etc. 3. The relative pace at which a musical composition is to be performed, as designated by its time signature, as Two-Four Time, Three-Quarter Time, Four-Four Time, etc. 4. The

401

duration for which a tone is sounded, as designated by a note. 5. The duration for which silence is maintained, as designated by a rest. AI. Time is one of the four characteristics of a tone. See TONE.

time signature: $\frac{2}{4}$ $\frac{3}{4}$ $\frac{4}{4}$ C ¢ etc.

MU. Any of the signs shown above. Reading from left to right, these designate Two-Four Time, Three-Quarter Time, Four-Four Time, Four-Four Time and Cut Time. AI. A time signature is written at the beginning of a musical composition to tell the time or tempo in which the piece is to be performed. In time signatures that are written like a fraction, the upper number designates the number of beats to the measure. The lower number designates the time value of each of these beats. For instance, in Three-Quarter Time there are *three* beats to the measure and each of these beats has a time value equal to that of a *quarter note*. In Four-Four Time there are *four* beats to the measure and each of these beats has a time value equal to that of a *quarter* note, etc.

time step

DG. 1. A tap-dance step done in *time* to music or an otherwise established rhythm. 2. A rhythm step. 3. The basic step used in tap dancing.

time value

MU. 1. The relative length of time a tone is played or sung. 2. The relative length of time a tone is heard, as designated by a note. 3. The relative time silence is maintained, as designated by a rest. AI. For instance, the time value of a half note is half that of a whole note. The time value of a quarter rest is twice that of an eighth rest, etc.

timing

TE. 1. The regulation of the time at which something is done. 2. The regulation of the speed at which a performance takes place. AI. For instance, the *timing* of a song, a singer's gestures, an actor's speech, the performance of a play, etc. might be said to be good or bad.

timpani

MU. 1. Kettledrums, plural. 2. A set of kettledrums. AI. Timpani

402

are usually used in pairs, called a *set*, one of which is tuned to the keynote, the other to the fifth of the key. Also spelled *tympani*. Singular, *timpano*.

timpanist

MU. 1. A percussionist who plays timpani. 2. A kettledrummer. AI. Also spelled *tympanist*.

timpano

MU. 1. A drum consisting of a hollow hemisphere, usually of copper or brass, and a parchment top that can be tuned, by tightening or loosening to change its pitch. Some timpani are made with a pedal which tightens or loosens the head, thereby changing the tone. 2. A kettledrum. AI. Also spelled *tympano*. Plural, *timpani*.

tin ear

MU. Anyone who cannot whistle, hum or *carry* a tune in any manner is said to have a *tin ear*. AI. Designating the opposite of *absolute pitch*.

tin pan alley

MB. 1. That part of the music business which deals in popular songs, no matter its location. 2. Formerly, the popular song business of New York City, its locale, life, world, etc. See MUSIC BUSINESS.

tipple

MU. An instrument of the guitar family, about half the size of a Spanish guitar, usually having eight strings which are tuned in pairs to correspond with the tuning of the first four strings of the Spanish guitar.

title

MB. 1. The name of a song. 2. A word or phrase by which a song is identified, as AFRAID, I CAN'T STOP LOVING YOU, THAT'S WHAT HAPPINESS IS, etc. AI. Also called *main title*, as distinguished from *subtitle*, if any. See FULL TITLE. 3. A complete song. AI. For instance, a music publisher might have *six titles in the racks*, meaning he has six songs offered for sale by rack dealers. LW. 4. The right to ownership, as that of a song. 5. A legal document designating such a right, as a *transfer of copyright or copyright assignment*.

title line

SW. The word, phrase or sentence in the lyric of a song that contains the song's title.

title page

PP. 1. The page of a song sheet, song book, etc. on which the title appears. AI. A title page usually also gives writer credits, copyright notice and the name of the publisher. 2. Usually the first music page of a song sheet.

title phrase

SW. The musical phrase that accompanies a song title. AI. For instance, the five notes (tones) to which the song title IT HAD TO BE YOU are sung.

title song

MP. 1. A song that has the same title as the motion picture in which it is sung and/or played. TE. 2. A song that has the same title as the (stage) musical show in which it is sung and/or played. AI. Typical title songs are CHARADE, THE PINK PANTHER, A SHOT IN THE DARK, THE GREAT RACE MARCH and DEAR HEART.

Toby

SB. 1. Any exaggerated rural comedy character, usually typified by a red-hair wig, freckles and a missing front tooth. 2. The featured character in a *Toby show*.

Toby show

SB. A stage show, musical or otherwise, in which the character Toby is featured. AI. There are a number of plays and musical comedies written about the character Toby. Typical Toby shows travel from town to town, in the midwestern part of the United States, presenting one or more of these plays, usually under canvas.

tom tom

MU. 1. A small American Indian or Oriental drum of indefinite pitch, played with a stick, sticks or the hands. 2. An imitation of such a drum, usually used by drummers in dance bands. See TAM TAM.

tone

MU. 1. A distinct and identifiable musical *sound*, caused by regular and constant vibrations, of constant pitch, as distinguished from *noise*. 2. A *musical* sound, long or short, loud or soft. AI. A musical tone has four characteristics. These are *pitch*, *time*, *intensity* and *quality*. Compare with NOTE. 3. The *interval* that corresponds to one degree of the scale or staff. 4. An interval equal to two half tones or two semitones. 5. A *major tone* or a *whole tone*. See DEGREE.

tone color

MU. 1. Timbre. 2. Quality.

tone deaf

MU. 1. Designating the inability to distinguish accurately the difference in musical pitch. 2. Being unable to recognize one tone from another.

tone value

MU. The relative pitch of a tone as designated by a note.

tongue

MU. v. To modify and/or interrupt the tone of certain wind instruments by use of the tongue. AI. Also called *tonguing*.

tongue

MU. n. 1. A reed, as used in wood-wind instruments. 2. The end of such a reed that vibrates.

tonic

MU. 1. The first degree of a scale. 2. The keynote. 3. The keytone. AI. For instance, in the scale of C major, the tonic is the tone of C.

tonic chord

MU. 1. A triad built on the tonic. 2. A three-tone chord which has the *tonic* as its root. AI. For instance, the tonic chord in the key

key of C is the chord of C. The tonic chord in the key of F is the chord of F, etc.

tonic sol-fa

MU. A system of musical notation based on the relationship between the tones of a key, using the English syllables of solmization, instead of the usual staff symbols or notation. The English syllables of solmization are: *doh, ray, me, fah, soh, lah, te, doh.* AI. Tonic sol-fa was the invention of Miss Sarah Ann Glover, of Norwich, England, about 1812. It was perfected by Rev. John Curwen, sometime after 1841 or thereabout, and is in popular use in England today. The majority of songs printed in England have the melody indicated in abbreviated solmization just above the melody or vocal stave, using the first letters of the syllables, thus: *d, r, m, f, s, l, t, d.* A method for learning and remembering the syllables of tonic sol-fa is given in the song hit DO RE MI, from *The Sound of Music.*

top

SB. v. 1. To surpass or excel. 2. To outdo. AI. For instance, one song might *top* another song in popularity. One gag might *top* another gag. One performer might *top* another performer, etc.

top

MU. n. 1. The beginning of a song. 2. The *top* of the first page. AI. For instance, an orchestra leader might say, "Let's take it from the *top*," meaning *let's play it from the beginning.*

top billing

SB. 1. The position of being featured, usually prominently so, over someone or something else. 2. The most prominent listing, as in an advertisement, on a theater program, a show card, etc. AI. For instance, a song might receive top billing over another song in a music trade publication advertisement. An actor might receive top billing over other actors on the program for a musical show, etc.

Top 40 Reviewer, The

MB. A weekly music-business trade publication which lists the top forty songs currently being played on a number of radio stations located in major-market areas of the United States. Address: 1606 North Argyle Avenue, Hollywood, California 90028.

topical song

MB. Any song with a lyric about currently popular subject matter, as an event or a personality that is in the daily news. AI. Calypso songs are often of a topical nature.

top tune

MB. 1. A song that enjoys wide popularity. 2. A song high up in the charts, as the *top 40*, the *top 100*, etc. 3. A survey song. AI. Also called *top song*.

torch singer

MB. A singer, usually a female, who specializes in singing *torch songs*.

torch song

MB. An intensely emotional song avowing an all-out declaration of (usually unreturned) love. AI. The designation comes from the expression *carry a torch*. Typical torch songs are WHAT WILL I TELL MY HEART, ALL OF ME, I'LL NEVER SMILE AGAIN, BODY AND SOUL, YOU'LL NEVER KNOW and I'M DANCING WITH TEARS IN MY EYES.

touch

MU. 1. The manner and method of striking or pressing the keys of a keyboard instrument, as a piano. 2. The force and/or pressure applied to the keys of a keyboard instrument. AI. For instance, it might be said that a pianist has a *light touch*, a *heavy touch*, an *elastic touch*, a *soft touch*, etc.

tour

SB. A trip, as that made by a singer, performer, theatrical company, etc. to give performances in a number of towns and cities. AI. Anyone on tour is also said to be *on the road*.

tr or tr〰〰

MU. The symbol shown above meaning trill. See TRILL. See TREMBLEMENT.

tr (tee-ahr)

PG. A typographical sign used in marking a proof sheet, as that of a song, meaning *transpose*. To a printer this correctly means *interchange one thing with another*. AI. For instance, if the word *roll* and the word *rock* were each circled and connected by a line in the three words reading *roll and rock* and *tr* were written near this, the printer would reset these three words to read, *rock and roll*. Care should be employed in using this mark correctly, so that it can not be confused to indicate the musical symbol meaning *trill*. See TRANSPOSE.

trad

MB. An expression of English origin meaning *traditional*, as usually used in connection with jazz music. AI. For instance, a *trad band* means a traditional jazz band. A *trad performance* means a performance in the *traditional Dixieland jazz style*, etc.

trade

MB. 1. The occupation or means by which one earns a living, as the songwriting trade, the singing trade, the music-publishing trade, etc. 2. Customers and clientele, as the sheet-music-buying trade, the record-buying trade, etc. 3. Customers, as to interests, as the pop trade, the country (music) trade, the rhythm-and-blues trade, etc.

trade journal

PP. A publication, as a magazine, devoted to the interests of a particular trade or business, as the music business, as distinguished from a *consumer publication*.

trademark

LW. 1. A symbol, design, letter, etc. created and used by a manufacturer, dealer, etc. to distinguish his products from those of his competitors. AI. Trademarks are usually registered and protected by law, similar to the manner in which songs are copyrighted. One of the oldest trademarks, if not the oldest, in the music business is that of RCA-Victor showing a dog listening to an old-fashioned phonograph, entitled *his master's voice*. 2. A distinctive and individualized musical phrase, as used by a particular musician, band or orchestra. 3. A particular and individualized style of singing or playing, as that of a particular singer, musician, band or orchestra.

trade press

MB. 1. Trade publications, collectively. 2. Trade journals in general.

408

trade publication

MB. 1. A trade journal. 2. A magazine or newspaper that devotes its interests to a particular trade or business, as the music business. AI. For instance, leading music-business trade publications are *Billboard*, *Cash Box*, *Record World*, *The Top 40 Reviewer* and *Variety*.

trade union

MB. 1. An association of workers organized to promote and protect its members' interests, primarily by collective bargaining. 2. A labor union, as the AFM, AFTRA, etc.

traditional

MB. 1. Designating a custom, practice, manner, style, etc. so long continued that it is almost the force of law. 2. Conforming to a tradition. 3. In a manner that has been handed down from the original. 4. Authentic. AI. For instance, *traditional* folk songs, as distinguished from modern imitative works, *traditional* jazz, *traditional* race music, *traditional* mountain music, etc.

train songs

MB. A classification in songwriting as to subject matter. AI. Typical train songs are: FIREBALL MAIL, CHATTANOOGA CHOO-CHOO, ALABAMY BOUND and ON THE ATCHISON, TOPEKA AND THE SANTA FE.

transcribe

MB. 1. To make a handwritten or typewritten copy, as of a musical composition. 2. To make a musical arrangement. RG. 3. To record, as on tape or a phonograph record. RO. 4. To record a musical performance, a program, a commercial, etc. for later broadcast. GI. 5. To make a transcription.

transcription

MU. 1. An arrangement or adaption, as that of a musical composition. 2. A copy. RO. 3. A recording made for radio broadcasting purposes, as an *electrical transcription*.

transfer of copyright

LW. 1. An assignment, exclusive license or any other document of alienation by which the ownership of a copyright is changed from one person or organization to another. 2. A written agreement to transfer or assign a copyright from one person or organization to another. 3. An assignment of copyright. AI. A transfer of United States copyright should be promptly registered in the United States Copyright Office. A transfer of Canadian Copyright should be promptly registered in the Canadian Copyright Office.

transient

MU. Designating a temporary thing or condition. AI. For instance, a *transient chord* is one used in shifting from one key to another and which is foreign to both keys. A *transient modulation* is a brief shift from one key to another, soon followed by a return to the original key or a shift to a third key, etc. A *transient key* is one to which a modulation is made but briefly.

transition

MU. 1. A musical passage, usually brief, leading from one theme to another. 2. A brief modulation. 3. An abrupt change of key. 4. A passing note (tone).

translate

MB. To replace the words of one language with words that mean the same thing in another language, as to translate the lyric of a song.

translation

MB. Words that have replaced other words, having the same meanings, in a different language, as the *English translation* of a Spanish song or vice versa. AI. A *literal translation* means a word-for-word, meaning-for-meaning translation. A non-literal, or *figurative translation means* one in which only a semblance of the original idea is retained. Because of the technicalities involved, the majority of song translations are non-literal translations. Many, in fact, consist of words conveying an entirely different idea, written to the same music. For the sake of accuracy, this kind of treatment should be called a new *version*, as a *French* version, a *German* version, etc. See LOCAL LYRICS.

translator

MB. One who translates, as a *song translator*.

410

transmittal, letter of

SW. See LETTER OF TRANSMITTAL.

transpose

MU. 1. To write out or perform a musical composition in another key. 2. To change from one key to another. AI. For instance, a song originally written in the key of C might be transposed to the key of G. A song originally written in the key of G might be transposed to the key of F, etc. Songs are transposed in order to better fit them to the range of a singer, etc. PG. 3. A term used in proofreading, meaning to change the positions of, as one word with another, one letter with another, etc. 4. To *interchange*. AI. *Transpose* does *not* mean to move one thing (only) from one place to another, as is often erroneously assumed. Abbreviated *tr*, not to be confused with the music symbol, composed of the same letters meaning *trill*.

transposing instruments

MU. Instruments whose natural scale is written in a different key. AI. Typical of transposing instruments are the B♭ or A clarinet and the B♭ or A trumpet. Also, the piccolo (for which music is notated an octave lower in order to avoid the extensive use of leger lines).

trap drum

MU. 1. A snare drum. 2. A drum to which traps are attached. See SNARE DRUM.

trap drummer

MU. A percussionist who uses *traps*. AI. Among the first, if not *the* first trap drummer, is Tony Sbarbaro, of the Original Dixieland Band, later known as the Original Dixieland Jazz Band.

traps

MU. Noise producing contrivances used by trap drummers, as clog boxes, jingles, cymbals, clackers, bells, shakers, etc. AI. So called because these devices were originally attached to the *trap* (snare) drum.

treatment

SW. 1. The manner of handling, as in writing a song. 2. The method

411

by which a song is written, including the form and/or manner in which it is written. 3. The result of a, usually special, writing process. 4. The manner in which a musical composition is performed. 5. The performance of a musical composition.

treble

MU. 1. High in tone or in compass, the soprano. 2. Designating the highest voice or part in harmony. 3. High frequency audio tones.

treble clef

MU. The G clef. See G CLEF.

treble staff

MU. 1. The staff on which the treble clef is written or printed. 2. The upper staff in a two-staves-to-the-system piano arrangement.

treble trio

MU. 1. A vocal or instrumental trio whose parts are written on the treble staff. 2. A vocal or instrumental combo whose parts are high in pitch. 3. An all-girl vocal trio.

tremblement: ︵︵︵︵

MU. 1. The symbol shown above. 2. A heavy, wavy line used after the letters *tr* to designate trill. AI. Also a *mark of continuation*. See TRILL.

tremolo

MU. 1. A trembling, fluttering or quavering produced by repeating a tone or a chord with great frequency or rapidity, or by the rapid alternations of a chord, as on the piano. 2. An unsteady, tremulous tone in singing. AI. A tremolo is produced on the guitar by a rapid up-and-down strumming, of the fingers or plectrum. A tremolo is produced on a violin by a rapid up-and-down movement of the bow.

tremulous

MU. 1. Trembling, palpitating, fluttering, quavering. 2. With a rapidly trembling effect.

trend

MB. A general movement or liking, as that of the public. AI. For

412

instance, it might be said that there is a *trend* toward country music, a *trend* toward big bands, a *trend* toward phonograph record albums, etc.

triad

MU. 1. A chord composed of three tones. 2. A chord made up of a *root*, its (major or minor) *third* and its (perfect, augmented or diminished) *fifth*, in ascending order in the scale. 3. A common chord. AI. There are four kinds of triads: major, minor, augmented and diminished. For instance, the C major triad (C) is made up of the tones C-E-G. The C minor triad (Cm) is made up of the tones C-E♭-G. The C augmented triad (Caug) is made up of the tones C-E-A♭. The C diminished triad (Cdim) is made up of the tones C-E♭-G♭.

trial and error

SW. The method or process of making repeated trials in order to achieve satisfactory results, as in writing a song, a lyric, a melody, etc. AI. The formula for trial-and-error procedure is given in the maxim *if at first you don't succeed, try, try, again.*

triangle

MU. A percussion instrument made of a heavy steel rod bent in the shape of a triangle, suspended from a hook or a cord, which is played by striking with a metal wand or beater, to produce a tinkling sound of high, but indefinite pitch.

trill: *tr* or *tr*〰〰〰

MU. 1. Two adjacent tones (a degree or half a degree apart) alternating in rapid succession. 2. A *shake*. AI. The lower note (tone) in a trill is called the *principal*. The higher note (tone) is called the *auxiliary*. A trill is designated by either of the signs shown above. These are the letters *tr*, in a special style, or the letters *tr* followed by a wavy line called a tremblement, which is also a *mark of continuation*.

trimeter

PY. A line having three metrical feet. AI. Musical counterpart, a three-measure phrase.

trim size

PP. 1. The overall size of a page, as that of a song sheet or song book.

413

2. The size to which a page is cut (trimmed), as distinguished from the size of the *printing area* on a page.

Trinidad

MB. An island in the West Indies, home of *calypso* songs and music.

trio

MU. 1. A group of three. 2. A group of three harmony singers, as a girls' trio, a mixed trio, etc. 3. A group of three instrumentalists. 4. A three-piece combo. 5. A musical composition for three voices or three instruments.

triple

MU. 1. Consisting of three. 2. Three times as many. 3. Three parts. 4. Three-fold.

triple rhyme

PY. 1. A three-syllable rhyme. 2. A rhyme word or rhyme phrase in which the rhyme falls on the second from the last syllable. AI. For instance, *pret'ti-est* and *wit'ti-est*, *end'less-ly* and *friend'less-ly*, *dream'a-ble* and *schem'a-ble* are triple-rhyme words. *Best of it* and *rest of it* are triple-rhyme phrases.

triplet:

MU. A group of three notes of the same time value played or sung in the time of *two* similar notes, as shown above. AI. The figure *3*, with or without a tie or bracket, is used to designate a triplet, when written above or below any group of three notes of the same time value.

triple time

MU. Any time in which the number of beats to the measure can be evenly divided by three, as Three-Four Time or Six-Eight Time. AI. Also called *three time, three beat* and *three-beat time*.

trite

SW. 1. Used so often as to be common, as a word, a phrase, an expression, etc. 2. Worn out by repetition. 3. Hackneyed.

414

trochee (troh′kee)

PY. A metrical foot of two syllables in this order: an accented syllable, an unaccented syllable, or —‿. Example, *ba′by*. The opposite of iambic. Musical counterpart, Two-Four Time. AI. Trochee is one of the four kinds of English meter. See ENGLISH METER.

trombone

MU. A brass wind instrument of the trumpet family, commonly with a U-shaped slide which is adjustable at will in seven positions. Each position gives a fundamental tone and its harmonics. Less popular is the *valve trombone* which is made with valves, instead of a slide, and is played like a trumpet. AI. The trombone is usually made in four sizes: alto, tenor, bass and contrabass. The tenor is most ordinarily used. See TAILGATE.

trope (trohp)

RC. 1. A figure of speech. 2. A word or phrase used in its nonliteral sense to give beauty of expression and/or vividness of literary style. RN. 3. One of the numerous formulas in the Gregorian chant.

troubadour (troo′ba-dor″)

MU. 1. One of a class of poet-musicians that flourished from about the year 1150 to 1300. 2. A medieval songwriter. MN, SW. 3. Facetiously, a modern songwriter or musician, as said by one to another.

truism

RC. Any relatively brief statement of undeniable fact, as *haste makes waste, love is blind* and *beauty is only skin deep.*

trumpet

MU. 1. A metal wind instrument with a cupped mouthpiece connected to a flaring bell by a tube in the shape of a long oval or loop and small secondary looped tubes, in which are connected three valves for producing changes in tones. AI. The trumpet is a transposing instrument. Its tone is high, brilliant and penetrating. Its compass is about two octaves. MN. 2. A musician who plays the trumpet.

try out

SB. v. To test, to determine fitness and/or appeal by performance, as a singer might *try out* a new song, a producer might *try out* a new musical, a comedian might *try out* new material, etc.

tryout

S.B. n. 1. Something that is tried out, as a song, a musical, a gag, etc. 2. The act of trying out. AI. For instance, a songwriter might give one of his songs to a singer for a *tryout*, etc.

tuba

MU. 1. A metal wind instrument of ponderous tone. 2. A bass horn. AI. The term is often loosely applied to almost any brass instrument whose compass is in the bass (except the bass trombone).

tubo

MU. Same as *chocolo*.

tune

MU. v. 1. To adjust to a musical standard, as to tune a piano, tune a guitar, etc. 2. To regulate pitch, as that of a string on a stringed instrument.

tune

MU. n. 1. An air. 2. A melody. SW. 3. A complete song.

tunesmith

MB. 1. A composer. 2. A songwriter. 3. Loosely used to mean one who writes both music and lyrics.

tune the lyre

MN. A somewhat facetious expression meaning *get ready* to play and/or to sing, as for a performance, a rehearsal, etc.

tuning fork

MU. A small steel instrument, having two prongs, which upon being struck gives a certain tone, used for designating true pitch in tuning musical instruments.

tuning peg

MU. See PEG. See MACHINE HEAD.

416

tuning pin

MU. Same as *tuning peg*.

turkey

SB. 1. A failure, as said of an unsuccessful song, musical show, play, etc. 2. Almost any endeavor in show business that fails to succeed, especially one that is heavily promoted.

turn

SW. 1. A, usually sudden, change in thinking, as that occasioned in the surprise ending of a song. MU. 2. A melodic embellishment used in serious music. TE. 3. A short performance, as that given as part of a variety show. 4. A routine. 5. An act. 6. A series of acts, as those in the floor show of a night club. 7. The performer or performers in such acts.

turned v

MU. Same as *upside-down v*.

turntable

MB. A disk-shaped, revolving plate or platform on which phonograph records are played, as on a phonograph, playback equipment, juke box, etc. AI. To say that a certain record is *on the turntables* means that the record is being played by the majority of disk jockeys. To say that a certain record is *on the turntable* of a certain disk jockey, or radio station, means that the record is being played by this particular disk jockey, or station, etc.

tutti (too-te)

MU. 1. All. 2. A musical direction for all instruments and/or voices to play and/or sing at the same time. 3. A musical passage played and/or sung by all performers. 4. A tonal effect produced by the concerted playing and/or singing of all performers, as contrasted with *solo*. AI. Also *tutta, tutte,* or *tutto*.

tweeter

RO. A small loud-speaker that is especially constructed to produce tones of high pitch, as distinguished from a *woofer*.

417

twice accented: ″

RC. 1. Designated by the twin-acute accent mark shown above. 2. Designating the syllable of less stress or secondary stress as so marked. AI. For instance, in the word *sweet′heart″* the first syllable (*sweet*) is marked for the chief stress and the second syllable (*heart*) is *twice-accented* or marked for the weaker stress. See ACCENT.

twilight zone, the

MB. 1. The phony world of the song shark and others who prey on would-be songwriters, as distinguished from the legitimate music business. 2. The make-believe song business pictured by song sharks in their advertising and literature. 3. Collectively, those in the business of preying on would-be songwriters by misrepresentation, their world, etc.

twist

SW. 1. A different, and usually unexpected, meaning, as that in a song. 2. Distinctive treatment, as that used in writing a song. AI. For instance, it might be said that a songwriter gave a song or a song idea a new *twist*. DG. 3. A dance popular in 1961-1962. 4. The music for this dance.

two: 2 or II

MU. 1. The Arabic numeral used as the upper figure in the Two-Four Time signature, designating two counts (beats) to the measure. 2. The Arabic numeral used to designate the second ending of a song. 3. The Arabic numeral used to designate an interval of a second. 4. The Arabic numeral used to designate the second or middle finger in the English system of fingering. 5. The Arabic numeral used to designate the first or forefinger in the German method of fingering. 6. The Roman numeral used to designate the second degree, or supertonic, in the diatonic scale.

two-act

SB. An act performed by two performers, as singers, dancers, etc.

two beat

MU. See DUPLE TIME.

two-color

PP. Designating the use of two colors (black + one other color),

418

as used in printing, as the cover of a song sheet, song book, advertisement, etc.

two-deck

RB. Same as *double deck.*

two decker

RB. A double-deck phonograph record.

two flats:

MU. The key signature of B♭ major, as shown above.

Two-Four Time:

MU. 1. The time designated by the time signature shown above. 2. The time that has two counts (beats) to the measure, with each beat being equal to a quarter note in time value. AI. Two-Four Time is one kind of *Two-Part Time,* or *duple time.*

two-lined octave

MU. The first octave, on the piano, above middle C. AI. The keys (tones) to this octave are designated c², d², e², etc.

two part

MU. 1. Designating music for two voices or two instruments. 2. Designating a duet arrangement. 3. An arrangement for a duo. 4. Two-part harmony. 5. Designating a musical time that has two counts (beats) or multiples of two counts to the measure, as *Two-Part Time,* or *duple time.*

two sharps:

MU. The key signature of D major, as shown above.

two-sided

MB. 1. Designating a phonograph record with a hit song on each side, as a *two-sided hit.* 2. A double-barrel hit.

419

two-staff arrangement

MU. 1. An arrangement written on a two-stave system. 2. A piano arrangement. 3. A four-part harmony arrangement of a song, written on a two-stave system, as used in choir, barbershop and other forms of group singing. 4. Also called *hymn arrangement, hymnal arrangement, quartet arrangement* and *barbershop arrangement*.

two step

MU. 1. A ballroom dance in somewhat slow Two-Four Time. 2. The music for this dance. AI. The two step was popular in the 1920's. Also called *slow fox,* or *slow fox trot*.

two-syllable rhyme

PY. A feminine rhyme. See FEMININE RHYME.

two-track monaural

RG. A method of pick-up and/or recording on tape. AI. The same as *dual track*.

two-track stereophonic

RG. A method of pick-up and/or recording on tape. AI. Also called *two-track stereo*. The same as *stereophonic*.

two-way hit

RB. A phonograph record with a hit song on each side.

two-way lyric

SW. A lyric that can be sung either by a boy or a girl, as distinguished from boy lyric or girl lyric. See BOY-AND-GIRL SONG.

two-way record

RB. A two-way hit.

two-way song

SW. A song with a two-way lyric.

tympani, tympanist, tympano

MU. See TIMPANI, TIMPANIST, TIMPANO.

420

type

SW. v. 1. To write with a typewriter, as the lyric of a song. 2. To typewrite.

type

MB. n. 1. A kind, as a group or class generally having the same distinguishing characteristics. AI. For instance, a pop song is one *type* of song, a country song is another *type*. PG. 2. An especially made piece of metal, plastic, wood or other material on which there is a raised character, as a letter, numeral, symbol, etc. in reverse, for use in printing. AI. The words you are now reading were first set in type in order that they might be printed. There are many different kinds of type classified as to style, thickness or thinness of line, size, etc. The most modern method of printing music is from camera-ready Masters, the form in which music typographers furnish complete music typography, as that for a song. This includes both words and music. *All music and music illustrations in this book were typset by music typographers.*

type face

PG. The letter, character, etc. on the impression surface of printers' type, as that used to print the words and music of a song or the type from which these words were printed.

typesetter

PG. One who sets type for printing.

typographer

PG. 1. One who is especially skilled in typography, as a *music typographer*. 2. A highly specialized, expert typesetter.

typographical

PG, WE. Having to do with the type used in printing or typewriting. AI. For instance, a *typographical error*, as might be made in typing the lyric of a song on a typewriter, etc.

typography

PG. 1. The art of selecting, setting and arranging type or types for printing, as in printing music. 2. The skillful choice, arrangement, style and general appearance of type for printing.

tzigane (tsee"gan')

MU. Designating a (Hungarian) gypsy tribe, its customs, practices, world, etc. as *tzigane songs, tzigane music,* etc.

tzigane music

MU. 1. Music in the wildly abandoned style of the tziganes, usually played at a fast tempo. 2. Gypsy music. 3. Music in imitation of the tzigane style.

u

U

U.C.C. or UCC

LW. Abbreviation, *Universial Copyright Convention.*

uke

MU. Short for *ukulele.*

ukulele (yu″ke-lae′le)

MU. A small Hawaiian stringed instrument which was developed from a Portuguese guitar. The ukulele, played like a guitar, has four strings which are usually tuned a^1-d^1-$f\sharp^1$-b^1 (sometimes g^1-c^1-e^1-a^1). AI. Music for the ukulele is usually in tablature form called *ukulele diagrams.*

ukulele diagram:

MU. 1. A diagram like that shown above. 2. A diagram showing the fingering of a chord on the ukulele. AI. Ukulele diagrams sometimes appear on printed song sheets, just above the top staff line in each system, in the same manner in which guitar diagrams are shown.

um (oohm)

MU. The syllable used to represent an accented note or tone as played on the tuba, as *um*-pah, *um*-pah in Four-Four Time, *um*-pah-pah in Three Quarter Time, etc.

423

unaccented octave

MU. The small octave, on the piano, which begins with the first C below middle C and extends upward. AI. The keys (tones) in this octave are designated by small letters without other markings, thus: c, d, e, etc.

unaccented syllable

PY. 1. An unstressed syllable. 2. A *short* syllable, as distinguished from a *long* syllable. AI. The opposite of accented syllable.

unaccompanied

MU. 1. Without accompaniment, as a song performed without instrumental accompaniment. 2. A cappella.

unacknowledged note

MU. 1. An unessential note. 2. A passing note.

unauthorized

LW. 1. Without right. 2. Without permission, as that of a copyright owner. AI. For instance, an unauthorized performance means the performance of a song without permission or consent of its copyright owner. An unauthorized record is a bootleg record, etc.

uncopyrighted

LW. 1. Not copyrighted. 2. Without copyright. AI. Some music publishers prefer that songs which are submitted to them be uncopyrighted, as this permits the longest possible copyright protection after the song is published (and then copyrighted as a published work).

under

MU. 1. Lower, as in pitch. 2. Lesser, as in volume. 3. Behind, as in the background. 4. To the left, as on the piano keyboard.

under canvas

SB. In a tent. AI. For instance, a traveling musical show might be presented *under canvas*.

under song

MU. A song or refrain sung as an accompaniment to another song. AI. For instance, in the musical show *Music Man,* the ballad GOOD NIGHT MY SOMEONE is sung as an under song to the stirring march SEVENTY SIX TROMBONES.

understudy

TE. v. To act as an understudy.

understudy

TE. n. A performer, as a singer, dancer, actor, etc., as in a musical show, who studies the part of another performer so that he can serve as a substitute, as and if necessary.

undertone

MU. 1. A low tone, especially one that is lower than other tones with which it is played or sung. 2. A tone that is heard in the background, as behind another or other tones. 3. A tone of lower pitch and/or lower volume than others. 4. A sub-tone.

unequal voices

MU. Designating a vocal group or vocal arrangement, as SATB, using both male and female voices.

unessential notes

MU. 1. Notes that form no absolutely necessary part of the harmony or melody. 2. Passing notes. 3. Changing notes.

unessential tones

MU. Tones designated by unessential notes.

union

LW. 1. A grouping together or combining, as of nations, for some mutually beneficial purpose, as the Berne (Copyright) Union. MB. 2. A trade or labor union, as the AFM, AFTRA, etc. MN. 3. Facetiously, a band, an orchestra or any group of (union) musicians, as the house band in a theater or radio station, etc. might be called *the union.*

425

union card

MB. A card which identifies its bearer as a member in good standing of a designated labor union, as that carried by union musicians, union actors, union singers, etc.

union scale

MB. The rate of pay established and enforced, for its members, by a labor union, as the AFM, AFTRA, etc.

unison

MU. 1. The same or identical pitch, as that of two or more tones, voices, instruments, etc. 2. A tone of the same pitch as a given tone, as jointly performed by different voices or instruments. AI. Such voices or instruments are said to be *in unison*. 3. A tone of the same pitch—by extension, as a given tone, as jointly performed, as the interval of one or more octaves, called the *zero interval*. AI. For instance, any C on the piano keyboard is *in unison* with any other C. Any D is *in unison* with any other D, etc.

unit

SB. 1. A group of performers, as those who might travel from town to town to perform in a musical show. 2. A troup (of performers). 3. A (theatrical) road company.

United States

LW. This designation as used in this book means the *United States of America*, a country mostly in North America, made up of fifty states and the District of Columbia, whose territories include the Panama Canal Zone, the Virgin Islands, Guam, etc. AI. Abbreviated, *U.S.* or *US*.

United States of America

LW. The United States. Abbreviated, *U.S.A.* or *USA*.

unity

MB. 1. The state of being united. 2. Skillfully combined and blended. 3. Oneness. AI. A song is said to have *unity* when its lyric, melody and/or harmony have been artistically unified. See FUSION.

426

Universal Copyright Convention, the

LW. An international treaty, subscribed to by some forty-odd countries, including the United States, which came into force September 16, 1955, for the purpose of simplifying the international protection of creative works, as musical compositions, by reducing to a minimum the formalities required for securing copyright among participating countries. Abbreviated, U.C.C. AI. The Universal Copyright Convention is not to be confused with the so-called "International (Berne) Copyright Convention" (to which the United States does not belong) or with the various Pan-American Copyright Conventions. A current list of U.C.C. member countries is given in *annex a of circular 37*. Procedure for securing copyright under the U.C.C. is explained in *circular UCC 1*. Both of these circulars may be had free of charge on request to the United States Copyright Office.

unprotected song

LW. A song for which a date of existence has not been established and for which copyright has not been secured.

unpublished

LW. Not published, as distinguished from published, as a song. AI. A musical composition, as a song, is generally considered to be unpublished if it has never been offered for sale, in printed or an any other form, if it has never been publicly distributed and if it has never been publicly exploited. AI. United States Copyright Law requires that it be stated whether a song is an unpublished (or published) work when application for registration of a claim to copyright is made.

up

MU. 1. High or higher in pitch. 2. Great or greater in volume. 3. Loud or louder in tone. 4. To the right on the piano keyboard. 5. Faster, as in tempo. 6. Away from the body of a stringed instrument and toward the head. AI. The opposite of down.

upbeat

MU. 1. The upward stroke of the conductor's hand or baton, in beating time. 2. The weak beat. 3. The unaccented part of a measure. 3. An accelerated (upped) tempo, as that used in playing and/or singing an *upbeat* tune. 4. A lively, somewhat fast, tempo (or beat), with pronounced accents. AI. The opposite of down-beat.

upped tempo

MU. 1. An accelerated rate of speed at which a musical composition is played. 2. A faster tempo, usually with a pronounced beat. AI. The opposite of *downed tempo*. Also called *up tempo*.

upright

MU. An upright piano, as distinguished from a grand, baby grand, concert grand, etc.

upright bass

MU. A large brass wind instrument somewhat in the shape of a trumpet but with the bell pointing upwards (upright), as distinguished from a helicon or Sousaphone. AI. Also called *tuba*.

upright piano

MU. A piano in which the case is upright, with the strings and soundboard in a vertical position and at right angle to the keyboard. AI. Compare with *grand piano*.

upside-down v: ʌ

MU. The accent mark shown above. AI. Also called *turned v* and *inverted v*. See ACCENT MARKS. See CARET.

upstage

TE. v. 1. (For a performer, as a singer or actor) to place one's self in a position on the stage so as to hinder the audience from seeing the face of a fellow performer. 2. To move upstage, away from the audience. 3. To treat (anyone) in a disdainful manner. 4. To act in a haughty manner.

upstage

TE. n. 1. That part of the stage away from the audience. 2. That part of the stage that is furthest to the rear in a theater.

upstem notes: ♩ ♩ ♪ etc.

MU. 1. Notes like those shown above. 2. Notes with stems going up from their heads, as distinguished from downstem notes. AI. In writing lead sheets, notes below the middle line of the staff are upstem notes. Notes on the middle line can be either upstem or downstem notes, whichever presents the best appearance.

up tempo

MU. A direction meaning to increase the rate of speed at which a musical composition is played. AI. The opposite of *down tempo.*

up tune

MB. A lively song with pronounced beat. AI. Typical of songs that are *up tunes* are I'M GOING TO SIT RIGHT DOWN AND WRITE MYSELF A LETTER, HONEYSUCKLE ROSE, RUNNING WILD and CHATTANOOGIE SHOE SHINE BOY.

U.S. or US

LW. Abbreviation, *United States.*

U.S.A. or USA

LW. Abbreviation, *United States of America.*

U.S.A. label

PG. A printed notice which states that the matter on which it appears, as a song, was printed in the United States of America. AI. Wordings used to serve this purpose are: *Made in U.S.A., Manufactured in the United States of America, Manufactured in the U.S.A., Printed in the U.S.A.,* etc. The U.S.A. label usually appears as a footnote, often in connection with copyright notices.

use credit

MB. The credit allotted a copyright owner for the performance (use) of a musical compositon, as in the accountings of a performance-rights society.

V

II III

V

MU. 1. The capital letter used in Roman numerals to mean five. 2. The small letter used, upright, on its side or upside-down, as an accent mark, meaning sforzando. 3. The small letter used upright to mean up-bow (in violoncello music). 4. The small letter used upside-down to mean down-bow. 5. The small letter used upright to designate toe (in organ music). 6. The small letter used upside-down to designate heel. 7. The small letter used as a breathing mark. 8. The small letter used as an abbreviation for vocal. 9. The small letter used as an abbreviation for violin (singular v, plural vv). PG. 10. The small letter used upside-down as an insert mark, or caret, in marking printers' proofs, as those of a song.

value

MU. 1. The relative duration a tone is sounded, as designated by a note. 2. The relative duration that silence is maintained, as designated by a rest. AI. Also called *time value*, as that of a note or rest.

valve

MU. A device used on certain brass wind instruments to change the pitch. AI. Typical of instruments on which valves are used are the cornet, French horn, bass horn, tuba, etc.

vamp

MU. 1. An instrumental prelude to a song. 2. A succession of chords that establish a rhythm.

431

vamp 'til ready

MU. A direction meaning, *repeat the vamp over and over again instrumentally*, until the singer or singers are ready to begin singing.

vanity publication

PP. Any publication, as a song, a book, etc., which a writer has printed or published, at his own expense, solely for self-satisfaction.

variation

MU. One of a series of variations. See VARIATIONS.

variations

MU. Repetitions of a theme (song) in new and varied aspects, as harmonic, rhythmic and melodic changes, the form and outline of the composition being preserved while the different passages are embellished, ornamented and amplified.

variety

TE. 1. Entertainment of the kind given in a variety show. 2. Vaudeville.

Variety

SB. A weekly show-business trade journal which features news of the theatrical and motion-picture industries and which devotes a portion of its space to the music business. Address: 154 West 46th Street, New York, N. Y. 10036.

variety show

TE, MP. 1. A show on stage, screen, television, etc., which is made up of (a *variety* of) different kinds of acts, as acrobats, singers, dancers, comics, etc. 2. A vaudeville show. AI. Typical of variety shows is the television show *Hollywood Palace*.

varsity

GI. Designating a team, usually athletic, that represents a college, university or school in competition, as football, baseball, track, etc.

varsity song

MU. A rousing song, written to inspire and cheer a *varsity*, as a football team, as distinguished from an *alma mater*.

432

vaudeville

TE. 1. A variety show. 2. Same as *vodvil*.

vernacular (ver-nak'yoo-ler)

GI. 1. The native speech, language or dialect of a country, or place. 2. The common, everyday language of ordinary people in a particular locality, as that in which folk songs are written. 3. The shop talk or idiom of a trade or profession, as the vernacular of the music business.

verse

SW. 1. The foreword of a song. 2. That part of a song which serves to introduce the chorus, as distinguished from the chorus, itself. PY. 3. A sequence of words arranged metrically, in accordance with a rule or rules of design. 4. Metrical composition, rhymed or unrhymed, as distinguished from prose. AI. MOONLIGHT IN VERMONT is an example of a song written in unrhymed verse.

verse libre

PY. Same as *free verse*.

versification

PY. 1. The art, practice and/or theory of poetic composition. 2. The form or style of a poem. 3. Metrical structure.

verso (ver'so)

PP. 1. Any left-hand page, as that of a song book, hymnal, etc. 2. The back of a leaf, in a book. AI. The opposite of *recto*. The United States Copyright law says, "The copyright notice for books shall appear on the title page or verso thereof."

vertical

MU. 1. Perpendicular, exactly upright. 2. Straight up and down. GI. For instance, the lines used for bars are vertical lines, as distinguished from lines that make up the music staff, which are horizontal lines.

vertically

MU. 1. In a vertical manner. 2. Straight up and down. AI. For instance, music is written and read in two ways: horizontally and *ver-*

433

tically. The noteheads that make up a chord are written or printed one above the other, or nearly so. This means that they are written and read *vertically*. Notes that are written *vertically* designate tones that are to be sounded *at the same time*. See HARMONY.

vibes

MU. A vibraphone. AI. Also called *vibe*. Two all-time great vibe players are Adrian Rollini and Red Norvo.

vibraphone

MU. A percussion instrument made of graduated metal bars which are struck with special mallets to produce tones. Below each bar is an open tubular chamber for added resonance. The instrument gets its name from the gentle *vibrato* produced by motor-driven fingers which revolve between the bars and the sound chambers.

vibration

MU. 1. The act of vibrating. 2. A rhythmic motion back and forth. 3. A quiver. 4. The movement that produces sound. AI. The faster the vibrations, the higher the tone is in pitch. The slower the vibrations, the lower the tone is in pitch.

vibrato (vi-brah'toh)

MU. A tremulous effect obtained by rapidly alternating the original tone with a very slight change in pitch, as is effected by the rapid shaking motion of the finger on a violin string. AI. Sometimes used to mean the same as *tremolo*, as applied to the voice and or singing.

vicarious

PS. 1. Imaginatively substituting one's self in the place of another. 2. Enjoying or suffering the emotions of another in one's mind. 3. Experiencing the experiences of another in one's mind, as *vicarious* pleasure or *vicarious* pain.

vicarious appeal

PS. 1. The urge to imagine one's self in the role of another, as that in a song. 2. The attraction to mentally participate in the joy or sorrow of another. AI. Songs with proven *vicarious appeal* are NOW IS THE HOUR, AMONG MY SOUVENIRS, IT'S ALMOST TOMORROW and I CAN DREAM, CAN'T I.

vice versa

GI. 1. Conversely. 2. The other way around. 3. The reverse order. 4. The reverse relationship. AI. For instance, music is important to a lyric and *vice versa*.

vide (vi'de): *vi - - - - - - de*

MU. The Latin word meaning see. AI. A term used to call the attention of a singer or musician to a particular portion of a musical composition where a *cut* is to be made. When written in a score, with two syllables divided, as shown above, this directs the performers to skip from *vi* to *de*, omitting all words and all notation in between.

video

TV. Designating the television picture, as distinguished from audio (the television sound).

video tape

TV. A magnetic tape on which complete television programs (both audio and video) can be recorded as for broadcasting at a later time.

viewpoint

SW. See POINT OF VIEW.

viol (vi''l)

MU. Any of several ancient instruments of the violin family which had fretted finger boards. AI. The term is sometimes erroneously used in connection with the word bass, as *bass viol*, to mean the contrabass or double-bass.

viola (ve-oh'la)

MU. 1. The second member of the violin family. 2. The tenor violin. AI. The viola is about one seventh larger than a violin, is tuned a fifth lower and has a somewhat veiled, slightly nasal tone color.

violin

MU. 1. The familiar modern stringed instrument, which has four strings, an unfretted finger board and is bowed. The highest-pitched instrument in its family. AI. The violin family popularly includes

435

four members: the violin, the viola, the violoncello and the double-bass. CM. 2. A fiddle.

violoncello (vee″a-lon-chel′oh)

MU. 1. The third member of the violin family. 2. The "little-big violin," familiarly called the *cello*. AI. The violoncello is held between the knees when being played and produces low, sonorous tones.

virtuosity

MU. Exceptional technical skill, particularly in the performance of music.

virtuoso (ver′tchoo-oh′soh)

MU. 1. A person having exceptional technical skill, particularly in the performance of music. 2. A highly skilled singer. 3. A highly skilled musician. 4. One who excels in musical performance.

vocable (vo′ka-b'l)

SW. 1. A word or vocal sound, regardless of meaning. 2. A word or syllable regarded as a unit of sound rather than a unit of meaning. 3. A scat syllable. AI. For instance, *wah* or *dah* in *wah-dah*, as used by background singers.

vocabulary

RC. 1. All the words used by a particular person, class, profession, etc. AI. For instance, the vocabulary of the music business. 2. Sometimes, all the words recognized and understood by a particular person, although not necessarily used by him in speech or writing.

vocal

MU. 1. Having to do with the voice. 2. Belonging to the voice. 3. Designating music that is intended to be sung. 4. Designating music that is adapted or arranged for singing.

vocalism

MU. The art of singing.

vocalist

MU. A singer, especially one of a cultivated or trained voice.

436

vocalize

MU. 1. To sing. 2. To practice singing. 3. Particularly to practice singing tones on vowels.

vocal music

MU. Music written for voices, as solo, duet, trio, quartet, chorus, etc., with or without accompaniment.

vocal range

MU. 1. The extent over which the human voice is effective when singing. 2. The extent between the highest tone and the lowest tone that can be comfortably sung by a human voice. AI. The approximate ranges that can be sung by average voices are shown below. Highly trained soloists have voices with greater ranges.

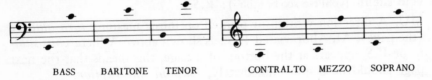

BASS   BARITONE   TENOR   CONTRALTO   MEZZO   SOPRANO

vocal score

MU. See SCORE, VOCAL.

voce (voh′che)

MU. Voice. AI. As *mezza voce*, meaning *with half the power of the voice*, and *sotto voce*, meaning *in an undertone*. Plural, *voci*.

vodvil

TE. The same as *vaudeville*. AI. This shorter spelling came into being in the 1920's, in order to use less space on the electric signs in front of vaudeville theaters.

voice

MU. v. To arrange or write voice parts, as those for a vocal trio, a quartet, a choir, etc.

voice

MU. n. 1. The sound produced by the human organs of speech. 2. The *singing* voice. AI. Male voices are divided into three categories. From high to low, these are tenor, baritone and bass. Female voices

437

ordinarily are divided into three categories. From high to low, these are soprano, mezzo-soprano and contralto. In female barbershop-quartet singing, while the four voices are called lead, tenor, baritone and bass, these are generally higher in register than men's voices by the same names. See VOCAL RANGE.

voice part

MU. 1. A vocal part, as distinguished from an instrumental part. 2. An individual part of a choral composition. AI. For instance, the part of soprano, alto, tenor or bass. Also called *voice*.

volti (vohl'tee): *V.*

MU. A direction written or printed on music meaning *turn over* (the page). AI. Abbreviated *V*, as shown above.

volti subito (vohl'tee soo'bee-toh"): *V.S.*

MU. A direction written or printed on music meaning *turn quickly* (the page). AI. Abbreviated *V.S.*, as shown above. Where *volti subito* or *V.S.* appears at the bottom of a page, this means that the next page should be begun immediately, *without interruption*.

volume

MU. The fullness of a sound or tone. AI. The loudness or softness of a tone depends on its volume. The greater the volume, the louder the tone. The less the volume, the softer the tone. See INTENSITY. See DYNAMICS.

v-on-its-side: >

MU. 1. The accent mark shown above. 2. A half-turned v. AI. Not to be confused with the much longer marks used to designate crescendo or diminuendo.

vowel

RC. An open vocal sound as distinguished from a closed, stopped, mute or consonant sound. AI. The vowels in the English language are *a, e, i, o, u* and sometimes *y*.

V.S. or VS

MU. Abbreviation, *volti subito*.

vv

MU. Abbreviation, *violins* (plural).

438

W

W

wail

MB. 1. To sing, particularly the blues. 2. To play a horn, particularly a trumpet, with deep feeling.

wailer

MB. 1. A blues singer, usually used to designate a female. 2. A horn player, usually one who plays trumpet.

wah-dah

MB. 1. Scat syllables often used by harmony singers for fill-ins and backgrounds. 2. Hence, any syllables used for this purpose. AI. Also used to designate a kind of fill-in and/or background, as *wah-dah fill-in*, *wah-dah background*, etc.

wah-dah singers

MB. 1. Singers who sing wah-dah or similar syllables. 2. Therefore, background singers, as a *wah-dah group*, *wah-dah trio*, *wah-dah quartet*, etc.

wah-wah

MU. 1. The sound of a muted trumpet. 2. Hence, the effect thus produced. AI. For instance, an orchestra leader might tell a trumpet player to "give us some *wah-wahs* through the last four measures," etc.

walking bass

MU. 1. A style of bass performance that produces the effect, or gives the impression, of *walking* back and forth. 2. A style of bass playing used in the performance of boogie-woogie. 3. A musical composition done in this style. AI. An example of walking bass is Henry Mancini's instrumental WALKIN' BASS.

wall-to-wall

MU. Solid, as said of a musical performance, a performer or performers, or an arrangement. AI. The term is used in the highest esteem, as "he is wall-to-wall" or "that was wall-to-wall," etc. Also, *solid wall-to-wall.*

waltz

MU. 1. A round dance, usually in moderate triple time, of Austrian origin. 2. The music for such a dance, usually characterized by an accompaniment pattern of a low bass note (tone) on the first beat, followed by two chords in the middle register on the second and third beats. 3. A song written in waltz time. AI. There is an old saying in the music business, "If it's a *waltz* hit, it is the biggest hit of all." Typical waltz hits are THREE O'CLOCK IN THE MORNING, NOW IS THE HOUR, IT'S A SIN TO TELL A LIE and TEN-NESSEE WALTZ.

waltz clog

MU. 1. A clog dance done in waltz time. 2. Music in waltz time for such a dance, characterized by a pronounced beat.

wand

MU. 1. A slender rod made of highly polished wood, metal, plastic or other material, used by orchestra leaders in conducting an orchestra. 2. An orchestra leader's baton of a particularly slender design. 3. A slender metal rod used by percussionists to play the triangle, also called a *beater.*

wander

MN. 1. To improvise rather freely, as in playing a song. 2. To drift. AI. The opposite of *staying with the book.*

440

warble

MU. 1. To sing. 2. To sing, usually melodiously, with embellishments, as bird-like quavers, trills and runs.

war cry

MN. See MUSICIANS' WAR CRY.

warmed-over

MB. Designating a melody, lyric or complete song that has been taken from another melody, lyric or song, with very little change, as a *warmed-over melody*, *warmed-over lyric*, etc.

warm up

MN. v. To practice informally, as done by musicians and/or singers.

warm-up

MN. n. A period of time devoted to warming up. AI. Also called warm-up session, warm-up period, etc.

washboard

CM. A board or frame with a ridged metal surface, made for washing (scrubbing) clothes, used as a rhythm-percussion instrument. AI. The washboard is usually held as one holds a small harp and played, in a somewhat similar manner, by metal thimbles which are scraped over the ridged surface. The method of playing a washboard is described in the song CONEY ISLAND WASHBOARD MELODY.

washboard band

CM. 1. Any instrumental group in which one or more washboards are used as rhythm-percussion instruments. 2. A washboard combo.

watch the stick

MN. 1. To stay on beat. 2. To keep in time. 3. Literally, to watch an orchestra leader's baton, as he conducts or beats time.

wavy-stem notes: ♩ ♩ ♩ ♩

MU. Notes with stems like those shown above. AI. Wavy-stem notes can be of any time value, as half notes, quarter notes, eighth notes, etc. In tambourine music, notes with wavy stems call for a roll. Also called roll notes. See JINGLE NOTES.

wax

RG. v. 1. To record, as a song. 2. Figuratively, to put a song on wax (meaning a *wax record*).

wax

RB. n. A phonograph record, regardless of the material from which it is made. AI. The term comes from the fact that phonograph records were originally made of wax.

wax business

RB. The phonograph record business.

waxworks

RB. 1. Originally, an exhibition of life-size wax figures, usually of well-known persons. 2. Currently, a phonograph record company. 3. A recording company. 4. A recording studio.

wayside songs

FK. 1. Songs that were sung, or heard, at the wayside, where travelers stopped to rest. 2. Hence, folk songs that were originally sung by those who traveled the highways. AI. Also called *wayfarer songs*. Typical of modern wayside songs are: CINDERS, SONG OF THE OPEN ROAD, CRY OF THE WILD GOOSE and RAMBLIN' MAN.

weather songs

MB. A classification in songwriting as to subject matter. AI. Typical weather songs are STORMY WEATHER, RAIN, WINDY AND WARM, APRIL SHOWERS, BLUE SKIES and THUNDER OVER PARADISE.

weeper

MB. A song which is intended to cause tears, as those of vicarious sorrow, pity, sympathy, etc. AI. Typical weepers are I WENT TO YOUR WEDDING, TEEN ANGEL and MOODY RIVER.

weighting formula

MB. The method used by ASCAP in establishing and assigning credit values to its members for the performance of works under its control. AI. Also called *credit-weighting formula*. Incorrectly called *weighing formula*.

western

MB. A ballad written about western subject matter. AI. Also called western song. Typical *westerns* are WAGON WHEELS, TUMBLING TUMBLEWEEDS, EMPTY SADDLES, I'M HEADED FOR THE LAST ROUND UP and THERE'S A HOME IN WYOMIN'.

wf or w.f. (dub'l-yu-eff)

PG. A typographical sign used in marking printers' proofs, as those of a song, meaning *wrong font*.

Whiffenpoofs (wihf′en-poofs)

MU. An honorary singing society composed of senior students at Yale University. Membership is by appointment, this year's members designating those who are to be members next year. AI. The activities of the Whiffenpoofs are described in the well-known WHIFFENPOOF SONG.

whistle

MU. 1. Usually, a small, simple end-blown flute with six finger holes, made of wood, metal or plastic, played by a trap drummer. 2. Any small, simple instrument that produces a single tone when blown.

white sound

RM. 1. The unmistakable sound of the voices of white singers, as distinguished from the sound of voices of those of other races, particularly those of the Negro race. 2. An (acceptable) imitation of the sound of the voices of white singers as performed by those of another race, particularly those of the Negro race, as distinguished from the *brown sound*.

white tones

BY. Tones sung with little or no vibrato, as used in barbershop harmony. AI. The opposite of *color tones*, or *colored tones*.

whole note: o

MU. 1. The character shown above. 2. The note consisting of only an outlined, white notehead. AI. A whole note represents a time value twice that of a half note, four times that of a quarter note, etc.

whole rest: ▬

MU. 1. The character shown above. 2. The rest that is in the shape of a solid black rectangle, that is suspended from a staff line or a leger line. AI. When written or printed in the staff, the whole rest hangs down from the *fourth* staff line. A whole rest represents a time value twice that of a half rest, four times that of a quarter rest, etc. The time value of a whole rest is equal to that of a whole note.

whole step

MU. The equivalent of two half steps. See DEGREE.

whole tone

MU. The equivalent of two half tones or two semitones. See TONE.

wind instruments

MU. Those instruments, the sounds of which are produced by wind (compressed air) supplied by the breath, a bellows or a pump. AI. Wind instruments for which wind is supplied by the breath are the trumpet, the trombone, etc. Wind instruments for which the wind is supplied by a bellows are the accordion and the concertina. Wind instruments for which the wind is supplied by a pump are the melodeon and harmonium, or pump-organs, each of which also uses a bellows (which is pumped).

wing

MN. 1. To improvise. 2. To ad lib. AI. To *take it on the wing* or to *wing-it* means to jam. See JAM.

wing-ding

MN. a. 1. Untrained, as a *wing-ding* singer, a *wing-ding* banjo player, etc. 2. Free in style, as that of a performance. AI. The term is not necessarily disparaging. A *wing-ding* pianist can be a very good pianist, an adept performer.

wing ding

CM. n. 1. A gay time. 2. A jamboree. 3. A gathering to dance and/or sing, especially boisterously and with abandon. 4. An exceptionally gay time.

with

PG. See O. K. WITH.

wobble board

MU. An instrument related to the percussion family, consisting of a flexible board approximately a yard square, which produces a *wobbling* tone when held by two opposite edges and flexed or wobbled. AI. The wobble board was first recorded as a background for the song hit TIE ME KANGAROO DOWN, SPORT.

wolf

MU. 1. A discord due to the improper tuning of an instrument, as the piano, organ, etc. 2. An unpleasantly harsh tone, as that of an instrument in the violin family, due to faulty construction, adjustment, etc.

woodpile

MN. A xylophone.

woodshed

MN, SW. 1. To rehearse intensely, as a singer or musician. 2. To apply one's self to an intense session of songwriting. 3. To work diligently, as at songwriting. See HACK.

wood wind

MU. 1. An orchestral instrument made of wood. 2. An orchestral instrument which was originally made of wood, regardless of the material from which it is now made. AI. Typical wood winds are the flute, piccolo, oboe, clarinet, bassoon, etc.

wood wind section

MU. That part of an orchestra which is made up of wood wind instruments, as distingiushed from *brass section, rhythm section,* etc. AI. Also called the *wood winds.*

woofer

RO. A large loud-speaker that is specially constructed to produce bass tones, as distinguished from a *tweeter*.

wordage

SW. 1. Words collectively, as those of a song. 2. The number of words, as those in a song.

words

SW. 1. The words of a song, as distinguished from the *music*. 2. The lyric. 3. Text. 4. Subject matter.

work

MB. v. 1. To promote, advertise and exploit, as a song. 2. To plug. AI. For instance, a music publisher might be said to be *working* on a certain song, meaning that he is attempting to popularize that particular song.

work

MB. n. 1. Something that has resulted from an effort or activity, as a song results from the effort or activity of songwriting. 2. Something that has been written or composed, as a musical composition, a song. AI. Collectively, works (plural), as the *works* of Cole Porter, etc.

working rough

SW. A song idea in any rough, unfinished form.

working title

SW. A temporary song title, used while working out another one, or while waiting for a better one to come to mind.

work made for hire

LW. 1. A work made, written, arranged or prepared by an employee within the scope of his employment. 2. A work done on special order or commission, as a musical composition, a song. AI. The employee who makes such a work forfeits all rights of authorship to his employer. The employer has full and legal rights to such work or works. The employer is legally entitled to name himself as sole author, sole proprietor and sole copyright claimant. Works are usually made for hire by contractural agreement.

work song

FK. 1. A folk song of the kind originally sung by laborers. 2. A folk song about laborers. AI. Typical work songs are I'VE BEEN WORKING ON THE RAILROAD, DRILL YE TERRIERS DRILL and WATER BOY. Among the modern work songs that have become hits are SIXTEEN TONS, BIG JOHN and DAY-O (The Banana Boat Song).

would-be

MB. Anyone who makes an inadequate attempt toward becoming a songwriter, with little or no idea as to how to go about it. AI. Also called a *would-be songwriter*.

wow

RG. A term applied to distorted sound, particularly that of a phonograph record caused by variations in speed of the turntable. AI. When a record produces such distortions for this reason it is said to be *wowing*.

wrenched syllable stress

SW. A device used in writing and/or singing calypso songs, in which the accent is placed on the wrong syllable. AI. For instance, placing the accent on the word *syl-la'ble* instead of (correctly) on the first syllable of the word syl'la-ble.

writer

MB. 1. A songwriter. 2. Usually a lyricist, as distinguished from a composer. 3. One who writes the words for a song or songs. 4. One who writes both music and words for a song or songs. See SONG-WRITER.

writer's copies

MB. 1. Copies of sheet music, usually of their own songs, which are furnished to songwriters free of charge by most music publishers. 2. Copies of phonograph records, usually of their own songs, which are furnished to songwriters by most phonograph record companies and/or music publishers.

447

wrong font

PG. A printer's type face that is the wrong style and/or size. AI. For instance, the *n* in the word so*ng* is obviously from a wrong font, as it does not match the style of the other letters with which it appears. Abbreviated, *wf* or *w.f.*

X

X

MB. 1. The capital letter used in Roman numerals to mean ten. 2. The small letter used in the English method of fingering to designate the thumb. 3. The small letter used in place of a notehead to form an x-note.

x-note (eks note):

MU. The character shown above. AI. X-notes are used (a) in percussion notation, (b) to replace melody notes where words are to be spoken instead of sung and (c) to designate hand claps. For instance, the hand claps used in the song DEEP IN THE HEART OF TEXAS are designated by *x-notes*.

xylophone

MU. A percussion instrument consisting of a series of wooden bars graduated in length so as to sound tones of the scale when struck with special-made small wooden hammers or mallets. AI. The xylophone usually has a range of four and a half octaves and belongs to the same family as the marimba and the vibraphone. AI. Also called the *marimba-xylophone*, the *marimba-zylophone* and the *zylophone*.

Y

Y

yellow contract

MB. The songwriter-publisher contract approved by the American Guild of Authors and Composers, titled *1947 Revised Uniform Popular Songwriters Contract*. AI. So called because this particular contract is printed on yellow paper.

yodel

MU. v. To sing with abrupt, alternating changes between the normal chest voice and falsetto.

yodel

MU. n. 1. The act or sound of yodeling. 2. A song or refrain sung to meaningless syllables, with abrupt changes from natural tones to falsetto and back. 3. A warble common among the Swiss and Tyrolese mountaineers.

you angle

SW. The point of view used in songwriting that pictures the narrator (singer) of a song as speaking (singing) directly to one specific person (you). AI. Although the phrase is often used to mean *love angle*, many songs are written from the *you angle* that have no love interest at all. Examples of these are KING FOR A DAY, YOU'VE GOT TO HAVE HEART and SANTA CLAUS IS COMING TO TOWN. Examples of songs written from the you angle that do have love interest are YOU'RE THE CREAM IN MY COFFEE, UNTIL THERE WAS YOU and HONEST AND TRULY.

Z

zero

JZ. a. 1. Exceptionally cool, as used to designate a jazz performance or a jazz musician or musicians. 2. Delightfully cool, skillfully so. See COOL.

zero

ET. n. The point marked *0*, from which positive measurements are reckoned upward, as those of sound, on the graduated scale of an audiometer. 2. Nothing.

zero audibility

ET. The level at which no sound is heard. AI. Also called *zero level* or *zero sound level*. See LEVEL.

zimbalon

MU. An improved dulcimer which has a scale of four octaves and is provided with dampers. AI. The zimbalon is identified with Hungarian music.

zither

MU. A simple form of stringed instrument having a flat sound board, over which some thirty or more strings are stretched, which

453

are stopped with the fingers of the left hand and plucked with those of the right hand.

zylophone

MU. Same as *xylophone*.

coda

456

44 KEYS

44 KEYS

Middle C

Middle C

A_2 B_2 C_1 D_1 E_1 F_1 G_1 A_1 B_1 | C D E F G A B | c d e f g a b | c^1 d^1 e^1 f^1 g^1 a^1 b^1 | c^2 d^2 e^2 f^2 g^2 a^2 b^2 | c^3 d^3 e^3 f^3 g^3 a^3 b^3 | c^4 d^4 e^4 f^4 g^4 a^4 b^4 c^5

§ | DOUBLE CONTRA | CONTRA | GREAT | SMALL | ONE-LINED | TWO-LINED | THREE-LINED | FOUR-LINED | FIVE-LINED

§ DOUBLE CONTRA
† FIVE-LINED

The nine names shown above are the names of the octaves in absolute pitch, as double-contra octave, contra octave, etc. Both double-contra octave and five-lined octave extend beyond the range of the standard (88-key) piano.

An individual key (tone) is designated by the octave in which it is included. Example: double-contra C, contra great C, small C, etc. All keys (tones) above middle C are treble. All keys (tones) below middle C are bass.

coda

$\oplus$

The practice of using written directions to tell how musical compositions should be played and/or sung began in Italy. The long-accepted, universally-used language for this purpose is therefore largely Italian.

While it might be desirable to use the English language to tell how songs with English lyrics should be performed, it might also be desirable to duplicate these markings in the universally-accepted-and-understood language on all copies intended for export.

The most-generally used markings, as they are universally accepted, are herein given:

TEMPO MARKINGS

Grave	Very, very slow (solemn)
Largo	Very slow
Larghetto	Slower than *adagio*
Adagio	Quite slow
Adagietto	Somewhat slower than *lento*
Lento	Slow
Andante	A normal walking pace
Andantino	Somewhat faster than *andante*
Moderato	Moderate
Allegretto	Moderately fast
Allegro	Quick (cheerful)
Presto	Fast
Prestissimo	Very fast

TEMPO MARKINGS DENOTING A CHANGE IN TEMPO

Accelerando	Gradually quickening the speed
Affretando	Increasing the speed (hurrying)
A tempo	Return to original speed (in time)
L'istesso tempo	At the same speed of previous section
Meno mosso	Slower
Piu mosso	Faster
Rallentando	Gradually lessening the speed
Ritardando	Gradually getting slower
Rubato	Quickening here and there

AUXILIARY TEMPO MARKINGS

Comodo	At a comfortable speed
Con moto	Rather quick
Mosso	In motion
Moto	Motion
Ritenuto	Held back
Stringendo	Pressing onward
Tempo primo	First tempo
Vivance	Lively (sprightly)
Vivo	Briskly (lively)

MARKINGS DESIGNATING DYNAMICS

Crescendo	Gradually getting louder
Decrescendo	Gradually getting softer
Diminuendo	Gradually getting softer
Forte	Loud

Fortepiano	Attact loudly and sustain softly
Fortissimo	Very loud
Mezzo forte	Moderately loud
Mezzo piano	Moderately soft
Piano	Soft
Pianissimo	Very soft

MARKINGS DESIGNATING BOTH TEMPO AND DYNAMICS

Allargando	Getting slower and louder
Calando	Gradually getting slower and softer
Morendo	Dying away
Perdendo	Fading away
Perdendosi	Fading away

MISCELLANEOUS MARKINGS

Al fine	To the end
Al segno	To the sign
A piacere	Freely
Da capo	Repeat from the beginning
Da capo al fine	Repeat from beginning to end
Dal segno al fine	Repeat from the sign to the end
Del capo	The top
Fine	The end
Giusto	Exact (just)
Mano destra	Right hand
Mano sinistra	Left hand
Ordinario	Customary (ordinary)
Poco a poco	Gradually (little by little)

Segue	Continue smoothly without pause
Subito	Immediately (quickly)

MARKINGS DESIGNATING TONAL PRODUCTION

Forzato	Forced (strongly accented)
Legato	Smoothly connected
Leggero	Lightly
Leggiero	Lightly
Marcato	With emphasis
Pesante	Heavy
Pieno	Full
Portamento	Sliding from one note to another
Sforzando	Strongly accented
Sforzato	Strongly accented
Sostenuto	Sustained
Staccato	Detached
Tenuto	Held for the full value

MARKINGS DESIGNATING EXPRESSION

Affetto	With tender feeling
Affettuoso	Tender
Amabile	Graceful (amiable)
Amorevole	Gentle (lovingly)
Animato	Spirited (animated)
Animo	Spirit
Appassionato	Passionate
Bravura	Dexterity (skill)
Brillante	Sparkling (brilliant)
Brio	Animation (pep)
Calmo	Tranquil (calm)
Calore	Warmth
Cantabile	In a singing style

462

Capriccioso	Impulsively
Deciso	Determined
Dolce	Sweet
Doloroso	Sad
Espressione	Expressive
Espressivo	Expressive
Forza	Force
Fuoco	Fire
Furioso	Furious
Gaio	Gay
Giocoso	Playful
Gioviale	Genial
Grazioso	Graceful
Maestoso	Majestic (stately)
Marcia	March
Marziale	Martial
Mesto	Sad
Misterioso	Mysteriously
Piangevole	Tearful
Pomposo	Pompous
Ponderoso	Heavy
Preciso	Exact (precise)
Risoluto	Firm (resolute)
Scherzando	Jokingly (playful)
Scherzo	Joke
Secco	Dry
Semplice	Simple
Sentimentale	Sentimental
Sentimento	Sentiment
Sereno	Serene
Serio	Serious
Spiritoso	Spirited
Teneramente	Tenderly
Tranquillo	Calm (tranquil)

SUPPLEMENTARY WORDS FOR MARKINGS

A, alla   at, in   as *a tempo* (back to original speed)
Assai   very   as *adagio assai* (very slow)

Ben   well   as *ben marcato* (well marked)

Con   with   as *con animo* (with spirit)

Di   of   as *tempo di marcia* (speed of a march)
Dúe   two   as *due voci* (two voices)

E   and   as *dim e rit* (gradually softer and slower)

In   in, at   as *in tempo* (in strict time)

Ma   but   as *ma non troppo* (but not too much)
Meno   less   as *meno mosso* (less motion—slower)
Mezzo   half   as *mezzo forte* (half loud)
Molto   much   as *molto meno mosso* (much slower)

Non   not   as *non troppo* (not too much)

Piu   more   as *piu mosso* (more motion—faster)
Poco   little   as *poco a poco* (little by little)
Poi   then   as *poi a poi* (by degrees)
Primo   first   as *tempo primo* (first tempo)

Quasi   almost like   as *quasi presto* (like a presto)

Secondo   second   as *secondo* (second part or voice)
Sempre   always   as *sempre legato* (always smooth)
Senza   without   as *senza organo* (without the organ)
Si   it   as *si segue* (proceed with it)
Simile   like   as *simile* (in a like manner)
Stesso   same   as *lo stesso tempo* (the same tempo)

Tanto   so much   as *allegro non tanto* (not too fast)
Troppo   too much   as *non troppo* (not too much)

Un, una   a   as *un poco piu mosso* (a little faster)

Va   go   as *va con* (go with)

Fine

COMMON ABBREVIATIONS

Accel.	Accelerando	*mf*	Mezzo forte
Accomp.	Accompaniment	M.M.	Maelzel's Metronome
Ad lib.	Ad libitum	*mp*	Mezzo piano
All.	Allegro	Obbli.	Obbligato
B.C.	Basso continuo	Op.	Opus
B.H.	Both hands	Ott.	Ottava
Brill.	Brillante	*p*	Piano
Cantab.	Cantabile	*pp*	Pianissimo
Cres.)		Pizz.	Pizzicato
Cresc.)	Crescendo	Rall.	Rallentando
Dal S.	Dal segno	Recit.	Recitative
D.C.	Da capo	R.H.	Right hand
Decres.)		Rit	Ritardando
Decresc.)	Decrescendo	Riten	Ritenuto
Dim	Diminuendo	Seg.	Segue
D.S.	Dal segno	Sim.	Simile
f	Forte	*sf, sfz*	Sforzando
ff	Fortissimo	Stacc.	Staccato
fp	Fortepiano	Sub.	Subito
Forz. or *fz*	Forzato	Tempo I	Tempo primo
Leg.	Legato	Ten.	Tenuto
L.H.	Left hand	V.S.	Volti subito

♪ ♪ ♪ ♪

465